MACBETH

Arden Early Modern Drama Guides

Series Editors:
Andrew Hiscock
University of Wales, Bangor, UK and Lisa Hopkins,
Sheffield Hallam University, UK

Arden Early Modern Drama Guides offers practical and accessible introductions to the critical and performative contexts of key Elizabethan and Jacobean plays. Each guide introduces the text's critical and performance history but also provides students with an invaluable insight into the landscape of current scholarly research through a keynote essay on the state of the art and newly commissioned essays of fresh research from different critical perspectives.

A Midsummer Night's Dream edited by Regina Buccola
Doctor Faustus edited by Sarah Munson Deats
King Lear edited by Andrew Hiscock and Lisa Hopkins
1 Henry IV edited by Stephen Longstaffe
'Tis Pity She's a Whore edited by Lisa Hopkins
Women Beware Women edited by Andrew Hiscock
Volpone edited by Matthew Steggle
The Duchess of Malfi edited by Christina Luckyj
Richard III edited by Annalise Connolly
The Alchemist edited by Erin Julian and Helen Ostovich
The Jew of Malta edited by Robert A Logan
Macbeth edited by John Drakakis and Dale Townshend

Further titles in preparation

MACBETH

A Critical Reader

Edited by
John Drakakis and
Dale Townshend

B L O O M S B U R Y
NEW DELHI • LONDON • OXFORD • NEW YORK • SYDNEY

First published in India 2017
First published 2013

Bloomsbury Arden Shakespeare
An imprint of Bloomsbury Publishing Plc

This edition published with permission from Bloomsbury Publishing Plc,
50, Bedford Square, London WC1B 3DP

British Library Cataloguing-in-Publication Data
A catalogue record for this book is available from the British Library.

ISBN 978 93 86349 90 3
10 9 8 7 6 5 4 3 2 1
For sale in the Indian subcontient only

Bloomsbury Publishing India Pvt. Ltd
Second Floor, Building No.4
DDA Complex LSC, Pocket C – 6 & 7, Vasant Kunj
New Delhi 110070
www.bloomsbury.com

Exclusively distributed in the Indian subcontinent by
Manohar Publishers & Distributors
4753/23, Ansari Road
Darya Ganj, New Delhi 110002
Tel.: 23284848, 23289100
Email: sales@manoharbooks.com, manoharbooks@gmail.com

Library of Congress Cataloging-in-Publication Data
A catalog record for this book is available from the Library of Congress

Typeset by Fakenham Prepress Solutions, Fakenham, Norfolk NR21 8NN
Printed and bound in India by Replika Press Pvt. Ltd.

CONTENTS

SERIES INTRODUCTION

The drama of Shakespeare and his contemporaries has remained at the very heart of English curricula internationally and the pedagogic needs surrounding this body of literature have grown increasingly complex as more sophisticated resources become available to scholars, tutors and students. This series aims to offer a clear picture of the critical and performative contexts of a range of chosen texts. In addition, each volume furnishes readers with invaluable insights into the landscape of current scholarly research as well as including new pieces of research by leading critics.

This series is designed to respond to the clearly identified needs of scholars, tutors and students for volumes which will bridge the gap between accounts of previous critical developments and performance history and an acquaintance with new research initiatives related to the chosen plays. Thus, our ambition is to offer innovative and challenging Guides which will provide practical, accessible and thought-provoking analyses of Early Modern Drama. Each volume is organized according to a progressive reading strategy involving introductory discussion, critical review and cutting-edge scholarly debate. It has been an enormous pleasure to work with so many dedicated scholars of Early Modern Drama and we are sure that this series will encourage you to read 400-year-old playtexts with fresh eyes.

Andrew Hiscock and Lisa Hopkins

NOTES ON CONTRIBUTORS

Sandra Clark is Senior Research Fellow at the Institute of English Studies, School of Advanced Study, University of London. She has published widely on Shakespeare and early modern drama, and is Series Editor of the Arden Shakespeare Dictionaries. She is currently editing *Macbeth* for the Arden Shakespeare Third Series.

Christy Desmet is Josiah Meigs Distinguished Teaching Professor at the University of Georgia (US). She is the author of *Reading Shakespeare's Characters: Rhetoric, Ethics, and Identity* and Editor of *Shakespeare and Appropriation* (with Robert Sawyer), *Harold Bloom's Shakespeare* (with Robert Sawyer), *Shakespearean Gothic* (with Anne Williams), and *Helen Faucit*, in the Lives of Shakespearian Actors series. With Sujata Iyengar, she is co-founder and co-General Editor of *Borrowers and Lenders: The Journal of Shakespeare and Appropriation* (http://www.borrowers.uga.edu).

John Drakakis is Emeritus Professor of English Studies at the University of Stirling. He also holds Visiting Professorships at Glyndŵr University, where he has been awarded an Honorary Fellowship, and the University of Lincoln. He has published widely in the area of Shakespeare Studies and is the editor of *Alternative Shakespeares*, the joint editor of *Gothic Shakespeares*, and three other books of collected essays; he is also the editor of the recently published Arden 3 Series *The Merchant of Venice*. He has contributed essays to edited collections and articles and reviews to a number of leading literary journals. He is currently a trustee of the British Shakespeare association, and chair of its Fellowships sub-committee. He is a Fellow of the English Association and a member of the Academia Europoeia. He is currently general editor of the Routledge *New Critical Idiom* series, and is the general editor in charge of the revision of Geoffrey Bullough's *Narrative and Dramatic Sources of Shakespeare*.

Terence Hawkes is Emeritus Professor of English at Cardiff University, Wales. He is the author of *Metaphor* (Methuen, 1972), and *Structuralism and Semiotics* (Routledge, 1977, second edition, 2003), as well as a number of books on Shakespeare, including *Shakespeare and the Reason* (Routledge 1964, 2005), *Shakespeare's Talking Animals* (Arnold, 1973), *That Shakespeherian Rag* (Methuen, 1986, Routledge, 2005), *Meaning By Shakespeare* (Routledge, 1992) and *Shakespeare In The Present* (Routledge, 2002). He was co-editor, with Hugh Grady, of *Presentist Shakespeares* (Routledge, 2007). He has also acted as the general editor of the *New Accents* series and of the *Accents on Shakespeare* series published by Routledge, and was an editor of the journal *Textual Practice*.

Laury Magnus is Professor of Humanities at the US Merchant Marine Academy in Kings Point, New York. She has co-edited *Who Hears in Shakespeare? Auditory Worlds on Stage and Screen*. Her chapter, 'Shakespeare on Film and Television' appeared in the *Oxford Handbook of Shakespeare.* She is editor of the New Kittredge editions of *The Taming of the Shrew* and *The Comedy of Errors*, and co-editor of *Romeo and Juliet* and *Measure for Measure.* She has frequently written on Shakespeare in performance in *The Shakespeare Newsletter*. Her articles and reviews have also appeared in *Literature and Film Quarterly, Connotations, Assays, and College Literature.* Her non-Shakespearean books include *Lexical and Syntactic Repetition in Modern Poetry* and a co-translation of Ivan Goncharov's *The Precipice.* Magnus is also a member of the editorial team of Hamletworks.org.

Lauren Shohet is Luckow Family Professor of English at Villanova University (USA). The recipient of fellowships from the National Endowment of the Humanities, the Shakespeare

Association of America, the Folger Library, the Huntington Library, the German Academic Exchange Service, the Fulbright Foundation and the Bogliasco Foundation, she is the author of *Reading Masques: The English Masque and Public Culture in the Seventeenth Century* (OUP 2010) and numerous articles on Renaissance poetry and drama, adaptation and genre studies. She is currently editing an *Othello* i-pad app for the Luminary Shakespeare.

Adrian Streete is Senior Lecturer in Renaissance Literature in the School of English, Queen's University, Belfast. He is author of *Protestantism and Drama in Early Modern England* (CUP, 2009), editor of *Early Modern Drama and the Bible: Contexts and Readings, 1570–1625* (Palgrave, 2012), and co-editor of *The Edinburgh Companion to Shakespeare and the Arts* (EUP, 2011), *Filming and Performing Renaissance History* (Palgrave, 2011) and *Refiguring Mimesis: Representation in Early Modern Literature* (UHP, 2005). He is currently writing a book on apocalypse and early modern drama.

Dale Townshend is Senior Lecturer in Gothic and Romantic Literature at the University of Stirling, Scotland. His publications include *The Orders of Gothic: Foucault, Lacan, and the Subject of Gothic Writing, 1764–1820* (AMS, 2007), four volumes in the *Gothic: Critical Concepts in Literary and Cultural Studies* series (with Fred Botting, Routledge 2004), and *Gothic Shakespeares* (with John Drakakis, Routledge 2008). He is currently at work on three major projects: a monograph entitled *Gothic Antiquity: History, Romance and the Architectural Imagination, 1760–1840*, *Ann Radcliffe, Romanticism and the Gothic* (with Angela Wright, Cambridge University Press, 2014), and *The Gothic World* (with Glennis Byron, Routledge, 2013).

TIMELINE

1564	William Shakespeare born; baptized in Stratford-upon-Avon on 26 April 1564
1566	Birth of James I, King of Scotland from 1567
1577	Publication of first edition of Raphael Holinshed's *Chronicles of England, Scotlande, and Irelande*
1582	Shakespeare marries Anne Hathaway on 28 November 1582
1583	Birth of Shakespeare's eldest daughter, Susanna
1585	Birth of Shakespeare's twins, Hamnet and Judith
1587	Publication of second edition of Raphael Holinshed's *Chronicles*, Shakespeare's primary historical source for *Macbeth*
1590–1	*Two Gentlemen of Verona*
1592	James Carmichael's popular account of witchcraft in North Berwick, Scotland, published in London in the pamphlet *Newes from Scotland: Declaring the Damnable Life and Death of Dr. Fian, a Notable Sorcerer, who was burned at Edenbrough in January last. 1591*
1594	Lord Chamberlain's Men Theatre Company founded
1596	Burial of Hamnet Shakespeare in Stratford-upon-Avon
1597	James VI's *Daemonologie, In Forme of a Dialogue, Divided into three Bookes* published in Edinburgh Shakespeare buys New Place, Stratford
1599	Globe Theatre built in Southwark, London, by Shakespeare's playing company, Lord Chamberlain's Men
1600–1	*Hamlet*

1603	James VI of Scotland becomes James I of England and Ireland; Union of the Crowns
	Lord Chamberlain's Men Theatre Company renamed as The King's Men and patronized by James VI/I
1605	Gunpowder Plot
	King James VI I attends, at St John's College, Oxford, a pageant involving Banquo's meeting with three 'fatal sisters'
c.1606	*Macbeth* debuts at the Globe
1606	King of Denmark visits English Court, possibly viewing there a performance of *Macbeth*
1607	Gunpowder Plot trials
1611	Simon Forman in his *Book of Plays* records attending, possibly in error, a performance of *Macbeth* at the Globe Theatre on 20 April 1610. The correct year of Forman's attendance is now generally accepted as being 1611, and the play itself a revival of an earlier production
1613	Globe Theatre destroyed by fire
1614	Globe Theatre rebuilt on original site
c.1615	Thomas Middleton's *The Witch* performed at Blackfriars Theatre
1616	Death of Shakespeare on 23 April 1616; burial in Stratford-upon-Avon
1623	*The Tragedie of Macbeth* published in the First Folio of John Heminges and Henry Condell, *Mr William Shakespeares Comedies, Histories, & Tragedies*
1642	Globe Theatre closed by the Puritans, along with other theatres
1660	Restoration of Monarchy with the reign of Charles II; reopening of theatres
1664	Sir William Davenant revives and produces an operatic, highly spectacular *Macbeth* for the Duke's Company
	Samuel Pepys records in his diaries his attendance of a performance of *Macbeth*

1667	Samuel Pepys records in his diaries at least three more performances of *Macbeth*
1674	Sir William Davenant's *Macbeth; A Tragedy. With all the Alterations, Amendments, Additions, and New Songs* published in London
1744	David Garrick debuts as Macbeth
1748	Hannah Vaughan Pritchard begins to play Lady Macbeth to Garrick's Macbeth
1765	Samuel Johnson publishes his edition of *Macbeth* in the sixth volume of *The Plays of William Shakespeare, In Eight Volumes*
1769	Elizabeth Montagu provides a fulsome critical assessment of *Macbeth* in *An Essay on the Writings and Genius of Shakespear*
c.1779	Sarah Siddons first plays the role of Lady Macbeth in the provinces
1785	Sarah Siddons first plays the role of Lady Macbeth in London
1794	Ghostless version of *Macbeth* produced for John Philip Kemble's inauguration of the new Theatre Royal, Drury Lane
1817	William Hazlitt, in *Characters of Shakespeare's Plays*, defends *Macbeth* against the terms of Samuel Johnson's critique
1823	Thomas De Quincey publishes his influential essay 'On the Knocking at the Gate in *Macbeth*' in the *London Magazine*
1834	Sarah Siddons's 'Remarks on the Character of Lady Macbeth' published in Thomas Campbell's *Life of Mrs. Siddons*
1847	Première of Giuseppe Verdi's operatic *Macbeth*
1849	Rivalry between William Charles Macready and Edwin Forrest; Astor Place Riots in New York
1888	Ellen Terry debuts as Lady Macbeth in Henry Irving's production of *Macbeth* at the Lyceum Theatre, London, with Irving in the title role

1904	A. C. Bradley publishes two influential lectures on *Macbeth* in *Shakespearean Tragedy*
1913	Première of *Macbeth* in Tokyo, Japan, translated by Ogai Mori and directed by Sojin Kamiyama
1930	Publication of G. Wilson Knight's *The Wheel of Fire*, with two chapters devoted to *Macbeth*
1933	Publication of L. C. Knights's riposte to A. C. Bradley in 'How Many Children Had Lady Macbeth? An Essay in the Theory and Practice of Shakespeare Criticism'
1936	Staging of Orson Welles's 'Voodoo' *Macbeth*
1947	Publication of Cleanth Brooks's influential essay 'The Naked Babe and the Cloak of Manliness'
1948	Release of Orson Welles's film *Macbeth*, starring Welles in lead role
1951	*Macbeth* edited by Kenneth Muir for Arden 2
1955	Production of *Macbeth* at the Memorial Theatre, Stratford-upon-Avon, starring Laurence Olivier and Vivien Leigh, directed by Glen Byam Shaw
	British–American crime drama *Joe MacBeth*, directed by Ken Hughes
1957	Akira Kurosawa's filmic adaptation of *Macbeth* – *Throne of Blood/Kumonosu-jō/Castle of the Spider's Web*
1960	Debut of George Schaefer's production of *Macbeth* for American television, starring Maurice Evans and Judith Anderson
1969	Publication of Dennis Bartholomeusz's *Macbeth and the Players*
1970	BBC production of *Macbeth*, starring Eric Porter and Janet Suzman, directed by John Gorrie
1971	Roman Polanski's film *Macbeth*
	Welcome Msomi's *uMabatha*, the Zulu *Macbeth*, first staged at the University of Natal, South Africa
1976	Production of *Macbeth* at The Other Place, Stratford-upon-Avon, starring Ian McKellen and Judi Dench, directed by Trevor Nunn

1977	Publication of *Twentieth Century Interpretations of Macbeth*, edited by Terence Hawkes
1978	Publication of Marvin Rosenberg's *The Masks of Macbeth*
1982	BBC production of *Macbeth*, starring Nicol Williamson and Jane Lapotaire, directed by Jack Gold
	Publication of *Focus on Macbeth*, edited by John Russell Brown
1985	Publication of Gordon Williams's *Macbeth: Text and Performance*
1990	Yukio Ninagawa's *Macbeth* debuts at the Opera House, Brooklyn Academy of Music, New York
	Filmic adaptation of *Macbeth* as *Men of Respect*, directed by William Reilly
1991	Publication of *Macbeth: Critical Essays*, edited by S. Schoenbaum
1992	Publication of *Macbeth: New Casebooks*, edited by Alan Sinfield
1997	*Macbeth* edited by A. R. Braunmuller for the New Cambridge Shakespeare
1999	RSC production of *Macbeth* at the Swan Theatre, Stratford-upon-Avon, starring Antony Sher and Harriet Walter, directed by Greg Doran
2002	Revival of Yukio Ninagawa's *Macbeth* at the Brooklyn Academy of Music, New York
	Billy Morrissette's filmic adaptation of *Macbeth – Scotland, PA*
2003	North American premiere of Vishal Bharadwaj's film *Maqbool*
2004	Publication of Bernice W. Kliman's *Shakespeare in Performance: Macbeth*
2005	Arthur Byron Cover and Tony Leonard Tamai's *Macbeth: The Graphic Novel*
2006	Moises Kaufman's production of *Macbeth* at the Delacorte Theater, New York
	Premiere of Geoffrey Wright's film *Macbeth*, starring Sam Worthington, Victoria Hill and Lachy Hulme

2007	*Macbeth* performed at the Chichester Festival Theatre, starring Patrick Stewart, directed by Rupert Goold
2008	Publication of *Macbeth: New Critical Essays*, edited by Nick Moschovakis
2009	Premiere of Alexander McCall Smith and Tom Cunningham's *The Okavango Macbeth* opera in Botswana
2010	*Macbeth* performed at Theater for a New Audience, New York, starring Annika Boras and John Douglas Thompson, directed by Arin Arbus
	Publication of *Weyward Macbeth: Intersections of Race and Performance*, edited by Scott L. Newstok and Ayanna Thompson
2012	Alan Cumming's one-man *Macbeth* debuts at Tramway Theatre, Glasgow, directed by John Tiffany and Andrew Goldberg

Introduction

John Drakakis

Johnson Against *Macbeth*

In the autumn of 1773 Samuel Johnson and James Boswell toured Scotland and got as far as the Western Isles. At the end of his short account of travel in 'The Lowlands', Dr Johnson observed that after visiting Elgin:

> We went forward the same day to Fores, the town to which Macbeth was travelling, when he met the weird sisters in his way. This to an Englishman is classic ground. Our imaginations were heated, and our thoughts recalled to their old amusements.[1]

Boswell's account seems to have been a little more 'heated' and certainly less partisan than Dr Johnson's, since early on he describes his companion, perhaps like Shakespeare's Duncan, as being 'somewhat susceptible of flattery'. 'His mind was so full of imagery', Boswell continues, 'that he might have been perpetually a poet',[2] but he was also 'somewhat disfigured by the scars of that *evil* [scrofula] which it was formerly imagined the *royal touch* could cure'.[3] At Laurencekirk, Boswell notes that 'Dr Johnson repeated with solemn emphasis Macbeth's speech on meeting the witches',[4] although given Johnson's own scepticism about the veracity or, indeed, the seriousness of what he called 'the scenes of enchantment' in Shakespeare's play,[5] and by implication his antipathy towards Scotland in general, it is difficult to gauge the level of irony implied by the phrase 'solemn emphasis'.

Elsewhere Johnson's response to *Macbeth* was mixed. For example, he could applaud the arguments that Lady Macbeth used 'to persuade her husband to commit murder' since they 'afford a proof of Shakespeare's knowledge of human nature',[6] but he seemed incredulous that when Lady Macbeth intends to 'gild the faces of the grooms withal/For it must seem their guilt' Shakespeare intended 'to play upon the similitude of *gild* and *guilt*'.[7] Johnson was even more critical of the lines 'Here lay Duncan,/His silver skin laced with his golden blood', lines in which, he claimed, 'every word is equally faulty' and that could only be emended 'by a general blot'.[8] In conclusion, Johnson's view of the play was that the 'propriety of its fictions' could be celebrated, but that it had 'no nice discriminations of character' and that 'the events are too great to admit the influence of particular dispositions, and the course of the action necessarily determines the conduct of the agents'.[9] For Johnson the play was, in part, 'improbable' because it was rooted too securely in Shakespeare's own time: 'I know not whether it may not be said in defence, of some parts which now seem improbable, that, in Shakespeare's time, it was necessary to warn credulity against vain and elusive predictions.'[10]

Johnson's lofty Augustan appeal to an historical relativism in order to explain the alleged 'improbabilities' of *Macbeth* sits uneasily with modern interpretations, performances and adaptations of the play. In his 1977 introduction to a volume of *Twentieth Century Interpretations of Macbeth*, which appeared on the eve of a major revolution in Shakespeare Studies, Terence Hawkes observed that the play had 'increasingly impressed twentieth century critics' as one 'with a peculiarly modern bearing', going on to suggest that

> Despite its evident involvement with an older world, with witches, their incantations and their spells, those who have written about the play in our own time indicate a growing sense that its protagonist speaks within a modern political and moral situation, about modern matters.[11]

To be sure, Hawkes had other models of modernity in mind in 1977 when he observed that '*Macbeth* contains elements that the twentieth century experience repeatedly recognizes and responds to',[12] but we might augment the list he compiles with reference to more recent political controversies cast in the discourse of 'regime change' or fundamentalist terrorism, as well as some of the larger conceptual questions involving the operations of global 'power', since *Macbeth* can undoubtedly be read in relation to these. Moreover, and in addition to its thematic resonances and its susceptibility to creative adaptation, since the early 1930s the play has also become a touchstone of the efficacy of the various shifts that have taken place within the institution of Shakespeare Criticism itself.

The Occasion of *Macbeth*

Commentators have been as wary about the dating of *Macbeth* as they have been about deciding whether it is a 'topical' or an 'occasional' play. The arguments in favour of its topicality as an early Jacobean play cite the accession to the throne of James I, the son of the executed Mary Queen of Scots and the *de facto* uniting of the thrones of England and Scotland in 1603, along with sundry references to the Gunpowder Plot to assassinate the new monarch in November 1605. Various issues known to have been dear to James, such as witchcraft, monarchy and governance – topics on which he had already written – are also adduced as inspiration for Shakespeare's play. The case for *Macbeth* as an 'occasional' play revolves around the visit of King Christian IV of Denmark, James's brother-in-law, in July and August 1606,[13] although in his book *The Royal Play of Macbeth*[14] Henry N. Paul speculates upon a meeting in Oxford involving James and Shakespeare where the idea of some kind of court performance is alleged to have been originally proposed.[15] More recently, and in the wake of the appearance of the Wells and Taylor-edited Oxford *Complete Works of William Shakespeare* (1986) and the controversy surrounding the textual provenance of the First Folio *Macbeth*, questions have been raised concerning the extent to which the play may have been a collaboration between Shakespeare and his prolific contemporary Thomas Middleton.

Most commentators are agreed that *Macbeth* was written and performed some time during late 1605 and 1606 and that references to 'farmer' and 'equivocator' in the Porter's speech at II.iii.4 and 9 may well refer to the equivocating Jesuit Father Henry 'farmer' Garnet who, having been accused of involvement in the Gunpowder Plot of 1605, was tried and executed on 28 March 1606. Kenneth Muir, the Arden 2 editor of the text, dismisses the suggestion that such references may have been added to an already extant text of the play,[16] nor does he accept the case for a connection between the play and Matthew Gwynne's deployment of '*tres quasi sibyllae*' in an entertainment at St John's College, Oxford, as part of the celebrations to mark James I's visit on 27 August 1605. Muir is also sceptical about the relevance of the dating of echoes in Shakespeare's text of plays such as John Marston's *The Wonder of Women, Or the Tragedy of Sophonisba* (1606); indeed, he concludes from the evidence that 'It is more likely that Shakespeare picked up one of Marston's best images ["Their large spread winges, which fanned the evening ayre/ Where the Norweyan Banners flowt the Skie,/And fanne our people cold"] from the second scene of *Sophonisba* than that Marston imitated several passages from one of the weakest scenes in *Macbeth*.'[17] Leaving aside the implication that a superior gloss on the evidence is always to be attributed to Shakespeare – although Muir is careful to balance his account with the claim that *Macbeth* contains 'weak' scenes – it would not be surprising to find that, in addition to 'source' material and contemporary extra-theatrical stimuli, there should be in circulation a lexicon of contemporary topics, images and expressions available to the alert writer.

Immediately available to Shakespeare, of course, was the account of Scottish history that formed part of Raphael Holinshed's *The Chronicles of England, Scotland and Ireland* (1587). Although *The Chronicles* contains the fullest account of the events that

Shakespeare chose to dramatize, various elements of the text of *Macbeth* as it appeared in the Folio of 1623 can be traced to a variety of other texts, and Geoffrey Bullough provides a full list of 'sources', 'analogues' and 'probable sources' in Volume VII of his *Narrative and Dramatic Sources of Shakespeare*. It is, of course, difficult to determine a clear causal pattern of influence or indeed to speculate with any authority about the circulation of these narratives, but Bullough has shown convincingly some of the ways in which the play, as we have it, clearly departs from the historical narrative and that these details are coupled with certain conflations that distinguish *Macbeth* from other texts that either treated or alluded to aspects of Scottish history.[18] For example, in Holinshed, Duncan and Macbeth are cousins by marriage[19] and not, as in Shakespeare's play, king and vassal, although the descriptions of Macbeth and Duncan are ones to which Shakespeare appears to have given some attention:

> one Makbeth a valiant gentleman, and one that if he had not been cruell of nature, might have beene thought most woorthie the government of a realme. On the other part, Duncane was so soft and gentle of nature that the people wished the inclinations and maners of these two cousins to have beene so tempered and enterchangeablie bestowed betwixt them, that where the one had too much of clemencie, and the other of crueltie, the meane virtue betwixt these two extremities might have reigned by the indifferent partition in them both, so should Duncane have proved a worthie king, and Makbeth an excellent capteine.[20]

Shakespeare's Duncan cannot be accused, as Holinshed claims, of being 'negligent' in his punishment of offenders, as the fate of Cawdor in the play demonstrates, and Shakespeare's narrative appears to hint at a much deeper and more complex cause of political disturbance than the simple claim that 'manie misruled persons tooke occasion thereof to trouble the peace and quiet state of the common-wealth, by seditious commotions which first had their beginnings in this wise'.[21] In *Macbeth*, Duncan is the 'worthie king' and Macbeth the 'excellent capteine', while the former, by Macbeth's own admission, 'Hath borne his faculties so meek, hath been/So clear in his great office, that his virtues/ Will plead like angels, trumpet-tongu'd against/The deep damnation of his taking off' (I.vii.17–20).[22] Modern productions have tended to take their cue for the characterization of Duncan from Macbeth's comment, but the perfunctory treatment of the rebel Cawdor, earlier at I.iv.1 and following, suggests a king capable of decisive violence when the occasion demands. The challenge from MacDonwald, who in Holinshed accuses Duncan of being 'a faint-hearted milksop, more meet to govern a sort of idle monks in some cloister, than to have the rule of such valiant and hardie men of warre as the Scots were',[23] is contained in the play and linked with the rebellion of Cawdor, 'a gentleman' on whom Duncan had 'built/An absolute trust' (I.iv.12–13). The play, unlike Holinshed's narrative, offers no reason for the rebellion against Duncan, and we are to assume that at the heart of the conflict is the impulse generated by unrestrained political 'ambition' that is the underside of the loyalty demanded by the king. In Holinshed, Banquo is active in support of Macbeth in overcoming MacDonwald, and it is the brutality of Macbeth in the service of Duncan that is emphasized:

> remitting no peece of his cruell nature with that pitifull sight [of MacDonwald's dead body], he caused the head to be cut off, and set upon a poles end, and so sent it as a present to the king who as then lay at Bertha. The headlesse trunke he commanded to bee hoong up upon an high paire of gallowes.[24]

Clearly Shakespeare retained some of this detail for the end of the play when Macduff enters at V.ix.19 with Macbeth's head.

Shakespeare deals more perfunctorily than Holinshed with Macbeth's cruelty, choosing rather to explore the extreme psychological tension between the loyalty of the 'subject' and the impulse to rebellion that is paradoxically generated by the ambition that the fact of quasi-feudal subservience generates. Moreover, this anxiety repeats the archetypal conflict between God and Lucifer that was one of the key pre-historic narratives used to explain some of the vicissitudes of certain forms of human behaviour during the period. Such accounts amalgamate the emphasis on secular politics in the manner expounded in texts such as Machiavelli's *The Prince* (c.1532) and developed in Tacitean accounts of the detailed tensions revealed by the political divisions that emerged in histories of the Roman empire on the one hand and a commitment that James I was known to have shared to the 'divine right' of kings on the other. Indeed, as many commentators on the play have observed, the act of regicide, the events leading up to it and its devastating consequences are central to the dramatic action. Shakespeare had embarked on a dramatization of the villain-as-hero much earlier in his *Richard III* (c.1592–1563, first printed in 1597), although Richard is clearly regarded in that play as a terminal 'effect' of the regicide of *Richard II*; Shakespeare returned to the issue of regicide in a carefully nuanced dramatization in *Richard II* (c.1595, first printed in 1597). *Hamlet* (c.1601, first printed in 1603 and then again in 1605) begins the process of giving some attention to the inner psychological turmoil of the regicide Claudius but contains it in another archetypal struggle that is rooted in the biblical mythical/historical narrative of the killing of Abel by his brother, Cain. Although these narratives sit uneasily with the micro-political suggestions in Holinshed of the ruler's inadequacies, Shakespeare's play imprints them on the political conscience of the tragic hero who is, in Aristotle's terms, better than the average, but who also gets caught up in actions that reverberate well beyond the 'character' of Macbeth. The drama is now located in a secular world where the fitness of a king such as Duncan – clearly, in terms of his monarchical values, out of his time – is pitted against a ruthless but conscience-driven opponent, torn between the demands of secular power and a feudal 'conscience', whose challenge to monarchical rule is imbued with both quasi-religious *and* secular political preoccupations. The tension that emerges is presented as a universal effect of a particular political structure while at the same time re-affirming the monarchical order upheld in theory and in practice by James I himself as being superior to any political alternative.

Two further elements treated by Holinshed are worthy of note: the role of the three 'Weird Sisters' and that of Lady Macbeth. These three figures appear in a Latin analogue, Matthew Gwynne's *Vertumnus Sive Annus Recurrens* (1607), as '*tres quasi Sibyllae*',[25] but in Holinshed's *The Chronicles* Macbeth and Banquo encounter 'three women in strange apparel, resembling creatures of elder world' who prophesy that the former will be Thane of Cawdor and 'hereafter shalt be king of Scotland'. To Banquo the 'first' of the women says that:

> We promise greater benefits unto thee, than unto him [Macbeth], for he shall reigne in deed, but with an unluckie end: neither shall he leave anie issue behinde him to succeed in his place, where contrarily thou in deed shalt not reigne at all, but of thee those shall be borne which shall govern the Scottish kingdom by long order of continuall descent.[26]

In Holinshed, these prophecies are the subject of light-hearted jest between the two vassals, although he goes on to say that

> afterwards the common opinion was, that these women were either the weird sisters, that is (as ye would say) the goddesses of destinie, or else some nymphs or feiries, indued with knowledge of prophesies by their necromanticall science, because everie thing came to passe as they had spoken.[27]

Macbeth and Femininity

Much critical ink has been spilt on apportioning the responsibility for Macbeth's actions in securing the crown and in recent decades questions have been asked about why these apparent forces of 'destiny' should be ambivalently female. Holinshed's claim that Macbeth was motivated by a sense that Duncan's nomination of Malcolm as his successor was tantamount to a 'defrauding' him of 'all maner of title and claime'[28] is presented in the play simply as an obstacle that Macbeth himself recognizes will prevent the Weird Sisters' prophecies from coming to fruition. But at the end of the play, when he comes to realize that his life is now emptied of any significance and when the final conditions of his apparently magical invincibility are shown to be no longer effective, he begins 'To doubt th' equivocation of the fiend/That lies like truth' (V.v.42–43) and questions their veracity:

> And be these juggling fiends no more believed
> That palter with us in a double sense,
> That keep the word of promise to our ear
> And break it to our hope. (V.viii.19–22)

The slipperiness of language and the uncertainties of meaning are here attributed to a satanic source that the play locates externally in the Weird Sisters and internally in the tortured psychology of the tragic hero. To give too much weight to the former, however, would deprive the tragedy of its force and to give too much weight to the latter would elicit no sympathy, as Johnson thought, for what would otherwise be a pathological criminality deserving of extreme punishment.[29] That this allegedly pathological criminality and its association with a demonic force should be identified, even if only partially, with femininity raises some serious questions concerning the assumptions that the play makes about the shaping of gendered subjectivity.

Lady Macbeth extends the process of the demonization of femininity in the play, although here Shakespeare clearly follows Holinshed initially in the suggestion that Macbeth was 'greatlie incouraged' by the words of the Weird Sisters, supplemented by the urging of his wife who 'lay sore upon him to attempt the thing, as she that was verie ambitious, burning in unquenchable desire to beare the name of a queene'.[30] In Holinshed, Banquo is an accessory to the murder of Duncan, but in Shakespeare's play that role is allotted exclusively to Lady Macbeth, while Banquo restrains himself from acting precipitately to bring about the Weird Sisters' prophecies. Early in the play, Lady Macbeth and Macbeth appear to exchange roles, with the latter being accused of 'feminine' humanity in contrast to her steely inhuman masculinity. However, Shakespeare reverses this polarity so that after the murder of Duncan Macbeth himself assumes control – 'Be innocent of the knowledge, dearest chuck,/Till thou applaud the deed' (III.ii.45–6) – and Lady Macbeth falls victim to the psychological pressures that follow on from the crime itself. In the case of both the Weird Sisters and Lady Macbeth, the stimulus to regicide is rooted in the patriarchal myth of an ambivalent feminine desire that proves to be both destructive and ultimately incapable of fulfilment. It is also important to emphasize that the Weird Sisters do nothing in the play and that when it comes to the act of regicide even Lady Macbeth is prevented from acting by virtue of a residual patriarchal imperative: 'Had he not resembled/My father as he slept, I had done't' (II.ii.12–13). This is the first sign that the play gives us of a vacillating resolve that temporarily rectifies itself: 'Infirm of purpose!/Give me the daggers. The sleeping, and the dead,/Are but as pictures; `tis the eye of childhood/That fears a painted devil' (II.ii.52–5), but then in the second half of the play she collapses into madness.

Historicizing *Macbeth*

From what we glean from Bullough's arrangement of the 'sources' for the play it is clear that Shakespeare extended what he may have read in a number of texts and for the most part re-shaped his material to produce a tragedy of moral, political and ethical complexity that spoke to concerns of early Jacobean England. Critics have become increasingly sceptical that the play was 'occasional', although modern performances gesture towards historical veracity by embedding them in a range of extra-dramatic and theatrical material. For example, a cursory glance at some of the programmes from a small selection of theatre performance from 1989 onwards reveals an increasingly heavy emphasis upon 'historical' contextualization. Adrian Noble's 1989 RSC production at Stratford-upon-Avon, though sparse in its contextualization, devotes a short passage to 'Date and Sources' and then offers a brief photographic palimpsest 'history' of modern performances from 1952 onwards. A foreword by Terry Eagleton, who some three years before had argued that the Weird Sisters were the unsung heroines of the play,[31] provides an abstract and universal envelope for the historical material, but in subsequent productions, such as Tim Albery's RSC *Macbeth* (1996) and Dominic Cooke's 2004 production, the programmes are fleshed out with substantial critical material (1996), augmented with specifically historical accounts of seventeenth-century witchcraft (2004). In a recent Sheffield Crucible production of *Macbeth* (2012) and in the wake of current debates about Scottish devolution and its political aftermath, specific emphasis is tellingly placed upon what the programme describes as 'A Scottish king in London: *Macbeth* and James I'. It is perhaps worth noting that, under the innovative direction of Daniel Evans, Andrew Jarvis's Duncan in this production attempted self-consciously to amalgamate the dual perceptions of the king portrayed alternatively as a 'Christ-like' figure and as an efficient, implicitly ruthless regal executive.

One further 'historical' question, however, requires some consideration. During the last two decades attention has turned more seriously, although not necessarily any more effectively, than before to questions of authorship, and given the fact that *Macbeth* did not appear in print until the Folio of 1623, some seven years after Shakespeare's death, the issue of Shakespeare's alleged collaboration with other contemporary writers has received renewed attention. The Folio refers to two songs that appear in Thomas Middleton's *The Witch* (c.1613–16), a play not printed during Middleton's own lifetime but probably acted by

Shakespeare's company, The King's Men, at Blackfriars. There have been doubts expressed about the methodology utilized by the champion of this alleged collaboration, Gary Taylor, to determine which parts of Shakespeare's play may have been written by Middleton, although the argument has settled around the suggestion that Middleton may have been the reviser of the play for performance some time after Shakespeare's death.[32] Perhaps we should also distinguish what is in part a marketing ploy to advance the more general cause and reputation of Thomas Middleton from judicious editors such as A. R. Braunmuller, who do not go beyond the acknowledgement that the play was 'adapted' by Middleton.[33]

A recent production, that of Alan Cumming's one-man *Macbeth* (2012) directed by John Tiffany, spans the divide between 'performance' and 'adaptation' in its attempt to explore the deeply psychotic nature of a man inhabiting the roles of other characters in the play and sinking deeper into insanity as he is forced to relive his crime and to suffer the trauma of psychological fragmentation of personality while being confined within the heavily policed clinical walls of a lunatic asylum. Reviewers have argued that in strict terms the Tiffany production is an 'adaptation' rather than a performance of the play, and it is indeed the case that *Macbeth*, as several chapters in this volume demonstrate, has generated a host of adaptations, theatrical, cinematographic and otherwise. Indeed, despite the attempts to anchor the play in a recognizable 'history', its themes, its emphases and finally the sheer intensity of its poetic language have all lent themselves to contemporary re-writings. The nature of the play's preoccupations with the anxieties and pitfalls of 'power' have, in our post-Foucaldian world, led to some of the most innovative 'adaptations' of any Shakespeare play, in particular those involving a generic shift into the cinematic form of the 'gangster' movie where extreme violence and Machiavellian practice innovatively combine. In addition to frequently creative performances, each sharpened by the extra-theatrical social awareness of audiences of the consequences of political devolution, the play has migrated into the cinematic genre of film noir. The Paul Douglas–Ruth Roman 1955 *Joe Macbeth* translates the play into the genre of the Hollywood mafia film, a tendency further extended in William Reilly's 1990 version, *Men of Respect*, which utilizes many of the elements of the earlier film. More recently, this type of adaptation has migrated to India in a Bollywood version, *Maqbool* (2004), which derives much from its two predecessors. For a fuller discussion of *Macbeth*'s afterlife in modern and contemporary rewritings and adaptations, see the chapters 'The State of the Art' and 'Resources' in this volume.

Political *Macbeth*

In much the same way that *Macbeth* as a performance text has encouraged various forms of adaptation, shaped to respond to current political concerns as well as shifts in aesthetic taste, so the play has become a touchstone for shifts in critical practice within the academy and the business of Shakespeare scholarship itself. We saw briefly how Adrian Noble's 1989 production of the play managed to co-opt the intellectual energies generated from within a burgeoning radical criticism, but the history of *Macbeth* criticism from A. C. Bradley onwards has been linked to changes in scholarly concerns that span more than a century. The shift in sensibility, there in William Hazlitt, who regarded *Macbeth* as being distinguished by 'the wildness of the imagination and the rapidity of the action',[34] is exemplified by Thomas De Quincey's essay 'On the Knocking at the Gate in *Macbeth*' (1823): here, De Quincey reads a crucial moment in the play not as a piece of 'comic relief' but as the means of making known

> audibly that the reaction has commenced; [that] the human has made its reflux upon the fiendish; [that] the pulses of life are beginning to beat again; and [that] the re-establishment of the goings-on of the world in which we live, first makes us profoundly sensible of the awful parenthesis that had suspended them.[35]

This essay signalled a movement towards revaluing a structure and mode of representation that an Augustan critic such as Samuel Johnson had dismissed out of hand. A. C. Bradley followed Hazlitt by admitting *Macbeth* to a pantheon of Shakespearean Tragedy whose boundaries were to remain in place well into the twentieth century. Though Bradley was sensitive to the dynamics of theatrical performance, he treated the play and its dramatic characterization in particular as though it were a nineteenth-century novel. It was Bradley who in a casual footnote started the hare of Lady Macbeth's 'children' and it was to this that L. C. Knights responded in his essay 'How Many Children Had Lady Macbeth?', a spry demolition from one of the progenitors of the *Scrutiny* school of English criticism that preferred to regard the play as a poem than as an exercise in the vicissitudes of novelistic characterization. This model was further refined in Cleanth Brooks's 1947 essay 'The Naked Babe and the Cloak of Manliness', which ostensibly co-opted the play for the cause of American New Criticism, while, coterminous with L. C. Knights, G. Wilson Knight sought to formulate an alternative to the Bradleyan mode of 'character' criticism by claiming that the key to a Shakespeare play lay in a process of 'symbolic personification'. For a fuller account of these and other early critical debates, see 'The Critical Backstory' chapter in this volume.

Macbeth Our Contemporary

Throughout the first three quarters of the twentieth century the debate oscillated between different perceptions of Shakespeare: as novelist (Bradley), with the emphasis on depth of 'characterization'; as a historical exemplar writing for a particular kind of theatre; and finally departing from the figure of the 'author' to emphasize the integrity of the text as a repository for 'Shakespearean' themes (L. C. Knights), and with a particular emphasis on Shakespeare's 'poetry' (Knights, Brooks). Alongside this concern was a focus on Shakespearean texts as blueprints for theatrical performance, a concern that had begun in earnest in the nineteenth century, but which had become more controversial as the process of textual editing, accelerated from the 1950s onwards by the new bibliographical methods developed by Fredson Bowers, began to concentrate more fully on authentication rather than on the predilections of editorial taste or the egotism of leading actors. The *Scrutiny* school of criticism led by F. R. Leavis began in the 1930s with what, with hindsight, appears to have been a left-wing bias. But the emphasis of some of its adherents, such as L. C. Knights, built on the writings of socialist historian R. H. Tawney, emerging in books such as *Drama and Society in The Age of Jonson*.[36] Moreover, M. C. Bradbrook's *Themes and Conventions in Elizabethan Tragedy*,[37] an influential source of material concerning stage practices, was subsumed into a more general account of the history of the Elizabethan theatre and was augmented by the writings of commentators such as E. M. W. Tillyard. In the case of editors and critics such as Kenneth Muir, a number of these emphases came together in an amalgam of textual scholarship, 'themes' criticism, 'source' hunting and a form of left-Leavisite social critique, in essays, editions and monographs that Muir produced over some forty years as a leading Shakespearean. Much of the writing of the period was un-theoretical if not at times hostile to theory, and it was not until the 1970s that a serious challenge was mounted to its hegemony.[38]

One book that exerted considerable influence on the trajectory of Shakespeare Studies, while spanning the divide between Shakespearean scholarship and theatrical practice, was Jan Kott's *Shakespeare Our Contemporary*.[39] Noted more for its linkage of *King Lear* and Beckett's *Endgame*, Kott's brief chapter on *Macbeth* indicates an approach that has remained influential in Shakespeare Studies despite the much more rigorous shifts in the direction of 'theory' from the late 1970s onwards. After a discussion of the play that could fit into any one of the paradigms of an earlier 'traditional' Shakespeare criticism, Kott contrasts the figures of Richard III and Macbeth, indicating that Richard is fully aware of 'the Grand Mechanism' of 'history' and submits himself to it, whereas Macbeth conceives it as 'nightmare'.[40] The nature of that nightmare is distinctively modern, as Macbeth passes through what Kott calls 'the "Auschwitz experience"', one in which 'everything is easy'.[41] Kott's vision is one of a post-Holocaust world, haunted by death and living in the shadow of an oppressive totalitarianism that casts its shadow on all artistic endeavour. This is the way, according to Kott, that we make sense of our own cultural experience, filtering the art of the past through the lens of a history coming rapidly to its end.

Kott's annexation of Shakespeare to an essentially nihilistic reading of twentieth-century post-Holocaust experience was influential but not long lasting. The positive *and* negative accounts generated from within feminism, alongside newly revived Marxist and non-Marxist materialist accounts of Shakespearean texts, breathed a new life into what was beginning to be regarded as a partisan 'establishment' practice. A retrospective glance at the 1970s and the 1980s reveals a much less dramatic conflict than seemed to be the case at the time, and many of the dialogues that were opened then have since continued. We are now, perhaps, in a much better position to evaluate more fully the appeal to modern sensibilities of a play such as *Macbeth*, having, as it were, a much firmer grasp of the secular operations of power, more nuanced understandings of the institution of monarchy in the early seventeenth century and a better grasp of what critics such as Bradley understood by the term 'characterization'. Eagleton's extravagant and brief excursion into *Macbeth* notwithstanding, questions concerning the nature and practices of witchcraft,[42] anthropological accounts of Tragedy and the place of the play within it,[43] new historicist and cultural materialist accounts of the ways in which 'art' represents experience and human subjectivity, the manner of representing gender in tragedy, and of the ways in which contemporary religious, constitutional and political concerns are filtered into theatrical form have all played their part in the continuing history of the reception of *Macbeth*. For an account of these and other recent critical impulses, see the discussion in 'The State of the Art' chapter in this volume.

It seems appropriate to end this Introduction with some

reference to what is arguably the most explicit critical methodology into which all others have been subsumed, one that was launched by Terence Hawkes even before a name for the practice had been formulated as such. Throughout the history of Shakespeare criticism it is possible to detect a certain partisanship even in those forms that advertise themselves as being 'objective'. In 1977, and after having produced two major books on 'historical' themes,[44] Hawkes became acutely aware of the intricate differences that may be traced through the alignment of the present with the past. With the benefit of hindsight, Hawkes observed the consequences in the mid-seventeenth century of the Gunpowder Plot of 1605 and the beginnings of an Irish 'plantation' – organized colonization of Ulster by Scots and English – in 1607 whose effects were to be felt throughout the twentieth century and beyond. His own contribution to this volume amplifies that awareness and extends it into the 'present'.

On the day of the completion of this Introduction, 15 October 2012, Alex Salmond, the First Minister of Scotland under a devolved parliament, and the British Prime Minister, David Cameron, met and agreed on the terms of a referendum to be put to the Scottish people, seeking to determine whether Scotland should secede from a union that was established in 1603 with the accession of James I and ratified a century later in 1707. The England of 1606 had a very good idea of what James thought of the Union, and in certain respects *Macbeth* acknowledged the royal preference, although, perhaps, not in so obviously laudatory a manner as some critics of the past have believed. To date we do not know what Elizabeth II thinks of the forthcoming referendum, but whatever it is, its implications for any future reading of *Macbeth* will be far reaching.

The Critical Backstory

SANDRA CLARK

The Beginnings

The seventeenth century has more to contribute to the critical backstory of *Macbeth* than to most of Shakespeare's plays, and so it seems appropriate to begin here. *Macbeth* is one of the few pre-Restoration plays to be described by an eyewitness, in this case Simon Forman, who saw it at the Globe in April 1611. His somewhat rambling account is largely descriptive and he makes no critical judgements on the performance, but he was evidently impressed by certain aspects of it, especially the indelibly blood-stained hands (which he attributes to Macbeth as well as his wife) and the appearance of Banquo's ghost. Lady Macbeth's sleepwalking also stuck in his mind. His account concludes: 'Observe Also howe Mackbetes quen did Rise in the night in her slepe, & walke and talked and confessed all, & the docter noted her wordes.'[1] One cannot deduce much at all from this about how the play appeared to its early audiences, but the two extant seventeenth-century promptbooks contribute by implication a little more information as to how the play was shaped for performance, and hence what audiences did or did not like. The so-called Padua promptbook,[2] of uncertain but certainly pre-Restoration date, is based on a text of the First Folio marked up with cuts and some stage directions for performance. It testifies to an interesting historical continuity in that the cuts made here anticipate what was to happen to the text over the next three centuries: they occur mostly in the Porter's scene (II.iii), Macbeth's first interview with the Murderers (III.i), the scene of commentary on the state of Scotland during Macbeth's tyranny (III.vi) and the long scene centred on Malcolm and Macduff (IV.iii). This promptbook also makes cuts to some of Macbeth's more verbally dense speeches in I.iii and I.vii, suggesting that from early on the play's language, in speeches now considered to be the most poetically complex, was found too testing in the theatre. The other early promptbook, from the Smock Alley theatre in Dublin (c.1680),[3] postdates the Restoration and is influenced in part by the version created by Davenant. Again, the Porter's scene is the target of cutting, this time more extensively; the Apparitions in IV.i also disappear, as does Lady Macduff's son. Alterations to the language reflect what Blakemore Evans calls 'the desire to clarify what seemed involved, difficult, or obsolete'.[4]

Davenant's adaptation of the play for Restoration audiences (printed in 1674, though written at least ten years earlier), which held the stage in preference to Shakespeare's till the middle of the next century, also constitutes an implicit criticism of Shakespeare's *Macbeth*. Davenant, of course, alters the play to conform to the theatrical tastes of the new era, for instance building up the roles of Macduff and his wife to provide a moral corrective to those of the Macbeths and, notoriously, enlarging the parts of the Weird Sisters with episodes of song and dance; but his revision of Shakespeare's language – usually making it either simpler or more genteel – speaks to a criticism of the play implied in the Padua and Smock Alley promptbook versions, first expressed by Dryden (though only in passing),[5] but taken up and considerably developed in the next century by Johnson and others: that it was obscure and even bombastic. Dryden's view that Shakespeare's style was 'pestered with figurative expressions'[6] was shared by Davenant, who in his version of *Macbeth* irons out ambiguity and dispenses with subtle word-play. The opening eleven lines of Macbeth's rich and complex soliloquy in I.vii, beginning 'If it were done when 'tis done, then 'twere well/ It were done quickly', are rendered as follows:

> If it were well when done; then it were well
> It were done quickly; if his Death might be

> Without the death of nature in my self,
> And killing my own rest; it would suffice;
> But deed of this complexion still return
> To plague the doer, and destroy his peace.[7] (I.vii.1–6)

In his wish to avoid bombast, he omits classical references and levels out linguistic registers. In Shakespeare, Macbeth's horror at his bloodstained hands issues in a tortured cry which combines Latinate polysyllables with plain native monosyllables:

> What hands are here? Ha: they pluck out mine eyes.
> Will all great Neptune's ocean wash this blood
> Clean from my hand? No: this my hand will rather
> The multitudinous seas incarnadine,
> Making the green one red. (II.ii.62–65)

In Davenant, Macbeth's emotion is less graphically expressed:

> What hands are here! Can the sea afford
> Water enough to wash away the stains?
> No, they would sooner add a tincture to
> The Sea, and turn the green into a red. (II.ii.60–63)

In the scene when Duncan's murder is revealed, Davenant's Macbeth says nothing of the king's 'silver skin laced with his golden blood', and does not include the much discussed image of the daggers 'unmannerly breeched with gore'. He describes the body in more straightforward terms:

> I saw Duncan
> Whose gaping wounds look'd like a breach in nature,
> Where ruine enter'd. There I saw the murtherers
> Steep'd in the colour of their trade; their Daggers
> Being yet unwip'd, seem'd to own the deed
> And call for vengeance. (II.iii.77–82)

Insofar as is consistent with a poetic drama, the neo-classical preference for a 'close, naked, natural'[8] idiom is everywhere apparent.

The Eighteenth Century

In the eighteenth century, early editors found themselves obliged to negotiate between their admiration for Shakespeare's works and their awareness that it did not meet the standards of neo-classical taste. In the theatre this was not such a problem since until Garrick produced his own version of *Macbeth* in 1744 and disingenuously billed it 'as Shakespeare wrote it' it was Davenant's more 'correct' version that held the stage.[9] The first of all Shakespeare's editors, Nicholas Rowe, allowed that 'it would be no very hard task to find a great many faults' in Shakespeare's works if judged by Aristotelian standards. He did, however, admit that, as Dryden in *An Essay of Dramatick Poesie* (1668) had argued, 'the times were ignorant in which [Shakespeare] lived', a view widely held during this period, and found many virtues to compensate for the faults. Early critics thought *Macbeth* lacking in poetic justice, since 'the Guilty and the Innocent perish promiscuously; as in the cases of Duncan and Banquo, and Lady Macduff and her Children'.[10] The play was popular onstage from the beginning of the century onwards; Downes in *Roscius Anglicanus* (1708) called it 'a lasting play', even though Gildon, in his *Remarks on the Plays of Shakespeare* prefixed to Rowe's edition, felt it undeserving of praise because 'the Plot is a sort of History and the Character of Macbeth and his Lady are too monstrous for the Stage'.[11] But positive features soon began to emerge and the capacity demonstrated in the play for arousing terror made for favourable comparisons with classical tragedy. William Smith in his translation of Longinus (1739) commends Euripides for his representation of Orestes' distraction after the murder of his mother as 'natural' and touched 'with a happy dexterity', sentiments also to be found in Shakespeare's handling of Macbeth's imaginative torment as he prepares for the murder of Duncan. He especially admires the conception of the dagger speech: 'His Eyes rebel against his Reason, and make him start at Images that have no Reality'.[12] T.W., writing in *The British Magazine* (1767) with Aristotle's view of the emotive function of tragedy in mind, asserted that 'If the chief end of tragedy be to excite terror and compassion, that of *Macbeth* must be allowed to surpass all others, whether ancient or modern.'[13] Gildon, who was capable of arguing on both sides, had stated, when challenging Rymer's *Short View of Tragedy*, that the moral aspect of *Macbeth*, along with *Hamlet* and 'most of Shakespeare's plays', could 'prove a lesson of mightier consequence than any in Sophocles except the *Electra*'.[14] Praise for *Macbeth* as morally instructive – even 'the most instructive tragedy in the world'[15] – was frequently expressed. It was seen, simplistically, as exemplifying 'the fascinating power, and insensible progress of Vice'[16] or as a warning against succumbing to unchecked ambition in William Richardson's *A Philosophical Analysis of […] some of Shakespeare's Remarkable Characters* (1774). Richardson, having traced the 'decay of virtue' in Macbeth, concludes:

> Thus, by considering the rise and progress of a ruling passion, and the fatal consequences of its indulgence, we have shown how a beneficent mind may become inhuman, and how those who are naturally of an amiable temper, if they suffer themselves to be corrupted will become more ferocious and more unhappy than men of a constitution originally hard and unfeeling.[17]

His analysis illustrates the propensity in this period for extracting general principles of moral conduct from the plays. Elizabeth Montagu more subtly reads the play's lessons from the moral agonies that Macbeth, whom she regards as a man basically 'of a generous disposition and good propensities', undergoes:

> Other poets thought they had sufficiently attended to the moral purpose of the drama in making the furies pursue

> the perpetrated crime [...] but Macbeth's emotions are the struggles of conscience, his agonies are the agonies of remorse. They are the lessons of justice, and warnings to innocence.[18]

An anonymous writer, reviewing a performance of Garrick as Macbeth, commended the audience for its moral response to a praiseworthy sentiment. When Macbeth rebuts his wife's charge of cowardice by saying 'I dare do all that may become a man;/ Who dares do more, is none', they 'saluted him with a clap; which I could not help being much pleased with, as it not only showed a good judgment to applaud so fine a sentiment but at the same time a refin'd humanity'.[19]

In the eighteenth century moral purpose was conventionally viewed as a priority of all literature and evidently audiences looked out during performances of plays for moments that offered moral lessons. Individual speeches were singled out for admiration in this respect, as instanced by the comment of Francis Gentleman on Macbeth's response to the news of his wife's death in 'She should have died hereafter': 'The foregoing speech has the first principle of intrinsic merit to an eminent degree, moral instruction.'[20] But in Shakespeare's case, what was deemed to be his unparalleled understanding of the human heart was almost equally important. Upton (1746) praised him for his 'knowledge of the secret springs and motives of human actions' as exemplified in Macbeth's 'wavering character' and hesitancy before agreeing to the murder of Duncan.[21] Upton's view of Macbeth as an initially virtuous man vacillating between good and evil was to establish the keynote for criticism of his character up to the time of William Hazlitt.[22] Arthur Murphy, commenting on a performance of the play at Drury Lane in 1757, thought that the way in which Shakespeare showed Macbeth's guilty torments leading him into further crimes gave 'amazing Proof of our Author's insight into Nature'.[23] This knowledge was seen as the source of his power of characterization. T. W. comments admiringly on the dagger soliloquy

(II.i.33–48) as illustrative of a natural human response in such circumstances:

> There cannot be a more admirable representation of the state of mind of a man who has conceived a design replete with horror, and is meditating upon the means of putting it into execution. Nothing is more common at such a juncture than for the mind to hold a sort of conference with the instruments to be used in effecting the bloody purpose.[24]

Elizabeth Montagu believed that in *Macbeth* Shakespeare exhibited his skill in 'the just imitation of nature' to finest effect in his use of soliloquy:

> But more amazing is the art with which he exhibits the movement of the human mind and renders audible the silent march of thought; traces its modes of operation in the course of deliberating, the pauses of hesitation, and the final act of decision; shews how reason checks and how the passions impel; and displays to us the trepidations that precede and the horrors that pursue acts of blood.[25]

Along with the understanding of human nature that Shakespeare displayed in *Macbeth*, the eighteenth century also admired the play for the evidence of poetic genius in the Bard's handling of the supernatural. Rowe was influential here in his view, shared by Theobald, that 'the greatness of this Author's Genius do's nowhere so much appear as where he gives his Imagination an entire Loose, and raises his Fancy to a flight above Mankind and the Limits of the visible World'.[26] Rowe mentions the Witches in *Macbeth* in this context, but the scene with the Apparitions in Act IV was also seen in this light. Commenting on it, William Duff remarks that the genius of Shakespeare 'delighted in the most uncommon and astonishing combinations of ideas, and it never appears with so much strength as when he bursts into the ideal world, and presents to our view the characters and offices of supernatural beings'.[27] Francis Gentleman, too, thought that the supernatural afforded special opportunities for Shakespeare to display his genius, though he feared for the effect that the Witches might have on 'credulous or heated imaginations'. Elizabeth Montagu, on the other hand, seems to enjoy such a shudder, and opens her account of *Macbeth* by admiring the 'new sources of terror, new creations of fancy' that the play produces. She does, however, in the manner of the age, proceed to moralize about the positive effects of being exposed to the supernatural: 'It keeps up in our minds a sense of our connection with awful and invisible spirits to whom our most secret actions are apparent, and from whose chastisement innocence alone can defend us.'[28] Elsewhere, she took a more pragmatic view of the 'popular superstitions' and 'preternatural beings' that went into the creation of the supernatural elements in *Macbeth* and other plays, ascribing them to Shakespeare's need to appeal to 'his fierce and barbarous audience'. Like others of her time, she believed that Shakespeare lived 'in the dark shades of Gothic barbarism', and that many faulty elements in his work could be explained, and excused, on these grounds.

But the Witches were problematic for other reasons. The sceptical Johnson's view that belief in witchcraft belonged to a less enlightened age, and one to which Shakespeare was obliged to pander, was not uncommon, and he gave Shakespeare credit for the accuracy with which he conformed to 'common Opinions and Traditions' in depicting the 'infernal ceremonies'. It was not Shakespeare's text but the staged version of the play derived from Davenant with enlarged roles for the Witches that made for the difficulties, as Horace Walpole, reviewing Garrick's production of 1772, pointed out: 'The witches in Macbeth are by the folly of the actors, not by the fault of Shakespeare, represented in a buffoon light. They are dressed with black hats and blue aprons, like basket women and soldiers' trulls.'[29] He did not mention that fact that they were played by men. Elizabeth Montagu also blamed the actors for destroying the effect of the apparitions scene: 'The solemn character of the infernal rights [*sic*] would be very striking, if the scene was not made hideous by a mob of old women, which the Players have added to the three weird sisters.' The comic Witches had been popular on the stage since at least the beginning of the century, as Addison had noted, but it was only gradually that critics started to become uneasy with comic elements in the play, and they were not portrayed seriously until a production at Covent Garden in 1768.[30] Thomas Davies in 1784 felt that it was a testimony to Shakespeare's 'infallible judgment and sagacity' that he included 'some mixture of merriment', in which he included the Witches, who 'though not absolutely comic, never fail to produce laughter' in his tragedies,[31] but Maurice Morgann thought that what he called the 'machinery' in *Macbeth* had become dated, since 'the Gallery now laughs in some places where it ought to shudder'.[32] Francis Gentleman was also conscious of inappropriate responses, as for instance when Malcolm and Donalbain prepare to go their separate ways after their father's murder, 'nine times out of ten the audience are thrown into a horse-laugh'; by all accounts, many also behaved this way during the scene of Banquo's murder.[33] Steele observed that Lady Macbeth's feigned surprise at the news of Duncan's murder – 'What? In our house?' – was often 'received with a loud Laugh',[34] and it was probably for this reason that for many productions during this century her presence was cut from the scene.

It must be remembered that for a large part of the period *Macbeth* was staged in versions deriving from or at least strongly influenced by Davenant, even after Garrick in 1744 – in a pioneering venture by no means universally admired – attempted to return to something like the Folio text. Before this, the editorial tradition was firmly established with the work of Rowe and Theobald, but until Garrick it had little influence on the theatre. By mid-century there were several editions of Shakespeare's works which produced texts based to different degrees on collations of the Folios and Quartos by Rowe (1709, 1714), Pope (1723, 1728) and Theobald (1733, 1740). Those of Hanmer (1744), Warburton (1747), Johnson (1765), Capell (1761), Malone (1790) and Steevens (1793) were to follow. Garrick, whose powerful adulation of Shakespeare led him to reform Shakespearean acting as well as the texts used in the theatre, found Davenant's *Macbeth* unsatisfactory. Influenced by Samuel Johnson, of whom he was a close friend, Garrick – somewhat unusually for an actor of this time – took a scholarly approach to Shakespeare's texts. Johnson's edition of Shakespeare did not appear till 1765, but he had already written (though not yet published) a pamphlet entitled *Miscellaneous Observations on the Tragedy of Macbeth*. It was with the advice of Johnson and Warburton, whose edition was completed by 1744 but not published till 1747, that the acting version of Garrick's *Macbeth* was created. This production, described on the playbill as being 'as Shakespeare wrote it', represents 'an unprecedented collaboration between the theatre and the new traditions of textual scholarship'.[35] Garrick based his acting text of *Macbeth* on the second edition of Theobald (1740),[36] the most recent one available, made by a far-sighted and sensitive scholar. He made his own emendations to it on the advice of both Johnson and Warburton. He accepted some now-familiar emendations of the original Folio text by earlier editors, such as 'Who dares *do* more is none' (I.vii.46); Rowe's emendation for F 'no', 'Tarquin's ravishing *strides*' (II.i.49); Pope's emendation for F 'sides' and 'this bank and shoal of time' (I.vii.10); and Theobald's emendation for F 'school' (though not Theobald's 'weird' for the Folio 'weyard' and wayward'). He also accepted the less-familiar reading of 'My *may* [instead of 'way'] of life/ Is fallen into the sear' (V.iii.22), which Johnson, later followed by his collaborator George Steevens though not many other editors,[37] proposed. He followed some, but not all, of Johnson's suggestions for the repunctuation of the Folio, for instance saying 'It will have blood – they say it will have blood' (III.iv.122) instead of 'It will have blood they say:/Blood will have blood', as in the Folio. Johnson, who considered the punctuation of Shakespeare's text to be 'wholly in [his] power' as an editor,[38] justified his view of these lines by an interpretation of Macbeth's thoughts at this point in the action (just after the appearance of Banquo's ghost):

> Macbeth, having considered the prodigy which has just appeared, infers justly from it that the death of Duncan cannot pass unpunished: 'It will have blood.' Then after a short pause declares it as a general observation of mankind that murderers cannot escape.[39]

Of all the eighteenth-century editors, Johnson was the one most interested in *Macbeth*. Rowe, Pope and Theobald had all contributed new readings which were to become standard, and Theobald in the Preface to his edition had first proposed the idea that the play was designed to flatter James I, but for Johnson the play had a special significance. His *Miscellaneous Observations* on the play constituted his first piece of Shakespearean scholarship, staking his claim to editorial expertise; according to Boswell, he quoted from it on his deathbed.[40] Despite strictures on the 'affected obscurity'[41] of some of its language, as well as his dislike for 'imperfections of diction such as Lady Macbeth's "dunnest smoke of hell," "knife," "peep" and "blanket of the dark"' (I.v. 49–51),[42] Johnson clearly studied the play's language carefully and it provided him with more examples for his *Dictionary* than any other Shakespeare play. Yet few of his editorial emendations are now accepted, and the summarizing comments on the play in his edition appear almost dismissive. He felt that

> it has no nice discriminations of character, the events are too great to admit the influence of particular dispositions and the course of action necessarily determines the conduct of the agents [...] The passions are directed to their true end. Lady Macbeth is merely detested; and the courage of Macbeth preserves some esteem, yet every reader rejoices at his fall[43]

Johnson perhaps led the way for editors in the increasing awareness of Shakespeare's verbal art, which developed in parallel with the 'rage for emendation' that set in from the mid-century onwards. Murphy was percipient in his observation that what he called the 'peculiar' verbal style of Macbeth was integral to the play: 'The Language takes a Tincture from the Subject, which, being dark and gloomy, it thence follows that the Poets Choice of Words, and their Arrangement, are calculated to fill the Mind with Imagery of the most solemn and awful Aspect.'[44] There was also a gradual restoration of Shakespeare's text in *Macbeth*, in that scenes cut or omitted on various grounds by both editors and actors, such as the Porter's scene, were allowed to be part of the play. Capell in the Notes to his edition makes a point of reinstating it, as necessary for the action and 'masterly in its way [...] open to no serious objections but such as lye against all comic mixture with things serious'.[45] Steevens in his edition of 1793 also supported this scene and endorsed the scene where Macbeth kills Young Siward (V.vii): 'This short scene is injudiciously omitted on the stage. The poet designed Macbeth should *appear* invincible, till he encountered the object destined for his destruction.'[46] It was Steevens who discovered the manuscript of Middleton's *The Witch* and noted various similarities with *Macbeth*, but believing it to have been written well before 1603, assumed that Shakespeare had plagiarized from it.[47] The presentation of witches in the two plays was compared by Samuel Badcock, reviewing the Johnson–Steevens edition of 1780; Badcock found that, in contrast to Middleton's 'light, frisky beings', Shakespeare's were transformed into 'an instrument of terror'.[48] As the century wore on, the Witches were taken more seriously, and this was reflected in stage practice.[49] So too was Lady Macbeth, and an important development in the criticism of *Macbeth* in the period is the increasing interest in the characters and the psychological analysis of them. Macbeth, often compared with Richard III as two 'great bad men' in Kemble's phrase, is analyzed with some sensitivity by writers such as William Richardson in *Characters of Shakespeare* (1774), Thomas Whately in *Remarks on Some Characters of Shakespeare* (1785), Richard Cumberland in *The Observer* (1785–91) and Elizabeth Montagu's *An Essay on the Writings and Genius of Shakespear* (1769). Macbeth is perceived as a man with good characteristics ('valiant, dutiful to his sovereign, mild, gentle and ambitious [...] without guilt')[50] who is transformed into a heartless villain. The degree of mental torment he undergoes is stressed; Montagu asserts that 'it is impossible not to sympathize with the terrors Macbeth expresses in his disordered speech', and for her, even at the end of the play, 'the man of honour pierces through the traitor and the assassin'.[51] The expression of the despair in which Whately sees him taking refuge 'is perhaps one of the finest pictures that ever was exhibited [...] It is presumption without hope, and confidence without courage.'[52] The extent of Lady Macbeth's influence is one factor that distinguishes Macbeth from Richard III, and she begins in this period to become a character of interest in her own right. She is 'sublimely terrible' in her invocation to the spirits in I.v and in her 'I have given suck' speech injects 'a note of horror, screwed to a pitch that bursts the very sinews of nature', as Cumberland puts it.[53] She is associated with the Witches, but Cumberland says that her 'high and predominant' spirit makes her more important than they are in bringing about the main action of the play; had this not been the case, 'nature would have been excluded from the drama, and Macbeth would have become the mere machine of an uncontroulable [*sic*] necessity'.[54]

Romantics and Victorians

Cumberland's account of Lady Macbeth makes it clear that there was no complete break between the criticism of the eighteenth century and that of early nineteenth-century Romanticism, although some Romantic critics, particularly Samuel Taylor Coleridge and William Hazlitt, set themselves up in conscious opposition to Johnson. In this, they were following August Wilhelm von Schlegel, the German Romantic critic, whose *Lectures on Dramatic Art and Literature* had been translated into English in 1815. Hazlitt in the Preface to his influential *Characters of Shakespeare's Plays* (1817) drew explicitly on Schlegel for his counterblast to what he perceived as Johnson's rule-bound reductiveness and inability to appreciate Shakespeare's 'bold and happy flights of imagination': 'To him an excess of beauty was a fault; for it appeared to him like an excrescence.'[55] Shakespeare's star was high in the period – Schlegel had eulogized him in the most extravagant terms as being 'in strength, a demi-god, in profundity of vision, a prophet'[56] – and *Macbeth* had a special appeal to the Romantics for the qualities to which Hazlitt felt Johnson was blind; he praised 'the wildness of the imagination' and the 'tumultuous vehemence of the action',[57] the distinctiveness of its two main characters and especially its evocation in Macbeth of the criminal as hero, and a quality of sublimity that elevates action and characters above the reach of morality. Of all Shakespeare's plays, claims Jonathan Bate, *Macbeth* 'produced the most forceful writing about Shakespeare in the period'.[58]

Although Byron wrote nothing explicitly about the play he clearly felt an affinity with it[59] and Hazlitt saw Macbeth as a kind of Byronic hero 'driven along by the violence of his fate like a vessel drifting before the storm'.[60] For Lamb, in his essay 'On the tragedies of Shakespeare considered with reference to their fitness for stage representation' (1811), Macbeth is, along with Iago and Richard III, one of Shakespeare's 'great criminal characters', though Lamb submits that the crimes are less important than 'the ambition, the aspiring spirit, the intellectual activity which prompts them to overleap those moral fences'.[61] The comparison with Richard III, developed in the previous century, is pursued as character study by Hazlitt, to Macbeth's moral advantage. He is cruel 'from accidental circumstances' rather than nature and driven to criminal acts by a conspiracy of 'fate and metaphysical aid', creating for him 'an evil destiny' that he cannot escape. The pressure exerted on his mind by supernatural forces makes him uncertain as to what is real and what imaginary, whereas Richard 'in the busy turbulence of his projects never loses his self-possession'. Unlike Richard, Macbeth ultimately reclaims the sympathy of the audience, in 'that fine close of thoughtful melancholy' of his speech at V.iii, where he laments the decline of his life into 'the sere, the yellow leaf'.[62] Coleridge, though less sympathetic to Macbeth than Hazlitt, analyses Macbeth's propensity to what he calls 'self-temptation' in his *Lectures on the Characteristics of Shakespear* (1813) with great perception.[63] Schlegel's illuminating observation that the Witches 'surprise Macbeth in the moment of intoxication of victory, when his love of glory has been gratified'[64] gives a psychological underpinning to the discussions by Coleridge, Hazlitt and Lamb of Macbeth's succumbing to the forces of evil and subsequent tormented despair.

The Romantics were able to countenance the idea of entering into the 'murderous mind', as De Quincey called it, as neo-classical critics would not have done, and this is also one factor in their increased interest in the character of Lady Macbeth. Another is the influence of the interpretation of the role by Sarah Siddons, who first played it in 1785 but rose to her true greatness in performances between 1792 and 1812.[65] Coleridge, Lamb and Hazlitt had all seen her, and this may well have led them to stress the character's womanliness and to treat her as a much more complex and interesting figure than the monster whom Johnson called 'merely detested'. For Coleridge, Lady Macbeth is a fantasist, deluded by unsustainable dreams of ambition, punished by remorse and a death 'in suicidal agony'.[66] Hazlitt, on the other hand, sees her as 'a great bad woman' whose 'obdurate strength of will and masculine firmness' set off by contrast her husband's 'faultering virtue'. But in the end she suffers from 'an excess of that strong principle of self-interest and family aggrandisement, not amenable to the common feelings of compassion and justice'. Her ambition is for her husband, not herself, a view strongly endorsed by Anna Jameson in *Shakespeare's Heroines: Characteristics of Women, Moral, Poetical, and Historical* (1832), the first book to provide separate studies of a range of Shakespeare's women characters. It is often treated as a product of the Victorian era, though this is not the case. Jameson, writing with the awareness of a critical tradition going back to Johnson, aims to rescue the character of Lady Macbeth from the neglect she has so far suffered, in comparison with her husband. She allows that Hazlitt offered some fine criticism, but feels that 'it is a little superficial, and a little too harsh'.[67] She is dismissive of 'the German school' and its followers for the 'sentimental jumble of great crimes and dazzling virtues' with which they insult moral feeling,[68] but is nonetheless able to observe Lady Macbeth's 'amazing power of intellect, her inexorable determination of purpose and her superhuman strength of nerve' without condemning these qualities as unfeminine. For Jameson the key to the character is that although she is intellectually superior to her husband, her ambition is directed solely towards achieving power for him, and there is a 'touch of womanhood' behind her ambition. She is not egotistical or vulgar, never desirous of the 'mere baubles and trappings of royalty'. Jameson separates herself from Romanticism to a point, but nonetheless she does not escape its imaginative style. Lady Macbeth in the 'rapture of her ambition' and 'the towering bravery of her mind' is Luciferan: 'Hers is the sin of the "star-bright apostate," and she plunges with her husband into the abyss of guilt.'[69] Yet she can find 'a touch of pathos and of tenderness' in her restraint at the end of the banquet scene and feels that 'our human sympathies are touched' by her helpless downfall in the sleepwalking scene, which she regards as 'sublime'.

Jameson was another of those nineteenth-century Shakespeare critics who was clearly inspired by Sarah Siddons's performances as Lady Macbeth; Siddons's view of the character, expressed in her 'Remarks on the Character of Lady Macbeth' (1834), Jameson knew of, but had not read. Siddons is keen to present the character in as attractive a light as possible, so sexually appealing – 'fair, feminine, nay, perhaps, even fragile' – that her husband is in thrall to her, yet 'of a naturally higher toned mind' than he.[70] Although she is, in her incitement to the murder, a 'perfectly savage creature', she is so not by nature but becomes like this through the ambition she has for her husband's success. Latterly she is pitiable, selflessly suppressing her own anxieties in order to give all her support to him. Siddons romanticizes her as a figure of Gothic horror in the sleepwalking scene: 'Behold her now, with wasted form, with wan and haggard countenance, her starry eyes glazed with the ever-burning fever of remorse, and on their lids the shadow of death.' She stresses the importance of the marriage as a partnership, and her final image for the couple is Miltonic: 'Unlike the first frail pair in Paradise, they spent not the fruitless hours in mutual accusation.'[71]

Hazlitt was also influenced by his recollection of Siddons and her performance, which he thought 'something above nature', and probably contributed to his view of her as 'sublime' through 'force of passion'.[72] In this, he contrasted her with the witches and their 'cold, abstracted, gratuitous, servile malignity'. But the witches held a strong appeal for the Romantics, for whom the play epitomized what Bate calls 'the Shakespeare of the terrible, the sublime, and the supernatural'.[73] Mysteriously powerful, sublimely contemptuous of humanity, awful in the fullest sense, they rise far above their stage representation, and the critics are unanimous in decrying what Coleridge called 'the vulgar stage error which transformed the Weird Sisters into witches with broomsticks'.[74] It should be remembered that at this time the witch scenes were usually performed with Davenant's additions, which were not omitted until much later in the century, and the parts played by male actors. They constituted a distinct element of the comic in the play, which offended Coleridge; he also objected to the Porter scene as 'low' and 'disgusting', probably 'written for the mob by some other hand'.[75] His ideal Macbeth displayed an 'entire absence of comedy, nay even of irony and philosophic contemplation [...] because wholly tragic'. For Lamb, similarly a purist who thought Shakespeare's plays 'less calculated for performance on a stage, than those of almost any other dramatist whatever'[76] and believed that, in any case, the supernatural lost all its proper terror onstage, the witches were turned instantly 'into so many old women, that men and children are to laugh at'.[77] Blake held the same view of them: 'Those who dress them for the stage, consider them as wretched old women, and not as Shakspeare intended, the Goddesses of Destiny.'[78] Hazlitt, quoting Lamb's *Specimens of English Dramatic Poets* and the German critic Heinrich Heine, contrasted Shakespeare's witches with those of Middleton, as being more mysterious and 'infinitely more imposing'.[79] But Lamb allows that in both playwrights the witches have power over the mind, concluding that 'they raise jars, jealousies, strifes, like a thick scurf o'er life'.

In a way, the most effective tribute to the power of the supernatural in the play is De Quincey's brilliant essay 'On the Knocking at the Gate in Macbeth' (1823), which is ostensibly focused on accounting for the intense emotional charge created by a few moments at the end of II.ii. Implicitly, he contrasts what has taken place during the murder of Duncan with the restoration of normality at the beginning of II.iii: the Porter scene. In the murder scene, a horrific transformation takes place:

> Here [...] the retiring of the human heart and the entrance of the fiendish heart was to be expressed and made sensible. Another world has stepped in; and the murderers are taken out of the region of human things, human purposes, human desires. They are transfigured [...] both are conformed to the image of devils; and the world of devils is suddenly revealed.

The violent knocking that signals the arrival of Macduff at the gate 'makes known audibly that the reaction has commenced; the human has made its reflux upon the fiendish; the pulses of life are beginning to beat again'.[80] De Quincey is concerned to explore how it is possible for an audience to enter into the minds of the murderers. In his view the temporary suspension of all human nature and feeling in Macbeth and his wife – which he terms 'an awful parenthesis' – to enable the murder creates 'the murderous mind'; subsequently, ordinary life resumes. The audience is taken into this mind [...] and then released from it. De Quincey, like Hazlitt, sees the play as a whole, and alludes with tantalizing brevity at the end of his short essay to the 'proofs of design and self-supporting arrangement where the careless eye had seen nothing but accident'. Hazlitt's account of how the 'principle of contrast' operates to organize what might otherwise seem like abruptness and 'violent antitheses of style' suggests an awareness of overall structure and design unusual in a period more concerned with individual characters and effects.

Post-Romantic and Victorian critics were also favourably disposed towards the play, though less attracted by the heroic criminality of Macbeth. Some, like George Fletcher in *Studies of Shakespeare* (1847), viewed him as inherently evil in a particularly unattractive way, referring several times to his 'extreme selfishness' and 'most irritable fancy'. Fletcher was keen to challenge the 'respectful sympathy' with which Macbeth was treated by Hazlitt and Lamb, to rid the stage of the 'sentimental butcher' (presumably a reference to Kemble's interpretation) and to reinstate a properly villainous Macbeth. Fletcher was dismissive of the idea that Macbeth's imaginative language could create sympathy for him, referring to his lament in V.iii for the loss of 'honour, love, obedience, troops of friends' as 'mere poetical whining'.[81] Fletcher's views were more extreme than most, but he was not alone in regarding Macbeth as a man with an innate propensity to evil which was brought out by the encouragement first of the witches, then of his wife. Although moved by 'the splendid despair of his closing hours', Joseph Comyns Carr, in *Macbeth and Lady Macbeth*, thought that Macbeth possessed 'a soul dyed in blood' before he ever set eyes on the Witches and wanted to reassess the balance between him and his wife. What he saw as the popular assumption 'that his enfeebled virtue was overborne by the satanic strength of her will' stood in need of correction; to begin with they are equal in evil, but after the murder of Duncan and Macbeth's success in gaining the crown he can deal with what is to come whereas she 'sinks appalled at the dark vista of unending crime'. Carr sees the play as a study in 'the contrasted characteristics of sex', though his view of gender roles is essentialist in the extreme; men anticipate, women remember, hence Macbeth is stronger in restraint and his wife in remorse: 'Where she only follows, she sometimes seems to lead.' This paves the way for an increasingly sympathetic view of Lady Macbeth in this period, with particular stress on the revelation of her mental torment in the sleepwalking scene (in which, of course, Siddons excelled). Carr refers here to her experiencing the 'thick-crowding thoughts of that one fatal hour, when her spirit shot like a flame across the sky, and then fell headlong down the dark abyss of night'.[82] Richard Moulton, in *Shakespeare as a Dramatic Artist*,[83] analyses the whole play as 'a study in character-contrast'. For him, Macbeth and his wife illustrate the opposition between the inner and the outer life, with, perhaps surprisingly, Macbeth as the practical man of action and his wife 'quick, delicate, sensitive', obliged to struggle against her softer nature. He has already begun his surrender to evil before the witches get to work on him, and he takes a positive delight in evil deeds. Everything Lady Macbeth does is for him; like the ideal Victorian wife, 'she has no sphere but the career of her husband'.

This view of the marital relationship is widely held. 'Love for him is her guiding passion', asserts William Maginn in *The Shakespeare Papers*,[84] also referring to the significance of the sleepwalking scene in showing how much Macbeth's wife has sacrificed for him and 'how dreadful was the struggle she had to subdue'. Downplaying the strength of Lady Macbeth allows for more emphasis on the power of the Witches. Although it is widely accepted that Macbeth is already wicked before he meets them, even that they 'encounter him because he has projected the murder',[85] they are nonetheless sublime and terrible, spirits of darkness and agents of destiny, to be distinguished from the 'broomstick' witches that held the stage for most of the century. Edward Dowden, from whom the expression comes, devotes much of his section on *Macbeth* in *Shakspere: A Critical study of his Mind and Art* (1875) to describing their contribution to the 'mysterious, spiritual powers' that permeate the play. He stresses that they are more than projections of the evil that is within Macbeth; they 'may take their place beside the terrible old women of Michael Angelo, who spin the destinies of man'.[86] Fletcher objected to the 'merely picturesque and poetical' view of them, and also to the 'low gambols and grimaces' with which they entertained audiences in the additional scenes written for them by Davenant. Like other critics of the period, including Joseph Hunter, F. J. Furnivall and Dowden, he was concerned with issues of authenticity and textual corruption. Coleridge's proposition that the Porter scene was not Shakespeare's was not generally accepted, and Fletcher justified its change of tone by the need for 'a gravely comic turn' between Macbeth's appearances in II.ii and II.iii, though he accepted that 'modern decorum' required the omission of most of the Porter's dialogue.[87] That Davenant's still-popular additions changed the character of the witch scenes was more generally recognized, and this was the time when Middleton's relationship to the play began to be seriously examined. Although there had been some interest in comparisons between Middleton's witches and Shakespeare's, for instance by Lamb, *The Witch* had hitherto been used mainly for purposes of dating. However, W. G. Clark and W. Aldis Wright, editors of the nine-volume *Cambridge Shakespeare* (1863–6), produced a separate edition of *Macbeth* in the Clarendon Press Series of Select Plays in 1869, arguing for Middleton as author of about three hundred lines in the Folio text of *Macbeth*, including sections of I.ii, III.v, and IV.i. F. G. Fleay followed them in his *Shakespeare Manual* (1876), adding thirty more lines. Fleay, like the Cambridge editors, believed that Middleton had revised and also abridged the play after 1613, when Shakespeare retired from the stage, and these views gradually became influential. Henry N. Hudson accepted them in his edition of the play, marking with an asterisk all the passages ascribed by Fleay to Middleton.[88] Fletcher, who knew nothing of this, defended some of the suspect lines in IV.i (the First Witch's speech after the show of Kings), which he considered 'most profoundly characteristic of [the witches'] diabolical nature'. Interested in restoring an authentic version of the play, he discussed at some length what he called 'stage corruptions', that is, authentic passages omitted in performance, such as Lady Macbeth's appearance in II.iii, the commentary scene III.vi, and especially the appearance of Lady Macduff and her son in IV.ii, vital to establish 'the presence of the affectionate family' in contrast to the Macbeths. Dowden in his essay *Shakspere* (1877) noted the views of Wright and Clark on the question of the presence of Middleton in the play, but without conviction. He also defended the Porter scene. The Variorum edition of *Macbeth*, edited by Horace Howard Furness, appeared in 1873. The revised edition of 1903, produced by Furness's son, included a discussion of *The Witch* in the section on dating, along with Dyce's text of all the witch scenes. Furness gives a synopsis of editorial and critical positions on the play's relationship to *Macbeth*, but offers no views of his own. His massive editorial apparatus also includes extracts from Davenant's adaptation and the text of Simon Forman's eye-witness account of a performance of the play at the Globe in 1611, the manuscript of which was discovered by John Payne Collier in 1836.

Although the primary focus of critics of *Macbeth* in this period was on characterization, other aspects of play began to attract attention. Moulton was unusual in his interest in elucidating the structure of the play, which he did by tracing 'how nemesis and destiny are interwoven'. In the first half, Macbeth's rise takes place against the fall of Banquo, culminating in his murder in III. iii; after this turning point, Macbeth falls as Macduff rises, and Macduff acts as the agent of nemesis for both the public and private wrongs of Macbeth. Moulton includes what he calls 'a technical analysis' of the plot, noting how the elements of parallelism, contrast and balance contribute to its neat shape. Other critics explored the language, Comyns for instance noting the importance of images of light and darkness. E. A. Abbott published his book *A Shakespearian Grammar* for the use of schools in 1888 and at the back included a list of notes and questions derived from the language of Act III of *Macbeth*.[89] Abbott's work was to become the standard point of reference for the explication of Shakespeare's grammar until the late twentieth century.

The Twentieth Century

The first critic of this century was A. C. Bradley, whose lectures on *Hamlet*, *Othello*, *King Lear* and *Macbeth*, delivered while he was Professor of Poetry at Oxford, were published as *Shakespearean Tragedy* in 1904. Bradley, like most Shakespeare critics of the century, at least the latter part, was an academic; *Shakespearean*

Tragedy was both the first and the single most influential piece of professional Shakespearean criticism. His account of *Macbeth* is influenced by Romantic attitudes, and he calls both Macbeth and his Lady 'sublime' several times, but he also challenged his predecessors in producing unsentimental character readings of both, developed from the premise that 'character in action' is the foundation of tragedy. Macbeth is distinguished by his imagination, but this is an ambivalent gift, 'productive of violent disturbance both of mind and body' yet also a moral faculty, keeping him in touch with his better nature. His reactions after the murder of Duncan are those of a man petrified by an 'imagination [which] presents to him the parching of his throat as an immediate judgement from heaven'. His wife, by contrast, takes all the practical decisions. The keynotes of her character are self-control and strong will, but she lacks imagination and is literal-minded. Bradley is dismissive of the nineteenth-century view of her, influenced by Siddons, as fragile and delicate; nor does he believe that her hold over her husband was due to 'seductive attractions'.[90] His criticism is intensely character centred, and he regards Macbeth as Shakespeare's 'most remarkable exhibition of the *development* of a character' (Bradley's emphasis). In Additional Notes he considers questions such as 'Did Lady Macbeth really faint?' and 'When was the murder of Duncan first planned?', but he also engages with issues relating to the text and possibilities of interpolation or abridgment, the dating of the play, and Shakespeare's use of Holinshed and Seneca. He is conscious of contributing to a growing body of information about the play.

After Bradley, *Macbeth*'s critical backstory begins to open out into multiple and diverse areas of interest. Although his focus on character seems very different from the interest in language and poetic imagery of critics such as Caroline Spurgeon (*Shakespeare's Imagery and What it Tells Us*, 1935), G. Wilson Knight (*The Wheel of Fire*, 1930 and *The Imperial Theme*, 1931), and L. C. Knights ('How Many Children had Lady Macbeth?',1933), his account of the conjunction of images of darkness and blood, his evocation of the play's densely poetic atmosphere, and his discussion of the violence of the language in relation to themes and structure certainly paved the way for these later studies. Spurgeon's work was regarded as pioneering and influenced much subsequent criticism. She aimed to produce a systematic study of Shakespeare's imagery in order to find clues to his personality, in the belief that his choice of imagery was largely unconscious. Despite the Freudian possibilities of this premise, she did not explore its psychological implications, and the figure of Shakespeare that she constructs – 'healthy in body as in mind', courageous, humorous, 'Christ-like' – is risibly idealized. But her account of *Macbeth*, a play which she felt was more rich, varied and imaginative in its imagery than any other, and in which she draws out images of ill-fitting clothes, illuminates both aspects of the characterization of the protagonist and also the play's larger moral and political themes; it did much to counter the view of the 'sublime' Macbeth in Coleridge and Bradley. According to her analysis, Macbeth, at least at the end of the play, is 'a small, ignoble man encumbered and degraded by garments unsuitable to him'.[91] She also considered the role of iterative images in creating the strong emotions produced in and by the play, and especially its exploration of the demoralizing effects of fear, regarded as the ruling passion in the play in a contemporary work by Lily B. Campbell, *Shakespeare's Tragic Heroes: Slaves of Passion* (1930), which examined the tragic protagonists in the light of Elizabethan theories of the passions.[92]

The contribution to the play's peculiar qualities, especially its disturbing intensity, by its language has been regularly examined throughout the century, sometimes quite technically, in terms of both local and larger effects. William Empson's analysis of 'Light thickens, and the crow/Makes wing to the rooky wood' (3.2.31) from *Seven Types of Ambiguity* (1930) is that of a poet, also serving to illuminate much else in the play.[93] M. M. Mahood has an excellent account of language and time in *Macbeth* in *Shakespeare's Wordplay* (1957)[94] and, supplementing this, Francis Berry in *Poets' Grammar* (1958) examines verb tenses in the play, observing the domination of the future indicative.[95] All editors are indebted to Hilda Hulme's *Explorations in Shakespeare's Language* (1962) for bringing her unrivalled knowledge of contemporary idioms to bear on verbal cruxes and hidden meanings in the play's language.[96] Laurence Danson in *Tragic Alphabet* (1974) is illuminating on linguistic inversions in the play, such as the 'potentially reason-destroying rhetoric' of the Witches and 'the 'implication of language in the propagation of evil' through equivocation; but his conclusion that 'the unnatural serves the natural', and that the paradoxes are only apparent and thus easily resolvable, is disappointing.[97] Michael Goldman in his fine chapter on *Macbeth* in *Acting and Action in Shakespearean Tragedy* (1985) illustrates the extent to which the play's power 'to involve us in the mental life of the hero' stems from verbal effects, such as the way that thickening sounds relate to thickening fluids such as blood, rain and the sea. Macbeth's language shows him like an actor, who 'observes carefully and with surprise the psychic readjustments by which he becomes a criminal'.[98] In *'If It Were Done': Macbeth and Tragic Action* (1986), James L. Calderwood devotes a chapter to the meanings circulating around uses of 'done' and 'undone', connecting related images and linguistic patterns with themes of sexuality as well as those of time and deferral.[99] Like Goldman, he sees Macbeth as an actor, here involved in enacting the ritual of murder. Two editors who have dealt particularly well with the play's language are Kenneth Muir (1951)[100] and A. R. Braunmuller (1997).[101]

A major influence on Shakespeare studies in the earlier twentieth century was George Wilson Knight, who examined first the 'metaphysic of evil' and then 'life-themes' in *Macbeth*, treating the play through what he called a 'spatial' rather than a 'temporal' perspective, like a dramatic poem. His approach was to define the components of the sense of evil that pervades the play through images and symbols, in particular storms, blood and animals. In defining 'life-themes' such as warrior-honour, imperial magnificence, sleep and feasting, creation and nature's innocence, he drew out the interplay of opposed strands of imagery, for example, hospitality as opposed to murder. For him, 'the whole play may be writ down as a wrestling of destruction with creation'.[102] His work had some influence on L. C. Knights, who used *Macbeth* in his provocatively named essay 'How Many Children Had Lady Macbeth?' as a manifesto to challenge Bradley's character-centred criticism and to exemplify the idea that 'a Shakespeare play is a dramatic poem', generically more akin to *The Waste Land* than *A Doll's House*. His approach is entirely language–centred, exploring how images work to create larger patterns of meaning but without any historicizing of the context within which they operate. Knights returned to *Macbeth* in *Some Shakespearean Themes* (1959) to show how, if the reader is sufficiently attentive to the 'thick clusters of imagery', he or she may see how meanings below the level of plot and character 'take form as a living structure'.[103] Cleanth Brooks's essay 'The Naked Babe and the Cloak of Manliness' (1947) takes a similar approach, using the play to demonstrate how techniques for analysing lyric poetry could also be applied to drama. He focussed on 'difficult' passages, the 'naked new born babe' of I.vii and the daggers 'unmannerly breeched with gore' in II.iii, as points of entry into larger symbolic patterns.[104] His reading of the speech from I.vii was challenged by Helen Gardner in *The Business of Criticism* (1956) as deriving rather from the preoccupations of North American New Criticism with irony, ambiguity and paradox than from clues provided from other Shakespearean contexts, but Gardner does not question the centrality of image analysis to the interpretation of the play.[105] It is the method used also by John Holloway in *The Story of the Night: Studies in Shakespeare's Major Tragedies* (1961).[106] Holloway points out a prevailing pattern of images of riders and horsemen, which he links with the Four Horsemen of the Apocalypse, and he connects the imagery of the coming of Birnam Wood to Dunsinane to the greenery of a Maying procession, celebrating the triumph of life over death. Using 'sensational' in its meaning of causing sensation, Paul A. Jorgensen in *Our Naked Frailties: Sensational Art and Meaning in 'Macbeth'* (1971) examined the language for its contribution to the play's 'almost uniquely tangible impact' on the feelings of the audience.[107] He writes especially effectively on Macbeth's own feelings, and the difficulty of separating somatic from psychosomatic suffering. Language is used as a way into character.

Critics of the mid-century generally subscribe to what has been called a 'dualistic' mode of interpretation, whereby the play is seen in terms of clearly distinguished moral polarities of good and evil. Common to almost all such readings is an acceptance of Malcolm, referred to by Tillyard as the type of 'the good ruler',[108] as an instrument of providential deliverance, affirmed in his closing speech.[109] The post-war climate of the times may have had some impact here. G. R. Elliott, proposing a Christian account of the play in *Dramatic Providence in Macbeth: A Study of Shakespeare's Tragic Theme of Humanity and Grace*,[110] felt that after World War I 'many critics have been impelled by modern evils to emphasise heavily Shakespeare's sense of evil'.[111] This was certainly the case in Roy Walker's book *The Time is Free* (1949), which also analyses the play from a Christian perspective as the triumph of good over evil, finding many allusions to and echoes of events in the Bible.[112] In Elliott's reading Macbeth is an almost Faustian protagonist, his soul caught between human pride and divine providence, which offers him the chance of grace. Herbert R. Coursen, deploying a similar schema, saw in the play Shakespeare's dramatization of the 'myth' of 'the fall from a state of grace' whereby Lady Macbeth plays a role equivalent to the serpent in the garden of Eden and Macbeth falls like Adam. Malcolm's restoration demonstrates 'divine governance [...] God's ultimate control of destiny'.[113] Leonard F. Dean summarizes trends in mid-century criticism of the play in '*Macbeth* and Modern Criticism' (1958), as does G. K. Hunter in '*Macbeth* in the Twentieth Century' (1966).[114]

But the twentieth century has seen a diversity of approaches that problematize the play's moral scheme and its ending in several very different ways. Freud's brief account (1916) is partly based on his usual method of analyzing the characters as he would his psychoanalytic subjects, according to which he saw the Macbeths' childlessness as the key to most of their actions; but he also drew on a paper by Ludwig Jekels, treating the couple as 'two disunited parts of a single psychological entity'.[115] His insights were not developed for some time, but bore fruit in later criticism based both on gender studies and on psychoanalysis. Before this, however, Macbeth's flawed masculinity came in for scrutiny. Eugene Waith, while still writing very much in the dominant mode of character-based criticism and before the advent of feminism, examined him in relation to the contradictions between different ideals of manhood; his inner torment arises from his awareness of the conflict between manliness narrowly defined as courage in battle, and man as a being with a 'moral nature'.[116] Matthew Proser explored the discrepancies between a protagonist's self-conception and his 'full humanity as it is displayed in action' in *The Heroic Image in Five Shakespearean Tragedies* (1965), finding that Macbeth is urged to pursue a spurious idea of manliness by his wife, which brings about his destruction.[117] This was a popular idea at the time, found also in D. W. Harding's 'Woman's Fantasy of Manhood: A Shakespearian Theme', where women (Lady Macduff included) want their men to play out 'bogus' masculine roles comprising ambition, action, courage and aggression, ignoring what might be the gentler and more humane aspects of manliness.[118] Coppélia Kahn developed this theme with the aid of psychoanalytic insights in *Man's Estate: Masculine Identity in Shakespeare* (1981), but instead of blaming women for men's failures in achieving a fully formed identity, she acknowledged the role played by a (rather broadly conceived) patriarchal society in creating women's fantasies and desires. Macbeth 'murders the babe of pity within himself'; he 'has not fully separated himself from the feminine source of his identity', and in his 'sexually confused fantasy world [...] only a violent and unnatural separation from woman can make a man whole, able both to feel and to fight, to be a father and to be valiant, as Macduff is'.[119] Janet Adelman's influential book *Suffocating Mothers: Fantasies of Maternal Origin in Shakespeare's Plays* (1992), parts of which appeared earlier, is based, like most of this work, on the unexamined Freudian premise that 'a staged person has an interior being, including motives that he himself does not fully understand'.[120] Hence, Macbeth must rid himself of an infantile dependency on the feminine, especially in terms of 'vulnerability to the mother', and his harping on the idea of a man not born of woman springs from his 'fantasy of escape' from this universal condition. In Adelman's reading, the play moves towards a 'radical excision of the female site of origin', in which all female characters, including the witches, are 'excised' and 'nature itself can in effect be reborn male'. The moving of Birnam Wood does not represent the restoration of fertility and life to Scotland, as Wilson Knight and Holloway, among others, believed, but only the kind of family tree envisaged in the play – one without women. Macduff is not the ideal of humane manliness that Harding thought him to be, but able only to achieve full power when 'energized' by the eradication of his family.[121]

A critic who influenced Kahn and Adelman was Harry Berger Junior in his articles 'The Early Scenes of *Macbeth*: Preface to a New Interpretation' (1980) and 'Text Against Performance: The Example of *Macbeth*' (1982), though he also broadened the scope of *Macbeth* criticism beyond the foci of feminism.[122] In the latter piece, 'Text Against Performance', Berger argues for the primacy of text, ascribing the restorative view of the play to the reaction of an audience in the theatre, where in his view the complexities revealed by a study of the text are radically diminished. Here, he enlarges on another aspect of the play subject to similar reduction: 'the ongoing dialectic of gender conflict and role reversal' which is concealed by 'the Christianized ideology of restoration'. He sees 'man's fear of being unmanned [as] the basic theme of the play as text'. The men in the play are motivated by a 'generalized dread of vulnerability and impotence' and a fear of 'feminine contamination', but all this, like the significance of the witches as threatening to manhood, is obscured in performance.[123] In 'The Early Scenes' Berger challenged what he regarded as the (then) traditional view of the play, ascribed to Wilson Knight especially, in which 'security and peace'[124] are finally restored to war-torn Scotland by the virtuous Malcolm and his loyal supporters. By means of an extensive and detailed analysis of the play's first three scenes, he aimed to create a more unsettling and ambiguous vision. For him, the characters themselves articulate the 'pietistic restoration view', but are self-deceived in doing so. In tracing links between what happens in the early scenes and the ending of the play, he finds a kind of circularity: he sees 'only a degree of difference' between Duncan's problems with civil war in Act I and Macbeth's in Act V. Rather than bringing about a conclusion to a distinctive era of violence and bloodshed, Macduff merely enacts what is a 'recurrent feature of the political process by which the kingdom periodically rids itself of the poison accumulating within it as a result of normal institutional functions'. 'In killing Macbeth, Macduff steps into his role.'[125] Stephen Booth, in a brilliant section of his book *King Lear, Macbeth, Indefinition and Tragedy*, also finds in Malcolm's final speech 'a vague, free-floating sense that the old cycle is starting over again',[126] though he approaches the play from a completely different viewpoint. Booth uses the play as a case-study to demonstrate his argument that Aristotle's definition of tragedy applies only to the play as structure and not to the actions within it. 'The play, as play, has definition – a beginning, a middle, and an end – but its materials [...] provide insistent testimony to the artificiality, frailty, and ultimate impossibility of limits.' He goes on to illustrate how the play is pervaded by 'a sense of limitlessness' and a lack of finality. The Macbeths cannot complete the murder of Duncan, the dead Banquo keeps returning, Macbeth cannot say 'Amen'; time is 'limitless and directionless'.[127] Booth analyses scenes and speeches in detail to support this view, including I.ii, in a way similar to Berger, and also finds Malcolm problematic as a hero.

A similarly dark view of the play had already been expressed by the Polish critic Jan Kott in his explosive book *Shakespeare our Contemporary* (1964). He saw in *Macbeth* the cyclic operation of what he called the 'Grand Mechanism' of history, by which

> having suppressed a rebellion, Macbeth is placed near the throne. He can become a king, so he must become a king. He

> kills the rightful sovereign. He then must kill the witnesses of the crime, and those who suspect it [...] Later he must kill everybody [...] In the end he will be killed himself.[128]

Kott's views were strongly influenced by his personal experience of life under a repressive totalitarian regime, but criticism of *Macbeth* that rejected restorative readings by means of an exploration of its historical and political aspects, sometimes regarding the play as an intervention in history, became a strong trend in the 1980s and 1990s. However, the view, now taken for granted, that the play was 'profoundly shaped by the political and ideological pressures [...] of its time'[129] and by its cultural context was first extensively explored by Henry N. Paul in his groundbreaking book *The Royal Play of Macbeth* (1950).[130] Paul set out, with the aid of documentary evidence and some speculation, to demonstrate that the play was written for King James with his intellectual and political interests in mind and first performed for him at court in August 1606. Hence Shakespeare, who is assumed to be familiar with the king's writings as well as with Scottish historiography, included content designed for royal appeal, such as Scottish history, witchcraft, views of kingship and the problem of tyranny, and the Gunpowder Plot. Paul's claims about the play's first performance have been taken as read by many later critics, although he produces no hard evidence for them, and the implication that *Macbeth* directly flatters the king is questionable. (This is taken up again by Alvin Kernan in *Shakespeare: The King's Playwright* [1995], which refers to the play as 'this consummate piece of patronage art'.)[131] But the view that the play's context could be more profitably defined in terms of political theory and current events than metaphysical and philosophical antitheses was an important one, yet to find its time. Wilbur Sanders in *The Dramatist and the Received Idea* (1968) aimed to reconsider the relationship between 'the artist and culture' and to question any overly simplistic connections made between the drama and the social and political thought of its time (as he found, for instance, in Tillyard's work on Shakespeare's history plays, or W. C. Curry's

Shakespeare's Philosophical Patterns,[132] which explains the witches in terms of medieval Christian demonology). But his method in the account of *Macbeth* relied on freeing up the play from prescriptive explanations of it derived from monolithic concepts of 'the Elizabethan world picture' and arguing for openness of interpretation. 'There is a danger of resolving things in *Macbeth* which Shakespeare deliberately left unresolved':[133] this view of the witches was to become important in subsequent decades. The impetus provided by Paul's work to the study of *Macbeth* in the context of Scottish history may have been strengthened by the appearance of Arthur Melville Clark's book *Murder under Trust, or, The Topical Macbeth and other Jacobean Matters*, which argued – not always convincingly – for the presence of much topical content such as the 1600 Gowrie conspiracy to kidnap James VI and 'the weaving-in of specialities from recent Scots law and procedure in relation to treason and murder under trust' to appeal to 'knowledgeable spectators'.[134] Michael Hawkins in 'History, Politics and *Macbeth*' (1982) aimed to consider the play in the light of what were important political questions raised at the time, while recognizing that precise correlations needed to be resisted. At the end of his essay he challenged a number of points made by Paul and his reading complicates the idea of *Macbeth* as a 'royal play'. His focus was very much on the way that the play is informed by the institutional structures of feudalism. While the banquet is 'the most significant affirmation of feudal loyalty', feudal ties were in themselves ambiguous, 'an expression both of loyalty to death and of common self-interest'.[135] While Duncan behaves like an absolute monarch, he is not a successful one, and one misjudgement he makes is in the nomination of Malcolm as his successor. Hawkins observes that the issue of hereditary succession is 'as clouded as most of the other political topics in the play'.[136] Macbeth is a failure as a ruler not because he is evil or dominated by his wife but because he 'cannot make the transition from a good "second in command" to that of chief politician'.[137]

David Norbrook's densely argued article '*Macbeth* and the Politics of Historiography' (1987) also situates the play in the context of topical politics, particularly those relating to the institution of monarchy. He examines the representation of Scottish history, attitudes towards different methods of succession and the Scottish readiness to dethrone tyrannical leaders in the works of George Buchanan, a republican, and Hector Boece; these constituted troublesome source materials for Shakespeare, writing as he was during the reign of a king who believed in absolute monarchy and primogeniture. He considers *Macbeth* to be 'an attempt to revise the more radical views implicit in [its] sources'. From a close reading of the text he argues that Shakespeare's revisions are conveyed in 'a subtle, oblique, carefully weighed manner' and the play retains elements of the attitudes [it is] rejecting'. He suggests that the audience may be able to sympathize with Macbeth 'because vestiges remain of a worldview in which regicide could be a noble rather than an evil act'.[138] Alan Sinfield uses *Macbeth* as part of a broader programme to suggest radical alternatives to prevailing political ideologies, drawing on Buchanan to support his 'oppositional' reading. In '*Macbeth*: History, Ideology and Intellectuals' (1992) he explores the ways in which the play 'handles anxieties about the violence exercised under the aegis of absolutist ideology', drawing on similar evidence in the text to Norbrook and Berger to reveal 'an undertow of circumstances militating against James's binary' (i.e. the King's view in his political writings of the clear distinction between good king and unlawful tyrant).[139] Garry Wills's book *Witches and Jesuits: Shakespeare's Macbeth* also argues for topical content in the play, but from a different standpoint.[140] In seeking to explain the play's tendency to fail on the modern stage (and assuming its original success), he argues that its first audience would have seen it as a post-Gunpowder Plot play, with a focus on topical concerns such as plotting, Jesuits and, especially, witchcraft. Witchcraft he finds pervasive, suggesting that Macbeth becomes a witch, that Lady Macbeth is tortured by 'witch fantasies', and that Malcolm's dramatic function is as a 'counter-witch' to Macbeth.

Topical aspects of the play's Scottishness are explored in relation to the King's attempts in the first years of his reign in

England to bring about a union of the kingdoms in two articles by Arthur Kinney. In 'Shakespeare's *Macbeth* and the Question of Nationalism' (1991) Kinney suggests that the play 'is about either the promise or the fear of a new imperial theme in England, or about both'.[141] In 'Scottish History, the Union of the Crowns and Right Rule' (1993) he is more specific, regarding the play as a warning to the King 'of the inherent dangers of imperialist and absolutist thought'.[142] He compares Malcolm's distribution of titles at the end of the play with Duncan's act of naming him Prince of Cumberland: 'The play has come full circle; Malcolm seems to have learnt nothing. This is surely meant to be the case in Holinshed, where in time Donalbain will attack his brother and seize the throne and new cycles of bloodshed and regicide will take over Scottish history once again.'[143] The potential circularity of the play's ending has often been observed, for instance by Berger, Calderwood and others.[144] Roman Polanski's film of the play (1971), scripted by Kenneth Tynan, also takes this line. Sally Mapstone in 'Shakespeare and Scottish Kingship: A Case History' focuses more narrowly on the Scottish 'pre-history' of IV.iii, comparing the treatment of the Malcolm/Macduff dialogue in the chronicles of Boece and Bellenden, Holinshed's sources. She shows how in this scene, 'one of the most popular and repeated episodes in Scottish historical narratives from the end of the fourteenth to the end of the sixteenth century', anxieties about the relationship between monarchy and tyranny are played out.[145] Nick Aitchison's book *Macbeth: Man and Myth* (1999) locates the original man in the context of the violent politics of eleventh-century Scotland and then explores the development of the varied mythology attaching to him and his reign, from early medieval verse chronicles up to Holinshed.[146] The earliest verses may have been commissioned by Macbeth himself, and are full of praise for his long kingship; the demonizing of him begins with the introduction of dark and supernatural elements two centuries later.

Witchcraft in the play is identified as a longstanding problem subject to two extremes of interpretation by Peter Stallybrass in

'*Macbeth* and Witchcraft':[147] at one end, from the perspective of 'historical minutiae' of early modern demonology, at the other, in terms of 'psychological symbolism'. While for earlier critics witchcraft was also central to the play's focus on evil, for feminists like Adelman it became subsumed into the play's misogyny. Stallybrass locates it within the belief systems of a period when it was 'normal' and also, for the play, 'a particular working upon, and legitimation of, the hegemony of patriarchy'.[148] Terry Eagleton, in his deliberately subversive reading of the play, asserted that 'to any unprejudiced reader [...] it is surely clear that positive value in *Macbeth* lies with the three witches. The witches are the heroines of the piece', agents who expose the self-deceptions found in the play by Berger and others. For Eagleton, the witches were proto-feminists, 'poets, prophetesses and devotees of female cult, radical separatists who scorn male power'.[149] Stephen Greenblatt in 'Shakespeare Bewitched' (1993) sees witches as 'a recurrent, even obsessive feature in Shakespeare's cultural universe', providing him with 'a rich source of imaginative energy' on which to draw for the creation of theatrical effects; in *Macbeth* he uses them for 'the effect of a nebulous infection, a bleeding of the demonic into the secular and the secular into the demonic'.[150] For Greenblatt, the theatricality of the witches, in which he was happy to include the Hecate scenes, was an intrinsic part of their 'histrionic life', whereas for Diane Purkiss in *The Witch in History*, Shakespeare, in what she regarded as his sceptical handling of witchcraft, was 'pandering shamelessly to the novelty-hungry news culture of Jacobean London'. The cauldron scene represented 'the sensationalism of the Jacobean stage at its worst'.[151] Stephen Orgel, making the twentieth century's last comment on the witches in '*Macbeth* and the Antic Round' (1999), accepted Berger's view of their role in the creation of the play's ethical ambiguity, but his main interest was in what the song cues in III.v have to suggest about the Folio text as a revised version of a lost original.[152] He concluded, without making any strong argument for the position, that the witches' parts were augmented 'to liven up an unpopular play' and that they 'open up a space for women' in what is otherwise 'an astonishingly male-oriented and misogynistic' work.[153]

The status of the Folio text and the issue of possible revision centring on the Hecate scenes have been concerns of all major editions during the twentieth century. Furness's New Variorum edition (1903) reprinted all the witch scenes from Middleton's *The Witch* and also those parts of Davenant's 1673 quarto which were not directly taken from the Folio. The New Bibliography (developed in the early part of the century by the endeavours of the textual scholars W. W. Greg, R. B. McKerrow and A. W. Pollard to trace, by painstaking bibliographical detective work, what kind of copy underlay the first printed texts of Shakespeare's plays) bore some fruit for *Macbeth* in the work of John Dover Wilson, Pollard's protégé. His speculation in his New Shakespeare edition (1947) that the play may have existed in a longer, pre-Jacobean version was never developed. His argument that the Folio text was an abridgment, made by Shakespeare but with passages rearranged and rewritten by Middleton, whom he terms a 'botcher', has been influential,[154] although many of his arguments were soon challenged by Kenneth Muir in the Arden edition (1951). In contrast to Dover Wilson's text, which is liberally peppered with explanatory stage directions, Muir presented a conservative text closer to the Folio than any since the seventeenth century. He did not, however, accept the extreme position put forward by Richard Flatter in *Shakespeare's Producing Hand* (1948) that the Folio text 'shows no evidence of "editorial" interference',[155] believing that III.v and parts of IV.i were 'spurious' and detrimental to the play as a whole, though not that Middleton was responsible. G. K. Hunter in the New Penguin edition (1967) produced another conservative text, closely attentive to the Folio; he gave short shrift to theories of cuts and revisions. He regarded the witch songs in III.v and IV.i as later insertions, but did not countenance the idea that Middleton had any involvement.[156] By contrast, the editors of the Oxford edition (1986), Stanley Wells and Gary Taylor, presented the play 'as adapted by Middleton' (though they distinguished this from collaboration) and found evidence of Middleton's hand in many parts of the play other than the Hecate scenes. They are the first to incorporate the full text of the songs as taken from *The Witch*, assuming that they would have been performed in full by the King's Men. In a challenge to the view of J. M. Nosworthy, who in *Shakespeare's Occasional Plays* (1965) examined the issues around the integrity of the Folio text in detail, they are convinced that Shakespeare did not interpolate the songs himself.[157] The two most recent editions of the play stand in contrast to each other. Nicholas Brooke (1990) takes the Oxford line still further, printing the songs in full and suggesting that Shakespeare and Middleton 'collaborated on the revision [of IV.i]'. He believed that 'the play as we have it is a generally sound, though not perfect, text of what was performed between about 1610 and 1620' while lurking behind it is 'an earlier version in which Hecate did not appear'.[158] A. R. Braunmuller, in the widely praised New Cambridge edition (1997), is far more cautious on the Middleton question, although he accepts the 'almost unarguable presence' of another author. His text, like that of Hunter, to whom he frequently refers with approval, is conservative. He regards the search for 'a "snapshot" of a pre-Folio Shakespeare–Middleton Macbeth' as futile, and relegates the songs as 'suspect text' to an appendix.[159]

Performance History

LAURY MAGNUS

Shakespeare's *Macbeth* stands out as one of the few plays that inspired a riot over the relative merits of two actors playing the lead role, both in New York City, in 1849. The Astor Place Riots were violent enough to leave many innocent bystanders as well as rioters dead or injured. American audiences objected violently to a British actor–manager (William Charles Macready) playing the leading role a few blocks away from the performance by an esteemed American actor (Edwin Forrest). Their quarrel was longstanding, and was fundamentally a class issue. Macready represented wealth and arrogance, while Forrest came from, and appealed to, the lower classes. Both actors, who had been friends after Macready had praised Forrest's acting, had become enemies when each believed that the other, attending his performance, had made deprecatory remarks loud enough to be heard on stage. When the riots broke out, neither actor, rapt in his performance, was aware of the battle in the street, amplified by the stupidity of the trigger-happy militia in their attempts to contain the mob. At the conclusion of the Astor House performance, Macready had to be spirited away by his supporters, while the lower-class Americans, supporting Forrest, tried to storm the theatre.[1]

Critical Accounts

Though public reaction to these two performances was extreme, the Scottish Play has always evoked a strong critical response. Four distinguished works of criticism are dedicated to *Macbeth*'s performance history. Dennis Bartholomeusz's *Macbeth and The Players* was the first of these, although he relegated to the margins of his discussion the various textual and interpretative problems that complicate *Macbeth*.[2] His subjects of enquiry were the promptbooks, interviews and playbills from which he reconstructed the way in which great actors through the ages have interpreted the roles of Macbeth and Lady Macbeth. Starting with Richard Burbage and the boy actor John Rice, Bartholomeusz discusses the landmark performances of Betterton, Garrick, Siddons, Kemble, Macready, Irving and Olivier, and he attempts (though not always successfully) to show the organic growth of their interpretations of their characters as the actors grappled with severe textual modifications of the Folio since Shakespeare's time, and with the pressures of directors' and audiences' expectations on their performances.

In 1978 Marvin Rosenberg broadened the focus considerably. As in his earlier *Othello* (1961) and *The Masks of King Lear* (1972), Rosenberg's *The Masks of Macbeth* was a truly encyclopaedic work on the history and nature of the play's productions.[3] Following the Folio text closely, *The Masks of Macbeth* examines every line and stage direction of the play, exploring the full range of interpretations from hundreds of productions Rosenberg saw or read about over the years. Long before the internet age, he kept abreast of all the play's significant productions around the world, and his extensive interviews with actors and directors provided an impressive archive. The book's 'Theatre Bibliography'[4] is arranged alphabetically by country, ranging from Argentina to Yugoslavia. While *The Masks of Macbeth* is not a book to be read from cover to cover, it is an invaluable reference resource for an understanding of the ways in which particular productions could, in the context of their times, bring specific lines and scenes to life in particular cultural idioms, but also set against a wider international awareness of Shakespeare performance. Rosenberg saw *Macbeth* as Shakespeare's totalizing exploration of character, and in his theoretical discussions of the play's dynamic movement, he was methodologically committed to unfolding the ways in which the play 'risk[s] to its limits the stance that nothing human is alien to us'.[5] Of all the productions he discusses, it is those that most adhere to what he calls 'polyphony' – performances that encompass the true range of Macbeth's and Lady Macbeth's character – that he values most highly. Though his book was published in 1978, it still remains the most exhaustive discussion of the play's performance history.

Gordon Williams's *Macbeth: Text and Performance* (1985)[6] is considerably more modest. It begins with an account of the performance implications of the text, but in particular it conceives of Macbeth as a Machiavellian hero. Following the path forged by Rosenberg, Williams focuses on such topoi as 'The Player King', 'The Banquet Scene' and 'Macbeth's Dearest Partner'. Moreover, like Rosenberg, Williams pursues comparisons of key moments in four or five major productions and the main film versions up to 1985. His discussions of varied cinematic approaches are pointed and intelligent. For example, while emphasizing Welles's and Polanski's mutual reliance on 'sustained [visual] imagery',[7] Polanski 'opts for [a] naturalism' that allows him to create warm domestic scenes contrasting with sequels of savagery.[8] Welles, on the other hand, grafts 'daringly extravagant'[9] innovations onto the text with the result that he 'has superbly realized that "violently sketched charcoal drawing of a great play" which was his declared aim'.[10]

Bernice W. Kliman's *Shakespeare in Performance: Macbeth* offers the fruit of meticulous research on the major productions of *Macbeth* to 2004.[11] Her introduction and first chapter address the paradox that though *Macbeth* 'is Shakespeare's experiment in unity of focus',[12] with all scenes having either Macbeth or Lady Macbeth at their centre, it is *not* a unified play in the modern sense, given both the grotesquely comic scene of the porter and the witches and the Hecate scenes; these scenes' excessive popular appeal is certainly at odds with the increasingly sombre tone of a play whose villain–hero is highly problematic. Kliman approaches what she sees as a bifurcation in productions: those that are 'actor-dominated, sometimes with little attention to the production as a whole', and those that are 'director-dominated, with interest diffused among the protagonists, the setting, other characters [...] and the production concept'.[13]

Detailed discussions of major performances include chapter-length analyses of specific variations in theatre/film performances, including versions of the play in other artistic forms, as evidenced in a section entitled 'Operatic Macbeths: What We Could Still Learn from Verdi' and a further chapter on important television interpretations of the play. Kliman's work is especially strong in tracing the full genesis and history of specific productions, often examining the ways in which performance choices change when productions shift venues or media (as, for example, in her examination of Orson Welles's Voodoo *Macbeth* and its film incarnation). As discussed below, she argues that twentieth- and twenty-first-century productions frequently involve what she calls 'chiasmus interpretations' in which Lady Macbeth dominates the first half of the play alongside a less forceful Macbeth, but then in the second half Macbeth assumes control, growing stronger and more ruthless as his Lady declines and falls prey to despair and madness. Kliman also traces film treatments of the play with the same care and attention to telling, intricate detail. To take just one small but precise example, Kliman notes that in Welles's *Macbeth*,

> Since Donalbain is cut, Malcolm and Macduff, after the discovery of Duncan's murder in II.iii, digest between them his few lines. Macduff runs off at the same time as Malcolm, in spite of his wife's entreaties to him to stay (her lines taken from IV, ii). Thus, instead of introducing a new character in a late scene as Shakespeare does, Welles has her enter here, making Macduff's betrayal of her consistent with the selfishness of those who will rule after Macbeth.[14]

Kliman manages, in one short paragraph, to keep in sharp focus the specifics of both text and Welles's verbal/scenic alterations, while also adumbrating their effects on a given performance. This is a consistent feature of her critical virtuosity.

Early Modern Performance

Though *Macbeth* is a play designed to produce a wide range of emotional responses, the riotousness at Astor Place in 1849 seems a far cry from what little we can glean of audiences' responses and the staging conditions of the play's first performances. A firm date for the play cannot be established, but allusions to the Gunpowder Plot in 1605 and to the conspirators' trials thereafter, particularly involving the figure of Father 'farmer' Garnet, suggest that it was written in the latter part of 1606. *Macbeth* seems to be designed to flatter King James VI of Scotland, who in 1603 succeeded Elizabeth I as King James I of England, and who quickly elevated Shakespeare's company to the title and status of 'The King's Men'. James did, in fact, descend from the lineage of Shakespeare's Banquo, a character who in the play resists the temptation to take an active role in bringing about the prophecies of the Weird Sisters in relation to his own future. Moreover, the play's witches can be taken as an acknowledgement of James's interest in witchcraft, evident in his own analysis of the phenomenon in the publication of *Daemonologie* (1597).

Strangely enough, though, Simon Forman's diary entry seems to be the only contemporary account of the play's performance, which perhaps can be explained by the fact that Shakespeare's supposed tribute to James may not have been quite as fulsome as critics have suggested. As usual with the playwright's depiction of kings, the play's ambiguities contain subversive elements that the new king might not have liked. For one thing, Shakespeare's choice of this particular episode of Scottish history from Holinshed's *Chronicles* might also have reminded James that the historical Banquo was Macbeth's partner in a conspiracy to kill King Duncan (albeit Duncan himself in the *Chronicles* is a usurper and Macbeth has legitimate claims to the throne). Also, although the murder of Duncan takes place offstage, its reverberations in the court at Inverness are terrifying, and despite the fact that Macbeth is a ruthless tyrant, the play's ending shows the defeat and beheading of an anointed king – two regicides in one play. As with the infamous deposition scene in *Richard II*, the staging of such events incurred some risks.

Whatever the uncertainty about the play's original audiences, the discovery of the Rose Theatre foundations and the archeological reconstructions of the Globe in the late twentieth and early twenty-first centuries have led to a number of 'original practices'[15] studies of the conditions of performance, telling us a great deal about *how* a play such as *Macbeth* would have been performed.[16] In an open-air theatre such as Shakespeare's Globe, performances took place in the afternoon, with actors and audiences equally visible to each other. On the very deep Globe stage, entrances from and exits back to the doors of the upstage tiring room demanded that each scene be complete in itself, and allowed for the witches 'appearing' from a trap door below the stage. They also allowed 'conversations' of varying groups of characters moving into a scene to occur upstage, while other characters, who may or may not have heard their remarks, remained downstage.[17] *Macbeth*'s singleness of focus is intense; according to Kliman, 'in all twenty-seven Folio scenes of the play, no matter what their structure, Macbeth is either on stage or being discussed. Lady Macbeth is present in nine scenes and discussed or mentioned in four more', but the stage's capacious ability to accommodate alternating groupings of various kinds of characters helped to compensate for this concentrated focus.[18]

Macbeth is a play not so much about Macbeth's and his Lady's murderously gaining of the power of kingship and the exercising thereof as it is about their nervous consciousness of the enormity of their action of regicide – and about how they perceive themselves and are perceived by others after the regicide of Duncan and Macbeth's accession to the throne. Both Macbeth and his Lady strain constantly to re-unite the shattered elements of language, action and thought, once they give themselves over to the consequences of the deed of regicide, and this is registered in the persistent and debilitating but shared consciousness of what they have done. And yet they draw others and audiences to them through the sheer magnetism of their tortured self-consciousness; indeed, in entering the workings of their minds, Shakespeare demands that we succumb to a greater force than mere verisimilitude, for a grander, mythical psychology rules the play, one that reductive Freudian formulations such as 'the return of the repressed' fail to capture. On stage, Shakespeare counterbalances the consistent focus on the protagonists' mental states by alternating the number of actors in each scene, with the result that this intensifies the dynamic interaction and movement among characters.

Shakespeare's witches open the play dramatically, and any attempt to stage the witches' scenes (I.i, I.iii and IV.i) must rise to the challenge of considerable textual ambiguity as to what exactly these creatures are and how they ought to contribute to the general shaping of a production. The challenge derives not only from their gender ambiguity – women with beards – but from the play's unusual and incomplete textual history. *Macbeth* is a play that has come down to us in a revised form that includes material from Thomas Middleton's play *The Witch* (c.1615–16) and that suggests changes in the conception of the witches in their last scene in the play (IV.i), when they appear with the quasi-mythological Hecate.

Even at the start of the play, however, we are not certain of who or what they are. They never refer to themselves as witches, but merely as 'Weird Sisters', and although they seem to have certain knowledge of future events, they are not directly shown as causing those events. As Kliman reminds us, 'The powerful and compelling idea of weird sisters' with their 'connotations of inevitable fate [...] so familiar from modern editions of *Macbeth*, is a later concept, emerging only after Lewis Theobald's 1733 emendation of the Folio's descriptive words weyward and weyard.'[19] There are also the problematic Hecate scenes and the witches' songs from Middleton's *The Witch* that modern editions of *Macbeth* usually print in full by comparison with the Folio's cryptic stage direction, 'Musicke and Song. Black Spirits etc.'[20] These scenes introduce a diverting, sometimes silly vulgarity and mischievous playfulness that are not just highly entertaining but which also, in the view of Gary Taylor and John Lavagnino, 'give the play a new dimension of theatrical magic'[21] supplied by the collaborating or revising Middleton. Kliman, from another perspective, reminds us that though such scenes may be jarring to modern audiences' notions of a unified tragic drama, spectacular scenes were nevertheless a familiar part of the drama in the seventeenth century and could well have been part of Shakespeare's original conception, for 'there is nothing odd about the juxtaposition of Macbeth thrown into despair by the show of kings [...] and dancing witches from the world of Hecate breaking into this mood, tripping before him'.[22]

Another feature of original staging largely lost on modern audiences is that Shakespeare's implied and explicit stage directions differentiate his thanes by their rank and power. Audiences in Shakespeare's time would have been familiar with each of the actors in The King's Men, and a few thanes, such as Rosse, are quite well developed, but like Macduff they seem to be motivated partly by their connection to the powerful, usurping king and partly by a larger function in the tragic pattern of the play. Only later in the play do Rosse and Macduff abandon Macbeth, and both of them fail to protect Lady Macduff and her children. Cawdor himself is a forerunner of Macbeth, whose rebellious tendencies Macbeth inherits with his title and who is distinguished by his primacy in the play. Other thanes have less power and eminence, and much less complicated roles, like Angus and Lenox, and some no role at all, like Menteith and Caithness.

These are subtle issues, however, compared to one other Elizabethan/Jacobean staging condition that created an absolute divide between early modern performances and those of future ages: Shakespeare's women, including the witches, were played by men, and given that gender ambivalence is a major thematic undercurrent of *Macbeth*, the actors' underlying masculinity would have lent a special kind of theatrical frisson to their performance of feminine roles. In *Macbeth*'s darkness, we descry a process that involves the gradual annihilation of any of the tenderness or sympathy that is normally equated with the feminine – with the nadir of these qualities reached in the hideous butchery of Lady Macduff and her son. Modern actresses' explorations of the nature of their 'femininity' and its interplay with strong masculine elements in the character of Lady Macbeth, then, are absolutely divorced from the gender complications of the original staging.[23]

This has bearing on Shakespeare's creation of the central protagonists and their audience appeal, since rarely has Shakespeare given us two 'partner[s] of greatness', that greatness lying, arguably, as much in the power of their language as in the boldness of their deeds.[24] But paradoxically, as the play progresses, the 'great' protagonists' power of language is increasingly placed in the service of the dark forces that they have unleashed. Macbeth's creator has endowed him with 'large discourse, looking before and after', but unlike Hamlet, who uses those gifts to parse out what he must do to expose and kill the usurping Claudius, Macbeth can use his large discourse merely to overcome his horror at the murder he himself has committed, and, as he grows more steeped in blood, to dissociate himself from his own thoughts about his deeds. Audiences are pulled into the fascinating processes of the dissolution. If 'worthy Macbeth', heroic man of battle, is his initial persona, he soon becomes the man obsessed by the full consciousness of what he must do to fulfil the prophecies of the Weird Sisters, and by the subsequent realization that he has sold his immortal soul for a crown that his actions have rendered worthless. That consciousness eclipses everything, even his loving partnership with his wife, and plunges him into nihilism and despair. And though Lady Macbeth is given hardly any soliloquies comparable to those of her husband, she is a singular, magisterial creation whose power of will is inscribed in language that is, at times, almost as memorable as his. The fact that she is a woman does not lessen her prestige or power, as is the case with other Shakespearean women, since her outspokenness, aplomb and control are never challenged in the stark, warrior-like patriarchal society to which her husband subscribes.

The Eighteenth and Nineteenth Centuries

Stage conventions of men and boys playing female roles lasted for some seventy years and after the closing of the theatres in 1642 acting did not resume until 1660 with the Restoration of the Monarchy under Charles II. From that point until 1744, although the Folio text went through four editions, it was entirely ignored in favour of Sir William Davenant's extensive rewriting of *Macbeth* as an operatic entertainment, with its 'new clothes, new Scenes, new machines, as flyings for the Witches, with all the Singing and Dancing in it', according to the promptbook of 1674.[25] The new play's operatic effects, according to Michael Dobson, included extravagant sets and witches 'who spent much of the play either singing, dancing or dangling from ropes' and 'a cloud on which Hecate descended from the sky'.[26] But, catering to the new roles for women on stage, Davenant also greatly expanded the role of Lady Macduff and her husband, with 'new scenes in which they meet and resist the witches and debate the moral problem of tyrannicide in rhyming couplets'.[27] More egregiously, Davenant watered down the language to avoid offence or 'translated it' to avoid its linguistic and metaphorical complexity, so that 'this my hand will rather/The multitudinous sea incarnadine' became 'No, they would sooner add a tincture to the sea, making the green one red.'[28]

The greatest Restoration actor of his generation, Thomas Betterton played over a hundred roles of all kinds, and the range and variety of the roles he undertook were remarkable. Though portly and ungainly, he was noted for what David Roberts describes as his 'Restraint, intelligence and mastery of the repertoire [which] made him, in the richest sense of the term, the first classical actor.'[29] With his superb vocal powers and sensitivity to the line-by-line nuances of his character, Betterton played a highly dignified Macbeth, labouring to create a kind of counterbalance to the showy, non-Shakespearean material, and, as actor–manager, he elicited audience responses that were restrained by the power of his speeches rather than reactions that tended towards bursts of raucous applause. In this he was joined by his wife Mary, whose actual mental fragility endowed her portrayal of Lady Macbeth with a psychological realism made possible by her special understanding of the role.

David Garrick succeeded Betterton both as the most famous actor of his generation and as actor–manager. He restored a great deal of the Folio text and, starting in 1744, played Macbeth for over twenty years. Both an extremely physical actor (unlike Betterton) and one with great vocal gifts, Garrick played Macbeth as a heroic, honorable warrior, a man of noble nature corrupted by his queen. According to Bartholomeusz, Garrick's Macbeth was an unaffected, sensitive character whose mind and spirit rebelled against the very limbs that had carried out the murder,[30] an appealing Macbeth, particularly when his talents were set against the frightening, remorseless cruelty of the powerful Hannah Pritchard's Lady Macbeth. Of the latter, Rosenberg informs us that she 'apparently represented archetypally the unfeeling "fiend" of "apathy"', i.e., that she knew no compunction and 'opened only to the knocking of horror' in her sleepwalking scene.[31]

In the late eighteenth and early nineteenth century, Sarah Siddons became arguably the most famous performer of Lady Macbeth ever known, and although her portrait was in the vein of Pritchard's terrifying Lady Macbeth, she virtually displaced her husband, played by her brother, John Philip Kemble. According to Kliman, Kemble was 'willing to submerge' his 'weak and poetic Macbeth [...] allowing her to take the lead in a role that she had constructed before he was given the opportunity to perform in *Macbeth* with her'.[32] Siddons played and studied the role assiduously for many years, writing extensively on Lady Macbeth's character.[33] Siddons's interpretation of Lady Macbeth's collapse stresses the fact that, unlike her husband, who unburdens himself to her, she has no such refuge against her unruly thoughts, and this recognition allowed Siddons's portrayal in the sleepwalking scene to be coloured with an alluring frailty that was strikingly moving, especially in its contrast to the towering figure that she begins as. This divide in her character begins to be visible in the banquet scene: Siddons defines the tight paradoxes that control the couple's behaviour in that scene, describing the royal couple as 'Surrounded by their court, in all the apparent ease and self-complacency of which their wretched souls are destitute',[34] and Lady Macbeth as 'dying with fear, yet with smothered terror' and 'attending to their 'wondering guests with frightful smiles, with over-acted attention, and with fitful graciousness'.[35] Siddons's masterful, nuanced portrayal of Lady Macbeth won her international fame.

Later nineteenth-century stagings of the play moved in two different directions: on the one hand, further progress was made in textual recovery, and by the mid-century Samuel Phelps had almost completely restored the Folio text. On the other hand, since sets became more and more illusionistic and elaborate, the textual sequence of scenes had to be rearranged to avoid drawn-out set changes, and the otherwise tight pacing of performance was attenuated. Romantic interpretations of the protagonists' characters, such as that of Edmund Kean and Ellen Terry, which focused on the inner processes of the Macbeths' unraveling, could hardly compensate for these mechanical disruptions of the play's quickly moving denouement. In twentieth-century stage history, a movement away from such grandiosely staged productions and back towards a general simplicity and reliance on the text would become the norm.

Macbeth on Film

While twentieth-century stage productions were restoring the supreme beauty and power of Shakespeare's 'original' textual version, the century also saw the burgeoning of film and its capacities to render Shakespeare's plays in all their complexity without straining the limits of the new medium. Ironically, film evolved to a standardized two-hour feature length, which Kenneth Rothwell largely equated with what he saw as the ever-present demands of 'tickling commodity' (i.e. the money factor) in Shakespearean filmmaking,[36] and this necessitated radical cuts of the text, replacing language with visual images that could bear part of the play's linguistic complexity and, in the hands of great film directors, become a rival art form. For a further account of *Macbeth* on film, see Lauren Shohet's 'State of the Art' and Christy Desmet's 'Resources' chapters in this volume.

Orson Welles's *Macbeth*[37]

Along with Sir Laurence Olivier, Orson Welles emerged as a major actor/director/auteur in the first half of the twentieth century. Their talents lent themselves both to stage and screen. But whereas Olivier was unable to raise the finances to film *Macbeth* (he succeeded later with *Hamlet*), Welles in 1936 with his live Voodoo *Macbeth* and its 1948 reincarnation on film became the first of several visionary film directors who adapted the play to screen. Welles's staging of the famous 'Voodoo *Macbeth*' had an all-black cast of hundreds and a lush Caribbean setting. By contrast, the film evokes the distinctly dark feel of a cold and elemental place of barren heaths and crags, a *mise-en-scène* of staircases leading nowhere, stone walls, arches, bridges, weird rock outcroppings and caves that suddenly materialize, all constructed of papier mâché, creating a haunting backdrop that at times is highly cinematic in its chiaroscuro, but also, at times, a throwback to the contiguous spatiality of stage. Like those of Olivier's 1948 *Hamlet*, its winding staircases can be empty of people – a dark void – or occasionally swarming with shield-carrying soldiers, officers, citizens.

'Tickling commodity' ever shadowed Welles: his breathless three-week shooting schedule forced him to improvise costumes and take many shortcuts. Occasionally, costume elements like bargain-basement Teutonic-looking helmets mar the supreme artistic control of his bizarrely surreal shots. Welles's large liberties – taken as an internationally recognized auteur – also led him to make a number of odd performance choices for his *Macbeth* film. He invented and interpolated a priestly figure who plays a darkly ambiguous but significant part in the hero's actions. His actors' 'Scottish' accents were generally unspeakably bad.

Yet there is much of the Wellesian magic. The film begins with an all-enveloping fog, a boiling, bubbling elemental spume out of which spring the silhouettes of the three hags who mould and deliver up a clay effigy of Macbeth to him and Banquo. A Welles-narrated voiceover introduction asserts that Christianity, though superseding the older religion, has not brought enlightenment or mercy. This is borne out by the barbaric-looking execution of Cawdor: the priest wields his Celtic cross, his shadow creeping up on Cawdor while the executioner's blade is wielded to the merciless drumming of a tom-tom. At many critical junctures, and in extraneous invented scenes between the Thane of Cawdor and his wife, the priest appears to work his negative spell on Macbeth. While he is clearly an enemy of the witches, the priest remains a sinister and evil figure, allowing us to sympathise with a Macbeth who has been overcome by the conjoined powers of darkness but who courageously fights on nonetheless. And although towards the end Macbeth hurls a huge staff into the priest's heart from high up on the battlements in an arresting shot, the witches and their spume swarm on to the scene at the end, their own staves in hand, chanting 'Peace, the charm's wound up.' By creating a Macbeth who maintains our sympathy as a victim of supernatural or priestly machinations, the film invokes the sense of society's tragic loss in that the victory seems to be that of dark, supernatural powers. Welles was never one to paint in nuanced shades, and though his free-wheeling adaptation mars the film's ultimate accomplishments, as an early experiment in filmed Shakespeare his flawed masterpiece remains an important milestone in the history of *Macbeth* in performance.

Visual Poetry in Akira Kurosawa's *Castle of the Spider's Web*[38]

Film, of course, offers many possibilities for creating the atmospheric darkness crucial to the terror of this play, and this has led to two twentieth-century masterpieces. In Kurosawa's Japanese adaptation of *Macbeth*, *Castle of the Spider's Web* (more popularly known as *Throne of Blood*), an impenetrably thick fog surrounds human deeds and destiny and forms the opening framework: a labyrinthine forest that enmeshes two Dante-esque riders trying to master their spooked and twisting horses in the thickets of a great wood. Here they reel about again and again till a hut magically appears with a Forest Spirit seated at her doubled-wheel loom, spinning silken threads. Some of Kurosawa's traditional images – visible in many of his non-Shakespearean masterpieces but especially prominent, too, in his later *Ran* (based on *King Lear*) – appear with arresting force in *The Castle of the Spider's Web*, including a ghostly-looking prophet (an androgynous figure who is female but with a male voice);[39] the slithering, snake-like movements and rustling dress fabric of a cold, mask-like Lady Macbeth, a traditional female figure whose stealth and stratagems embody the powers of darkness; the ominous fog that is a harbinger of the evil ensnaring human will and choice; and the shower of arrows raining down on a warrior confronting superior forces.

The opening scenes of Samurai warfare and internecine struggle suggest that masculine aggression is an ever-present force threatening to break out if it is not constrained by a fierce code of loyalty to an overlord, the one with the greatest power (the 'Great Lord'). The regal position of the overlord may represent tradition and a just locus of honorable fealty, but it is by nature unstable: the very fact that Washizu (Macbeth) has received the prophecy from the Forest Spirit is something that Miki (Banquo) will necessarily reveal to the King, who, as his wife Asagai argues, will necessarily feel threatened by this prophecy and move against Washizu unless, she further urges, he strikes first. Though, like McKellen's 1971 RSC *Macbeth*, Mifune's Washizu is seized from the very beginning by terror and self-loathing, manifested at times through a manic laughter, he is nevertheless stunned when his wife flatly confronts him with harbouring evil designs. Evidently, she knows the labyrinths of his mind better than he knows them himself, indicating that he is in a state of complete denial, and there is no ambiguity about her taking the lead here.

She calls to mind the spinning forest spirit whose double-spindled wheel is like a film reel – dispassionately unravelling what *is*, in the best documentary fashion; she pronounces upon the future definitively but without any discernible emotion. As Kenneth Rothwell has emphasized, her deadly stillness is in major contrast with the increasingly restless movement of her husband, and is Kurosawa's way of transposing the 'fair is foul'[40] opposition into cinematic terms.

The crimes of Kurosawa's Washizu are crimes against a society that has a sickness at its heart, part of its valorization of warrior mettle and the ambition that goes with it. Once Washizu yields to his wife's persuasions and gives himself over to his terrible deed, he is led inevitably to the other crimes. At first, each of the 'partners of greatness' seems to act with sure knowledge of the other, but without any sensitivity to, or tenderness about, what the other is feeling. With their gnawing sickness at heart comes isolation, followed, inevitably, by sterility as well: Kurosawa's story retains, even as he adjusts it, the potent motif of the Macbeths' childlessness. Washizu himself tells Asagai that he is about to name Miki's son as heir because they have no children, but she then announces that she is pregnant. The later scene in which a midwife tells Washizu that his child has been stillborn accompanies the news that the first and second castles have gone on the attack, but rather than seeing Washizu confronting or comforting Asagai, we see him approaching her anteroom instead, then looking miserably at a sceptre leaning against the wall and the 'fruitless crown', a crescented helmet nearby, while, thundering with rage and grief, he sits down violently and despairingly. Cut off from any promise of progeny, he compresses his anger into one word of self-reproach: 'fool!' Washizu's defeat by the chaotic forces of a labyrinthine forest that beckons to all men is also part of the film's closing conception, with no Malcolm figure to embody the possibility of futurity in this dark and 'gored' state.

Critics might disagree over whether or not Kurosawa has directed the greatest masterpiece inspired by Shakespeare, but few would quarrel with the notion that though 'Kurosawa's visual poetry is only one feature of this austere and beautiful film [...] it is the aspect that brings *Throne of Blood* close to the glory of *Macbeth*'s language.'[41]

Roman Polanski's *Macbeth*[42]

Roman Polanski's 1971 film of *Macbeth* has been viewed as an important milestone in Shakespearean filmmaking, despite its extraordinary violence and its initially hostile reception. Polanski's tragic biography partly explains the harshness of his adaptation. In addition to his being a child victim of the Holocaust, during a time of great social upheavals in the late sixties and early seventies in the USA (immediately before he began making the film) his pregnant wife Sharon Tate and three of the couple's friends were brutally murdered by the psychopathic but charismatic drug-addict Charles Manson and a group of his followers.

Polanski problematizes Shakespeare's tragedy and the audience's reactions to its events, showing that society, rather than the supernatural or the personal, determines the outcome of the tragedy by demonstrating that the recurrence of evil is a social rather than a supernatural phenomenon. It is ruthless and violent ambition, externalized in the grotesque figures of the Weird Sisters, that determines Macbeth's tragedy, but the evil to which he falls prey remains a permanent feature of the human universe. Polanski taunts audiences, too, as representatives of 'society' with their own voyeuristic interests in blood and mutilation. At the beginning of the film, the bleeding sergeant's account of his adversary in battle whom he has 'unseamed [...] from the nave to the chops' is the occasion of laughter. We are not surprised to see that bearbaiting turns out to be a popular and jocular entertainment. Polanski sets his tale in a rough, medieval Scotland of stone and sheepskin rugs, albeit his primitive Inverness is in stark contrast to the bright, courtly and light-filled spaces of Dunsinane. The castle at Inverness is a hive of social activity, its inhabitants eating, drinking and sleeping in close proximity to each other. Primal objects – chalices, cisterns, scythes, straw-strewn floors

– take on a mythic significance. Basins drip continually, and metal rings out at crucial times, as on the occasion when Macbeth's crown clatters to the floor. Intrigue is at the very heart and hearth of Inverness, personified not only in the youthful and beautiful Macbeth (Jon Finch) and his Lady (Francesca Annis) and in their animal sexual attractiveness, but also especially in the character of Rosse (played by John Stride), whom Polanski rewrites as a collaborator in Macbeth's murders and who is singled out as a social creature notable for his hypocrisy and his pandering to an increasingly tyrannical Macbeth.[43]

Polanski's intercutting is an important part of an artistry that stresses the social aspects of this tragedy. An extended example is the scene of Macbeth's soliloquy of I.vii: 'If it were done when 'tis done', contemplated in a voiceover as he and his wife sit at the banquet table on opposite sides of Duncan, Lady Macbeth flirting with the older man while being serenaded by Fleance ('O your two eyes will slay me suddenly' continues the young boy's Petrarchan song). Feasting, they break bread, and Duncan toasts 'worthy' Macbeth, the dark interior warmly lit up with torches while thunder rolls and lightning flashes outside. Though Polanski cuts many of his protagonists' lines and accompanies even the most poetic speeches with banal or unclean images (Macbeth's reflections on how his hands will 'incarnadine' or turn red the green sea are shot against a bucket of murky water), he also chose his two stars carefully – not just for their youthful sexuality, but for their well-modulated voices and ability to handle the verse. Critics, however, have sensed a lack of moral compass in both characters, which lessens their internalized sense of personal responsibility and hence of tragic seriousness.

Still, paradoxically, there seems to be a corollary between Polanski's personal suffering and the intense power and beauty of his narrative, which is full of arresting moments and the tormenting visions of the villain–hero. Polanski takes us behind the scenes to watch Macbeth's murder of the king, and the power of the filmic gaze (reflective of the viewers' gaze) is made an immediate causal factor in the killing: when Macbeth approaches him, conscious of stealing 'Tarquin-like' towards his victim, Duncan awakes in bed, naked, with Macbeth's sword at his heart, and the king's accusatory glance is what spurs Macbeth's cutting of the king's throat and frenzied, repeated stabbing of his victim. Similarly, there is a supercharged coherence between Macbeth's inner visions and the exterior action. For example, Polanski interpolates a dream in which a tall Fleance playfully grabs the crown and puts it on his head while the recumbent Macbeth laughs – but then Fleance grabs a slender steel file and is about to plunge it into Macbeth's chest when Macbeth awakes. When we later see Fleance escaping the assassins on horseback, his father draws a slender arrow to kill one of them, but successful at protecting his son, he himself falls victim to a battle-axe embedded in his back. Internal visualizations are realized externally: we see Macbeth drag the two drugged grooms out by the heels, covered in blood (so brutal an image that Lady Macbeth does indeed faint at it), just as court lackeys drag out the corpses of the poor baited bears, gored in blood. It has often been claimed that these images are a reflection of Polanski's own experience when he returned home to be confronted with the dismembered corpse of Sharon Tate.

Polanski's use of violence is not, as with many twenty-first-century filmmakers, gratuitous, but rather calls to mind the Artaudian Theatre of Cruelty, the violence of which is designed to 'break through language in order to touch life'.[44] External horror is matched by the internal dissolution of Lady Macbeth, so beautiful and self-possessed at the beginning of the film. Annis deploys her physical beauty to inform her acting as the exuberant and welcoming hostess, but her Lady Macbeth is one who embarks on a journey with no sense of the peril she has placed herself in by summoning the 'spirits that tend on mortal thoughts'. It seems that she is simply annoyed at her husband's lack of nerve, and that this irritation lies behind her goading him to commit regicide. Once the murder has been committed, however, and her husband's bloodlust is disclosed in a particularly gory scene revealing the slaughtered guards of Duncan, she genuinely swoons. Annis's Lady is quickly out of her depth and becomes increasingly isolated from a self-absorbed Macbeth; as Kliman, with regards to Annis's portrayal, observes, 'in the instance of vulnerable Lady Macbeths, a character's weakness can sometimes be evidence of an actor's skill'.[45] An arresting strategy on Polanski's part was filming the sleepwalking scene with Annis in the nude, yet managing to ensure that the scene remained peculiarly un-erotic. Annis's long red hair covers her breasts and flanks, and she holds her body rigidly, sitting down like an unseeing penitent Magdalene, blindly and compulsively rubbing her hands to rid herself of those invisible spots.

Both the gore and the lust for gore are chronicled in the closing scenes of the film. Finch's Macbeth rises courageously to the occasion of learning how foolishly he has relied on the witches' prophecies, and he strikes with power and prowess at Macduff. Yet when he yields and his tyrant's head is hoisted on a pole for all to view, a noisy laughter rings out, as at the film's opening. In Polanski's final sequence, Rosse's loud but solo 'Hail, King of Scotland' proclaims Malcolm king, followed by the furtive manoeuvres of the limping figure of Donalbain. As a kind of underhanded riposte to the idea of final stability, Donalbain has slyly ridden off to seek out the witches – with the implication that the world's evil is permanent and constant, that not only is there no catharsis but that human psychology frequently degenerates into pathological madness: fratricide, in fact, may replace regicide, and a new kind of 'rough beast' seems poised to inaugurate another cycle of carnage and terror.

Twentieth-century transpositions of the play to film, then, have shown no loss of intensity or invention. Those of our century, however, are a comparatively minor affair, generally dramatizing Macbeth not as a tragic hero but as a mafia criminal. Macbeth as a gangster film started with *Joe MacBeth* in 1955, directed by Ken Hughes, with Paul Douglas in the title role and with Ruth Roman as Lily MacBeth, a nagging wife who talks her husband into rubbing out a rival gangland boss. *Men of Respect* (1990) features 'the irreverent John Turturro play[ing] Mike Battaglia as a wild-eyed, desperate weakling, a mad-dog killer who would be at home in any modern gangster saga'.[46] *Scotland, PA*, which came out ten years later but was filmed before 9/11, is a hilarious spoof of *Macbeth* drawn also along misfit/gangster lines. It uses contemporary language to tell the tale of a murderous couple's takeover of the first drive-in hamburger joint, Duncan's, by the ambitious 'Mac' (James LeGros) and his long-suffering waitress wife Pat (Maura Tierney). The film turns on the ludicrous in human affairs: for example, while binding and gagging Duncan in planning to 'whack' him, the pair accidentally cause him to fall over into a deep-fryer. McBeth and his wife's tortured consciousness is reduced to ludicrously slick self-analysis, with lines such as Pat McBeth's idea of ambition: 'We're not bad people, Mac … just underachievers who have to make up for lost time.'[47]

Two other, much darker gangster-style versions also were also produced, the first made in 2003 in Hindi by the Indian director Vishal Bharadwaj. It tells the tale of Maqbool, who, with his mistress and the help of their corrupt police friends, slaughter the ageing leader of a criminal gang and in turn becomes the target of a rival gang. Sam Worthington's 2006 version of *Macbeth*, which uses Shakespeare's language, is chilling and slick, an Outback-style gangster film. Its opening minutes are a long, wordless 'shoot-'em-up' version of a drug deal that goes awry, with Macbeth saving his overlord. Long on blood, with several scenes of butchery that recall Polanski's violence but have none of the rich visual invocations of the language's imagery, the film's chief attraction is the smoothness with which the often inverted or transposed language is still potent, although in an entirely contemporary idiom. Nothing really remains of social commentary or even of the gripping storytelling involved in the dissolution of Macbeth's marriage. The film, in short, is full of sound and fury, signifying not so much nothing as nothing very much.

Major Twentieth-Century Stage Interpretations

On stage, as opposed to film, twentieth-century productions profited from a return to spatial simplicity and more minimal set design. This eliminated the need for scenic transpositions to accommodate the increasingly elaborate sets that had characterized the century before, and the focus began, once again, to be on character. By mid-century, a chiasmus design, a 'crossing over of the ascendancy of Lady Macbeth and Macbeth within one production', allowed each of the protagonists in turn to shine.[48] The most impressive example of this was the 1955 production of the play at the Memorial Theatre, Stratford-upon-Avon, starring Laurence Olivier and Vivien Leigh and directed by Glen Byam Shaw. The expressionist sets by Roger Furse, with their skewed-angled walls and arches, insistently conveyed the protagonists' inner disarray; the production's rough-textured men's costumes conveyed the warriors' stalwart masculinity and body-clinging women's costumes their strong sensuality.

As Kliman argues, the use of chiasmus design in this production compensated for the inherent problem in Macbeth's character that Orson Welles articulated, i.e. that 'The actor must be brutally simple and completely natural to play the first part, and extremely cerebral to play the second part.'[49] By focusing attention first on the Lady and then on the thane, Olivier's stage portrayal of Macbeth opposite Vivien Leigh's Lady Macbeth avoided this problematic bifurcation in Macbeth's character.

Leigh was curvaceous and extraordinarily beautiful, but her slender build suggested that her terrible passion and determination in the early scenes were a product of her tautly controlled will. Critics were slow to recognize Leigh's special contribution to the ensemble. Her viperous strength being so evident at the beginning of the play, her originality lay in her subtle switching over of power with Olivier's Macbeth and in her supreme success at showing Lady Macbeth's vulnerability, which, by the banquet scene, had begun to become evident. After Macbeth's unravelling in that scene, Leigh, in her anxiety for her husband, 'would urge him to rest softly, sorrowfully, [and] by private gesture would reveal her own loss of hope and happiness'.[50] Leigh's own battles with bi-polar disorder, like Hannah Pritchard's mental disorders, added psychological acuity, helping her simultaneously to convey and attempt to conceal a great softness and vulnerability that emerged subtly in her sleepwalking scene. Audiences were conscious, as Rosenberg informs us, of how tightly she kept her 'grim hold on her feelings; only small clues signified the feeling woman within who cried to escape the hard outer shell'.[51]

The chiasmus design also enabled Olivier as Macbeth to develop the protagonist's softer qualities at the beginning of the play and to keep them in reserve as touchstones in the latter part, a brilliant way to counterbalance the hero–villain's swift katabasis. Gibbs noted that

> This Macbeth was slow-spoken, reflective, kindly and noble. By a consistent return to this manner between the later wild passages of fear and passion, Sir Laurence kept recalling the essential character, making a wonderfully moving contrast between the man of honour and the man burdened by guilt.[52]

Always a highly physical actor, Olivier moved

> with the fluid and sinuous grace of a tiger, and he risked gestures that no one else could have pulled off, like the pushing movement he made when speaking of being pushed from his stool. [...] The most amazing scenes came at the end, when the audience was utterly convinced of Macbeth's evil, yet almost against their will were forced to sympathise with him and almost made to agree that the penalties exceeded the crimes. As the *Times* critic put it, 'The smouldering anger with the universe that had betrayed him to his own damnation flashes into flame and throws over the end of the bloody tyrant a sense of the tragic sublimity of his trespass against nature.'[53]

Peter Donaldson has shown the psychological dynamics involved in Olivier's daring leap from a parapet to kill Claudius in his 1948 film of *Hamlet*,[54] and Olivier's gymnastic virtuosity came to the fore once again in a breathtaking final duel, with Macduff forcing Macbeth to retreat backwards up the high, winding castle steps. The bravura show led into a grand finale, after which audiences applauded in thunderous ovation that kept the stars coming back again and again for curtain calls.

Trevor Nunn's Production of *Macbeth* (1976)

Trevor Nunn's acclaimed RSC 1976 *Macbeth* at The Other Place in Stratford-upon-Avon was a minimalist production designed in every way to induct audiences into the claustrophobic, nightmare world of its protagonists. The actors sat in a circle on packing crates and, like the audience, surrounded the players;[55] actors left the periphery of the circle to 'enter the stage' or to exit, later returning to their surrounding crates where, with the audience, they watched what was going on at the spot-lit centre of the circle.

With Ian McKellen as Macbeth and Judi Dench as Lady Macbeth, Thames Television reconstructed and broadcast the 1976–8 Stratford stage version – VHS and later DVD versions were made widely available. Though the recording omitted both the audience and the actors watching in the surrounding circle, an establishing bird's-eye-view shot of the circle of actors creates an overview of the acting ensemble and the play's 'community'. Against this frame, Nunn modulates to unremittingly intense close-ups of the faces of his two greatest actors, with almost everything else pared away and/or shot in darkness and fog.

The fact that both witches and other characters surrounded the centre created a kind of parity of natural and supernatural elements, yet the causal element in this production was man's nihilistic nature, embodied not only in the self-destructively ambitious Macbeth and his Lady but also in Griffith Jones's bland, mild-mannered and Christ-like Duncan, physically supported by his vassals, as well as in Malcolm, Banquo and the other thanes. They have been half asleep as Macbeth's evil genius has been gathering force. Roger Rees's portrayal of a gentle, perplexed and hesitant Malcolm, someone given to the spiritual life and who only with great reluctance joins the battle to defeat Macbeth, manifests this idea of the vulnerability and the inertia of the forces of goodness.

Dench and McKellen make a riveting pair. They share their plans for the murder while desperately kissing and caressing each other, as if they have an inkling of the path they are about to take but cannot think it through and so cling to each other. Dench's Lady Macbeth is someone we know. She starts out softly, meditatively; we have a sense in her perusal of Macbeth's letter that she is talking her husband through the idea of a regicide that he has hinted at, and this thrills her with a new daring. Dench calls on the 'spirits that tend on mortal thoughts' softly and tremulously: this is the first time she understands her own potential to realize such power, and she is visibly shaken that the spirits have responded. Dench's command of language is total, and like McKellen, she speaks with an authority and conviction that is frightening. In the theatre, the effect was electrifying, as the actors passed in very close proximity to the audience.

McKellen's every facial nerve communicates his inner turmoil, so there is no need for an actual dagger or a visible ghost of Banquo. Nunn deploys the actor's stunning mobility of expression at each juncture, only occasionally augmenting it with camera work. For example, in the lines of high poetry in which he speaks of how his hand will 'incarnadine' the seas, he stares, fascinated by the strange red-covered hand (his own), which the camerawork enlarges vastly, but we are mesmerized by the vacant eyes and pursed lips that foreshadow Lady Macbeth's response to invisible blood in her sleepwalking scene.

Dench's sleepwalking scene is one of the most remarkable scenes ever played for sheer intensity and soul-shattering pathos. Like McKellen's disconnected red hands, her white hands move furiously, repeatedly rubbing each other, unable to be still, and her eyes stream with tears. Her horror at her own dissolution is mixed with her compassion for Lady Macduff: 'The Thane of Fife had a wife/Where is she now?' (V.i.40–1).[56] Her wrenching cry at the end of her sleepwalking scene is surely that of a soul in hell. She arouses both fear and pity, because she is so convincingly a victim of self-delusion.

McKellen pulls sharply away from her during and just after the banquet scene, and even when he reassures her ('be ignorant of the knowledge, dearest Chuck'), it is clear that she has been the source of his strength and that his own has now allowed him to dispense with her support. He has steeled himself to do what must be done to protect what he has won, despite his attempts to deny 'the horror, the horror' within. The bitter nihilism of his despair increases, finally audible in the slow, unyielding utterance of his 'Tomorrow and tomorrow and tomorrow' speech, pronounced with his demonic face paradoxically devoid of affect.

Though the forces associated with the saintly Malcolm have won the battle, there is little cause for confidence that Macbeth's evil has been expunged, as the aura of human vulnerability still hovers, and it is not clear where Macbeth's defeat and death have left the kingdom. In the closing lines in which Malcolm takes up his responsibilities, Macduff is the only thane to voice 'Hail, King of Scotland!' (V.ix. 25), and no mention is made of the thanes being ennobled. One by one, the thanes exit, and next to an empty golden crown and a suspended royal robe, which Malcolm will presumably don at his investiture, two bloody swords are left, glowing in the emptiness before a final darkness falls.

Greg Doran's Production at the Swan Theatre (1999), Televised in 2001

The 1999 RSC production was brilliantly directed by Greg Doran and starred Antony Sher as Macbeth and Harriet Walter as his Lady. The production later went on tour both nationally and internationally and a televised version was aired in 2001. RSC actor Richard Armitage, who played Angus, explains the televised production as 'reconceived in gritty documentary-style for the camera, giving the impression, at times, of an under-cover report from near the front line of a Balkan war' and 'shot in that legendary venue, The Roundhouse, in 2000, empty and awaiting refurbishment' with 'its labyrinthine corridors and circular main space'.[57] The wandering, panning camera and heavy use of darkness lit sometimes only by flashlight created a sense of being lost in a demonic funhouse which may have sparked British theatre company Punchdrunk's production *Sleep No More* later in 2003.

In its gripping intensity, the descent of Sher's Macbeth into the abyss is swift and fear-inducing to watch: a sustained hysteria, both terrified and exultant, can be seen in his gleaming eyes and heard in his furious whisperings, whether to himself or others. As Ben Brantley comments, both Macbeth and Lady Macbeth 'begin at an improbable fever pitch and then keep growing hotter, moving imaginatively forward when you think they have reached a dead end'.[58]

Doran's witches set upon the Thane of Glamis in short order, and in the televised version seem to swallow him up whole, with their voracious tooth-blackened mouths in extreme close-up, before he even appears. From the very beginning of this modern-dress production, Macbeth is demonic-looking and semi-feverish with the elation of battle, hoisted on his comrade's shoulders, so that his move into tyranny and fear-mongering is almost glib, at times even smugly playful (as when he twice threatens Fleance bodily – 'in jest'); however, he is overwhelmed at the audacity of own conception and easy prey for his wife, the soft-spoken lady of deadly manipulation. Upper crust, tidy looking, she is an eager and similarly glittering-eyed devotee of evil. Walter's Lady Macbeth exudes a sexual voraciousness that jibes with the martial bonhomie and evident ambition of Macbeth. She is in a hurry, but without the least strain, she is in total command of every situation. Though Sher is so riveting that attention must be wrested from him, this is a challenge to which Walter rises with a natural sense of command.

In the televised production, touches of Doran's stage magic are augmented by the camera's special capabilities, especially its alternation of scenes between its long offstage corridors of deteriorating exposed brick and the decorous, candle-lit banquet hall or throne room that were a defined stage area. The corridors were quick-exit venues of asides – of conspiracy and the shared whisperings of horror. Close-ups, frequent direct addresses to the camera and occasional toned-down special effects are put to marvellous use. For example, the banquet scene shows us a suddenly empty stool, then the present Banquo, the guests scattering, Macbeth sauntering off, Lady Macbeth sitting down crying miserably at one end of the long table with all the lit candles to her back, and, finally, the thin tablecloth alight with the babbling witches who materialize in shadow *beneath* the table, rising up and sending the crockery flying. The witches rub their hands compulsively and babble out 'double, double, toil and trouble' as Macbeth bursts in on them; he pursues them with a flashlight through dark receding corridors of brick until he catches up with them bending over three cauldrons flaming up in the dark. The dagger which marshals Macbeth starts out invisibly and then, during the soliloquy, becomes a material dagger he later wields to kill the king. Such sudden materialization of a dagger is also his nemesis: in the final battle scene with Macduff, Macbeth starts out with the advantage of a sword against Madcuff's long metal rod, but Macduff pulls a dagger from the dead body of the young Siward, while Macbeth becomes frozen, rapt – indeed hypnotized – by this final vision of a dagger and thus loses his life to his mortal enemy who was not born of woman. Supporting actors bring in fine performances as well, especially Nigel Cooke as Macduff, John Dougall as Malcolm and Paul Webster as Rosse. The scene of Malcolm's self-maligning, usually straining to keep on the right side of ridiculous, comes through with restraint and conviction, finely contrasting with Macbeth's angry screaming and pent-up hysteria.

Doran's *mise-en-scène*, both of the stage play and televised version, evoked the Balkan war of the 1990s and, straddling the turn of the century, could be seen as inaugurating the great twenty-first century versions of *Macbeth* that were also, largely, a response to a sense of ongoing international warfare. As electronic platforms in the new century have opened theatre performances to the world, it is likely that Rupert Goold's production, starring Patrick Stewart, will not be the only one of those mentioned below to be available to worldwide audiences in our own century.

Major Stage Productions of the Twenty-First Century: Ninagawa (1990, 2002); Moises Kaufman (2006); Rupert Goold (2007–8); Arin Arbus (2011)[59]

Unlike *Hamlet*, which had a long history in Eastern Europe during the cold war as a crypto-political play, versions of *Macbeth* have only occasionally been played for purposes of direct-if-tacit political allegory.[60] On the other hand, no playwright ever born was as sensitive to the historical cycles of power or as alert to its inherent corruptions as Shakespeare, and given the catastrophic events of 9/11 and its aftermath it is not surprising that *Macbeth*, with its emphasis on 'regime change' and its possible tyrannical after-effects, has continued to be a popular production choice.

Paul Harvey and Bernice W. Kliman, in discussing the work of Yukio Ninagawa, have noted that in Japan, 'Since 1990 an average of five or more different productions have appeared every year [...] [and] at least sixteen published translations.'[61] Ninagawa's *Macbeth* has been recognized as the crowning achievement of an intense production history of the play in Japan. A revival ran very briefly at the Brooklyn Academy of Music in December 2002, some twelve years after it had gained international fame and a multi-national audience. Like the original version and like more recent adaptations such as *Sleep No More* and Alan Cumming's one-man *Macbeth* (2012), it was a 'performance event'. It was a multi-lingual, multi-media, multi-period production, combining both eastern and western sources and drawing on diverse periods for costume and music. Traditional Japanese gongs and church bells, for example, mingled with selections from Bulgarian polyphonic music, Verdi's 'Ave Maria' and Bach's organ works.

The Ninagawa *Macbeth* had achieved its world prominence in 1990 in large part because of its ambitious and stunningly beautiful staging, with set design by Kappa Seno, featuring its *shoji*, enormous sliding screens whose mirrored surfaces reflected an always subtly shifting plane of action. These could become transparent or translucent, shutting audiences out of the action behind the scenes or allowing them privileged insiders' views. In the 2002 version, the set designed by Tsukasa Nakagoshi retained the *shoji*, which were again augmented in their powerful effects with brilliant lighting design (this time by Tamotsu Harada). The *shoji* not only enlarged the action, creating distancing, ceremonial effects, but when tilted back at a slight angle showed reflections of offstage entrances (including those of arriving latecomers) blending with those of actors entering or exiting the stage and enhancing Shakespeare's way of creating variety through the changing number of those on stage at any moment. The shape-shifting sense of the real and unreal haunted the production, used to greatest effect in the shadow-play scenes of Macbeth's dagger illusion, the banquet, Lady Macbeth's madness and the moving of Birnam Wood.

Like Polanski's protagonists, Ninagawa's actors attracted audiences with their youth and beauty. Lady Macbeth (Shinobu Otake) first entered through the audience all in white, walking slowly and holding a giant lotus flower like a baby in her arms: like that of the bloody sergeant and the crowds of warriors who came pounding down the aisles, her closeness to audiences continued to implicate them in the action. Her loving relationship with her husband remained a constant feature, even after the banquet scene (when most productions show them as divided against each other), obviating the need for the chiasmus approach, with its divided emphasis.

Both actors are very slight in build and are foils to the burly warriors who surround them. In the 'indoor' banquet scene, distraught over Macbeth's hallucination, Lady Macbeth's delicacy is part of her public persona: she never forgets her manners; she speaks sharply to him but politely to her departing guests. The staging here is brilliant and provides an excellent solution to the difficult problem of Banquo's appearances and disappearances.

The set is filled with small tables covered with white tablecloths, a sophisticated scene mirrored over and over in the black reflective panels. The ghost appears among the many warriors and it is so difficult to distinguish it that, like the thanes, we are not sure what Macbeth sees it or whether it is a figment of his imagination. In her sleepwalking scene Lady Macbeth enters in white nightdress and peignoir and her image, replete with candle, is effectively multiplied in the black surfaces of the set, making it difficult to tell which images are real, which reflected. With her long black hair loose, she is a pitiable image of woe.

As in his 1990 adaptation, Ninagawa set the play in such a way as to depict centuries of violence in Japanese history. The warriors in long patterned skirts could be from the late medieval period or, with their trench coats, could be soldiers from World War II, inviting audiences to connect the history of sixteenth-century Japan with twentieth-century militarism and aggression, part of Ninagawa's personal interpretation of the significance of the *Macbeth* story. As Harvey and Kliman remind us in discussing the central conception behind Ninagawa's *Macbeth* productions,

> He meant us to ask: could Macbeth himself represent prewar imperial Japan, destroyed by the enticement to an overweening ambition? This latent interpretation became explicit at the end of the play, when Malcolm gave his final speech in the high-pitched ringing tones that characterized radio broadcasts from the war period.[62]

As in the earlier production, Malcolm's last words were muffled by the translucent screen devolving into a blank: although this is in the past, the screen seems to say 'it has happened before and will happen again'. While it encouraged emotional distance from individual characters, the overwhelmingly poignant formal beauty of the production created a visceral response to the ongoing sense of continuous warfare and constant, overreaching ambition – and to the inevitability of such tragic waste.

Moises Kaufman, award-winning director and playwright (best known, perhaps, for his *The Laramie Project* and *I Am My Own Wife*) could not have chosen a more appropriate Shakespearean play to mount three years into what seemed like an endless war in Iraq. The 2006 season choice for the Public Theater's Shakespeare in the Park coupled the play with Brecht's *Mother Courage*. Kaufman's brassy, updated *Macbeth* starred Liev Schreiber and Jennifer Ehle; both of the season's choices were framed in terms of the murderous business war unleashes and the inevitability of its cyclical recurrence, promoting the sense of the play's relevance to an American culture both aggressively at war and in denial about it on the home front.

On stage, visible detritus of war abutted the deteriorating blue-and-gilt facade of a 1930s-style modish manor house. The set design thus evoked what Ezra Pound famously called a 'botched civilization' that is 'gone in the teeth'.[63] The darker business of private murder took place just inside the balcony castle entry; bloody battle scenes fanned out on to the capacious downstage area; the centre-stage trap door lay in wait till after intermission when it released a special-effects spirits' cauldron to mix highly combustible ingredients with toil and trouble.

In a striking opening, the three Weird Sisters streamed across the stage in powdery-white battle fatigues, their strident incantations weaving a dark chain of events that would follow from scenes of battle that have just taken place. These masculinized women, soldierly versions of the 'bearded sisters', bespoke Kaufman-the-playwright's concern with violence and what it does to people. The hags' shadow-play is frequently visible, as when their ghostly hands drop a crown on the head of the seated Duncan and, significantly at the end, when they repeat this gesture with Malcolm. Two of the androgynous witches also play the drunken Porter and the Gentlewoman who attends Lady Macbeth before her mad scene, and all three together appear as dagger-wielding phantasmagoria, equivocating predictors, cauldron chef-conjurers, sword-bearing combatants, and, finally, as politics-staging prognosticators scripting an unwritten epilogue. The shape-changing witches thus seem both causal agents and allegorical figures of the botched civilization that naturally produces such men as Macbeth.

Such men necessarily have chic wives: Jennifer Ehle's Lady Macbeth was an American *femme fatale* (*à la* Wallis Simpson, perhaps) whose fatality seemed a product of her bored yet compulsive pursuit of social glitz. Ehle's icy performance and vacuous aplomb made her convincing as an ambitious wife who expects great things from her husband and is not too particular about how she gets them; Liev Schreiber's fiery, polyphonous Macbeth is a man continually surprised and appalled at the paths he has taken. Though his murderous action does seem to come from outside him, he displays his growing inner dread with suppressed hysteria that seems to overwhelm his tall, graceful frame, although he can be gruff and menacing enough as he becomes more and more steeped in blood. Macbeth and his Lady are occasionally strong partners: in the banquet scene, for example, Ehle's quick-witted *sang-froid* is perfect as she extenuates her husband's madness and virtually hoots the courtiers off stage. But she is too self-absorbed and without the strong give-and-take in his relationship with his Lady, Schreiber loses ground. This is most apparent when he must act precipitously, as when he caves in to his wife's taunting or suddenly decides to keep her ignorant of his recently acquired and even more bloody resolves. Schreiber's despair, however, fails to carry us with him into his bitter nihilism as he is pressed to deal with the exigencies of war and to push aside the news of his wife's death.

Notwithstanding these shortcomings, a stirring denouement unfolds as the lighting merges the great pine trees of Central Park with the movement of soldiers bearing their branches as Birnam Wood comes to Dunsinane. The highly stylized fight scene that ensues is beautifully choreographed, with soldiers marching onstage with their bayonets to be successively killed – they fall to the ground and create a battlefield strewn with bodies.

Gripping swordplay between the furious Macduff and the defiant Macbeth comes to a dramatic pause as the corpses came to life again with other ghostly victims, including Duncan and Banquo, all confronting Macbeth with his bloody past. Macbeth freezes, while Macduff wields his sword with finality in a shadow-play fight whose strokes we hear rather than see. Rhythmically, the dead soldiers' bayonets cross each other in clanking accompaniment to Macduff's thrusts, then are poised in mid-air to gather inexorable force anew, and finally wielded simultaneously once more in a fight-to-the-death.

This visceral sense of inevitability brought Kaufman's *Macbeth* to a memorable conclusion, one perhaps far more ominous than the text itself suggests. Rather than hearing the promised investiture of a new legitimate king at Scone, we hear the witches repeat their query: 'When shall we three meet again?' as Malcolm – like Duncan at the beginning of the play – receives the crown from their ghostly hands. In his production notes, dramaturge Robert Blacker stresses the notion of war as an endless cycle of violence that corrupts all who wield a sword. As at the end of *Mother Courage*, one senses that violence has become business as usual. Kaufman's textual cuts of references to suffering Scotland also suggest that since all violence begets violence valorous Malcolm will be caught up in the same bloodiness that led to the death of the tyrant Macbeth – who, himself, had once been a loyal vassal. Audiences may have felt relief that after the bestial descent of the once-heroic Macbeth, this tyrant who steeped his hands in blood was vanquished, but Kaufman's production demanded that they abandon any idea that Malcolm's investiture might lead to a future of peace and stability.

One year after Kaufman's production, in 2007, Rupert Goold's award-winning *Macbeth*, starring Patrick Stewart, was performed for the Chichester Festival Theatre. It then came to the Brooklyn Academy of Music in 2008 and in 2010 was filmed for BBC Television. Goold's warlike *mise-en-scène* was set in a vaguely World War I monochromatic netherworld haunted by terrifying sounds: part operating room, part hospital basement kitchen, part interrogation room. In this constricted world, slabs of flesh – human or animal – seem like interchangeable parts ready for refrigeration, the rubbish heap, or reheated and reincarnated as freshly minted dishes. Pea greens, hospital whites and khaki drabs coated the chipped walls, the same palette as that of characters' battle fatigues, caps and macintoshes. The production was a steady assault on the nerves, unmitigated in its horror, an ethos that was intensified in the televised version. The witches are field nurses who, in their necrophilic rap incantations around the cauldron, are ever ghoulishly serious. A terrifying Lady Macbeth, played by the ferocious Kate Fleetwood, commands her formidable husband in the initial scenes. The entire cast was strong if less than memorable, but at the production's centre was Patrick Stewart's performance.

Ben Brantley's *New York Times* review found the whole conception and execution undistinguished, but located its magnificence directly in

> Mr. Stewart's […] raw susceptibility, […] his thrilling recognition that his character is as close kin to the fatally introspective Hamlet as he is to power-wielding men of ill will like Richard III. His performance […] realize[s] completely what the scholar Harold Bloom means when he calls this play 'a tragedy of the imagination'.[64]

To some degree the televised version allows us to understand how carefully orchestrated Stewart's reactions are, as, for example, when Duncan bestows his estate upon his […] 'eldest'. The long pause lets us see the hoped-for-miraculous pronouncement that animates Stewart's features while after 'eldest' we watch him covering up the chasm that has opened before him as he comprehends that the witch's prognostications are not to be. The same thing happens just after the murder when Macduff greets Macbeth, extending his hand to shake and asking 'Is the king stirring?' Macbeth stands upright in his bathrobe but hesitates to take the proffered hand. Stewart's consummate acting skills allow his gestures and his expression to convey his recognition that his action of just a few moments ago will have consequences that will shadow him even into the life to come. Throughout the production, Stewart's Macbeth is enslaved by the nihilistic images that come to him compulsively, part and parcel of what he has steeled himself to become. The null point of his life is not his defeat by Macduff but his encounter with the gurney that bears the body of his dead queen, whose inert thing-ness repulses him and yet fascinates him, since this is what he is shortly to become. In the flickering hospital lights, his 'Tomorrow and tomorrow' speech seems to be the only logical response to having rolled down the sheet that covers her face. The production's searing nihilism resonated with the sense of waste that warfare and ambition had wrought, and the naked, bleeding head that Malcolm holds aloft at the end of the production mesmerized audiences who could scarcely concede that any good implicit in Malcolm's investiture might emerge out of 'the horror'.

No less compelling in its star performances, the 2010 *Macbeth* of the Theater for a New Audience, New York, featured Annika Boras and John Douglas Thompson and was directed by Arin Arbus. However, the stars' nuanced interpretations were complemented by first-rate ensemble acting. As Ben Brantley pointed out, Arbus's production differentiated itself from the increasingly loud war-panic of famed earlier productions by mining 'a humming silence beneath' the play's sound and fury. 'It's the kind of noiselessness in which a man's thoughts can creep up on him from behind and grab him in a stranglehold.'[65] Thompson's Macbeth fluctuates dangerously between fearful warrior and ordinary man, so that the play's causality seems to derive from this human oscillation. Central to the production, as well, is an allegory of an un-childed universe in which the idea that 'blood will have blood' refers largely to questions of issue and the protagonists' consciousness of their childless marriage.[66]

Part of Arbus's strategy to return to an emphasis on character may have derived from the small scale of the Duke Theatre,[67] with its intimate thrust stage, set just a step or two above the level of the audience. Costume was also kept simple, with metal-studded tunics for men and unadorned, clinging gowns for women; the unusual red boas that festoon the black attire of the royal pair at their coronation scene comprise the only stylized image of the blood that underlies their assumption of the throne.

In his initial guise as righteous warrior, Thompson's Macbeth is full of commanding energy, dignified in his bearing and majestic of voice; he seems aptly called 'worthy Macbeth' by a worthy king. Duncan's graciousness towards Macbeth also sets up Cawdor as a vicious attempted regicide whose treachery smacks of the 'vaulting ambition' that Macbeth comes to find in himself. Unlike Kaufman's *Macbeth*, this production offered almost no initial signs of blood or any suggestion that the kingdom's being 'steeped in blood' at the outset is responsible for the evil that will rise up in Macbeth and engulf all of Scotland. Similarly, the Weird Sisters, bearded young hippies in sackcloth, seemed to be merely unwashed mortals; they lacked ominousness and seemed superfluous either to the action or to the internal chaos they supposedly create. Arbus's cutting of the Hecate scene served to minimize the witch's influence, further emphasizing a Macbeth whose demons are largely internal. Thompson's delivery of 'this supernatural soliciting cannot be ill [strong beat], cannot be good' soliloquy expresses the covert hope, malice and self-distrust that Lady Macbeth goes to work on immediately after the prophetic temptation scene with the witches.

Annika Boras, with her magnificent vocal power and sensitivity to the verse, was an extraordinary Lady Macbeth. Slender, fair and curvaceous, she radiated confidence both as a woman who is the wife of a great thane and warrior and 'partner of greatness' and who is also youthful and attractive. Like Thompson, she played each moment fully, apparently unconcerned about the contradictions in her nature; sheer magnetism and total command of the entire space invoked the 'powers that tend on mortal thoughts'. They seemed to swarm down to 'unsex' her by filling her slender form from 'top to toe with direst cruelty', yet they never divested her of the sex appeal she used to call upon them, or banish vestiges of soft femininity. Indeed, she knew her husband's divided self by her own self-division.

The compelling love story of a Macbeth and Lady Macbeth who are enwrapped in each other is central to the ethos of this production. A misplaced erotic energy seems to fuel their deeds of ambition: Macbeth's 'Bring forth men children only' is full of affection and boastful approbation, but it somehow remains rueful, as though he is indulging in a lost fantasy rather than speculation about a likely futurity. Her later attempts to 'nurse' him back to health, cradling him on her breast like a troubled child, make sense in this context and support the view that a misplaced erotic energy charges their deeds of ambition.

Thompson's variety is impressive, first as the admired thane, then as the self-disgusted killer baffled by his own sacrilege, who, with his wife's help, smoothly puts on an 'outraged-swift-avenger' act. He becomes the sweating victim of a relentless self-abhorrence, the tyrannical force who demands his doubters' subjection, presenting his hand for Banquo to kiss – or dare to refuse to – and he eventually degenerates into an increasingly deranged killer whose secret evil grows in proportion to his nightmarish self-doubts. Boras delivers an equally powerful yet variegated performance, and we soon begin to see the couple as spooked by their killing: Lady Macbeth is in denial; Macbeth is in shock at what he has done, and for a while this keeps them together, clinging to each other for support. But once he restricts the knowledge of his plans for the deaths of Banquo and Fleance to the assassins, Boras's 'How now my lord why do you keep alone?' reveals her surprise at the deep fissure, a hurt and consequent dejection that will lead to her isolation and mental collapse.

The denouement is brought about swiftly and with an inevitable sense of justice. When madness later descends upon Lady Macbeth, she is alone, crouched at the centre of the stage in her white nightgown, blankly rubbing her hand of imaginary blood. 'The Thane of Fife had a wife/where is she now?' is a soft lament that conflates her own situation with that of Lady Macduff. The blood in her mind will not stint and her cries are harrowing as she fixates upon washing her own invisibly bloody hands. It is no mean feat for any actor to be utterly convincing both in a steely determination to murder without compunction and in pitiable vulnerability once abandoned.

But pity only takes us so far. Hearing of her death, Macbeth is now the one left alone to face his tripartite nemesis in the form of the three prophecies coming true. As Jan Kott explains, 'history, shown as a mechanism, fascinates by its very terror and inevitability. Whereas nightmare paralyzes and terrifies.'[68] Arbus's production has just such a paralyzing effect on us: we fear what there can be no escape from, a sense of irreversible katabasis. Rail as he may against the forces joined against him, Macbeth has tied himself 'to the stake' and must watch as he plays the nightmare of his own making out to the end. He rises to the occasion in daring, suspenseful swordplay with Macduff, deftly executed and with a minimal display of the tyrant's severed head. Though the nightmare seems to have come to a just end – it seems that a worthy Malcolm may now rule a chastened Scotland – audiences left this production still haunted by the inevitable swift descent into nightmare. Given the variegated landscape of the history of *Macbeth* in performance and the diverse directions that major productions of this century have taken, one concludes that the play will continue to exercise its fascination on future generations of actors, directors and audiences, challenging them to new interpretations and adaptations of the play. Nevertheless, with the exception of Arbus's production and its return to the domain of the personal, our century would seem to be bound up with what is violent and apocalyptic in this tragedy.

The play's richly textured language, riveting if self-tortured protagonists and scenes of enormous theatrical power will doubtless continue to make great theatre in new contemporary accents and to invite varied emphases. Future performances will likely be determined by the ongoing evolution of performance spaces in an electronic and media-saturated age, moving, it may be surmised, in two divergent directions: large-scale or re-originated performance events – whether in theatre or film – that radically reinvent the text, like those of Punchdrunk or the Alan Cumming one-man show on the one hand, and on the other, the proliferation of text-based theatrical versions performed on simpler, smaller and more intimate stages, delivering up close Shakespeare's absorbing story of loss of self and personal dissolution.

Macbeth: The State of the Art

LAUREN SHOHET

The past decade has seen lively extensions of traditional avenues for interpreting *Macbeth*, with new contributions enlarging the discussion of knowledge, agency, nation, gender and history in the play. Critics and artists also have illuminated the play as a resource for contemplating issues newly central since the turn of the millennium, among them time, space, historiography and inheritance (both literal and literary). *Macbeth*'s explorations of Scottish nationality have sponsored critical considerations of the 'Scottish' and the 'British' aspects of the play, not only in the play's original historical contexts but also in those energized by present-day developments in Scottish political autonomy. More abstract aspects of political relations in the play have made *Macbeth* equally appropriable for extra-British examinations of individual, sub-cultural and political identity and their intersections, particularly in certain post-colonial and American contexts. This chapter surveys this body of work, aiming less for comprehensiveness than to identify centres of interpretative energy that indicate the range of *Macbeth* engagements, scholarly and creative, from 2002 to 2012. It does not include live performance (for that, see the 'Performance History' chapter in the present volume), but does treat some works whose wide release on film or CD makes them part of the durable archive, although current rapid evolution in digital storage, access and proprietary rights makes any delimitation of that archive provisional, if not arbitrary. The chapter begins by treating critical work. It then turns to secondary studies of adaptation and performance history – a particularly energetic area of recent response among both scholars and artists. Indeed, we might say that the primary valence of 'state' in 'State of the

Art' has migrated from the political, in *Macbeth* criticism of the 1980s and 1990s, to the codicological sense of 'textual condition'. In discussing iterations and adaptations, the chapter's purview is limited to the past decade; however, the substantial body of recent scholarly work *on* adaptations often returns to older texts. The final part of the chapter considers three adaptations chosen to show the generic variety of current re-mediations of the play.

Epistemology and Hermeneutics

Beginning in fog and prophecy, *Macbeth* asks how we know what we know: how we recognize, misrecognize or fantasize appropriate interpretative strategies. Indeed, Kent Cartwright suggests that the play 'takes as an overarching concern the authenticity of vivid experience', which 'dramatizes a juncture in Renaissance epistemology'.[1] At this juncture, '*Macbeth* addresses the problem of scepticism by turning theatre into a way of knowing' that is useful rather than misleading, because its representations are at once frankly artificial and deeply vivid.[2] 'Scepticism, applied to drama [...] bring[s] attention to the texture of lived experience, to the sense impressions by which we construct understanding, to the intersection of materiality and consciousness.'[3] Sean McDowell explores the specific epistemological challenges of conjecture: that dangerous 'attempt to make sense of the jumble of information [...] within and flooding into the early modern soul-body'.[4] 'Every stage of Macbeth's progression from "worthy thane" to malicious tyrant depends on his (and others') flawed conjectures', McDowell concludes.[5] Arthur Kinney's study of the play's rhetoric of espionage, lent particular force by post-Gunpowder-plot Crown insecurity, scrutinizes a different angle of the play's problems of knowledge.[6] For Kinney's Macbeth, 'the need to know coupled with the fear of not knowing, promoting an anxiety and a *mentalité* of surveillance, captures in an individual the whole crisis of an historical moment of English civilization'.[7]

Art historian Stuart Clark takes *Macbeth* to be a 'vision-centred drama' emerging in a cultural moment between the

Reformation and the Scientific Revolution when 'vision was anything but objectively established or secure in its supposed relationship to "external fact"'.[8] Clark points out that *Macbeth*'s 'action repeatedly involves seeing and things seen [...] its poetry is rich in the language of the eyes and eyesight; and its drama relies heavily [...] on [...] the workings of optical illusions'.[9] As Clark continues,

> To hypocrisy in word and deed [...] *Macbeth* [...] adds a kind of hypocrisy of the eyes, where what appears as one thing might very well be (and thus mean) another, where images as well as words 'palter with us in a double sense'.[10]

This prompts us to 'transfer to the play's field of vision the rhetorical categories [...] usually reserve[d] for its poetry': 'riddling, punning [...] and irony'.[11]

Mary Thomas Crane suggests that a cognitive reading of the play yields a 'different view of the role of binary opposition[:] in contemporary critical theory, in this play, and in early modern logic'.[12] Cognitive theory, writes Crane, has denaturalized binary distinction in human cognition. At the historical moment when Cartesian binarism begins to take hold, *Macbeth* thematizes the laborious reduction of networks into binarism 'in situations where [characters] feel pressured to choose or defend a beleaguered position. The binary "machine" is thus exposed by the play as a cognitive tool, rather than an inescapable cultural structure.'[13] Richard Kerridge considers the play's use of environment as interpretative resource, 'so that animals, plants, weather and seasons, as well as traditional labor, are a constant source of metaphors, analogues and symbols to make sense of all kinds of experience'.[14] Kerridge claims that *Macbeth*'s natural environment serves as a representational as well as an epistemological resource, remarking that despite rapid early seventeenth-century urbanization, the play 'presents a deep familiarity with a local natural environment as a communal sensibility' and 'seems to expect [audience] recognition' in a way that either 'speaks to cultural memories of indigeneity' or – interestingly – 'asks [audiences] to recognize the depth of an indigeneity not their own'.[15] Like Crane, Kerridge suggests that the play's hermeneutics unravel dualist modes of logic: the 'attempt to see, and manage, the world and the self in dualistic terms becomes untenable and has to give way to holistic terms'.[16]

Space, Place and Time

Other critics explore the experiential consequences of these varied modes and models of cognition. Kristen Poole suggests that *Macbeth* is deeply concerned with 'the presence of space and time and the relationship between the two'. [17] In a chapter subtitled 'The World According to Calvin, Hooker, and Macbeth', Poole studies the 'conflicting latent spatial epistemologies' of early modernity.[18] She argues that *Macbeth* dramatizes 'the experience of inhabiting [the] contradictory spatial epistemologies' that derive from two dominant theological models: on the one hand, the mutability of a Calvinist notion of creation as 'subordinate to the fluctuations of God's providence'; on the other, the fixity that accompanies Hooker's emphasis on 'immutable divine laws'.[19] Poole considers the play's peculiar uses of time and space ('verb tenses and sentence constructions collapse, as past, present, and future repeatedly collide and compromise each other') in light of early seventeenth-century physics and metaphysics.[20]

Robert Weimann deploys his familiar questions about *locus* and *platea* – scripted and hierarchical theatrical space on the one hand, improvizatory and carnivalesque expanse on the other – for a fresh reading of *Macbeth*'s porter scene. Weimann analyses the porter's gate as a space 'in which a strong residue of the *platea* is made to intercept a particularly vibrant moment of stringently localized tragic action'.[21] The knocking at the Porter's gate is 'part of a hybrid purpose of playing where two different localizations mutually engage and at least partially suspend one another': the castle gate belongs both to 'the *platea*-related space of the devil-portering' reminiscent of medieval mystery plays where Hell is represented by a castle gate and 'the "necessary" office of the castle's south-gate custodian'.[22] These localizations belong to two 'modes of appropriating space and time', 'one [...] marked by immediacy and spontaneity [...] in an orally inspired assimilation of a space', the other governed by a 'more abstract mode of regulating and symbolizing things, relations and temporal processes in space'.[23] Although the latter mode of abstracting space subtends modern projects of 'mastery', the Porter, situated in the *platea*, is encoded as 'a contemporary, residing in the time and place of early Jacobean London'. His 'space is not of those who are represented but of those who are doing the representing and the watching of the play as a performed event'.[24] Martin Orkin provocatively explores relations between inhabited place and borrowed language. Proverbs are 'markers and bearers of communal, inherited [...] wisdom' at the same time that their frequent 'rewordings, manipulations, or reapplications' mark 'individual versions of or responses to generalized assertions' that can 'invite comment on particular subjectivity effects'.[25]

In his study of 'untimely matter', defined as the polychronous, multitemporal quality of material objects, Jonathan Gil Harris argues that audiences smelling the sulphurous explosive squibs used to produce stage fog in *Macbeth*'s first scene experienced 'a palimpsesting of temporally discrete events and conventions: the contemporary Gunpowder Plot, the older stage tradition of firework-throwing devils and Vices, and the abandoned sacred time of Catholic ritual'.[26] For Harris, 'the play's smells put pressure on the very notion of a self-identical moment as the irreducible ground zero of historical interpretation'. Instead, and violently impelled by the explosive squibs rather like Weimann's knocking, 'the past is made to act upon, and shatter the self-identity of, the present'.[27] Remarking on the uncanny power of smell 'to evoke multiple memories and associations from across a broad spectrum of time',[28] Harris claims that olfaction summons memories of a recent Catholic past, whose absence not only inflects the present but also dismantles clear distinctions between past and present. '*Macbeth*', Harris argues, 'powerfully evokes the scented rituals of the past, but that evocation less recovers the past than fractures the present',[29] as the play 'recogni[zes] that the Catholic past is less divided from the Protestant moment than all too present within it'.[30] This allows for 'audience recognition [...] of something missing in the olfactory spectrum of the "new" religious dispensation'.[31] Brayton Polka's study of the play's understanding of 'act' and its relationship to consciousness also treats less-than-linear time in his discussion of action's 'consequences' and the uncanny undoing of that 'sequence'. Polka argues that the action is 'at once temporal and eternal' to the extent that reprehensible deeds produce irreversible consequences at the same time that they also return to plague their perpetrators.[32] Duncan repeats the error of judgement with Macbeth that he made with Cawdor, and Macbeth repeats the challenge to Duncan that Cawdor represented; history repeats itself through the agency of the Weird Sisters, through the return of the ghost of Banquo, and especially in the behaviour of Macbeth.

In a short but extremely provocative argument offering a 'queer' reading of *Macbeth*, Heather Love suggests that attending to 'questions of linearity, temporality and succession' in *Macbeth* reveals a 'form of temporal dislocation or asynchrony' that operates as 'queer', distinct from 'the time of the family and the time of the couple'.[33] Positing that 'deviations from normative time – rather than any specifically sexual form of transgression' are legible as 'queer', Love reads ambition as 'a form of desire that does not respect temporal sequence'.[34] 'Jump[ing] the life to come' (I.vii.7) spurns dynastic history in favour of 'unlineal' succession, in historical company with 'that group of men known for their impatience and for their love of the barren sceptre'.[35] Love reads Macbeth through Lee Edelman's Lacanian notion of the '*sinthomo*sexual' – a figure who 'annuls the temporality of desire' for 'the unrestricted availability of jouissance'. [36] By contrast, Banquo is associated with Edelman's 'reproductive futurity'. Lady Macbeth, for her part, undertakes a 'sex change' that renders her *sinthomo*sexual as she collapses time, disavowing the traditional 'longing for an outcome located in the future' and embracing instead 'a constant enjoyment of the future in and as the present'.[37]

Subjectivity and Social Relations

Jennifer Lewin takes 'Macbeth's own mind' as the 'centre of the play's attention': the tragedy plumbs Macbeth's 'mental world, […] his intense mental energy and his capacity for speculation and rumination'.[38] Derek Cohen analyses the effect on Macbeth's mind of the play's anomalously scarce references to personal history. This creates an 'intensely present mood' of struggle; rendering the past with only 'abstract precision' underwrites bloodthirsty ambition when it 'seals connection to the present and […] distance to the past'. [39] Focusing on Macduff, Lynne Dickson Bruckner explores mental experiences of grief as the 'tension between internal affective mandates and the demands of the power structure', arguing that 'in *Macbeth* the dynamics of power intrude on and even organize affective experience, exploiting the way grief can readily be reconfigured as revenge'.[40] Game theorist Steven J. Brams cites *Macbeth* as an instance of Frustration and Self-Frustration games, a class – also including the Samson and Delilah story and *Lysistrata* – that moves towards 'nonmyopic equilibrium'. [41] Brams offers his model as a way to 'rationally explain […] seemingly irrational choices'.[42]

Katherine Rowe situates subjectivity within early modern affect theory. She shows that the discussion between Rosse and Lady Macduff of Macduff's departure (IV.ii) takes up 'a persistent concern of seventeen-century English passions theory': the 'natural turbulence' and contagiousness of 'undirected passions'.[43] For post-Stuart political theorists, such affective lability 'challenges a stable polity. Not knowing their own passions and swayed by sense, the commons' […] allegiance never can be secured.'[44] Rowe studies William Davenant's revival of *Macbeth* in the light of his proposal for state-supported theatre as an arena to redress this vulnerability with 'civic instruction of the passions'.[45] Rowe suggests that *Macbeth*, with its 'many scenes of sympathetic instruction', 'provided an especially rich ground for experiments in theatrical education'.[46] Davenant's revisions of the Shakespearean play replace 'a kind of affective exchange no longer suited to the internal disciplines Davenant promotes'[47] with scenes of 'emotional management'[48] that 'model [...] a very different mode of cognitive self-possession'.[49]

Challenges to self-possession emerge earlier in the century as well, complicating spiritual as well as civic projects. Abraham Stoll unpacks how *Macbeth* stages 'the functioning of conscience in the sinful mind' in relation to Reformist theories of conscience.[50] Stoll suggests that *Macbeth* betrays the possibility that 'conscience' names merely humoral disequilibrium, psychological projection, or (as for Hobbes) 'the human tendency to elevate personal opinion to the exalted level of truth, even divine law'.[51] For Stoll, the play 'counters the period's generally sanguine theorists by developing a vision of conscience as a tragically equivocal moral guide'.[52] By contrast, Richard C. McCoy rehabilitates equivocation, which critics traditionally suspect as Jesuit, arguing that 'equivocation [...] can be a force for good and a source of grace', 'a form of graceful performance'.[53] McCoy offers an account of Malcolm's perplexing scene of perjurious self-accusation: McCoy's Malcolm equivocates among 'grace' as 'political favour', 'artful elegance', and 'divine right' as a useful strategy that 'acknowledges and embraces his role as actor and player-king'.[54]

Lina Perkins Wilder investigates the role and manipulation of memory in fashioning the play's selves. The 'sweet remembrancer' Lady Macbeth (III.iv.37) consistently 'instructs Macbeth in the masculine discipline [of mnemonics] that [...] will allow him to act and not think about what he has done'.[55] Wilder illuminates the extensive vocabulary of memory and forgetfulness in the play, detailing its discourse of early-modern mnemonic training. 'Lady Macbeth's 'unsex[ing] refits her body not only for masculine and evil deeds but for a masculine control over her memory.'[56] Fragmentation, recall and manipulation of memory shape narratives for both characters and audience, epitomized when the sleepwalking scene 'is received by its audience as if it reveals past deeds [...] but in which Lady Macbeth "repeats" words she never speaks in the course of the play'.[57] As the tragedy's end approaches, 'each further catastrophe recalls an element of the prophecy [and] these heavily marked mnemonic devices teach the audience to forget and remember on cue, learning [...] the discipline that Macbeth and Lady Macbeth also attempt to learn'.[58]

Relations *among* the selves generated in these various ways have been studied as questions of friendship, paternity and marriage. Rebecca Ann Bach uses Alan Bray's model of 'voluntary kinship' among male friends to explore the play's 'love language that binds men to one another'.[59] Fred Tromly finds that, although the significance of father–son relationships is attenuated in plays after *King Lear*, Macduff's response to his family's murder 'expresses the deepest paternal grief in all of Shakespeare'.[60] Carol Thomas Neely analyses Lady Macbeth's 'language of distraction', claiming that 'the play introduces a new kind of female distraction and a new context for reading it'.[61]

Politics, Culture and Nation

Questions of nationhood and constructions of 'Scotland' continue to generate both critical discussion and artistic response. The past decade arguably has seen this area energized by the interplay between *Macbeth*'s inception during debates about the 1607 Act of Union joining England and Scotland on the one hand (see especially the arguments of Norbrook and Kinney, discussed in 'The Critical Backstory' chapter in this volume) and the 1997 devolution of Scotland and 1998 establishment of the Scottish parliament on the other. In recent analyses, historiography looms as large as history. Jonathan Baldo's '"A Rooted Sorrow": Scotland's Unusable Past' understands the unification of the imagined pasts of Scotland and England as part of the Union project – its stakes heightened by the relative novelty of the 'English' nationality laboriously forged under Elizabeth. Baldo links *Macbeth* to the Shakespearean history plays in their questions about the 'uses and disadvantages of history for a sense of nationhood'.[62] Malcolm Smuts takes *Macbeth* to relate 'the importance of indefeasible hereditary right in the transmission of political authority' to 'the social and biological processes that perpetuate royal bloodlines through time'.[63] Smuts argues that this question is given currency less by the play's brief image of Banquo as ancestor of King James than by political discussion in the play's recent past about choosing the successor to a virgin queen. In contrast to interrogation of the play's position in constructing seventeenth-century 'Scottishness', Rebecca Rogers claims that, at least in performance, '*Macbeth*'s stage-Scottishness was a relative late development in the play's post-Restoration afterlife.'[64] Only in the eighteenth century, according to Rogers, did the play 'acquire' 'national traits[,] at the time when the national identities of England and Scotland were being reformulated and Shakespeare's pre-eminent position in English cultural life was being consolidated'.[65]

Notably complex traditions underlie Scottish monarchical succession, that event so bloodily dramatized in *Macbeth*. Indeed, in an essay that critiques nominally 'historicist' critical practice for *appearing* to engage with the past by invoking markers of specific historical phenomena like 'The Gunpowder Plot' or 'Catholic equivocation', while actually voiding history through oversimplified and inadequately contextualized sampling, Kathleen McLuskie suggests that Macbeth's instrumental 'allegorization' of the past displays some homology with modern 'historicist' readings.[66] Historically, the Celtic practice of tanistry selected rulers from alternating dynastic lines, and in medieval Scotland both election and heredity played a role in accession. Macbeth's succeeding Duncan as ruler, and Malcolm's challenge to Macbeth, look quite different depending upon which available paradigm for succession is taken as salient. Critics and historians argue that these medieval Scottish practices are of more than antiquarian interest. Rather, their persistence in early-modern Ireland made these models known to Shakespeare's England, and widely read chroniclers like Holinshed remark on some aspects of them, albeit partially and sometimes inaccurately. Thus, Paul

Innes takes *Macbeth* to 'translate' complexities of actual Scottish history into terms more dramatically intelligible to English Renaissance audiences, reworking the 'half-remembered history of early medieval Scotland to produce the British *translatio imperii* ('transfer of rule') on the English Renaissance stage.[67] Historically – and, to students of *Macbeth*, surprisingly – King Malcolm's reign was 'a major initial stage in the developing historical enmity between Scotland and England'.[68] In the play, Innes writes, 'a buried layer [of history] remains just beyond the field of vision, haunting an unsettled play with the phantom of its origins'.[69] Similarly, Olga Valbuena claims that *Macbeth* 'suppresses' 'the violent means by which Duncan's own succession was secured against the Macbeths' dynastic interests', producing an 'unsettling colloquy [...] of disclosure and equivocation' in 'recasting that history into a play of praise'.[70] Valbuena remarks that critical accounts of successional conflict 'have not addressed the historical Lady Macbeth's dynastic claims and revenge motive lurking at the margins of historical and dramatic master texts'.[71]

'Scottishness' is constructed culturally as well as politically. Mary Floyd-Wilson analyses *Macbeth*'s geo-humoralism: the dominant early-modern affect theory that derives temperament from the ecology of humours circulating both within and around the individual body. Floyd-Wilson suggests that the accession-era flood of Scots into England 'put new pressures on the question of whether the English and Scots were humorally indistinguishable'.[72] She shows that the play draws on a tradition holding the ancient Scots to be naturally stoic, in accordance with their rugged environment, before their contamination, first in the Lowlands and eventually in the Highlands as well, by interaction with the temperamentally degenerate and self-indulgent English.[73] But the play 'inverts the ethnological claims' of this argument when it 'represents an already-degenerate Scotland desperately in need of anglicized civility and government'.[74] Indeed, the Highlander Macbeths are particularly vulnerable to permeation, not only by such Galenic 'non-naturals' as the weather so prominent in the tragedy, but by demonic spirits too. 'By demonizing the far north', Floyd-Wilson continues, 'Shakespeare's Jacobean play anxiously seeks to preserve a distinct English environment and disposition.'[75]

Criticism, performances and adaptations of *Macbeth* extend nationalist questions beyond Britain, mining the play's engagements with ambiguous insider–outsider status in an England newly ruled by a Scottish king. *Macbeth*'s 'Scottishness' is of course tenuous: Rosse's lament 'Alas poor country/Almost afraid to know itself!' not only capaciously encompasses ignorance ('afraid to know'), knowledge ('*almost*' afraid) and the space between, but further nuances ways that (partial) knowledge and (semi-performative) ignorance can inflect one another when these lines are spoken by an English actor in Jacobean London to varied audiences that included Scottish courtiers (IV.iii.164–5). But the very artificiality of *Macbeth*'s 'Scotland' allows consideration of nationhood *per se*.

The most recent studies of *Macbeth*'s politics find more nuance and ambiguity in the play, and in its relations to a complex political culture, than was usual in previous readings of the play as a myth of Stuart origins. Rebecca Lemon suggests that the play challenges absolutism 'while at the same time celebrating the role of legitimate and even mystical kingship in stabilizing the state'.[76] For Lemon, the play 'differentiates between two types of treason, one committed in the name of the state and the common good, and the other out of personal interest'.[77] When Malcolm purges 'traitorous thanes' from the political landscape, 'restor[ing] the rhetorical opposition of sovereign and traitor', this opposition is 'belied in Scotland by [Malcolm's] own treasonous sovereignty'.[78] In the end, the play 'makes the radical move of supporting rebellion, but it does so in the name of Malcolm's absolutist, patriarchal, Christian orthodoxy'.[79] Peter C. Herman sets the play in a singularly rich version of sixteenth- and mid-seventeenth-century political theories of the state. Like other Shakespearean plays of the early 1600s, Herman suggests, *Macbeth* 'reflect[s] upon the steadily escalating conflict between Jacobean absolutism, predicated on a monarchy that is above the law of the land, and the traditions of English liberty signified by [...] the Ancient

Constitution, in which the monarch follows and is subject to the law'.[80] While the former, absolutist, political paradigm was often the only one visible in New Historicist discussions of *Macbeth*, Herman shows that the latter was explicitly and robustly argued by English Parliamentarians like Sir Edward Phelps, *contra* James's assertions. Herman's *Macbeth* 'tests' and 'finds wanting' both political models.

Judith Weil's *Service and Dependency in Shakespeare's Plays* reveals political theory couched in the discourse of service, a practice with both domestic and divine aspects whose lexicon permeates the play. She argues that recognizing service as a locus for negotiating freedom and constraint reveals more expansive possibilities than were visible in previous analyses.[81] Against our 'readiness to surmise that an un-rationalized, customary dependency mystifies authority',[82] Weil counters that 'different kinds of "belonging" [...] can empower dependents through an interplay of subordinate roles [...] characters constrained by subject positions may nevertheless resist or transform the purposes which try to turn them into instruments or things'.[83] The language of service is spoken 'precisely' by Duncan and Macduff, but 'perverted' by both Macbeth and Lady Macbeth.[84] Elizabeth Fowler studies *Macbeth*'s political paradigms as a question of 'fit' or rhetorically modelled decorum: crisis ensues when characters are ill suited to the 'social persons they aspire to occupy'.[85] Fowler takes the play as an instance of forensic rhetoric that requires its audience to evaluate 'the origins and consequences of a breach of fit in the polity'[86] at a junction of historically based 'transformation' in 'categories of social person'.[87]

Anselm Haverkamp understands Macbeth as a Machiavel, Lady Macbeth as the 'most eloquent agent and theoretician' of the 'new violence' theorized by Machiavelli, and *Macbeth* as a play taking 'violence [...] as its theme, object and plot, impetus and tendency'. [88] Haverkamp holds that the

> moral of the story of *Macbeth* is not the vanquished past of the wild Scotland of clans, but rather the confrontation of

> [Shakespeare's] time with the ghostly present of a violence which, in a barbaric after-image celebrating grim primal circumstances, can in no way be limited to a gloriously overcome past.[89]

This is partly because representing violence is implicated in violence. Contemplating the 'mediatization of violence into a medium of progress',[90] Haverkamp argues that unlike the 'mystifications' of Machiavelli that put violence 'at an analytic distance'[91] *Macbeth* stages for our consideration 'the medial principle [...] of an endlessly ongoing theatrical inscription' as evidenced in Lady Macbeth's recitation of Macbeth's letter, 'starting the monologue in which the message become the medium of bloodshed'.[92]

In addition to considerations of politics and political theory in *Macbeth*, recent criticism studies uses of the play in politics. William C. Carroll discusses the widespread invocations of *Macbeth* in British political discourse from the early-seventeenth to mid-eighteenth century, and distinguishes between two different *Macbeth* traditions: one centred on the popular Shakespearean play, the other on a politically quite distinct anti-absolutist strain, deriving from George Buchanan.[93] John H. Astington studies recent Canadian and British examples of *Macbeth* citation, including journalistic and cartoon representations of unpopular political leaders. Astington also treats Howard Brenton's play *Thirteenth Night* (produced by the RSC in 1981) and the 1990s British TV mini-series *House of Cards*, adapted from novels by Michael Dobbs.[94] Stephen M. Buhler's 'Politicizing *Macbeth* on U.S. Stages' explores the 'resonances' of *Macbeth* in the American political culture of Barbara Garson's 1966–7 play *MacBird!* (which dramatizes the John F. Kennedy assassination) and the 1995 play *Jungle Rot* by Seth Greenland (which depicts the assassination of Patrice Lumumba of Congo).[95]

Katherine A. Rowe's 'The Politics of Sleepwalking: American Lady Macbeths' explores Lady Macbeth in American adaptations, centrally Charles Brockden Brown's 1798 novel *Wieland*, as 'the figure of the independent American woman' whose transformation from mastermind to sleepwalker offers a long-mined trope for the 'haunting' 'fear that a dishonourable instrumentality lies at the heart of [...] Jeffersonian [...] consent and feminizes each democratic subject in disabling ways'.[96] Gay Smith's book-length study of dalliances between Lady Macbeth and American politics cross-reads the history of portrayals of Lady Macbeth on the American stage with the character's deployment in political rhetoric. American political discourse consistently appropriates Lady Macbeth to figure concerns about the 'political wife able to influence her husband, as the couple climbs to the pinnacle of political power, precariously holds fast to it, and ultimately falls'.[97] Smith examines the portrayal, reception and political appropriations of Lady Macbeth in a chronology that begins with Cotton Mather, then extends through a long series of first ladies: Abigail Adams, Mary Todd Lincoln, Edith Galt Wilson, Eleanor Roosevelt and Hillary Rodham Clinton. We might attribute Lady Macbeth's availability for such wide appropriation to an intriguing textual feature of the play illuminated by Pamela Mason: no early text of the play names 'Lady Macbeth' as such.[98] Rather, as Mason remarks, she is variably termed 'Macbeth's Wife', 'Macbeth's Lady', 'Lady' and 'Wife'. More broadly, Mason suggests that the marked irregularities of the Folio text, encompassing inconsistencies concerning who is on stage, unusually abrupt stylistic variation and lineation problems, may account for unusually broad editorial interventions in lacunae ripe for appropriation.

Adaptation and Performance Studies

Studies of *Macbeth* adaptations on stage demonstrate continued interest in taking the play into new contexts, from the Restoration to the present, from London to Beijing. Simon Williams considers the *Macbeths* of Davenant, Garrick, Schiller and Verdi.[99] Paul Prescott analyses the history of playing the protagonist from 1744–1889.[100] Ruth Morse discusses adaptations of the play in modern French drama[101] and Juliet Dusinberre explores the play's influence on modern English poet Wilfred Owen.[102] Natasha Distiller studies how the reception of Welcome Msomi's 1974 *uMabatha*, the 'Zulu Macbeth', mutually reinforces notions of Shakespeare's transcendent genius and 'the authenticity of [white] experience of the "Zulu culture" on offer'.[103] Ruru Li surveys a range of post-war Chinese stage adaptations and Bi-qi Beatrice Lei describes *Macbeth* adaptations in Chinese opera of the 1980s and 1990s.[104] Stephen Purcell's book-length study of 'simulation and subversion' in contemporary popular stage adaptations of Shakespeare, prominently including *Macbeth*, observes how parodic appropriations 'suggest a synergy between Shakespeare and pop culture at the same time as deriving comic effects from their perceived disparity'.[105]

Recent discussions of *Macbeth* on screen treat both older films and new ones. Sarah Hatchuel explores how cinematographers process *Macbeth*'s focus on the seen, the unseen and the visually horrible, examining the screen vocabularies of 'presence and absence, revelation, and concealment' in Orson Welles's, Roman Polanski's and Jeremy Freeston's *Macbeths*.[106] Peter Holland, attesting that 'the Scotland of *Macbeth* films is always aware of the limits of its power as well as of its geography', discusses the intersection of the play's construction of nation with the contemporary political force – or lack thereof – of post-devolution Scotland.[107] Holland argues that the 'location' of Scotland in the films he analyses – the *Macbeths* of Welles (c.1950) and Polanski (1971), plus *Joe MacBeth* (Ken Hughes, 1955), *Throne of Blood* (Akira Kurosawa, 1957) and *Men of Respect* (William Reilly, 1990) – 'enables the film audiences to read the play'.[108] Focusing on more recent versions, Mark Thornton Burnett suggests that in Freeston's film *Macbeth* (1996) and the television productions by Michael Bogdanov (1997) and Gregory Doran (2001), 'in keeping with one strand of globalization, what is witnessed is the gradual disappearance of Scotland: these reworkings of Shakespeare's drama plot a path in which the local is first prioritized and finally blanked out'.[109]

Kim Fedderson and J. Michale Richardson analyse the corpus

of film adaptations in light of 'SHAKESPEARE', which they render typographically in capital letters to designate as 'imperial brand'.[110] Fedderson and Richardson delineate a 'complex dynamic of compliance and resistance as the margin writes and rewrites the cultural commodity exported by and imported from the center'.[111] Similarly, Courtney Lehmann's 'Out Damned Scot: Dislocating *Macbeth* in Transnational Film and Media Culture' remarks that

> Scotland, and, more specifically, the dislocated 'Scotland' that figures so prominently in twentieth-century media adaptations of Shakespeare's *Macbeth*, suggests a compelling metaphor for the transnational playground wherein the challenges and possibilities of globalization may be traversed.[112]

Considering *Macbeth* films from 1990 to 2002, Lehmann analyses the longstanding cinematic tradition of 'viewing Scottish scenery and history through the lens of other national fantasies'.[113] A special issue of *Borrowers and Lenders: The Journal of Shakespeare and Appropriation* treating Asian Shakespeare films is devoted to the 2004 Hindi *Macbeth* adaptation *Maqbool* (dir. Vishal Bhardwaj) and the Mandarin *Hamlet* film *The Banquet* (dir. Feng Xiaogang, 2006).

The volume *Weyward 'Macbeth': Intersections of Race and Performance* treats adaptations of the play in sundry genres, united by their playing a 'role in American racial formations'.[114] The collection proposes that the play is 'much more racially engaged than is conventionally assumed'.[115] *Macbeth*'s constructions of Scottishness render the play 'always already marked as a potentially racialized project', as Francesca Royster remarks in her contribution on Polanski's *Macbeth*.[116] Beyond this, however, co-editor Ayanna Thompson argues that *Macbeth*'s 'rhetoric of blood and staining' 'seeps into early American racial rhetoric'; the 'indelible quality of blood' in the play 'unnervingly coincides with early American debates about the nature – the essence

– of race'.[117] Despite this, and despite its demonstrably robust presence throughout American history, *Macbeth*'s 'not readily announc[ing] itself as already weywardly racialized' frequently occludes its 'long history of literary and performance intersections with race' (p. 6).[118] The collection demonstrates *Macbeth*'s ubiquity in antebellum abolitionist and anti-abolitionist rhetoric alike,[119] studying Frederick Douglass's appropriations of Shakespeare,[120] documenting *Macbeth*'s prominent position in early African American theatre[121] and minstrelsy,[122] and examining adaptations from Welles's Voodoo *Macbeth* to hip-hop. Charita Gainey-O'Toole and Elizabeth Alexander discuss the extensive allusions to *Macbeth* in African American poetry from the nineteenth century to the present. Examples are legion (poets include Gil Scott-Heron, Amiri Baraka, Gwendolyn Brooks and Claudia Rankine); the essay focuses on uses of the weyward sisters in poetry of Rita Dove, Julia Fields, and Lucille Clifton to engage 'a parallel tradition of conjuring within the African-American literary tradition'.[123]

Adaptation studies range into further media too. An unusual book by the historian Alexander Nemerov uses *Macbeth*, the play at whose performance Abraham Lincoln was shot, as a kind of lens to filter a full range of Civil War-era American contexts.[124] Nemerov attends to resonances between American experiences and the play (very popular at the time), playing the tropes and rhetoric of *Macbeth* over paintings, architecture, documents and encounters of 1860s America. Bruno Lessard's study of hypermedia *Macbeths* contends that 'digital adaptations of *Macbeth* [...] actualize visually the [...] cognitive mechanisms readers of *Macbeth* perform when they read the play'. [125] Lessard contends that digital editors bring to life 'how unstable and uncertain textual editions of Shakespeare have always been',[126] suggesting that the Voyager Shakespeare 1994 CD-ROM and Digital Artisans' 2001 *Hyper Macbeth* 'give voice and "body" to the [...] themes of return and haunting'.[127]

Adaptations

Among the past decade's *Macbeth* films that use the Shakespearean script the two most widely viewed are the broadcast version of Rupert Goold's Chichester–New York production (discussed in the 'Performance History' chapter of the present volume), which was broadcast by the BBC and PBS in 2010 and has since been available online,[128] and Geoffrey Wright's 2006 film, set in contemporary Melbourne and featuring the Macbeths (Sam Worthington and Victoria Hill) as a prosperous gangland couple suffering from the recent loss of their child.[129] Wright's *Macbeth* opens with destruction, in a cemetery (perhaps the one where the Macbeths' child is buried). The witches are schoolgirls gleefully hacking at tombstones with chisels and sledgehammers, wielding red spray paint. Defacing monuments offers another a provocative figure for adaptation – perhaps unfortunately apt, for this lukewarmly received film – as does the youthful vitality of the witches whose violence disfigures, and also thereby reshapes, the tombstones.

The habitus of fraternal bonds and feudal webs of obligation among *Macbeth*'s thanes, which are set against the larger and only vaguely represented 'English' court, are transliterated into gang affiliations in a variety of global film settings. In addition to Wright's *Macbeth*, these include *Maqbool*, set in Mumbai in an adaptation that combines 'Bollywood gangster film, Muslim social drama, ethnography and postmodernist artwork', Greg Salman's 2004 *Mad Dawg*, set in Los Angeles, and Liberian director Gerald Barclay's 2003 *Bloody Streetz*, set in New York.[130] Additionally, the more glancingly allusive 2006 Kevin MacDonald film *The Last King of Scotland*, adapted from Giles Foden's 1998 novel, plays out *Macbeth* elements in its representation of Idi Amin's Uganda.

Concerns with clan, lineality, inheritance and the relationships between clan and nation inform both *Macbeth*'s initial Jacobean framework and the later contexts of adaptations. The setting of *Maqbool* in the same Mumbai underworld that invests in

Bollywood production, meta-cinematically acknowledged in the film, invites cross-reading with Stuart court patronage of London theatre.[131] Similarly, the background array of paternal icons in Billy Morrissette's 2002 *Scotland, PA*, including wall photos of Richard Nixon, are congruent with *Macbeth*'s evocations of the ways in which King James constructs political paternity.[132] In felicitous re-situations, the operations of each arena can throw into relief the workings of the other. Thus David Mason reads the religious tension subtending *Maqbool* to reveal what is 'brutal, savage, relentless, *Elizabethan*' in Hindi–Muslim violence in recent South Asian history as well as to illuminate *Macbeth*'s inflection by 'the cyclic storms of religiously fomented violence' of confessional conflict in Tudor–Stuart England.[133]

One 'State' of the Art (adaptation on film): *Scotland, PA* (2002)[134]

Scotland, PA sets *Macbeth* in a diner in rural 1970s Pennsylvania. Early in the film the waitress Mrs Lennox checks to see if anyone is watching, then grabs a bite of a customer's half-eaten burger as she clears the tray. Sneaking a leftover offers a provocative figure for adaptation, as new works take nourishment from what went before, consuming parts but leaving other bits untouched as they transport the remains to new venues, whether to the kitchen, or to more urbane new contexts. Checking to see who might register her raid, Mrs Lennox conveys the particular relationship of many self-deprecating, parodic or highly mediated adaptations to their high-culture source material: who will notice the appropriation? is it culturally authorized?

Cross-reading Mrs Lennox gulping a crust in the Morrissette movie, Patrick Stewart's Macbeth making sandwiches for the murderers he hires in the Goold film and Macbeth's own lexicon of banqueting and butchering can throw into relief the figurative economies of nurture, sustenance, ingestion and communion circulating in the play's discourse. Morrissette's diner setting reminds students of Shakespeare that food imagery saturates the play. As Duncan's first dialogue with Macbeth concludes, Duncan remarks that Macbeth 'is full so valiant,/And in his commendations I am fed;/It is a banquet to me' (I.iv.54–6). This sets up a model of mutual nourishment whereby reports of Macbeth's valour nourish King Duncan at the same time that Macbeth is nourished by Duncan's promoting him, creating the metaphorical 'feast' of successful community. The play's peripety scene is a banquet, where Macbeth's fortunes change as he proves unable to sit at table with his thanes. Lady Macbeth remarks on the transubstantiation that Macbeth's hesitance subverts when she mines the homology of 'meat' and 'meet' to admonish him that 'the sauce to meat is ceremony;/Meeting were bare without it' (III.iv.35–6). The descent into tragedy plays out in the lexicon of 'ravining' ('famished') 'ambition' (II.iv.29) that renders Macbeth in the end a 'dead butcher' (V.ix.35). Woven among these three structural pillars of the action are many references to food.

Scotland, PA makes burgers the foundation of Joe McBeth ('Mac's') bid for power, first manifested when he o'erleaps the service counter to rout unruly thanes engaged in a food fight; the advent of the drive-through service window at his employer's, 'Duncan's', catalyses his ambition. The witches are three stoned hippies who frequent a local carnival, munching fried chicken on a Ferris wheel of fortune. When Pat and Mac McBeth murder Norm Duncan in a deep-fat fryer, investigative pressure from police lieutenant Ernie McDuff incites Mac to murder potential witnesses, including his friend Banko, and Pat succumbs to hallucinations of a severe grease burn on her hand. At the McBeths' downfall the film intercuts scenes of Pat seizing a cleaver to chop off her hand with Mac's attempt to choke McDuff with a burger – an effort foreclosed by McDuff biting Mac's hand. *Scotland, PA* mines many of *Macbeth*'s food images. For example, the 'milk of human kindness' ostensibly overfilling Macbeth (I.v.17) and which apparently once brimmed sufficiently in Lady Macbeth for a 'babe' to 'milk' her (I.vii.55), manifests in *Scotland, PA* in the soft-serve ice cream cones that Pat's leering manager figures as breasts ('The tip of that mountain's going to go right into our customer's mouth, and make him happy […] Mr McBeth, get out here, and have a look at your wife's beautiful cones'). Frozen, artificial food substitutes seem unlikely to effectively nourish *Scotland, PA* just as the barren Shakespearean Macbeths fail to succour their subjects in old-world Scotland. Nor are other Pennsylvania women any more effective: the local matron trying to provide dairy refreshment to the widower Norm Duncan at a football game, sighing that Malcolm 'is just crying out for a new Momma', comes up empty: '*Damn* this cocoa! Damn this cocoa! We're out of cocoa, Norm.'

Food is the medium through which the McBeths might be able to exercise some control over their destiny. But acquiring the restaurant and transforming it into 'McBeth's' [*sic*] imprisons them in abject obsession that ends in death. The images of Pat's hand on the cutting board, Mac's hand in McDuff's teeth and the dead Duncan's bound hands hanging out of the fryer encapsulate the traversable boundary between the agency that hands can exercise and represent, on the one hand, and inert flesh, always ripe for ingestion or decomposition, on the other. Extending beyond individual agency, *Scotland, PA's* diner offers a synecdoche for the new commodification of the 'eating experience' that historically swept across rural America in the 1970s: a homogenization of locales that both enfranchizes and erases them, a transformation of individuals into consumers. Indeed, the film's prophesying witch first mistakes the restaurant in her vision for a bank.[135]

Scotland, PA transliterates the play's negotiations of Scottish and English power into carnivorous and vegetarian subculture. Congruent with the play's seeking remedy 'from gracious England' (IV.iii.43), the film brings urban police lieutenant McDuff to town to investigate Duncan's murder. McDuff arrives in Scotland as a vegetarian, bearing an exotic plate of baba ghanouj to Duncan's wake. By contrast, the locals socialize over burgers and hunt deer. Mac draws attention to diet as the figure for cultural difference when he asks nastily whether McDuff is 'gracing our home with a vegetable dish' as a sign of 'how the better half lives'. But just as Scottish–English relations are more complicated in the play than they might initially seem, the politics of food in *Scotland, PA* prove prone to oversimplification. McDuff misperceives Scotland as pastoral, romanticizing the homicide-inducing diner's capacity to nurture its customers ('Do not underestimate what you do, sir! Workin' the grill, fryin' the fries, feeding hungry people') and misreading citizens' hugging him at the end of interviews as warmth, when in fact the embraces stem from the serial mistake of each discomfited witness awkwardly imitating the previous one. And when McDuff seizes upon his dream to take over the restaurant, in a wordless coda, the film shows him forlorn, holding a carrot in an empty parking lot bereft of custom for the 'garden burgers' advertised on his new sign.

One 'State' of the Art (adaptation on the page): *William Shakespeare's Macbeth: The Graphic Novel* (2005)[136]

Like Morrissette's black comedy, this graphic novel by Arthur Byron Cover and Tony Leonard Tamai, set as science fiction, adapts *Macbeth* into a popular form. *William Shakespeare's Macbeth: The Graphic Novel* uses the words of Shakespeare's play, with only occasional alterations and somewhat more frequent elisions, in hybrid print form, re-mediating Shakespearean material with an inventive (if not always fully artistically satisfying) deployment of its own representational repertoire. In its black-and-white drawings, for instance, variably dense cross-hatching conveys variable ontological status (Banquo's ghost is transparent) and intensity of affect (the bereaved Macduff is strikingly dark, as saturated with ink as Banquo's ghost is sparing, his grief rendering him intensely real).

The unfamiliarity of the graphic form in relation to the Shakespearean words disorients the reader, thereby presenting the witches to Banquo, Macbeth and to us in ways consonant with early modern witch encounters. The novel confronts us with the temporal, ontological and generic displacement that disorients Macbeth and Banquo on the witches' heath. It opens with a single-frame page whose situation bubble announces 'Stardate

1040: the forces of King Duncan are engaged in battle against those of the rebel Macdonwald'.[137] It also depicts battle-forces mounted on dragons. Is this science fiction or fantasy? Will the codes be medieval or futuristic? A dialogue bubble in the bottom right-hand corner of the page reads 'When shall we meet again? In thunder, lighting, or in rain?' without any visible source for the words. Who is speaking? An apposite question not only for this story but for any adaptation. Here, it may be intensified by the elision of 'three' from the familiar opening line: how many witches will there be? more broadly, what relationship to the play will the text develop?

The top frame on the second page depicts the witches, letting us know who answers 'When the hurly-burly's done'.[138] But, like *Macbeth*'s Weird Sisters, these witches confound their interlocutors' category expectations. Where the play verbally records indeterminacy of gender and cosmic status, *William Shakespeare's Macbeth* graphically records indeterminacy of species. We cannot tell if these conjurors are human figures wearing gas masks and body armour jointed even to the fingers, or whether the carapaces are prostheses, or if we are seeing the unencumbered bodies of a very different species. The mixing of graphic novel and Shakespearean play likewise leaves us unsure which generic conventions govern at any given moment: the top panel of the second page graphically renders explosive battle noise as hollow-capital-letter 'THOOM!!';[139] the top panel of the next page, as the witches prepare to exit, has a follow-up 'DOOM!!'.[140] Is the latter another sound effect? or prophecy?

B: One 'State' of the Art (opera on CD): *The Okavango Macbeth* (first performance 2009, CD release 2011)[141]

Macbeth is deeply concerned with the constitution of the human, which it defines in distinction to the animal, the superhuman and the monstrous. Both Macbeth's plaint 'I dare do all that may become a man' (I.vii.46) and Lady Macbeth's imperative 'unsex me here'(I.v.42) leave unspecified what might lie beyond the boundaries they evoke. Is the opposite of 'man' 'woman'? 'boy'? 'servant'? 'monster'? 'beast'? When Malcolm urges the bereaved Macduff to 'dispute' his family's murder 'as a man' and the latter replies 'I must also feel it as a man' (IV.iii.219–21), Macduff switches the lexicon from gender or maturity to humanity. When Lady Macbeth and Macbeth debate Macbeth's resolve, uses of 'man' ricochet from 'manliness' ('I dare do all that may become a man' [I.vii.46]) to 'not-animal' ('What beast was 't then/That made you break this enterprise?' [I.vii.48–9]) to 'hierarchically elevated social actor' ('you would/Be so much more the man' [I.vii.50–1]).

The chamber opera *The Okavango Macbeth* plays out in these boundaries of the human. Performed first in Botswana in 2009, then in Edinburgh, the work's release on CD in 2011 makes it part of the durable archive of adaptations. With libretto by Alexander McCall Smith and music by Tom Cunningham, the opera stages its *Macbeth* plot among a troop of baboons and a team of primatologists in the delta.[142] The stylistic eclecticism among movements, drawing in both classical and musical-theatre idioms, is part of what positions this 'chamber opera', as its creators designate it, to address a variety of audiences – as early modern theatre did. Some movements draw out resonances between Renaissance dance beats and African rhythms: in both movements of the first act, for instance, compound metres set syncopated subdivisions within strongly duple dance measures. The hollow-sounding woodwinds in the orchestra similarly evoke both Renaissance recorders and African flutes.

The Okavango Macbeth's characters comprise both jungle animals and people: both humans playing humans (the primatologists) and humans playing animals, who are themselves 'playing' humans insofar as some take on the Shakespearean character names 'Macbeth', 'Lady Macbeth' and 'Duncan'. The opera draws in the supernatural with its scientists, who serve as both witches and chorus. Scientific method stands in for fate: 'Science is a hard-hearted/Mistress, who lets things/Happen [...]/[...] Even death must be watched:/Dispassionately', opines the Male

Primatologist (II). The Male Primatologist arrogantly assumes this observational capacity to be uniquely human ('As God is to man/In his grant of free will, [...]/So are we to these/Dumb creatures' [II]), but the baboons prove equally aware of the humans' presence, and, in fact, make precisely parallel claims: [BABOON 1] 'We must watch them'/[BABOON 2] 'But never interfere' (II). Expanding *Macbeth*'s ambivalent representation-suppression of clan relationships and its ruminations on the bonds of 'kinship' (for instance, Macbeth's chagrin that he holds Duncan in 'double trust' as his 'kinsman' [I.vii.12–13]), the opera's primatologists designate the baboons 'this cousin of man,/In whose ways/We may see our own' (II).

In the plot that spins out among these 'cousins', Lady Macbeth is herself the coveted prize held by Duncan: she is to mate with him, the highest-status male, but prefers Macbeth. She urges the latter to kill Duncan in his sleep, screwing Macbeth's courage to the sticking place in a waltz-timed duet that fashions a glorious persona for Macbeth. Moulding him into 'the one who is all glorious,/In my eyes' (II), Lady Macbeth addresses Macbeth as 'My lover bright, in courage spun; [...]/[Who] plucks the eagles as they fly/With talons drawn, and dashes them' (II). This evokes both the Shakespearean Captain's ironic report that Macbeth feared Macdonwald 'as sparrows eagles' (I.ii.35) and the horrified accounts of nature inverted by Duncan's murder (II.iv). The Okavango aria continues in a duet wherein Lady Macbeth completes Macbeth's half-line demurrals, transforming them to affirmations.

> MACBETH. Is that me whom you describe?
> Am I so brave who once was ...
> LADY MACBETH. Brave, and always was.

The melody in this part of the dialogue recapitulates the theme Lady Macbeth has just established, successfully drawing Macbeth into her project. Later in the movement, Macbeth follows Lady Macbeth into a less melodic, more recitative style, to similar effect:

> MACBETH. Still, I am only ...
> LADY MACBETH. Only one, you are the one and
> Only one I think of
> When I'm lonely.
>
> (II)

In the end the baboon Lady Macbeth is killed by a leopard; Macbeth's nemesis is not death but solitude, the exact inversion of what the simian Lady Macbeth promised, and his last line in the opera is 'I am alone, I am alone' (IV).

Conclusion: 'with a glass in his hand'

A banquet disrupted by a ghost: not an unprovocative figure for adaptation. The guests that a tale invites to its banquet include tellers, listeners and re-users. The haunting presence–absence of the source (used with varying degrees of completeness, acknowledgement and recognition) can, like Banquo's ghost, discomfit the gathering, but it is also generative. Perhaps the most dramatic staging of this in recent adaptations is Martin Turner's Banquo striding furiously across the banqueting table in the Goold film. Banquo's street shoes violating the snowy linen cloth, his footsteps stamping past brimming platters as the camera pans out from tight focus on his feet, are as shocking as the glare he fixes on Patrick Stewart's Macbeth when he comes to the end of the table and the camera reaches his face. Later, as the end of the film approaches, Macbeth sits alone at that same table, surrounded by poultry carcasses and empty wine bottles, which rattle and spill in the shockwaves of exploding shells fired by Malcolm's approaching army. The munitions evoke the 'crack of doom' which alone, Macbeth fears, will end the infinite multiplication of kings in the vision the witches show him. The wordless power of this pageant of spectral heirs, the last of whom re-mediates and further multiplies the regal figures with his mirror (IV.i), yields another provocative metaphor for adaptation.

Goold's bottles recall how often film adaptations make use of glass – appropriately enough, given the double sense of 'screen'. In *Scotland, PA*, thick dirty spectacles screen what Banco, laconic and sometimes drunk, but always perceptive, sees. *Maqbool* begins with the corrupt policemen who occupy the witches' role riding in a car through a rainstorm, one tracing a horoscope on the automobile's fogged windows. The semi-opacity of these films' foggy windscreen, smeared spectacles and half-drunk wine bottles lets us glimpse the source text behind the adaptation, while interposing an undeniable layer of mediation that offers an inscribable surface (for the blunt fingertips of Bhardwaj's policeman, for the detritus of use on Morrissette's spectacles, for the printed labels on Goold's wine bottles) even as it partially blocks our view of the source. Some adaptations certainly spill the vintage wine in their bottles. But if the vessels themselves are part of what carries the play forward into vibrant future uses, then even if the bottles tip over in the blasts of anachronistic artillery, what they have lost, Macbeth hath won.

CHAPTER ONE

Macbeth and 'Sovereign Process'

JOHN DRAKAKIS

Hamlet as Textual Precursor

> [T]he kingdome of Englande is farre more absolute than either the dukedome of Venice is, or the kingdome of the Lacedemonians was. In warre time and in the field the Prince hath also absolute power, so that his word is lawe, he may put to death, or to other bodilie punishment, whom he shall thinke so to deserve, without processe of lawe or forme of judgement.[1]

This passage from Book 2, Chapter 3 of Sir Thomas Smith's *De Republica Anglorum: The Maner of Government or Policie of the Realme of England* (1583) is part of a larger discussion of the role 'Of the Monarch King or Queene of Englande' and it pinpoints clearly occasions when 'absolute power' – because it is 'absolute' – can subsume into itself or even depart from the 'processe of lawe or forme of judgement'.[2] Smith's emphasis on 'war' presupposes an external enemy whose existence must be 'existentially' negated, and it remains, in the words of the jurist Carl Schmitt, 'a real possibility for as long as the concept of the enemy remains valid'.[3] What Sir Thomas Smith pinpoints (and the contrast that he sets up between the limited power of the prince in the republic of Venice and the balanced monarchy of ancient Sparta is telling)[4] is the connection between the 'Prince', the right to exercise physical power and his relationship to the law.[5] Venice and Sparta in Sir Thomas Smith's lexicon are opposites, exceeded only by the power accorded to the sovereign monarch in 'the kingdome of Englande'.

My concern in this chapter is not to investigate what Smith implies is a particularly violent, albeit implicitly divinely sanctioned, departure from 'process', but rather to attempt to analyze the deep structural connections between 'sovereignty', 'process' and 'violence' and the ways in which they chart a shift from a theological to a political focus in Shakespeare's *Macbeth*. The cue for this lies in an earlier Shakespeare play that is not normally closely associated with *Macbeth*, where what becomes the tragedy of the later play is pre-figured and contained. That play is *Hamlet*, and the precursor of the later protagonist is the player-king Claudius.

It is not until Act III that Claudius articulates the duplicitous practice through which he enacts the role of the sovereign. Following her father's tutoring of Ophelia in the art of deception, Claudius 'privately' affirms Polonius's observation that 'with devotion's visage/And pious action we do sugar o'er/The devil himself' (III.i.45–9).[6] The phrase 'pious action' reduces religious ritual to the level of a strategy, with the result that the sovereign's public persona resembles 'The harlot's cheek, beautied with plast'ring art' that 'Is not more ugly to the thing that helps it/Than is my deed to my most painted word./O heavy burden!' (III.i.49–54). The theological residue in this utterance is clear, but like the invocation of the principle of 'divine right' later in the play, it is strategic rather than conceptual, in a regime whose disposition of sovereign power is radically political.

Two scenes later, Claudius is provoked into analyzing his predicament in more detail. Here his concern is with the psychological turmoil that a collision between past, present and future has generated; he begins with a horrifyingly instrumental recognition of the operations of 'justice' and 'law' in a post-lapsarian world:

> In the corrupted currents of this world
> Offence's gilded hand may shove by justice,
> And oft 'tis seen the wicked prize itself

> Buys out the law. But 'tis not so above:
> There is no shuffling, there the action lies
> In his true nature, and we ourselves compell'd
> Even to the teeth and forehead of our faults
> To give in evidence. (III.iii.58–64)

Here the player king *imagines* the legitimizing moment of sovereign authority when he is compelled to articulate, as though in a court of law, an act of rebellion that is both a repetition and a cue for abandonment. Claudius has already identified with figures from an 'historical' past: there is the surreptitious identification with Cain (I.ii.105), and there is the double repetition of the murder of Gonzago (III.ii), which itself repeats Claudius's regicide. Gilles Deleuze's axiom that 'Repetition is a condition of action before it is a concept of reflection' could not have a more apposite demonstration.[7] Claudius imagines an ultimate divine juridical process, and in doing so recapitulates the originary moment of a divine politics in which the 'player' sovereign reverts to being a subject. In other words, Claudius will be forced to relinquish the sovereign role to which he has become accustomed, of being, in the words of Carl Schmitt, 'he who decides on the exception'.[8] Moreover, the internalization of a series of archetypal struggles in the realms of the human and the divine inaugurates a process of separation between an over-determined, and policed, afterlife and a post-lapsarian human world in which there opens up a gap between a theologically authorized sovereignty and an order subject only to relations of power, in which the latter legitimizes its practices in and through the rhetoric of the former. In other words, 'deeds' may be subject ultimately to divine judgement, because they retain an 'essence' that is harnessed to a particular theological 'concept of truth', but 'words' can now be deployed as counters in a complex algebra of signification in which 'the struggles and antagonisms of real life' (88–90) and their political investments take precedence. The shift is from the monarch as a transparent representative of 'God' and towards a division between the 'public' and the 'private' in which a decisive element of 'political power' is, first of all, isolated, and then developed as a political practice. *Hamlet* recognizes the nature of the struggle between these two 'mighty opposites'.

Horatio's initial narrative account of the confrontation between Old Hamlet and Old Fortinbras, two kings whose actions were 'Well ratified by law and heraldry' (I.i.90), but who, by virtue of their sovereign power, were possessed of the authority to make writing coincide with action, and, in the words of Giorgio Agamben, to 'make sense coincide with denotation', establishes a norm.[9] But in Horatio's narrative of this event, which is an attempt to make sense of the appearance of the Ghost, it is difficult to decide whether the two sovereigns are presented and represented, represented but not presented, or presented but not represented. In what is, in effect, a gloss on Alain Badiou's tri-partite division of the possible types of membership of a mathematical set, Agamben observes:

> The sovereign exception is thus the figure in which singularity is represented as such, which is to say, insofar as it is unrepresentable. What cannot be included in any way is included in the form of the exception. In Badiou's scheme, the exception introduces a fourth figure, a threshold of indistinction between excrescence (representation without presentation) and singularity (presentation without representation), something like a paradoxical inclusion of membership itself. *The exception is what cannot be included in the whole of which it is a member and cannot be a member of the whole in which it is always already included.* What emerges in this limit figure is the radical crisis of every possibility of clearly distinguishing between membership and inclusion, between what is outside and what is inside, between exception and rule.[10]

In a further gloss Agamben extends this structural account into the sphere of the 'sovereign claim' of language, which achieves a stabilization of meaning by 'abandoning' its *denotata* and 'withdrawing from them into a pure *langue* (the linguistic "state of exception")'. It is here that he finds a space for 'deconstruction' which posits 'undecidables that are infinitely in excess of every possibility of signification'.[11] This is what Agamben calls 'The logic of Sovereignty':

> The sovereign decision traces and from time to time renews this threshold of indistinction between outside and inside, inclusion and exclusion, *nomos* and *physis*, in which life is originarily excepted in law. Its decision is the position of an undecidable.[12]

This suggests that the 'structure of sovereignty' is not 'an exclusively political concept', nor 'an exclusively juridical category', nor 'a power external to law' nor, indeed, simply that which fulfils the function of 'the supreme rule of the juridical order'.[13] The modern gloss on 'exception' is 'emergency', although it is worth pointing out that both *Hamlet* and *Macbeth* begin in 'states of emergency'. It is, perhaps, no accident that the 'meaning' of the figure of the Ghost in *Hamlet*, or the Weird Sisters in *Macbeth*, is 'undecidable' in the manner suggested by Agamben's 'logic'. Each points in the direction of a dangerous energy that the structures of political power attempt to domesticate in different ways: the Ghost, located in the liminal space of a backward-looking Purgatory, and the Weird Sisters who are the nominally female 'irrational' transgressors of order. Collectively, they represent different facets of a dangerous 'otherness' which art is attracted to, even as it attempts to neutralize and to socialize it.

I want now to turn to a particular aspect of what is already becoming a complex configuration of concepts: the distinction between the originary violence that inaugurates law, and that which preserves law, that Claudius's private ruminations inadvertently uncovers. In Aristotle's *Politics*, a text that appeared in translation in 1598, the section on 'kingship' draws together the issues of 'force' and 'authority' in a manner that anticipates the connection between Walter Benjamin's distinction between creative violence and preservative violence:

> [I]s the intending king to have about him a force with which he be able to impose his will on those who seek to resist his rule? How else is he to exercise his authority? For even if his sovereignty is such that he can act only in accordance with law, and do nothing of his own volition that is illegal, it will still be necessary for him to have sufficient armed force to give the laws protection.[14]

What frightens Claudius is the threat of a reversion to an originary structure of which the living Old Hamlet, present to himself, had been the entirely un-selfconscious, 'god-like' representative. His closing couplet in the prayer scene – 'My words fly up, my thoughts remain below./Words without thoughts never to heaven go' (III.iii.97–8) – reiterates the dilemma that arises when 'action' and 'language' are separated from each other, where representation is itself the question. Consequently, he posits a *difference* between the operation of divine justice, and the ruses available to him 'in this world'. What he fears most is not so much the 'application' of divine law to his case as its consequence, final 'abandonment': a removal from the regimes of representation altogether. There he will be 'at the mercy of *the* 'originary force of law' and he fears an exclusion that the ending of the play will make permanent. However, in seeking 'freedom' – 'O limed soul, that struggling to be free/Art more engaged!' (III.iii.68–9) – we may wonder if he is expressing that 'daemonic desire' that Jonathan Dollimore has identified as an 'untamed, unsocialized, and at heart non-human' energy, that in its 'amoral core becomes the more potentially destructive of the human as a result of the human attempts to tame it'.[15] The more he struggles to free himself from the constraints of divine sovereignty, the more his own apparently demonic 'sovereignty' is, paradoxically, compromized.

This momentary insight into what Agamben would call 'the structure of the ban' is superseded by Claudius's final soliloquy at the end of IV.iii that audaciously enlists the audience's support for a plan that both exposes his desire, while, at the same time, preserving his formal sovereignty.[16] 'England' is asked to discharge 'our sovereign process, which imports at full,/By letters congruing to that effect,/The present death of Hamlet' (IV.iii.66–8). Thus far, the double signification of Claudius's language invites us to read the phrase 'our sovereign process' ironically. What is Claudius protecting at this point? Is he protecting his 'crime'? Or is he protecting, in accordance with Aristotle's defence of force, 'the law'? Or is he acting above (or beneath the surface of) the law, as Smith would say: 'without process of law or forme of judgement'?[17] Or does this gesture reveal the sovereign who can act according to nothing that is 'codified in the existing legal order', but who, in 'a case of extreme peril, a danger to the existence of the state', has recourse to action that 'cannot be circumscribed factually and made to conform to a pre-formed law'?[18]

We may think that the answer to all these questions is obvious: here is a villain who wishes to neutralize a threat that could expose his crime of regicide, and in so doing is behaving in a manner that parodies sovereignty. But two scenes later Laertes enters at the head of what seems a popular rebellion. The imagery deployed by the anonymous Messenger is that of 'primal chaos', of a time immediately before the institution of the rule of law: 'And as the world were now but to begin,/Antiquity forgot, custom not known –/The ratifiers and props of every word –' (IV.v.103–5). In *Hamlet*, law, it would appear, follows language and informs a symbolic order that unites language and sovereignty. For Schmitt, 'Sovereignty is the highest, legally independent, underived power', whereas for Agamben, as we have seen, the *structure* of language and sovereignty are identical in that both are able to enact 'a state of exception'. Here, however, the 'rabble' that supports Laertes do not revert to a formless 'life' (*zoë*); rather, they elect a 'king' (*bios*): 'They cry, "Choose we! Laertes shall be king"' (IV.v.106). Laertes's 'rebellion' recapitulates a titanic struggle, but it also places him in a 'state of exception' and it threatens to repeat, in a different register, the regicide of Claudius. But Claudius forces further the comparison between his own and a divine sovereignty through an appeal to the very metaphysical power that authorizes sovereign process:

> Do not fear our person.
> There's such divinity doth hedge a king
> That treason can but peep to what it would,
> Acts little of his will. (IV.v.122–5)

This audacious identification of his 'person' with the figure of the 'sovereign' is the 'satyric' (we might even say 'daemonic') version of the figure of Old Hamlet ('Hyperion'), but in confronting his own 'rebellion' he reverts to a formulation that both invokes even as it demystifies the ideology that sustains the institutions of sovereignty. Sovereign process in this play is not simply deciding upon a 'state of exception' while at the same time evoking 'wonder';[19] rather, it involves a repetition of the means whereby the 'sovereign' comes into being as a means of structuring what would otherwise be 'bare life'. What emerges is a bio-politics whose features are exposed, and in which accumulation figures as a primary motive. In the case of Old Hamlet, just as in the case of Duncan in *Macbeth*, we do not, as Georges Bataille observes, in a more general context 'see the sovereign moment arrive' because in both cases 'nothing counts but the moment itself'; in fact, Bataille's definition of 'sovereignty' is an enjoyment of 'the present time without having anything else in view but this present time'.[20] When rebellion imitates sovereignty it 'looks' giant-like, but, as in the later case of Macbeth, the incumbent is made to feel 'his title/Hang loose about him like a giant's robe/ Upon a dwarfish thief' (*Macbeth* V.ii.20–2).[21] No matter how the play *Hamlet* resolves Denmark's crisis of authority, the mystery of power to which Claudius appeals as part of 'sovereign process' is exposed as a political rhetoric that beautifies 'with plast'ring art' the harlot's cheek, a form of representation, equally available to sovereign and regicide alike. This is an efficient demonstration, should one be required, of the way in which 'Offence's gilded hand may shove by justice' (III.iii.58) and constitutes an important part of a fundamentally theatrical deception that obscures the symbolic order that sovereign authority legitimates and sustains.

The play *Hamlet* makes very little drama out of Claudius's private predicament, choosing to offer us only brief glimpses of the theatrical 'doubleness' that underpins his 'performance'. But in the passage from *Hamlet* to *Macbeth* it gradually comes to assume a greater interest and a more complex form in Shakespeare's theatrical imagination.

Macbeth and Sovereign Power

Henry N. Paul's *The Royal Play of Macbeth* (1950) has long been accepted as the definitive account of the occasion of the play, but it rests on an invented conversation between Shakespeare and George Buc, the acting Master of the Revels, some time during early September 1605:

> He must have been at Oxford during the king's visit charged with some oversight of the plays; and it would have been quite in order for Buc to tell the dramatist of the King's Company that since the king did not seem to like the sorts of plays he had been shown at Oxford, it would be well for him to write a better play for his king, with suggestions as to subject matter, which sent him to the story of Macbeth as found in Holinshed.[22]

Paul concludes that it was Shakespeare's own awareness that 'King James was to see the play' that shaped his language and dramatic choices, for 'as the dramatist sat at his desk and wrote, he was conscious of the face of the king looking straight at him'.[23] Evidently, embedded in *Macbeth* is a critical view of 'sovereignty', although it is one that makes this a far less laudatory theatrical event than Paul would have us believe, and that – among other things – Shakespeare may well have had the unfinished business of *Hamlet* in mind as he wrote it.

Many of the features present in *Hamlet* recur in *Macbeth* to the extent that we might argue that the latter is the tragedy of *Hamlet* re-written from the perspective of an exemplary hero whose lawful ambition, transformed into unbridled desire, is turned against the sovereign power that nurtures it. But what has also changed between the two plays is tone. Claudius's machiavellian confidence that can assert that 'In the corrupted currents of this world/Offence's gilded hand may shove by justice' (III.iii.57–8) is radically transformed into the fear of a circular, but secular, justice, inscribed in the very 'bloody instructions' that comprise the actor's strategy:

> We still have judgement here; that we but teach
> Bloody instructions, which, being taught, return
> To plague th' inventor: this even-handed Justice
> Commends th' ingredience of our poison'd chalice
> To our own lips. (I.vii.8–12)

Power may succeed in *containing* the violence that it needs to sustain itself, but because it must expose its strategies, what it teaches – the 'bloody instruction' – returns to its origins both as an 'even-handed Justice' *and* as a 'poison' reminiscent of the Derridean figure of the *pharmakon*.[24] Power is desired, but the means necessary to attain and secure it, disclose and render open to imitation what Agamben calls 'the originary structure in which law refers to life and includes it in itself by suspending it'.[25] The inner structure of this very Shakespearean expression of the *pharmakon* compels Macbeth to traverse the space between the 'sovereign exception' and what Agamben calls 'the ban' that he later describes as 'the originary exclusion through which the political dimension was first constituted'.[26] What Macbeth brings together in this extraordinarily prescient utterance is the identity of the sovereign both as he who decides on the 'exception', which is 'the value or the non-value of life as such', *and* he who is placed 'on the threshold in which life and law, outside and inside become indistinguishable'.[27] The utterance is prescient precisely because

Macbeth's own sovereignty will be gradually eclipsed by the very status of 'bare' life, that is, life that is 'abandoned' and, in the play, ultimately reduced to animality: 'They have tied me to a stake: I cannot fly,/But bear-like, I must fight the course' (V.vii.1–2).

This is not unlike Claudius's fate, as he appeals to his court 'O yet defend me friends, I am but hurt' (V.ii.329), and the moment at which Macbeth is driven to the realization that 'that which should accompany old age,/As honour, love, obedience, troops of friends,/I must not look to have' (V.iii.24–6). But it is also an acknowledgement of both the 'violence' *and* the accompanying discourse of political power upon which both sovereign and regicide depend: Claudius pleads for his 'friends' to defend him, while Macbeth, in a more fulsome account, can only look forward to 'Curses, not loud, but deep, mouth-honour, breath,/ Which the poor heart would fain deny, and dare not' (V.iii.27–8). It also indicates a movement away from the 'divine providence' that Hamlet comes to realize steers human history and towards a 'Jacobean' perception of the secular tension between originary force and the unforeseen consequences of human action. It is this awareness of the deep structural connection between desire and political expediency that spurs Macbeth into further violations after he has become king: 'To be thus is nothing, but to be safely thus' (III.i.47). But it succeeds only at great cost in that both he and Lady Macbeth register the *feeling* that such insecurity generates: 'Nought's had, all's spent,/Where our desire is got without content: 'Tis safer to be that which we destroy,/Than by destruction dwell in doubtful joy' (III.ii.4–7). In short, what Macbeth and his Lady have done is turn 'sovereignty' – and the 'human' – inside out in such a way that its hitherto mystified structure is exposed, revealing the explicit configuration of the originary moment of a Renaissance bio-politics as it does so. It is this that enables us to cast a critical glance at Duncan's 'sovereignty' and the violence (as well as the social structures) that sustains it, and also at Malcolm's intended sovereignty, and particularly at that of the English king who, as Derridean *pharmakeus*, is endowed with magical powers but who may also be the bearer of 'poison'.

Macbeth and 'Bare Life'

Macbeth and the Lady delude themselves into thinking that the fruition of true 'desire' will be safety and contentment. Theirs is a copy, a simulacrum, a 'mimetic desire', that is as incomplete as it is intense and whose incompleteness is articulated as an 'excess' that always eludes their grasp. This logic of the supplement that is always to be found at the source (embodied in Malcolm, Banquo, Fleance and, finally, Macduff) infects the language of the play and is responsible for its 'equivocations', those excesses of meaning that masquerade as stable and singular 'truths'. Macbeth's actions invert the natural flow of 'time' itself, and liberation from the resulting tyranny can only be guaranteed by an external power – one that in reality has already historically united the thrones of Scotland and England. It is a force that is external to the play, and one that is deeply political despite the metaphysical claims made for it, that initiates the process of recuperating the regicide's mimetic violence and the slipperiness of language that it produces, for a sovereign power that itself, paradoxically, works through equivocation, thereby demystifying precisely what it sets out to rehabilitate. To align the rhetoric with the violence that binds the structure of sovereignty and the feeling of 'wonder' that it generates is to suggest that the institution is, at one level, nothing more than the sum of its material supports and that its bio-politics derive from an eradication of the distinction between 'violence' and 'law'. Following 'the most ancient recorded formulation' of 'the principle according to which sovereignty belongs to law', Agamben concludes that 'the sovereign is the point of indistinction between violence and the law, the threshold on which violence passes over into law and law passes over into violence'.[28]

For Agamben, the 'state of nature' (external) and the 'state of exception' (internal) are two sides of a topological coin. As he puts it,

> The state of exception is thus not so much a spatio-temporal suspension as a complex topological figure in which not

> only the exception and the rule but also the state of nature and law, outside and inside, pass through one another. It is precisely this topological zone of indistinction, which has to remain hidden from the eyes of justice, that we must try to fix under our gaze.[29]

He is, however, concerned primarily with investigating the modern forms that the category of 'bare life' assumes as a consequence of an unpicking of the limited juridical concept of sovereignty. But in certain crucial respects *Macbeth*, and earlier *Hamlet*, anticipate Agamben's enquiry, and it is precisely these plays' reconstitution of 'sovereignty' through repetition and hence the exposure of its inner structure that allows us to read them against the grain. It is the regicide's secular *challenge* to an unselfconsciously theologically authorized sovereignty that, whether inadvertently or not, exposes its constitutive elements to full view. Moreover, once exposed, the figure of the sovereign and the institution that sustains it can never be the same again. The adjustment of critical perspective that this necessitates diverts attention away from the tragic heroes of both plays and towards the monarchical 'victims', Old Hamlet and Duncan, both of whom sustain their respective authorities through a violence that masks a deeply embedded initiatory political gesture. Both Old Hamlet and Duncan *must* have been responsible for acts of violence at some stage in a now mythologized past that served to inaugurate their respective political positions and of which we, as audience, are afforded the most peremptory of glimpses.

The Logic of Sovereignty

Ostensibly Macbeth's transgression and its consequences constitute the central action of the play, although his regicide is itself symptomatic rather than originary. One of Shakespeare's main 'sources' for *Macbeth* was Holinshed's *Chronicles of Scotland*, in which Duncan is portrayed as a weak and ineffectual king who is reluctant to punish wrongdoers, it being left to Macbeth and

Banquo to compensate for the king's lenient treatment of rebels. In Shakespeare's play, however, Duncan is presented differently, even though some directors have chosen to follow the line that has its origins in Holinshed. There is some textual evidence from the play to support this portrayal in Macbeth's soliloquy at I.vii.16–20:

> Besides, this Duncan
> Hath borne his faculties so meek, hath been
> So clear in his great office, that his virtues
> Will plead like angels, trumpet-tongued, against
> The deep damnation of his taking off [...]

But this description does not quite square with the ruthless manner in which the sentencing of Cawdor is authorized. However, the portrayal of Duncan represents a much more condensed and apparently less militaristic version of features that Horatio attributes to Old Hamlet, while the phrase 'so clear in his great office' indicates a sovereign subject '*as he appears to himself from within*'.[30] What Macbeth fails to internalize, and what Banquo manages to retain, is 'a bosom franchis'd, and allegiance *clear*' (II.i.27–8; emphasis added), the complementary facets of the *divinity* of sovereign power that 'concentrates the virtues of a miraculous presence'.[31] It is this capacity to perform 'miracles', projected on to the 'English' king, that will be re-asserted as part of a larger machiavellian armoury at the end, but not before the content of its charisma has been exposed.

Shakespeare's revision of Holinshed's narrative is telling in this respect. Instead of accepting a narrative of permanent regicide that begins with the provocation leading to Macdonwald's murder of King Duff, he casts the Thane of Cawdor and then Macbeth as loyal subjects who begin by following the dictates of sovereign Law, but who fall from grace and are then designated as prospective *exceptions*. Cawdor never gets as far as Macbeth, perhaps because the latter is cultivated by Duncan as a counterbalancing force. But in the case of Macbeth, both the decision concerning the 'exception' and the 'state of exception' are combined in a spatio-temporal framework that passes from 'revolution' through the semblance of sovereignty and comes to rest in a 'bare life' as the life that can be killed with impunity. Macbeth, like Claudius, and like Cawdor before him, must be 'abandoned' before he can be killed.

At the outset it is Macbeth, 'Bellona's bridegroom, lapp'd in proof' (I.ii.55), whose active allegiance underwrites sovereign power. However, unlike in the case of Laertes's rebellion and Claudius's unwitting identification of himself with Cain, the play *Macbeth* emphasizes that the primal trauma through which the eponymous hero passes will reiterate Satan's rebellion that fallen humanity is destined to replicate. This serves to re-position the originary moment of the politics of sovereignty in the mystery of 'divine right'. In undertaking to 'represent' the figure of the king, both as vassal and then as substitute monarch, Macbeth simply imitates the violent sovereign process that lies at the origin of the order over which Duncan presides. Indeed, Duncan's is the sovereign violence that brings the Law into being *and* that maintains its efficacy, but in the secular world the king occupies a position on the threshold between an originary and constitutive violence and the 'life' whose exclusion the Law is called upon to mediate. It is this threshold position that gives to sovereignty a 'sacred' value. It incorporates a 'bare life' that can be killed but not sacrificed, in so far as the king's death can have no meaning as part of any ritual practice undertaken to reinforce social order. The metaphysical upheavals and the social chaos that accompany regicide are all part of the moral structure of prohibition that functions to obscure the material political content of sovereignty while at the same time insisting upon a legitimizing transcendental authority. The sovereign violence that initiates Law also engenders a *politics* that regulates competing interests with the specific objective of instituting, stabilizing and harmonizing of social life at the same time as it obscures its practices through an appeal to a metaphysical reality that permits the exercise of 'free will'. If, as the play indicates, Duncan makes the same mistake twice, then there is clearly something in the composition of the figure of the king that is a reminder of an endlessly recurring sovereign violence that in a post-lapsarian world is projected onto the human subject. In this respect, Macbeth functions as Duncan's alter ego, through his progression from supportive to regicidal violence.

Duncan fulfils precisely the function that Agamben asserts in his theoretical account of 'the logic of sovereignty' when he says that 'The exception does not only confirm the rule; the rule as such lives off the exception alone.'[32] It is that capacity to determine the complex dialectic of 'rule' and 'exception' – in other words, to socialize desire – that those who aspire to sovereign power covet. Agamben goes on to tease out the inexplicable paradox that resides at the heart of sovereign power in the observation that 'what is excluded in the exception maintains itself in relation to the rule in the form of the rule's suspension'.[33] He aims to rethink Ernst Kantorowicz's account of 'political theology' in *The King's Two Bodies* (1957), in which the permanence of the 'corpus mysticum' of the sovereign is shown to compensate for the mutability of his physical body, but in which 'politics' is downplayed in favour of 'theology'.[34] But in a recognizably Derridean move, he also seeks to counter the structuralist claim, and that of Carl Schmitt, that the state of exception is 'the chaos that precedes order', arguing, rather, that the position of the sovereign is '*taken outside* (*ex-capere*), and not simply excluded'.[35] His concern is to map the metaphysical process whereby the originary violence that inaugurates 'the political dimension' of sovereignty collapses the distinction between the realms of the 'religious' and the 'profane'. He argues that what he calls 'the sphere of sovereign decision' is one in which the Law is suspended 'in the state of exception' so that it 'implicates bare life within it'.[36] By 'bare life' Agamben means 'life' outside and prior to all of those politically motivated ritual practices, and institutions that give it meaning. He puts the matter in this way:

> The political sphere of sovereignty was thus constituted through a double exclusion, as an excrescence of the profane in the religious and of the religious in the profane, which

> takes the form of a zone of indistinction between sacrifice and homicide. *The sovereign sphere is the sphere in which it is permitted to kill without committing homicide and without celebrating a sacrifice, and sacred life—that is, life that may be killed but not sacrificed—is the life that has been captured in this sphere.*[37]

This is a difficult point, but it explains the distinction in the play between the 'lawful ambition' that the sovereign authorizes and legitimates and which inhabits the political institutions it brings into existence, and unlawful or proscribed ambition (transgressive desire) that imitates the originary act of sovereign violence but which cannot be wholly divorced from it. This explanation helps to position Duncan – and, indeed, the figure of the sovereign generally – on the threshold, as Agamben would say, between the 'inside' and the 'outside', thus making 'the validity of the juridical order possible'.[38] Macbeth's 'Vaulting ambition' (I.vii.27) that is compelled to 'o'erleap' (I.iv.49) any obstacle that is placed in his way is encouraged by Duncan to the point where it challenges the authorized limits of sovereign law. Macbeth recognizes, however, that in placing himself beyond *the* limit, beyond *all ethical* limits, his ambition only 'o'erleaps itself/And falls on th' other' (I.vii.27–8). In this instance, 'th' other' is 'bare life' cut adrift from the structures that incorporate and seek to control it. Whereas Duncan's sovereign power already embodies both the 'norm' and the 'exception', Macbeth's repetition of Cawdor's treachery is a starkly reductive imitation of what is, in reality, the inexplicable paradox that resides at the heart of the institution of sovereignty itself. It is for this reason that under the guise of sovereign power he commits acts that are unlawful and which, in general, challenge the basis upon which 'the juridical order, and what is excluded from it, acquire their meaning'.[39] It is also why none of the social rituals that he enacts once he becomes king have any authoritative or restorative meaning. The mimetic energy of the regicide is here seen confronting its nemesis, producing a fracturing of the self that undoes the political logic of the sovereign power that Duncan represents in its most obscured form.

Duncan's confidence in the originary violence that inaugurates and sustains sovereign power allows him to remain detached from Cawdor's treachery to the point where he can generalize confidently upon human behaviour and upon the paradox of representation:

> There's no art
> To find the mind's construction in the face:
> He was a gentleman on whom I built
> An absolute trust – (I.iv.11–14)

In a play in which, as in *Hamlet*, meaning is radically unstable from the outset, Duncan's legislative aphorism is open to two mutually opposed interpretations: (a) that the human mind is un-representable or (b) that no *art* is necessary to represent the mind, since its machinations are 'naturally' and transparently figured in the face.

This doubleness finds a surprising but profound gloss in Malcolm's exchange with Macduff at IV.iii in that it treats precisely of the discrepancy present in the play between thought and deed, motive and action, origin and representation. Malcolm observes aphoristically that 'A good and virtuous nature may recoil/In an imperial charge' (IV.iii.18–20), but there is something deeply paradoxical about this formulation: power may corrupt, but in a post-lapsarian world 'good' cannot easily be distinguished from the 'evil' that seeks to imitate it, and moreover, it is defenceless: 'Angels are bright still, though the brightest fell:/All things foul would wear the brows of grace,/Yet Grace must still look so' (IV.iii.22–4). In this important scene, sometimes savagely cut in performance, Malcolm incorporates into himself all that sovereign power necessarily *excludes* or 'abandons' as ethically unacceptable, but that is symbolically central to its operation. He would 'cut off the nobles for their lands;/Desire his jewels, and this other's house' (IV.iii.79–80) – in short, indulge an 'avarice' that is without limit and that involves an outright rejection of all 'the king-becoming graces':

> As Justice, Verity, Temp'rance, Stableness,
> Bounty, Perseverance, Mercy, lowliness,
> Devotion, Patience, Courage, Fortitude,
> I have no relish of them; but abound
> In the division of each several crime,
> Acting in many ways. Nay, had I power, I should
> Pour the sweet milk of concord into Hell,
> Uproar the universal peace, confound
> All unity on earth. (IV.iii.92–100)

Of course, it is Macbeth who has already used his 'power' to 'pour the sweet milk of concord into Hell', and the linked imagery is not accidental, but Malcolm's description of 'bare life' through whose aegis he formulates sovereign power negatively serves to consolidate its place on the *threshold* where the constitutive process of inclusion and exclusion operates: the space, in short, where politics begins. Agamben describes precisely this situation as follows:

> The 'sovereign' structure of the law, its peculiar and original 'force' has the form of a state of exception in which fact and law are indistinguishable (yet must, nevertheless, be decided on). Life which is thus obliged, can in the last instance be implicated in the sphere of law only through the supposition of its inclusive exclusion, only in an *exceptio*. There is a limit-figure of life, a threshold in which life is both inside and outside the juridical order, and this threshold is the place of sovereignty.[40]

In this scene Malcolm demonstrates precisely why he is Duncan's legitimate heir, in that he has learnt from his father's errors of self-presentation.

Violence and its Discontents

The central concern of *Macbeth* is rebellion, cast in archetypal terms, but geographically located in the margins of the realm – Scotland. The play's immediate historical background was the Catholic terrorist conspiracy to assassinate the king and his parliament on 5 November 1605. Two years earlier, James I's accession to the throne had united England and Scotland and the Gunpowder Plot had sought to undermine that unity. But, of course, evidence of disunity and disorder is present from the beginning, *well before* Duncan's murder. Indeed, these forces constitute the very condition of marginality in the play, embodying a propensity for dissolution that provokes a counter-violence, the force through which sovereign power establishes itself, and part of that dialectic of inclusion–exclusion that resides in this play at the heart of 'Nature'.

In his essay 'Critique of Violence', Walter Benjamin noted 'a dialectical rising and falling in the law-making and law-preserving formation of violence' before going on to argue that:

> The law governing their oscillation rests on the circumstance that all law-preserving violence, in its duration, indirectly weakens the law-making violence represented by it, through the suppression of hostile counter-violence [...] This lasts until either new forces or those earlier suppressed triumph over the hitherto lawmaking violence and thus found a new law, destined in its turn to decay.[41]

This is a perception that Macduff's young son grasps briefly just before he is murdered. Benjamin opposes as 'pernicious' 'all mythical law-making violence, which we may call executive' and 'the law-preserving administrative violence that serves it', but he insists that 'Divine violence, which is the sign and seal but never the means of sacred execution, may be called sovereign violence'.[42] This helps us to understand the various forms of violence that appear in *Macbeth*: 'sovereign' violence represented by Duncan;

the violence of resistance encouraged by the Weird Sisters and furthered by Macbeth; and the sovereign 'counter-violence' that, in process, reveals the precarious basis of its own authority.

Just as *Hamlet* brings the motif of 'madness' into the orbit of the feminine, so *Macbeth* locates the subversive force of 'equivocation' in the sphere of the 'feminine', and it is the Lady (Macbeth) who augments the activities of the Weird Sisters. Macbeth himself echoes the grammatical formulations of the Weird Sisters even before he has met them: 'So foul and fair a day I have not seen' (I.iii.38), but at the end of the play he comes to realize the linguistic duplicity that they embody: 'And be these juggling fiends no more believed,/That palter with us in a double sense;/That keep the word of promise to our ear,/And break it to our hope' (V.viii.19–22).

The Weird Sisters represent linguistically and visually what happens when sovereign power, which authorizes representation and prescribes and legitimizes meaning, is laid bare: they invert reality, but in doing so they expose the mystery of patriarchal power for the ideological fraud that it is. In addition to making the Weird Sisters the heroines of the play, Terry Eagleton has claimed that 'the witches figure as the "unconscious" of the drama, that which must be exiled and repressed as dangerous but which is always likely to return with a vengeance'.[43] He goes on to argue that 'The unconscious is a discourse in which meaning falters and slides, in which firm definitions are dissolved and binary oppositions eroded: fair is foul and foul is fair, nothing is but what is not.'[44]

This is partly true, but the Freudian account of 'repression' is not at issue in the play, or at least, not in any straightforward sense. For example, while criticism has always focused upon the violence that Macbeth engages in – killing the king, then Banquo, and then engineering the murdering of Lady Macduff and her children – little is made of the violence that is endemic in Duncan's own rule. Duncan fertilizes his kingdom, the garden he tends, with human blood. He 'plants' Macbeth 'and will labour/ To make [him] full of growing' (I.iv.28–9). He implies the same for Banquo, although here the rewards are less tangible: 'Noble Banquo,/That hast no less deserv'd, nor must be known/No less to have done so' (I.iv.28–31). The king is 'indebted' to his vassals in that his regal obligations in rewarding them are a condition of his being included in a relation from which he is, as sovereign, excluded. As the origin of Law he is excluded from its quotidian operations, an issue that had perplexed state theorists for over half a century, and to which Marlowe had, in part, addressed his play *Edward II*. Agamben notes the sense of 'being-in-debt' as an originary sense of the term 'guilt', a form of recompense for the act of violence that inaugurates sovereignty. But the play *Macbeth* also explores two other crucial meanings of 'guilt' that both position the hero while at the same time testifying to a growing inability of sovereign power to legislate meaning. 'Guilt' is the term used to distinguish between the licit and the illicit, that the subject of power internalizes as the operation of 'conscience', a mechanism for regulating behaviour. The homophone 'gilt', on the other hand, richly theatrical in its suggestiveness, transforms obligation into a market transaction in which self-esteem and the ethics that sustain it can be bought like a theatrical costume, thus allowing Macbeth to buy 'golden opinions from all sorts of people,/Which would be worn now in their newest gloss,/Not cast aside so soon' (I.vii.33–5). This leads to the Lady's cynical manipulation of all these meanings in a reference to Duncan's 'golden' blood, a gesture that undermines radically the originary language of sovereign power: 'If he do bleed/I'll gild the faces of the grooms withal,/For it must seem their guilt' (II.ii.55–6). This is not 'repression' in the Freudian sense of the term so much as semantic plenitude, a plenitude that undermines hierarchies of meaning and the very process of representation itself.

Macbeth's consciousness is too full and too inclusive to allow us to talk about 'repression'. It is true that 'The Golden round' which the Lady thinks that 'fate and metaphysical aid doth seem/To have thee crown'd withal' (I.v.28–30) requires an act that Macbeth is reluctant to perform, because it carries with it a high moral price: 'guilt'. It is also true that she is willing to suppress her matriarchal feelings as a means of encouraging her husband, just as Macbeth himself must forget the etiquette surrounding Duncan's rewards for his loyalty. Indeed, in this play the dramatic characters appear to have no (Freudian) unconscious, and Macbeth's 'way of life […] fall'n into the sere, the yellow leaf' (V.iii.22–3) and the 'Tomorrow and tomorrow' speech (V.v.19 ff.) indicate a knowing, if retrospectively realized, collapse into 'bare life'. However, as auditors we recognize these variations in meaning as parapraxes or 'slips of the tongue'. They inaugurate a logic in which initial success leads to disaster for Macbeth and the Lady and ultimately to a restitution of the very political order that regicide has temporarily inverted, although, as we have seen, not before exposing the vulnerability of the ideological materials that shape that order. Eagleton's point is that it is the 'text' and not the characters that has an 'unconscious' – but is he right? What we need, perhaps, is a more historical (maybe even less rational) understanding of the 'unconscious' that the play sketches out.

In the early part of the play it is the Lady who usurps the masculine active role, although if we look a little more closely at it, we realize that it is a reduced masculinity – an inhumanity, even – that she encourages. Her invocation to those 'Spirits/That tend on mortal thoughts' to 'unsex me here,/And fill me, from the crown to the toe, top-full/Of direct cruelty!' (I.v.40–3) is a plea to evade 'guilt' itself by stopping up 'the access and passage to remorse' (I.v.44). It is also a plea to keep 'the compunctious visitings of Nature' (I.v.45) at bay, where 'compunctious' (a word that for Shakespeare is unique to the text of *Macbeth*) is a quality of Nature itself and refers to 'the pricking or stinging of the conscience or heart […] consequent upon sin or wrongdoing'.[45] It is precisely this debate that Macbeth conducts with himself from his first soliloquy at I.iii onwards. The moral and ethical implications that Lady Macbeth seeks to *suppress* (rather than repress) are precisely elements of 'that suggestion/Whose horrid image doth unfix my hair,/And make my seated heart knock at my ribs,/Against the use of nature' (I.iii.134–7) that Macbeth feels once he considers submitting himself to the logic of events inaugurated by the Weird Sisters' prophecy. The horrid image whose suggestion he contemplates unfixes much more than his hair. In precisely the same way that meanings of words like 'guilt' are unfixed, so Macbeth seeks to deny the inexorable logic that 'assassination' calls into being: 'if th' assassination/ Could trammel up the consequence, and catch/With his *surcease success*' (I.vii.2–4). 'Surcease' refers here to the act of 'desisting': it means both 'ceasing from some action' (*OED* 1a) and 'to come to an end, or to discontinue' (*OED* 3a), but it is also 'to give up or resign a position of office' (*OED* 3†b). The impersonal nature of Macbeth's language here serves to align the act of regicide with a voluntary resignation of power that will absolve him from guilt and elides two semantically opposed words that are imperfectly homophonic. As the play progresses, these 'equivocations' (or disturbances of linguistic hierarchy) multiply, and in the final stages the action turns upon how these linguistic signs are interpreted.

Sovereignty and Nature

It is clear that Macbeth and the Lady regard Nature as an enemy. It is part of the play's ideology that Nature *naturalizes* sovereign power, but sovereign power, as we saw earlier, places the king in a precarious position since he is both *inside* and *outside* the order of Law: the source of the originary act of violence that brings Law into being and is above the Law, but that incorporates into its sphere 'bare life'.[46] We can see what happens when a figure like Hamlet is forced to confront this threshold position; he begins to question the nature of 'being' itself. We can also see what happens when, in *King Lear*, the sovereign exception is stripped of all that makes him different from the 'life' over which he exerts power: Lear confronts the 'bare life' in himself. It is the secret of sovereign power that Macbeth glimpses in a much starker form as his actions systematically sever his ties with 'Nature', to the point where he declines into a 'player' king and finally an 'idiot' whose tale 'full of sound and fury' signifies *nothing*. His is the 'bare life' against which a hierarchical Nature concentrates its powers, reducing the figure of 'the player king' to 'a poor player,/ That struts and frets his hour upon the stage' (V.v.24–25), one that signifies 'nothing', and thence into a baited ('bear'/'bare') animal.

This suggests that there is something peculiar about 'the nature of Nature' in the play. Elsewhere in Shakespeare, the forces that seek to undermine order are usually potentially anarchic (possibly libidinal and almost certainly chaotic) energies. In *Hamlet*, Claudius's lust for power is perceived by Hamlet to involve a reprehensibly demonic sexual energy that comes to be focused on his mother and on Ophelia; in *Othello*, the figure of the 'Moor' that Shakespeare had begun to experiment with in a minor way in *The Merchant of Venice* becomes the site of competing forces in which a series of masculine Venetian values require to be defended against a barbaric 'otherness'. In *Macbeth*, the agency of subversion is the Weird Sisters, whose initial evaluation comes from Banquo, while Macbeth is too caught up in musing on the future that they map out for him. For Banquo, they appear to melt into Nature: 'The earth hath bubbles, as the water has,/And these are of them' (I.iii.79–80), and Macbeth notes that 'what seem'd corporal,/Melted as breath into the wind' (I.iii.81–2). But they also lead Banquo to question their corporeal reality, through the deployment of a metaphor that draws attention to Nature's capacity to pervert nourishment and subvert 'reason': 'Were such things here, as we do speak about,/Or have we eaten on the insane root,/That takes the reason prisoner?' (I.iii.83–5). Perhaps another way of putting this is to say that the linguistic stability that the sovereign process of naming initiates is a means of ordering and socializing the existence of particular situations.[47] It is significant that the Weird Sisters, like Macbeth himself later in the play, either cannot, or will not, name what they do. The 'truth' of monarchy that Macbeth is encouraged to replicate in such a way that his rule becomes a 'simulacrum', a theatrical representation of an institution, is shown to be dependent upon (or at least intertwined with) a demonic force that they embody.

And it is Banquo who sees this: 'And oftentimes, to win us to our harm,/The instruments of Darkness tell us truths;/Win us with honest trifles, to betray's/In deepest consequence' (I.iii.123–6). It is Banquo who acknowledges the evil that is secreted at the very heart of 'truth' itself and that Alain Badiou identifies in another context as 'that Evil which it recognises as the underside, or dark side, of these very truths'.[48]

Indeed, the play's antithetical logic shapes Nature as the space where opposed forces compete openly for supremacy to the point that we might say that, of all Shakespeare's plays, *Macbeth* is unusually 'conscious' of its own 'unconscious'. In a play where all that nourishes life can easily be transformed into its opposite, Banquo registers the effects of the resulting conflict, though he arrives at conclusions diametrically opposed to those of Macbeth. At the beginning of Act II, at Inverness castle, he feels the urge to sleep but cannot:

> Hold, *take my Sword*:
> There's Husbandry in Heauen,
> Their Candles are all out: take thee that too.
> A heauie Summons lyes like Lead vpon me,
> And yet I would not sleepe:
> *Mercifull Powers*, restraine in me the cursed thoughts
> That *Nature* giues way to in repose.
>
> *Enter Macbeth, and a Seruant with a Torch.*
>
> *Giue me my Sword*: who's there?[49]

The Folio lineation prompts a series of questions. Is Banquo saying that it is 'human nature' i.e. his 'nature' that yields to 'cursed thoughts' once he is asleep? Or is he saying that on those occasions when 'Nature' suspends its task of ordering 'reality', then its dark side, the 'cursed thoughts', rise to the surface? The Folio lineation, metrically imperfect though it appears to be, is poetically and dramatically very powerful in directing our attention. As Banquo relaxes, giving up his sword, so the embodiment of those 'cursed thoughts' (in the representational guise of Duncan's vassal) enters. We know that Macbeth has already begun to 'yield to that suggestion/Whose horrid image doth unfix my hair,/ And make my seated heart knock at my ribs,/Against the use of nature?' (I.iii.134–7). This involves a rebellion of the physical 'body', a perversion of its use that the sovereign power of Nature has authorized. The 'event' that generates this mental anguish – the meeting with the Weird Sisters – produces opposite reactions in Banquo and Macbeth. What for both are 'cursed thoughts' obscures what for Macbeth is a 'political sequence': if he leaves matters to 'chance' then he deprives himself of the power to effect his desire, but if he acts then he replicates but only at the level of a *simulacrum*, the originary violence that constitutes sovereignty. These are the 'cursed thoughts' – the descent into a secular politics that would separate sovereignty from the mystery of its own origins – that Banquo fears when the ordering power that he ascribes to Nature relaxes her control.

Much later in the play we will see the obverse of the situation that Banquo here experiences and describes when the sleep-walking Lady will be unable to eliminate from her dreams (as she manages to do effectively from her waking life) the regulating mechanism of 'conscience' and the force of the 'human' that she has hitherto suppressed. In a world where the pursuit of secular political goals has become the norm, the 'good' in Nature disrupts its own regenerative mechanism, sleep, to take on the role of a subversive 'other' that resists control. 'Fair is foul and foul is fair' indeed. In the intoxicated Hell of Macbeth's castle, where the drunken Porter stands as gatekeeper, there develops a gulf between 'desire' and 'performance'. In the impeccable comic logic of the Porter, alcohol is in relation to sexual performance what criminal accomplishment, and the mimetic strategies it deploys, is to the transgressive mechanisms of desire.

The disturbance that brings to the surface the negative force of 'nature' signals the decline of sovereignty into the nightmarish realm of a Darwinist secular politics of what Fulke Greville called 'flesh and blood'.[50] In the poem 'A Treatise on Monarchy' that may have been written around 1600 but that was not published until the late seventeenth century,[51] Greville distinguished between practice and principle:

> 33
> But in the world as thrones now mowlded are
> By chance, choice, practise, birth, or martiall awe;
> Where lawes and custom do prescribe how farr
> Either the Kinge or subject ought to drawe
> These mutuall tyes of dutie, love or feare
> To such a straine, as every man may beare.
>
> 34
> Which place what is it, but of reverence,
> A throne rais'd on mans reason, and affection;
> Where that well mixt and happy confluence
> Of earthly and celestiall reflection
> Should weave the publique, in the private good,
> And to protect both, governe flesh and blood.[52]

This is precisely the dilemma of early modern sovereignty that *Macbeth* stages: if there is no 'divinity' that can protect the sovereign from regicide, and if 'conscience' cannot be relied upon to regulate the behaviour of subjects, in what does sovereign authority and its hierarchical system of representations reside? The resulting descent into violence isolates 'power' from those ethical and moral imperatives 'That lymitt the excesses of a Crowne'[53] so that 'Whence neither makers now, nor members held/Men are; but blankes where pow'r doth write her lust'.[54] However, if sovereignty can be rendered vulnerable, imitated, deprived of its mystery, subject to the unrestrained exercise of 'power', reduced to 'process' and to theatrical performance, what is there that can prevent it from declining into tyranny, or from being overthrown?

There is no way of knowing if Shakespeare was familiar with Fulke Greville's *Treatise*, but he appears certainly to have been familiar with many of its sentiments. He was, on the other hand, almost certainly familiar with Timothy Bright's *A Treatise of Melancholie* (1586), a book that Shakespeare was thought to have consulted in relation to *Hamlet*, where dreams comprise a dialectic that is later echoed in part in Greville's poem. What for Greville are dreams of transgression are in Bright's *Treatise* 'sensible actions of the minde' that recall a pre-lapsarian existence, and that cannot be regarded as 'false' even though they span the gulf between daily practice and the memory of paradise; these are two sides of the same coin. The mind, Bright argues,

> seeth in dreames things past as present: for so it doth also future things sometimes: which rather may argue, that both past, and to come are both present vnto the mind, of such things as fall into the capacitie of her consideration. If anie man thinke it much to aduance the mind so high, let him remember from whom it proceeded, & the maner howe it was created, and the most excellent estate thereof before the fall, and no doubt it will sufficiently aunswer that difficultie, and confirme that which I haue said.[55]

Macbeth's tragedy lies in a conflict that folds a politically realized fantasy of power into the struggle between pre-lapsarian order and post-lapsarian desire. Banquo's 'cursed thoughts' are the excesses, reversions to undifferentiated similitude that a waking political existence regiments and contains. Macbeth's *actions* reject the controlling imperatives of Nature and catapult him into a world of nightmare in which human desire that is the dark side of a sovereign politics is doomed never to be satisfied. In the play, politics, like 'history', inaugurate the desire of the desiring subject. This suggests a different account of the play from that offered by H. N. Paul when, during his discussion of the *Basilicon Doron* of James I, he suggests that Shakespeare 'shows us in his royal play a good and kindly king cut off by the treason of an unnatural subject'.[56] What Paul overlooks is an issue that the play fudges: the origins of the prophecies of Macbeth's success. In *Basilicon Doron* James asserted that 'Prophecie proceedeth onelie from GOD: and the Devill hath no knowledge of things to come', but he then goes on:

> And that the Diuel is permitted at som-times to put himself in the liknes of the Saintes, it is plaine in the Scriptures, where it is said, that *Sathan can trans-forme himselfe into an Angell of Light*. Neither could that bring any inconvenient with it to the visiones of the Prophets, since it is most certaine, that God will not permit him to deceiue his own: but only such, as first wilfully deceiues them-selues, by running vnto him, whome God then suffers to fall in their owne snares, and justly permittes them to be illuded with great efficacy of deceit, because they would not beleeue the trueth (*as Paul* sayeth).[57]

In this passage James projects on to 'God' the determination of the 'exception', but in Shakespeare's play it is Duncan who inadvertently confirms the Weird Sisters' prophecy, and by doing so 'traces' and 'renews' what Agamben describes as a 'threshold of indistinction between outside and inside, inclusion and exclusion, *nomos* and *physis*, in which life is originarily excepted in law'.[58] We can now see why Shakespeare should have discarded Holinshed's account of Macbeth's successful years as ruler. To have followed this narrative strand would have been to capitulate to a pragmatic politics in which the yardstick of practical efficiency could be used as the sole measure of sovereign authority and legitimacy. The Anglo-Scottish royal presence that hovers just outside the boundaries of the play, and that would appear to sanction the recuperation of the 'equivocations' of the Weird Sisters for a benign but mysterious, if not magical, sovereignty, cannot quite contain those excesses – of language, of political action, of desire – that Nature itself periodically releases into human society and of whose warring forces he is, himself, the regal embodiment. Indeed, what the play invites us to observe is the returning of a disputed ground of politics to Nature, and once the mechanics of that ideological operation are laid open for display – as on a stage – then what they lose is their mystery and mystique.

CHAPTER TWO

Rooting for *Macbeth*: Parable Ethics in Scotland

Adrian Streete

In II.vi of *The Two Gentlemen of Verona* (c.1590–93) two servants, Speed and Lance, meet in the street. Speed asks Lance to the pub and tries to find out whether his master, Proteus, is still engaged to Julia. Lance refuses to answer Speed directly, inviting him instead to 'Ask my dog'. He then says, 'Thou shalt never get such a secret from me but by a parable' (II.v.30–4).[1] The obvious, physical humour of this exchange is, of course, caused by the participation in the scene of the dog, Crab, and also because Lance comically ascribes to the animal the temporary status of interlocutor and possessor of the knowledge desired by Speed. However, there is another kind of humorous resonance embedded verbally within the latter line, one that generates a less obvious and rather more subversive comedic effect. The key term here is 'parable', interestingly the only time in Shakespeare's works where he uses this word. Lance's line draws upon those chapters in the gospels of Matthew, Mark and Luke when the significance of Christ teaching by parables is explained.[2] As Matthew says,

> All these things spake Iesus vnto the multitude in parables, and without parables spake he not vnto them. That it might be fulfilled, which was spoken by the Prophet, saying, I will open my mouth in parables, and wil vtter the things which haue bene kept secret from the foundation of the world. (13:34–5)[3]

Two things are worth noting here. Firstly, by stating that he will only reveal his secrets in a parable, Lance briefly yet daringly assumes the mantle both of the Prophet and of Christ. His appropriation of parabolic biblical language allows him to tread an audacious line between comedy and blasphemy. By jokingly giving a mere servant access to the 'things which haue bene kept secret from the foundation of the world', biblical authority is at once affirmed and undermined.[4] Secondly, Lance's words, and the biblical verse from which they are taken, suggest that a division exists between those for whom parables are necessary ('the multitude') and another audience for whom the 'secret' is revealed more directly. The implication that someone of Lance's lowly class may be the keeper of such prophetically inspired secrets, and that Speed may not, is central to the comedic construction of this scene. The consequences of this division are made more explicit in the Gospel of Luke. Here, the disciples demand that Christ explain to them directly the parable that he has just told. He replies, 'Vnto you it is giuen to knowe the secrets of God, but to other[s] in parables, that when they see, they should not see, and when they heare, they should not vnderstand' (Luke 8.10). This piece of exegesis comes after Christ has told the Parable of the Sower.[5] In this story, some of the sower's seed is destroyed, eaten, withered, choked by thorns, or fails to take root in bad ground; the rest of the seed falls 'on good ground' and bears fruit (Luke 8. 5–8). Christ compares the seed to the 'word of God' and the seed that flourishes to those for whom 'nothing is secret': the seed that fails to grow is, by contrast, likened to those who 'haue no rootes'. Such people may 'for a while beleeue, but in the time of tentation [*sic*] goe away' (Luke 8.11–17). The 'secrets of God' will only ever be fully revealed to God's chosen. The divisive message of the parable is much more starkly expressed here than in Matthew's Gospel, a point that I will return to later.

Lance never does reveal his 'secret' directly to Speed. Instead, he turns the original invitation on its head, getting Speed to reveal indiscreetly that his master is a 'hot lover' (II.v.42) and then asking the other servant to go with him 'to the alehouse'. If he does not, says Lance, then 'thou art an Hebrew, a Jew, and not worth the name of a Christian' (II.v.44–5). By agreeing to go away to the pub, Speed assumes that he can avoid being condemned with the Hebrews and the Jews, thus reclaiming his status as a Christian. But the scene slyly reinstates the logic of the Parable of the Sower: by being 'tempted' into this series of small indiscretions, Speed is in fact associated with the 'voluptuous liuing' (Luke 8.14) of which the gospel parable warns. Lance keeps his 'secret' and Speed is marked as a doltish figure, one whose faith is, like his credulity, merely temporary.

Christ's gospel parables have attracted the attention of biblical interpreters, preachers and moralists since the beginning of the Christian era, and early modern England was no exception. Nevertheless, under the influence of Reformed theology, the parables were read in new and important ways. In this chapter, I want to examine the use of some of the gospel parables in *Macbeth*, focusing in particular on the Parable of the Sower, a story that assumes a particular significance in late sixteenth- and early seventeenth-century England. Unlike the passing reference in *The Two Gentlemen of Verona* with which I began this chapter, I will argue that the parables play a much more significant and extended role in *Macbeth* (1606) at both a linguistic and a thematic level. Language and imagery from these stories weave their way throughout the narrative in a number of intriguing ways. Important metaphors of seed, planting, roots, cultivation, growing, ground, secrecy, luxury, withering, time and death found in the play can all be connected to the Parable of the Sower, as well as to the Parable of the Reaper, the Parable of the Wheat and the Tares and the Parable of the Pearl of Great Price.[6]

However, I also want to suggest that the use of such imagery cannot simply be related, as G. Wilson Knight famously put it, to an expression of the 'ethical standards of the Gospels'.[7] Knight's guiding assumption is that the Bible offers Shakespeare a set of fixed ethical values which he then transplants into his plays and uses to interrogate various characters. Certainly at times the playwright will hold figures to moral account through the use of Scripture: Antonio and Shylock in *The Merchant of Venice* or Angelo and Isabella in *Measure for Measure* are two well-known examples. But more often than not, as more recent scholarship has argued, Shakespeare's primary use of biblical texts and his exploration of their various ethical possibilities is rather more sceptical, questioning and flexible. Indeed, as Stephen Marx has argued, Shakespeare's method of using the Bible can itself be termed a type of midrash: 'a technique of interpretation that expands and elaborates the biblical narrative. [...] Midrash unfolds symbolic meanings latent in the scriptural texts with analytical techniques [...] it generates new stories, dense revisions of the original, and more symbolic expressions that warrant further explication.'[8] Shakespeare does not simply 'apply' the Bible to his plays: rather, his plays are a space where the Bible and biblical ethics are actively interrogated. Such a reading/interpretative practice also allows him to consider the various theological implications of the parables. He is especially interested, as is suggested in *The Two Gentlemen of Verona*, in the potentially divisive nature of these gospel parables. Do all have access to God's 'secrets', for example, or are some excluded? As we will see, this question assumes a particular importance in *Macbeth*. By looking at the ways in which the gospel parables were understood in early modern England, we can explore the ways in which Shakespeare comments upon, amplifies, manipulates and at times challenges the dominant ethical and theological readings of these stories, a process that also feeds into the linguistic breadth and imaginative complexity of the play itself.

Sowing, Reaping and Cultivating

In addition to being the prime source of all religious doctrine for early modern Christians, the Bible offered an incomparably rich store of imagery and metaphor for writers. In a pre-industrial society where the division between city and country was not as marked as it commonly is today it is perhaps not surprising that biblical imagery drawn from the natural world was of particular interest.[9] There were a number of early modern texts dedicated to explicating just such imagery, such as *An Herbal for the Bible* by the well-known Dutch physician Levinus Lemnius published in an English translation in 1587. Drawing on the Parable of the Wheat and the Tares in Matthew 13, Lemnius promises the reader that:

> Neither is it possible for a man to reape anie the like benefit of plentiful knowledge and copious learning, nor to taste such foison of soueraigne foode both for soule and conscience, out of anie Works written by Philosophers, Orators, and Poets, as hee may out of the most plentifull storehouse, and aye lasting fountaine of Diuinitie.[10]

As this quotation shows, the Bible was a 'storehouse' unlike any other: the Reformed doctrine of *sola scriptura* meant that, even in a society where literacy levels were low, most individuals could be expected to have a decent working knowledge of Scripture from hearing it read and explicated at church, both in the Book of Common Prayer and during sermons. This meant in turn that playwrights could expect most of their audience to pick up biblical references in plays: stories or quotations from more recondite classical or historical sources were likely to have been recognized by a much smaller section of the audience.[11]

Natural imagery drawn from the Bible was of particular interest to early modern commentators. The first chapter of Lemnius's book begins by informing the reader:

> That noble Kings and renowned Princes in the old time (euen otherwise most busily encombred with garboils of wars) haue beene studiously addicted and singularly delighted in the serch [sic] and knowledge of the nature of plantes and herbes.[12]

It is interesting that Lemnius should insist that the study of nature is a properly monarchical pursuit, even in the midst of war. We may be reminded of Duncan's greetings to Macbeth and Banquo when they meet in Forres after the battle with Norway. To the former he says 'I have begun to plant thee, and will labour/

To make thee full of growing' (I.iv.28–9).[13] The horticultural language used here positions Duncan as a cultivator of nature, a posture that befits the patriarchal status of the monarch as the source of patronage and power. Similar to the Parable of the Sower and the Labourer in the Vineyard, he is one who plants his seeds in the hope that they will flourish.

Yet as we also know from these parables, the chances of this cultivation occurring well are decidedly mixed. Nature, biological and human, cannot be so easily co-opted. Consider the Captain's ominous words when he compares the 'Doubtfull' progress of the battle to 'two spent swimmers, that do cling together/And choke their art' (I.ii.7–9). As in Gertrude's invocation of the drowning Ophelia in *Hamlet* (IV.viii), Shakespeare implies not only that the drowning swimmers are choking on water; he likens them to clinging weeds that choke the life out of the flowering seed, in this case each other. As Matthew 13:22 warns: 'he that receiueth the seed among thornes, is hee that heareth the word: but the care of this world, and the deceitfulnesse of riches choke the word, and he is made vnfruitfull'. The potential malignity of nature is never far from the surface in *Macbeth*, always threatening to choke or drown at will: we might recall here Macbeth's invocation of 'Pity' and 'heaven's Cherubins' who 'Shall blow the horrid deed in every eye,/ That tears shall drown the wind' (I.vii.21–5). Invariably, this is a malignity that reflects human depravity. Significantly, when Lennox assents to 'purge' Scotland of Macbeth in V.ii, he brings imagery of weeds and drowning together, saying that it will be 'so much as it needs/To dew the sovereign flower, and drown the weeds' (V.ii.28–30). Only by spraying the weeds can Scotland's 'sovereign flower' be saved. Indeed, Lemnius relates weeds in the gospel parables to those who promote corrupt doctrine

> through the instigation of sathan with their pestilent gloses and suttle expositions, infect and poyson the mindes and consciences of men, and corrupt the pure word of the Gospel, by obtruding of falsehoode in steed of truth, and doting dreames in place of sincere doctrine.[14]

As a devilish figure (see IV.iii.52–60) associated with infection (see I.vii.10; V.ii.69) and bad dreams (see III.ii.22), Macbeth's crimes take on an intriguingly theological aspect.

When the king promises to 'infold' (I.iv.31)[15] Banquo in his heart, he replies in kind: 'There if I grow,/The harvest is your own' (I.iv.33). This comment interestingly echoes Banquo's earlier question to the witches on the heath: 'If you can look into the seeds of time,/And say which grain will grow, and which will not,/Speak' (I.iii.58–60). The various political futures faced by Scotland are compared throughout the play to the imminent growth of seeds.[16] Yet this is an inherently unstable comparison. At times, Macbeth dizzyingly evokes a natural world not governed by providence but by the random chance of germination, such as when he demands of the witches, 'though the treasure/ Of Nature's germens tumble all together,/Even till destruction sicken, answer me' (IV.i.58–60). His invocation of the 'swelling act/Of the imperial theme' (I.iii.128–9) can also be related to this idea. As the *OED* notes, 'Swelling' is a word with natural/horticultural uses in early modern English, connoting the gestation and dilation of natural seed or a disruption in the natural world (definitions 1a, 1b and 3a). But it can also relate to the 'Abnormal or morbid distension or enlargement of some bodily part or member' such as a cancer (2a) as well as 'Pride' and 'vanity' (5).[17] Macbeth's 'swelling' may, like the witches' prophecies, be 'ill' or 'good', an outcome that at the start of the play is impossible to predict (I.iii.131). This kind of verbal echoing takes on a demonic resonance in the play. For example, Macbeth wonders, in an aptly horticultural metaphor, whether he and Banquo have 'eaten on the insane root' (I.iii.84). Words are planted and cross-fertilize like scattered seeds that lead to doubtful roots: once released they cannot be controlled and, if incorrectly planted, may well return to plague the sower. Compare Banquo's complaint at the start of Act III, 'myself should be the root and father/Of many kings' (III.i.5–6), Macbeth's statement that his 'fears in Banquo/Stick deep' (III.i.48–9) like thorns or roots, and his words to Banquo's murderers, 'I will advise you where to plant yourselves' (III.i.128). It is the unpredictable *plurality* of seeds and the dangers inherent in the act of sowing that such imagery points to. At times, the wildness of *Macbeth*'s natural imagery seems positively Lucretian. In such a world, the political present and future is always unstable, invariably open to disruption. As Jonathan Gil Harris argued recently, the play's 'untimely temporality can never be characterised in the singular'.[18]

In terms of Scripture, these ideas find their germination in the Parable of the Wheat and the Tares. Here, Christ likens the kingdom of heaven to 'a man which sowed good seed in his field' (Matthew 13.24). After the sower had done this, 'there came his enemy and sowed tares among the wheate'. The man's servants ask him whether they should 'plucke vp' the tares, but the sower says no, and that he will gather the wheat and the tares together at harvest, burning the former and storing the latter. Christ explains this parable in unapologetically apocalyptic terms.[19] As he explains, the enemy who sows the tares is the 'deuill', the reapers are 'Angels' and the harvest signifies 'the end of the world' where the Angels will 'seuer the bad from amongst the iust' and there will be 'wailing and gnashing of teeth' (Matthew 13: 36–42). These small but important lexical connections between images of seeds, growth and harvest throughout the play gradually help to build up the various dramatic ironies that the tragedy trades in. Banquo will certainly be 'harvested', but not necessarily in the way that he anticipates: for the 'Devilish Macbeth' (IV.iii.117), the possibility of the 'seed of Banquo kings!' (III.i.69) being germinated in opposition to his 'fruitless crown' (III.i.60) must be resisted, even if this causes an apocalypse in Scotland.[20] Macbeth's observation that 'o'er the one half-world/Nature seems dead' (II.i.49–50) casts him as a hidden demonic sower and reaper. As he treads quietly on the 'sure and firm-set earth' (II.i.56), worried about whether the 'very stones prate of my where-about' (II.i.58), he proceeds to deal in 'wither'd Murther' (II.i.52). His words about the stones connote Luke 19.37–44, when Christ's disciples start to rejoice after his descent from the Mount of Olives. The Pharisees ask Christ to rebuke his followers but he refuses, saying 'that if these should holde their peace, the stones would cry'. Christ weeps over Jerusalem for the things that are 'hid from thine eyes'. He then predicts a day when 'thine enemies shall cast a trench about thee, and compasse thee round, and keepe thee in on euery side'. Macbeth's invocation of this line and narrative can be read as transgressive and prophetic, casting his hidden murderous intent as an anti-Christian harbinger of weeping[21] and also pointing towards his eventual destruction. Not for nothing has the critic Arthur Kinney termed *Macbeth* 'a Doomsday play'.[22]

Macbeth's response to the king when he announces his intention to travel to the castle at Inverness is also worth pausing over: 'The rest is labour, which is not us'd for you:/I'll be myself the harbinger, and make joyful/The hearing of my wife with your approach' (I.iv.44–6). Although on the surface this comment seems honourable and facilitative, a proper display of hospitality by a 'peerless kinsman' (I.iv.58), it is nevertheless somewhat disjunctive that Macbeth should figure his 'labour' as not being intended for Duncan. Indeed, the two men's conceptions of 'labour' differ markedly. These various uses of the term 'labour' could well have invoked for an audience the Parable of the Labourer in the Vineyard. In this story, the labourers chosen at the start of the day are paid as much as those hired later on. This causes complaints 'against the master of the house' (Matthew 20.11) who informs the labourers hired earlier that this is, in fact, a fair way of dealing since he agreed to pay them all the same regardless of how long they worked. The ethical equity of the hirer's actions, with their implications of mutuality and reciprocity, is consistently undercut in the play's invocations of 'labour', 'house' and 'host'.

For example, Lady Macbeth cynically tells Duncan on his arrival that 'Your Majesty loads our house' (I.vi.18), a comment that suggests an extension of hospitality, but one that also implies the various burdens invariably accrued by such a visit.[23] The audience have just witnessed her terrible invocation against the 'compunctious visitings of Nature' (I.v.45), her desire demonically to cultivate Macbeth by pouring her 'spirits' into his ear (I.v.26) and her anti-Edenic advice to her husband: 'look like th' innocent flower,/But be the serpent under't' (I.v.64–5).[24] In this context, the last word that Duncan trustingly speaks to Lady Macbeth before his death, 'hostess' (I.vii.31), is redolent with irony. Macbeth also meditates on the transmutation of more tranquil implications of these terms into something darker. In I.vii he notes that he is not just Duncan's 'kinsman and his subject', he is also 'his host/Who should against his murtherer shut the door' (I.vii.13–15). Macbeth occupies a conflicted space here. His transgression of the king's 'double trust' (I.vii.12) is a violation of the 'labour' that Duncan has expended on Macbeth. His status as host and killer, and Duncan's as guest and victim, points up the fact that the etymology of 'host' ('*hostem*', '*hostia*') connotes guest and stranger, and also, more ominously, a sacrifice (witness Macduff's reference to 'Most sacrilegious Murther' in II.iii.68).[25] In II.ii, Macbeth pointedly refers to slumber as a 'sore labour's bath' (II.ii.37) that he will no longer be able to enjoy now that the voice has cried '"Sleep no more!" to all the house' (II.ii.40). Even his hallucinations disturb the peace and protection that should be properly vouchsafed by a host within his household. As he accepts Macduff's invitation – 'a joyful trouble' (II.iii.49) – to 'wake' the murdered Duncan, he hypocritically comments that 'The labour we delight in physics pain' (II.iii.49–51), a perversely knowing inversion. And once the murder has been discovered, Lady Macbeth comments on the 'hideous trumpet' that 'calls to parley/The sleepers of the house' (II.iii.82–3), feigning shock that such a thing could happen 'in our house' (II.iii.88). In setting their labour against the king, denying the true rewards of just labour, labouring falsely, and by failing to maintain their household as a safe haven, the Macbeths align themselves with those in the parable who are ranged against the master and who fatally desire more than is their due.

Reading the Book of Nature: Knowledge and Time

As Lemnius says, a king should delight in the 'serch [*sic*] and *knowledge* of the nature of plantes and herbes' (my emphasis).

But as *Macbeth* shows from the outset, this is a world where secure knowledge of objects or of persons is hard to find. Think of the irony implicit in Duncan's words on arrival at Macbeth's castle – 'This castle hath a pleasant seat; the air/Nimbly and sweetly recommends itself/Unto our gentle senses' (I.vi.1–3). Banquo's speech at I.vi.3–10 also rhapsodizes the castle using natural and avian imagery, and commending, like the king, the delicacy of the air. These words not only reveal both men to be dangerously credulous; they also show them to be poor readers of signs, too open to the promise of the book of nature and insufficiently attentive to its potential opacity.[26] In such examples, and throughout the play more broadly, it would appear that Shakespeare is engaging with the somewhat paradoxical Calvinist belief that 'man is corrupted through natural vitiation, but a vitiation that did not flow from nature'.[27] For Calvin, only humans can be responsible for their own sins. This then enables him to assert that although nature is a gift from God, humankind is also estranged from understanding its true wonder because what we know about nature is, like what we know about God, imperfect and fallen. Humankind is, to quote Calvin, 'naturally depraved and faulty', a proposition whose premise *Macbeth* explores with considerable acuity.[28]

There is also a providential aspect to these considerations. The various disjunctions in nature reported in the first two acts, most notably the witches' 'supernatural soliciting' (I.iii.130) and their demonic manipulation of the natural world – they 'Melted as breath into the wind' (I.iii.82) – should serve as a warning, particularly to the king. Many in an early modern audience would have understood these natural disruptions as providentially presaging a dangerous alteration in Scotland's power structure.[29] Duncan's patriarchal belief in the fundamental benignity and knowability of nature renders him vulnerable despite his assertions of power and authority, something that makes Macbeth's 'breach in nature' (II.iii.113) all the more transgressive. In the king's case, imperfect knowledge is the source of his political weakness: his nurturing of his vassal's obligation contains the seeds of his own destruction. In Macbeth's case, it is a temporary source of political power. Significantly, Macbeth begins the play by asserting the transparency of knowledge. He is particularly keen to assert a link between self-knowledge and a stable identity: 'By Sinel's death I *know* I am Thane of Glamis' (I.iii.71; my emphasis). However, by the time he resolves to the kill the king, his attitude to epistemology has radically altered: 'False face must hide what the false heart doth *know*' (I.vii.83; my emphasis). Indeed, in order to embrace fully the political implications of his murderous actions, Macbeth must create a breach between self-knowledge and identity: 'To know my deed, 'twere best not to know myself' (II.ii.72). *Macbeth* shows us a world populated by imperfect knowers. But, daringly, Macbeth refuses to be cowed by this imperfection. We might even say that he actively harnesses the Calvinist doctrine of humankind's depravity, twisting it to his own political ends. He understands that in a Calvinist world, access to full self-knowledge and, by extension, identity is invariably chimerical. For a Calvinist, this understanding should properly lead an individual to repentance and, if applicable, to the workings of grace. But for Macbeth, 'renown, and grace, is dead' (II.iii.94). In the absence of such gifts, therefore, he embraces the freedom temporarily afforded to the depraved.

I have used the word 'temporarily' here because both the word and the idea were central to the explication and understanding of the gospel parables in early modern England, especially the Parable of the Sower. For the great Humanist scholar Erasmus, this parable is primarily an example of the presence of evil in the world. So while he does not doubt that there are those people 'who hear the words of heavenly teaching carelessly and listlessly', for him the blame lies mainly with 'the evil one, who lies in ambush and envies strong beginnings, [and who] immediately sends against the soul some transitory cares to destroy the seed before it grows into green stalks or puts down roots'.[30] Human responsibility is not denied, but the Devil's culpability is worse. When it comes to the issue of ethical responsibility, Erasmus is typically humanistic in his refusal to draw any specific theological implications from what he sees as a fairly common foible of humanity. For instance, the seeds that fall amongst the stony ground or that are clogged by stones are likened to a man who does not fix the message of the gospel 'deeply in the marrow of his mind, but in typical human fashion takes lightly – as a sort of passing whim – what he does'. For Calvin, on the other hand, this kind of interpretation is incorrectly oriented. In his popular *Harmony of the Gospels*, first published in England in 1584, he does not deny the agency of the Devil. But he focuses much more intently on the culpability of people. The seeds that fall on good ground are likened to the elect since 'not all bear the same measure of fruit'; those who do not understand the word 'because there is no preparation for it within their hearts' represent the reprobate.[31] Such an interpretation is stark, if hardly surprising. What is particularly significant is Calvin's discussion of the seeds that fall on stony ground. He likens them to those who possess what he calls 'temporary faith'. This is a 'promise of fruitfulness at the outset, but their hearts are not worked on well enough or deeply enough to make them soft to nourish seed'. Such individuals 'lack a living feeling (*affectus*) to confirm them in steadfastness. Everyone should examine himself inwardly, lest his readiness is merely a great flash which is soon gone like a stubble fire'.[32]

This passage is crucial for two reasons. Firstly, the doctrine of temporary faith represents both an innovation and a departure for Calvin. Generally, he is extremely wary of recommending that humans examine themselves inwardly.[33] Indeed, as he often notes, when undertaken incorrectly, such activity commonly leads man to 'empty assurance and puffs him up with pride'.[34] But the implications of the Parable of the Sower clearly led him to the conclusion that, because some people may be temporarily deceived in the assurance of their faith, increased interior scrutiny was justified in such cases in order to find out whether one was a reprobate or not. This inward turn is, I think, uneasily explored in Macbeth's obsessive interior examinations throughout the play. His claim that thinking 'Shakes so my single state of man,/That function is smother'd in surmise,/And nothing is, but what is not' (I.iii.140–2) pivots on the very uncertainty engendered by making inwardness the condition upon which epistemological truth might be tested. Secondly, the doctrine of the temporary faith of the reprobate, and the inwardness associated with it, assumed a particular significance in early modern England. This is especially the case in the work of the pre-eminent Calvinist of the period, William Perkins.[35] Perkins's theology, deeply influenced by the work of Calvin's successor in Geneva, Theodore Beza, placed much more emphasis on the division between the elect and the reprobate. In order to assuage anxiety about this matter and to help people examine their own election, he published a book in 1590 called *A treatise tending vnto a declaration whether a man be in the estate of damnation or in the estate of grace: and if he be in the first, how he may in time come out of it: if in the second, how he maie discerne it, and perseuere in the same to the end*. Reprinted a number of times in the years that followed, the text begins by quoting Luke 8.13 on the seeds that fall on stony ground: 'they haue no rootes: which for a while beleeue, but in the time of tentation [sic] goe away'. Perkins states that such people have knowledge of the word of God, give their assent to it, and to the convent of grace.[36] He goes on to list a series of thirty-three propositions that show just how far the reprobate may go in his temporary faith. He may zealously profess the word of God, be taken for a Christian, and may even appear sincere in his love of God. Of course, the reprobate is always eventually found out. Drawing on the Parable of the Sower throughout the text, Perkins notes that temporary faith 'may bee somewhat rooted in his heart and setled for a season, and may bring forth some fruits in his life, peraduenture very faire in his owne and other mens eies: yet indeede neither sound nor lasting, nor substantiall'.[37] In the end, reprobates will 'runne headlong to their own damnation, and perish finally'.[38]

Nevertheless, it really is quite remarkable just how much time, space and agency Perkins affords to the temporary faith of the reprobate. As he asks rhetorically in the final proposition, 'Seest thou howe farre a reprobate may goe?'[39] If the activities of the reprobate match those of the elect so closely, how is it possible, before the final judgement, to distinguish absolutely the one from the other? Such temporary faith almost seems, if not exactly attractive, then certainly politically expedient: Perkins regularly cites King Saul as the prime example of a ruler who is a reprobate yet who is able to wield considerable power during the period of his rule.[40] Macbeth's rule can be seen in a similar light.[41] Indeed, I think that Shakespeare's play demonstrates a fascination with the question of 'how farre a reprobate may goe' and how hard it is to tell the difference between the godly and the ungodly. As Malcolm strikingly puts it, 'Though all things foul would wear the brows of grace,/Yet Grace must still look so' (IV. iii.23–4). This uncertainty is reflected in the way that the gospel parables are used in the second half of the play to draw attention to Macbeth's ungodliness, as well as in the play's deep-seated concern with time itself.

As many scholars have noted, this is a play where time is horribly disordered. Kristen Poole has noted that 'any sense of a regular progression of time is thwarted as the play quickly enters a temporal morass'.[42] What is less frequently noted is the degree of agency that this temporal confusion affords to the Macbeths. Lady Macbeth's advice to her husband, 'To beguile the time/ Look like the time' (I.v.62–3), is so seductive because it holds out the possibility that the ungodly Macbeth (personified as the second 'time' in this line) may be indistinguishable from the godly 'time' of providence. The word 'like' does a lot of work in this sentence. Or as George Gifford put it in a 1583 sermon on the Parable of the Sower, 'it is one thing to seeme good before men, and another thing for to be good in deed before God'.[43] Certainly for most of the first two acts, this confusion affords the Macbeths considerable power: witness his desire to 'mock the time with fairest show' (I.vii.82). This temporal slipperiness may well be a fool's paradise that is based on nothing more than a cunning manipulation of metaphor. But it still has sharp consequences: 'cruel are the times' (IV.ii.18), notes Rosse. Only when Macbeth is facing defeat and contemplating his final judgement

– 'the last syllable of recorded time'– does the promise of 'to-morrow' cease to have meaning (V.v.17–19). His cry that life signifies 'nothing' can be read as realization that the freedom he has been afforded has been, indeed, temporary, a fact reflected in Macduff's words, 'the time is free' (V.ix.21). However, Macbeth's defeat and death are less important than the cruel fact that, in the providentially ordered universe imagined by theologians like Perkins, a temporal and political space can still be opened that allows a figure like Macbeth to wreak such pain and suffering. This space is, like the faith of the reprobate, temporary, but the acknowledgement of its temporariness always comes too late for figures like Duncan, Banquo and, most tellingly, Lady Macduff. By the point that time turns against Macbeth, the damage is irrevocably done.

Parable Ethics and Typology

In terms of the play's exploration of parable ethics, the turning point comes with the escape of Fleance. If the murderers had succeeded, says Macbeth, he would have been 'perfect' indeed: 'whole as marble, founded as the rock' (III.iv.20–1). But the possibility of solidity, mental and political, is fleeting. This line draws upon Christ's comment in Matthew 7.25 where he likens those who will be saved to the wise man whose house was 'grounded on a rock'.[44] Those who are not saved are compared to the man who builds 'his house vpon the sand' (Matthew 7.26). When Banquo's ghost appears in the scene that follows, the audience witnesses Macbeth's household disintegrating before their eyes: the 'host' (III.iv.40 is inexplicably distracted, is displaced by the ghost from his seat (see III.iv.77–81), calls on the 'earth' to 'hide' the uninvited guest (III.iv.92), and the assembly falls into confusion and 'disorder' (IV.iv.109).[45] As Macbeth says:

> It will have blood, they say: blood will have blood:
> Stones have been known to move, and trees to speak;
> Augures, and understood relations, have

> By maggot-pies, and choughs, and rooks, brought forth
> The secret'st man of blood. (III.iv.121–5)

The usurper figures forth a proto-Gothic fantasy where nature animates itself against him. As the conclusion of Christ's story about the man who built his house on sand has it: 'And the raine fell, and the floods came, and the winds blewe, and beate vpon that house, and it fell, and the fall thereof was great' (Matthew 7.27). Macbeth's 'fall' is imagined through this biblically derived rhetoric of 'nature': in his wife's words, 'You lack the season of all natures, sleep' (III.iv.140).[46] Ironically, his assertion 'blood will have blood' alludes to Genesis 9 when God is making his covenant with Noah: 'Who so sheddeth man's blood, by man shall his blood be shed: for in the image of God hath he made man' (Genesis 9.6). This is important because the form of biblical interpretation known as typology is concerned with how the Old Law of the Old Testament was replaced and superseded by the New Law of the Gospels, one that substitutes the kind of sacrificial logic that Genesis trades in for a new dispensation based on the singular sacrifice of Christ for humankind. We not only see the language of the gospels turning against Macbeth; more strikingly, the return of the 'man of blood' sees him aligned with the sacrificial logic of the Old Law and against the potentially saving grace of the New Law.

When Macbeth meets the witches for the last time, their prophecy about Birnam Wood elicits the following response:

> That will never be
> Who can impress the forest; bid the tree
> Unfix his earth-bound root? Sweet bodements! good!
> Rebellious dead, rise never, till the wood
> Of Birnam rise; and our high-plac'd Macbeth
> Shall live the lease of Nature, pay his breath
> To time, and mortal custom. (IV.i.94–100)

The irony that undercuts Macbeth's confidence in his 'lease of Nature' should, by now, be clear. Whereas Duncan placed too much trust in his role as sower, Macbeth puts too much trust in the security of his roots. Indeed, his political 'uprooting' begins with his overly rigid conception of what nature's laws might be, forgetting his earlier invocation of a Lucretian fluidity in nature. We might also think of that odd scene when Malcolm and Macduff discuss the state of Scotland in IV.iii. Malcolm spends much of the scene claiming that he is as 'Luxurious, avaricious, false, deceitful' (IV.iii.58) as Macbeth. His avarice is likened to a 'more pernicious root' (IV.iii. 85), vice is horticulturally 'grafted' (IV.iii.51) to him, and Macduff even predicts that Malcolm may 'hoodwink' time itself (IV.iii.72). He might go on to 'abjure/The taints and blames I laid upon myself' (IV.iii123–4), but surely by associating Malcolm with the kind of ambiguous natural and temporal imagery connected up to now with Macbeth, Shakespeare warns his audience against the political abuse of 'nature', from whatever source. Malcolm may be Scotland's political saviour from Macbeth, but can this be reconciled with his queasily plausible attraction to tyranny? Macduff is silent at the end of Malcolm's 'recantation'. When asked why, he says, 'Such welcome and unwelcome things at once,/'Tis hard to reconcile' (IV.138–9). Macbeth may be 'ripe for shaking' (IV.iii.238), but Malcolm's invocation of 'the Powers above' (IV.iii.238) is little more than a convenient obfuscation of his more nakedly political intent, a way of making his actions seem inevitable and, perhaps, even 'natural'.

As a new political dispensation emerges and wends its way towards the castle in seeming defiance of nature, Macbeth reflects that 'my way of life/Is fall'n into the sere, the yellow leaf' (V.iii.22–23). He is withering on the vine, a fruitless (and childless) tyrant whose wife's 'rooted sorrow' cannot be plucked from her 'memory' (V.iii40–41). The freedom of temporariness that Macbeth has traded on for so long finds its antidote in Macduff, a man who was, of course, 'from his mother's womb/ Untimely ripp'd' (V.ix.15–16). 'Nature' is reclaimed by the 'unnatural' means of a man 'of no woman born' (V.ix.31) and Macbeth's 'untimeliness' is supplanted by a different temporal order. Again, it would be wrong to assume that Shakespeare simply constructs this new political dispensation as unambiguously just and righteous. The regime change at the end of *Macbeth* also affords him the opportunity to offer a more pointed political intervention. As the gospel parables make clear, the blade that reaps the fruit brings forth 'the tares also' (Matthew 13.26). Malcolm's first act as king is to raise all his 'Thanes and kinsmen' to the peerage (V.ix.28), an act that seems curiously redolent of James VI and I's much-criticized profligacy in this area. Malcolm also plans to call back to Scotland all 'our exil'd friends abroad' (V.ix.32). It is worth asking whether Shakespeare's audience would have linked the arrival of this new Scottish king and his followers in *Macbeth* with the influx of Scots to England that followed James's accession, a source of considerable tension during this period. And, lastly, it is notable that this last act is described as being 'planted newly with the time' (V.ix.31). Kings will always seek to plant and to sow. Yet as *Macbeth* shows, the ethical implications of planting in early modern religious culture are decidedly fraught.[47] Putting too much trust in those who seek to plant, and who look to co-opt time itself, is politically and ethically extremely dangerous. Malcolm may assign his victory to 'the grace of Grace' (V.ix.38). And he could very well be right to do so. However, given what we have seen of the new king's ethics, and given what we know of early modern Calvinism, we might just as easily conclude that such security in his own justification could equally be spectacularly misplaced. In the stark words of William Perkins, 'Manie professors of Christ, in the day of grace, perswade them selues that they are in the estate of grace; and so the true Church esteemeth of them too: yet when the day of grace is past, they contrariwise shall find themselues to bee in the estate of damnation remedilesse.'[48]

CHAPTER THREE

Unsexing *Macbeth*, 1623–1800

DALE TOWNSHEND

In an arresting dramatic moment, Shakespeare's Lady Macbeth invokes the preternatural assistance of the Spirits in a willed and deliberate act of unsexing: 'Come, you Spirits/That tend on mortal thoughts, unsex me here,/And fill me, from the crown to the toe, top-full/Of direst cruelty!' (I.v.40–3).[1] Unrecorded in English lexicography until the publication of *The Tragedie of Macbeth* in the first Folio edition of the play in 1623, 'unsex', as transitive verb, appears to have been of Shakespeare's own coinage. However, when considered within the context of the semantic field of which it is a part, the neologism seems decidedly less striking and singular, for from its opening moments the language of the play is marked by the prefixing of 'un' to a range of familiar verbs, adverbs and adjectives: a soldier is 'unseam'd' by the valiant Macbeth in the opening battle with Norway (I.ii.22); the images called up by the witches' ludic prophecies 'unfix' Macbeth's hair (I.iii.135); Macbeth's faltering resolve in the act of regicide is said to 'unmake' him (I.vii.54); his anxieties are said to 'unbend' his noble strength (II.ii.44); alcohol 'provokes' and 'unprovokes' sexual performance (II.iii.28); the weapons of the framed assassins are 'Unmannerly breech'd with gore' (II.iii.115); Macbeth is 'unmann'd in folly' at the sight of Banquo's ghost (III.iv.73); he facetiously dismisses a literal interpretation of the Birnam Wood/Dunsinane Hill prophecy with the rhetorical question 'bid the tree/Unfix his earth-bound root?' (IV.i.96); and Rosse makes proud reference to the 'unshrinking station' where Siward's son valiantly fought (V.ix.8). Of the numerous instances of the 'un' prefix in the play, the *Oxford English Dictionary* notes that, as is the case with the verb 'unsex', the first recorded instance of the use of 'unprovoked', 'unshrinking' and 'unbend' (in the sense of slackening or weakening) is in *Macbeth*, while 'unmannerly' and 'unfix', though still new coinages by the time of the play's dramatic debut in or around 1606, appear for the first time in print in *Two Gentlemen of Verona* (1616) and *2 Henry IV* (1600) respectively. Though the *OED* lists earlier recorded instances of 'unmann'd', it would appear that the particularly gendered inflection that the term receives in III.iv of *Macbeth* was hitherto unprecedented.[2] 'Fair is foul, and foul is fair' (I.i.11) indeed, as the negative 'un' prefix is added to words of originally positive import in order to extract from them a sense of their opposite. The linguistic inventiveness displayed in Shakespeare's generation of neologism in *Macbeth* is significantly tempered by the prevailing sense of disquiet to which it gives rise, the misgiving that one is being confronted here with a tragic world in which language has strenuously to make and unmake itself if it is to have any role in representing it at all.

Lady Macbeth's Discursive Body

Lady Macbeth's body, the site of her desired unsexing, has received considerable critical attention in recent years. For Alice Fox, the play is replete with references to Renaissance obstetrical and gynaecological practices, so that Lady Macbeth's call to the Spirits to congeal and thicken her blood as a means of short-circuiting the 'compunctious visitings of Nature' becomes, in accordance with contemporary medical thought, a euphemistic reference to her desire to block, terminate or eradicate her own menstrual cycle, the sure sign of her more compunctious femininity.[3] Building upon similar insights, Jenijoy La Belle has pointed out that the soliloquy is informed by the early modern tendency to couple psychological characteristics with physiological states, to the extent that the change in sentiments for which the 'Lady' of the first Folio calls is ultimately anchored in precise changes to her sex that she wishes to undergo at the level of physical, corporeal existence.[4] More recently, Joanna Levin's reading of Lady Macbeth has drawn attention to the striking parallels between Shakespeare's play and the links between witchcraft, daemonology and hysteria explored in Edward Jorden's contemporary *Briefe Discourse of A Disease Called the Suffocation of the Mother* (1603).[5] But there remain other ways in which Lady Macbeth's famous 'unsex me here' soliloquy presents itself as the object of genealogical analysis, particularly if by 'genealogy' we mean a Foucauldian 'analysis of descent' that is situated 'within the articulation of the body and history', a sub-Nietzschean endeavour that conceptualizes the body as being 'totally imprinted by history' to the extent of its very constitution.[6] For it is to a particular historico-discursive construction of the body to which *Macbeth* continuously looks, this discourse providing the grounds for the intelligibility and consistency of the play's language and the resource from which its most enduring metaphors are hewn.

This historical inscription is disclosed from the outset, in the seemingly transparent meanings of the soliloquy's opening lines: 'Come, you Spirits'. In what may or may not be a compositorial idiosyncrasy, the first Folio of the text renders 'Spirits' in the upper-case, as follows: 'Come you Spirits,/That tend on mortall thoughts, vnsex me here' (I.v.392).[7] Of all early editions of the play, Edmond Malone's *Macbeth* in his authoritative *The Plays and Poems of William Shakespeare* (1790) identified the most historically likely source for this seeming act of supernatural invocation: Thomas Nashe's pamphlet *Pierce Penilesse His Supplication to the Devil* of 1592.[8] In recent criticism, too, it has become customary to read the line as a supernatural appeal, as an instance in which Lady Macbeth, uncannily doubling the necromancy of the Weird Sisters, calls upon the power of the supernatural in her anticipated act of unsexing.[9] As Mark Rose puts it, 'the third scene opens with the Witches alone, after which Macbeth enters and they hail him by his various titles. The fifth scene opens with Lady Macbeth alone, practising witchcraft. [...] And when Macbeth enters she, too, hails him by his titles.'[10] Indeed, the references to 'murth'ring ministers', 'sightless substances', 'thick

Night' and 'the dunnest smoke of Hell' in the subsequent lines of the speech appear, in their apostrophizing of the powers of literal and spiritual darkness, to set in place certain parallels between the supernatural invocations of the three witches and the 'domestic magic' of Lady Macbeth herself.

However, it is likely that, in Lady Macbeth's invocation, Shakespeare is also referring to an historically specific medical and anatomical debate concerning the origins of human action and agency, a debate, more natural than supernatural, that was centred around the complexities of the word 'Spirit' and its relations to the early modern body. While documenting a profound lack of consensus on the issue, William Harvey provided a useful retrospective gloss on sixteenth- and seventeenth-century thought concerning Spirit and the role it was thought to play in the motivation of human behaviour in the second of his *Two Anatomical Exercitations Concerning the Circulation of the Blood* (1653):

> For commonly ignorant persons when they cannot give a reason for any thing, they say presently that it is done by Spirits, and bring in Spirits as performers in all cases, and like as bad Poets, doe bring in the gods upon the Scene by head and ears, to make the Exit and Catastrophe of their play.[11]

Harvey's use of theatrical metaphor in this extract is striking, and his cynicism regarding explanatory recourse to Spirits as little more than irresponsible justification for morally dubious action casts a particularly wry perspective on Lady Macbeth's act of invocation. The point to be made, though, is that the ghouls and spectres of popular superstition these Spirits need not necessarily be, as Harvey proceeds to outline the major scientific schools of thought on the issue, including Galen, Hippocrates, medieval scholasticism, Fernelius (Jean Francois Fernel) and Erasistratus. For some thinkers, the Spirits, like the soul, were entirely incorporeal; for others, the Spirits were thought to join with, and enter into, the body at a particular point of intersection between the immaterial and the corporeal realms. While recounting these differences of opinion and the resultant conceptual vagueness concerning Spirits, Harvey eventually stakes out a useful definition of the term:

> yet for the most part all Physicians seem with Hippocrates to conclude, that our bodies are made up of three parts, containing, containd [*sic*], and enforcing, by the forcing he means Spirits. But if Spirits must be understood to be every thing which enforces in a man's body, whatsoever hath the power or force of action in living bodies must be call'd by the name of Spirits.[12]

For William Harvey, as for Lady Macbeth four decades earlier, Spirits, though partly supernatural beings, are also those unfathomable principles of 'enforcement' that motivate, drive, support and inform what Lady Macbeth refers to as 'mortal thoughts' or human intention and behaviour, a kind of vitality or life-principle that lies at the centre of subjective agency and action. True to his empirical bent, Harvey's position is that Spirit is a distinct and separate essence, having no existence beyond or independent of the vital substance that is blood, the same blood that, in the earlier *De Motu Cordis* (1628), he had shown to circulate throughout the body and its extremities via the system of arteries and veins that led to and from the heart: 'Those Spirits which passe out through the *veins* or the *arteries*, are not separable from the blood, no more than flame from the flakes about it. But the blood and the Spirit signifie the same thing, though divers in essence, as good Wine and its Spirit.'[13] Indeed, it soon becomes clear that for Harvey Spirit is the vitality principle that lends to blood its life-giving properties.

Certainly, Lady Macbeth's plea that the Spirits 'make thick [her] blood' remains thoroughly in accordance with Harvey's account of the palpable thickening that ensues when the blood is most replete with spiritual substance: 'Therefore blood when it is most imbued with Spirits, it does require and look after more room, because it is swell'd or leaven'd, and blown up by them.'[14]

The ultimate destination of her Spirit-thickened blood, of course, is not the receptacle that is her own body, but rather – via a transfusion-like process of decanting – the empty body of her husband Macbeth: 'Hie thee hither,/That I may pour my spirits in thine ear,/And chastise with the valour of my tongue/All that impedes thee from the golden round' (I.v.25–28); with Macbeth's agreement to the act of regicide in the lines 'I am settled, and bend up/Each corporal agent to this terrible feat' (I.vii.80–1), it would appear that the decanting of Lady Macbeth's unsexed, masculine Spirits through the ear and into her husband's body has been successful. Renaissance accounts of the thickening of the blood anticipate Judith Butler's argument concerning the unsustainability of the sex/gender divide: biological sex is always, already the fabricated, historically contingent effect of the latter, and both little more than the cultural by-product of on-going, continuous performativity.[15] Maintaining that 'For the Gravity of Blood may differ sensibly in several persons according to their Sex, Age, Constitutions, &c.', for instance, Robert Boyle in his *Memoirs for the Natural History of Humane Blood* (1683) claimed, in a revealing generic use of the term 'Man', that 'Mens Blood may be much more Phlegmatick or serous than that of others, which it self may be more or less spirituous according to the Complexion, Age, Sex, &c. of the person that bleeds.'[16] Lady Macbeth's call for a thickening of her blood as one of the desired consequences of her unsexing discloses a similar set of assumptions, and in Boyle and Shakespeare alike, conceptualizations of biologically determined sexual difference emerge as little more than a cultural fiction of gender-difference rewritten in essentialist terms. As anatomical as it is supernatural, and deeply imbedded in early modern gender-politics, Lady Macbeth's invocation of the Spirits as an aid to her unsexing is founded in a particular historical conceptualization of corporeality.

A range of other references to body fluids, body parts and the world of Nature in Lady Macbeth's 'unsex me here' soliloquy serve further to locate and anchor her utterance within a particular discursive construction of the body:

> Stop up th'access and passage to remorse;
> That no compunctious visitings of Nature
> Shake my fell purpose, nor keep peace between
> Th'effect and it! Come to my woman's breasts,
> And take my milk for gall, you murth'ring ministers,
> Wherever in your sightless substances
> You wait on Nature's mischief! (I.v.41–7)

With her act of 'unsexing' conceptualized as the prelude to a process in which an empty body is filled and made replete – 'And fill me', she implores, 'from the crown to the toe, top-full/Of direst cruelty!' (I.v.41–3) – the body and its parts are figured as a receptacle designed primarily for the containment of the fluids of blood and gall, a clear allusion to Hippocratic and Galenic medical and proto-psychological models of the four humours. Blood, of course, is the prevailing fluid of the sanguine temperament, while the functions of gall were thought to fall within the classificatory categories of yellow bile and choler. As Alexander Ross's *Arcana Microcosmi: Or, The Hid Secrets of Mans Body Discovered* of 1652 makes clear, gall was thought to serve as the primary means of absorption of the excess choler in the blood: 'nature hath made the Gall to receive choler, that the blood may not be therewith infected, as sometimes it is when the Gall is obstructed, whence comes the yellow Jaundice'.[17] Lady Macbeth invokes the humours of blood and gall as the ideal determinants of her intended murderous actions, themselves the anticipated consequences of the process of 'unsexing' that she seeks, with the motivating assistance of the Spirits, to effect.

Fluids and the Alchemical Body

Of all of Shakespeare's tragedies, *Macbeth* is not only the most bloody, but also the play in which blood assumes the most important medical, historical, ideological and metaphorical meanings. It thus seems fitting that Lady Macbeth's thoughts, both here and elsewhere in the play, are most heavily preoccupied with the workings, functions and meanings of the sanguine fluid, preoccupations compounded by the fact that, as several contemporary medical treatises show, blood was central to early modern constructions of sexual difference, and thus, of necessity, integral to the process of unsexing that she wishes to effect. Written, performed and published prior to the 'Copernican shift' that William Harvey's account of the circulation of the blood in *De Motu Cordis* (1628; trans. 1653) brought about within early modern anatomical discourse, *Macbeth* draws upon the older models of the blood, its constitution and its passage that were enshrined in Galenic and Hippocratic medicine. As Thomas Laqueur has influentially pointed out, Galen was the primary exponent of the so-called 'one-flesh' or 'one-sex model' of sexual difference, that pervasive pre-Enlightenment anatomical discourse according to which female genitals and reproductive organs were conceptualized as inverted, lesser-developed and hence inferior equivalents of masculine genitalia.[18]

It is difficult to overemphasize the extent to which the assumptions enshrined in Galen's one-sex model pervaded medical thought in late sixteenth- and early seventeenth-century England. Thomas Vicary, for instance, surgeon to the Tudor monarchs Henry VIII, Edward VI, Mary I and Elizabeth I, cited Galen, 'the Lanterne of all Chirurgions' (n.p.), as his primary authority in his *A Profitable Treatise of the Anatomie of Mans Body*, an emended and updated version of which was published posthumously by his colleagues at St Bartholomew's Hospital, London, in 1577.[19] The tract is wholly invested in the Galenic theory of the four humours: 'These are the places of the humors', Vicary declares, 'the blood in the Lyver, choler in the chest of gal, melancolie to the spleen, flegme to the Lunges.' Blood, though, assumes in this account greater anatomical significance over the other three liquids, as Vicary conceptualizes the body as a vessel that is fuelled and generated by the excesses of the four humours that are transformed, via a heat-driven process of conversion that occurs in the liver, into blood. While Aristotle conceptualized the heart as the centre of the body's blood-flow, Galen and his followers regarded the liver as the centre of the body's sanguine system. In line with earlier anatomists, Vicary's text distinguishes between the veins and the arteries, the former serving as vessels for what he terms 'blood nutrimental', or blood as it is commonly conceived, and the latter for the transmission and passage of 'spirite of lyfe', a kind of energizing principle of vitality or life-force that, again, throws a particularly anatomical inflection upon Lady Macbeth's appeal to 'Spirits' in the 'unsexing' speech. In line with Galenic precedents, and not unlike Lady Macbeth herself, Vicary renders the body primarily as a vessel or receptacle for the containment and processing of blood, a closed economy of sanguinity in which all excesses of the fluid are internally transformed, via a process of what he terms 'digestion' in the body's various 'Glandulus fleshe' or glands, into the secondary body-fluids of milk, semen and spittle:

> The profites of the Glandulus fleshe are these: first, that it turneth the blood into a cullour like to him selfe, as doth the fleshe of a womans paps turne the menstrual blood into mylke: secondly, the Glandus lus fleshe of the Testikles, turneth the blood into sparme: thirdly, the Glandus lus flesh of the cheeks, that ingendreth spittle.

Indeed, semen and breast-milk in Vicary serve as the clearest examples of the body's process of sanguine digestion. Commenting on the function of the glandular 'paps' that are anatomically perceivable in both men and women, Vicary notes that

> in women there is the generation of milke: for in women there commeth from the matrix into their brestes manye veines which bring into them menstrual blood, the whiche is turned through the digestive virtue from red colour into white, like the colour of the pappes, even as chyiley coming from the stomocke to the Lyver is turned into the colour of Lyver.

Following similar Galenic precedents, Thomas Cogan advanced identical views on the sanguine origins of breast milk in his *The Haven of Health* of 1596:

> Milke is nothing else but blood twice concocted: for until it come to the pappes or udder, it is plaine bloud: but afterward by the proper nature of the pappes it is turned into milke.[20]

The same process of conversion pertained to semen:

> there is left some part of profitable bloud, not needful to the partes, ordained by nature for procreation, which by certaine vessels or conduits serving for that purpose, is wonderfully conveighed and carried to the genitories, where by their proper nature and that which before was plaine bloud, is now transformed and changed into seede.[21]

As late as 1652, Ross could advance the claim that breast milk was nothing other than menstrual blood that had undergone a process of internal conversion: 'menstruous blood [...] is appointed by nature for nutriment of the infant, whilst it is in the womb; and after birth it is converted into milk'.[22]As this attests, Galen's one-sex model so thoroughly permeated medical discourse in late sixteenth-century Europe that its implications might be traced in anatomical treatises that do not, on the surface, appear to be concerned with the differences and similarities between male and female reproductive systems.

As it turns out, the body in its entirety is governed by a principle of sanguine conversion, for flesh is itself nothing other than congealed blood, while blood as it is commonly conceived, so-called 'blood nutrimental', is the product of the conversion of the body's 'spirite of lyfe' or Spirits into the crimson, animal fluid in the gland-like ventricles of the brain: 'And the aforesayde spirite or breath taketh a further digestion, and there it is made animal, by the elaboration of the spirite vital is turned and made animall.'[23] The Renaissance body thus conceived is an alchemical crucible designed for the conversion of the unsexed 'base-matter' that is blood into the at least partially sexed fluids of milk and semen. Like the alchemical process itself, this act of conversion depended ultimately upon the levels of available heat within the body, for men were invariably thought to be of a hotter constitution than women: as Alexander Ross put it, 'the male is hotter then [*sic*] the female, because begot of hotter seed, and in a hotter place'.[24] Lady Macbeth seeks in the 'unsex me here' speech to draw upon and exploit this body-as-crucible model in order to effect her unsexing through a reversal of the process of sanguine conversion: the milk that she has emitted from her 'woman's breasts', the same milk with which she later claims, however disingenuously, to have 'given suck' to 'the babe that milks me' (II.vii.54–5), must re-enter her body in order to be returned to its bloody origins, become thickened there with masculine Spirit, and, as either masculine blood or choleric gall, henceforth turn her murderous, bloody ambitions to corporeal action, or suit her physical make-up to her desired range of psychological objectives. As she realizes, this is to reverse the path of Nature so that no 'compunctious visitings' might 'Shake [her] fell purpose' (I.v.45–6), blocking and stopping up the internal, digestive passages to remorse through which more feminine humours, such as the blood that is emitted during menstruation, might flow: as La Belle has argued, in calling for a reversal and drying up of her reproductive system, Lady Macbeth wills upon herself the symptoms of amenorrhea that plague her throughout the remainder of the action, including swooning, fainting, melancholy and somnambulism.[25]

As the Lady envisages it, unsexing consists of a willed and deliberate process of reversed and inverted body-alchemy in which the external body fluids seemingly marked by ineradicable sexual difference return to the body's interiors to be converted into their hotter and thicker masculine equivalents. As a dramatic line, 'unsex me here' includes dimensions that are spatial, temporal and meta-theatrical: if accompanied with a hand-gesture, 'here' might have served as a self-conscious reference to the prosthetic breasts with which male players upon the Renaissance stage habitually signified their feminine roles.[26] Uttered just before a detailed anatomical account of the Lady's corporeality, 'here' might also invoke not only the breasts but the interiors and exteriors of her body in its entirety; uttered during an especially poignant scene, 'here' might also call attention to a particular theatrical space and a particular moment in dramatic time. Notable, indeed, is the ease with which the Lady envisages the act of unsexing. Effected by a linguistic command, unsexing is swift, deliberate and even effortless in nature, less a long, arduous and time-consuming process of traversing from one sex to the other than a sudden sex-change, inaugurated by a performative speech-act in which the external signs of sexual difference are reabsorbed by the body and summarily redirected.

To be unsexed as a woman, of course, is also simultaneously to be resexed as a man, just as a glove or reversible garment changes superficial appearance but not deep structure or shape when it is turned inside out. Even as he defended his account of ideal femininity from the misogynistic views advanced by Gaspare, the Magnifico Giuliano, in Book III of Castiglione's *The Book of the Courtier*, insisted upon the fact that masculine women constituted an assault upon contemporary gender codes.[27] While the channels of feminine compunction and remorse seem to have remained unstopped during that moment when, recalling her father in the slumbering figure of the king, her murderous resolve falters, Macbeth's later claim that her 'undaunted mettle should compose/Nothing but males' (I.vii.74–5) implies that her unsexing has been successful: not only has Lady Macbeth been resexed as male, but the seed to which her body within the one-sex model is thought to give issue will produce only male heirs. At the very least, she wields at this moment a considerable reproductive self-sufficiency, and, excluding himself from the procreative process, Macbeth figures his wife as capable of generating masculine offspring utterly independently of a male partner.

It would appear that the sanguine fluid that ran within the veins and arteries of the early modern body was decidedly sexless, and that it was only at the point at which blood, having undergone a 'digestive' process of internal conversion in the glands, exited the body that it became ineradicably marked by the signs of sexual difference. Blood becomes milk via the glands of the breasts, and an excess of blood becomes semen, seed or sperm following digestion in the testicles, both substances leaving the body and signifying the differences between female and male respectively as they do so. Here too, however, the sexing of body-fluids in early modern anatomical discourse provided anything but fixed and absolute certainties, and much like an uncontainable emission itself, the implications of the one-sex model leaked into attempts at classifying bodily discharges as either exclusively male or exclusively female. Thomas Laqueur calls this the 'fungibility' or the 'interconvertibility' of body-fluids in the period, a particularly clear example of which is early modern accounts of the conversion of blood into semen.[28] For instance, and as Vicary maintains, women have internal testicles of their own, but it is only in the outwardly visible testicles of men that blood undergoes a further process of digestion in order to become semen:

> Also there is founde two other vessels called, vaza seminatia or the spermatike vessels. And they come from Venakelis, bringing blood to the Testikles, as wel in man, as in woman, in the which by his further digestion it is made sparme or nature in men. They be put outward, for the Testikles be without, but in women it abydeth within, for their Testcies [*sic*] stande within, as it shal be declared hereafter.

Thus far, Vicary seems to reserve sperm as an exclusively masculine fluid. However, any easy identification of women with breast-milk and men with semen was complicated by Vicary's strongly Galenic claim that women, too, produce seed, its difference from that of males being only a matter of warmth, thickness and potency: 'Sparme', he claims, is

> made and gathered of the most best and purest drops of blood in all the body, and by the labour and chasing of the testikles or stones this blood is turned into another kinde, and is made sparme, which hath contrarie qualities, for the womans sparme is thinner, colder, and feebler.

Much the same applies to milk, for while it would appear that the act of breast-feeding is an exclusively female prerogative, Renaissance culture was by no means lacking in examples and accounts of lactating men. Laqueur cites the examples listed by Aristotle, Hieronymous Cardanus (Court physician to the King of Denmark), an Italian commentator on Cardanus, and Joubert.[29] Ross commented upon the possibility of the existence of milk-producing men in *Arcana Microcosmi*: 'I have read of men that have had milk in their brests, which is likely, if they were of a cold, moist, and feminine complexion, abounding in blood.'[30] Not even menstrual blood for Ross is a sure sign of the clearly sexed female body, as he records, alongside accounts of milk-producing males, at least one instance of a man who menstruated:

> As there be some masculine women, so there are some feminate men; such was he who from twenty to forty five, had his monthly vacaution of blood, as women have; by which it seems his constitution was altogether feminine, moist and cold; therefore was smooth skinned, having no Beard, not hair at all on his body.[31]

Much anti-Semitic discourse in the period, of course, peddled the myth that Jewish men menstruated. Though originating in the unsexed, internal pool of sanguinity, fluids and emissions that flowed beyond the body's borders provided no clear and absolute sign of the sex of the body from which they came.

The dramatic use of body-fluids in *Macbeth* register similar ambivalences. Somewhat more acutely, though, Shakespeare exploits the sexual indeterminacy of the body's secretions in a further elaboration upon Lady Macbeth's unsexing. The opening scenes of the play appear to take off in a direction quite distinct from that of the one-sex, sanguineous body through their setting up of a system of equivalences between blood, military valour and masculinity in the account of the bleeding Captain or 'bloody man' (I.ii.1) who has protected Malcolm in the battle against the Norwegians. The Captain's description of the actions of the Fortune-disdaining Macbeth only compounds this apparent attempt at gendering blood as male: 'with his brandish'd steel,/ Which smok'd with bloody execution,/Like valour's minion', Macbeth 'carv'd out his passage' through the foe (I.ii.17–19). Blood, the stuff of 'reeking wounds' (I.ii.40), is spilled through violent blood-letting in a masculine site of war in *Macbeth*, a space wholly different from the carnivalesque world of gender indeterminacy staged and represented by the Weird Sisters. Not even at the play's end has blood lost its masculine meanings and associations, as in the description of Malcolm's army as 'Those clamorous harbingers of blood and death' (V.vi.10). As Macbeth, feigning his commiseration with Malcolm and Donalbain after the murder of their father, disingenuously claims, the body of the king is a vital source of blood, not only for the natural family, but for the blood of the body politic as a whole: 'The spring, the head, the fountain of your blood/Is stopp'd; the very source of it is stopp'd' (II.iii.96–7). Lacking in the obstacles to action that so incapacitate her husband, Lady Macbeth taunts her husband's faltering resolve with the line 'When you durst do it, then you were a man' (I.vii.49): the murderous spillage of blood in the act of regicide is a thoroughly masculine action. Accordingly, the murder of Duncan is signified as a particularly bloody affair: in Macbeth's phrasing, it is a 'bloody business' (II.i.48); for Banquo, a 'most bloody piece of work' (II.iii.126); and for Rosse a 'bloody deed' (II.iv.23) indeed. The murder of Banquo, in time, becomes steeped in blood too, and Macbeth points out to the murderer that 'There's blood upon thy face' (III.iv.13). Being that time in the play during which the most blood is spilled, night-time, the same thick, pall-like blanket with which Lady Macbeth in the unsexing speech wishes to cover up the wounds inflicted by the knives of her intent becomes for Macbeth an insatiably blood-thirsty presence – 'It will have blood, they say: blood will have blood' (III.iv.121). And later, with anxiety and paranoia closing in upon him, he figures himself as a man who, wading through a bloody river, is in danger of drowning: 'I am in blood/Stepp'd in so far, that, should I wade no more' (iii.IV.135–6).

However, despite all these associations between blood and the violent actions of men performed upon the bodies of other males, it soon becomes clear that the meanings of blood in the play cannot be so easily arrested, fixed or sexed. Far from being a true sign of absolute murderous culpability, blood may be smeared on the bodies of the slumbering grooms in order to mark their innocence as guilty: 'When we have mark'd with blood those sleepy two/Of his own chamber, and us'd their very daggers,/That they have done't' (I.vii.75–8). When Donalbain and Malcolm, misnamed by Macbeth as 'our bloody cousins' (III.i.29), flee war-torn Scotland, they carry with them the bloody guilt that has been fallaciously linked with their names. Transferred, in the words of the *OED*, to an object, person or action that is different from but analogous to that to which it is literally applicable, blood in *Macbeth* assumes metaphorical values and functions, opening itself up to a potentially limitless range of transferrals, substitutions and gendered implications. As metaphor, its most obvious function is as a signifier of Macbeth's culpability, a culpability localized in his own murderous hands: 'Will all great Neptune's ocean wash this blood/Clean from my hand? No, this my hand will rather/The multitudinous seas incarnadine,/Making the green one red' (II. ii. 59–62). Though it stains the hands of a male, Lady Macbeth, in conversation with her guilt-ridden husband, is quick to notice that 'My hands are of your colour' (II.ii.63). This transportation of blood, from the masculine realm of assassination into one that is at least notionally feminine, is intensified during the sleep-walking scene, in which the hallucinating Lady claims 'Here's the smell of the blood still: all the perfumes of Arabia will not sweeten this little hand' (V.i.47–8). Though Rosse maintains that his war-torn native country 'cannot/Be call'd our mother, but our grave' (IV.iii.166), Malcolm comes metaphorically to deploy Scotland as a haemorrhaging maternal body, not unlike the torn and bleeding womb of the mother from which Macduff was 'Untimely ripp'd' (V.viii. 15): 'I think our country sinks beneath the yoke;/It weeps, it bleeds; and each new day a gash/Is added to her wounds' (IV.iii.39–41). No longer associated exclusively with masculinity, but metaphorically transferred onto the hands and mutilated bellies of women, the blood that haemorrhages from the body in the play is as unsexed, as resistant to classification by the male/female gendered and sexual divide, as Lady Macbeth herself.

The unsexing of bodily secretions in *Macbeth* becomes even more pronounced in the case of milk, the other body-fluid that, together with blood and semen, preoccupied early modern anatomists working within the discursive assumptions of Galen's one-sex model. In the lines 'I have given suck, and know/How tender 'tis to love the babe that milks me' (I.vii.54–9), Lady Macbeth manipulatively invokes what is more than likely a fictional, phantasmatic past of fecundity, maternity and child-rearing in an attempt at galvanizing her reluctant husband to action; as seemingly at odds with the couple's childlessness as this claim might be, it nonetheless firmly relies upon, and perpetuates, a conventional range of associations between femininity, maternity and the production of breast-milk. Shortly prior to this, though, Lady Macbeth's private assessment of her husband's character is that 'It is too full o'th'milk of human kindness,/To catch the nearest way' (I.v.17–18). Although, as Richard G. Moulton has argued, 'human kindness' in this line ought more accurately to be glossed if not printed as 'humankind-ness' in order to express Macbeth's 'instinctive tendency to shrink from whatever is in any way unnatural', the emphasis here falls more effortlessly on Lady Macbeth's sense of her husband as an effeminate, lactating man, a male who produces milk in ways that are possible only from within the one-sex anatomical model of sexual difference.[32] Indeed, in the one-sex world of the play it is not entirely inconceivable that even Malcolm, a man otherwise representative of a hyper-masculinity, might lactate, and in rejecting such virtues as justice, perseverance, fortitude and mercy he himself elects to 'Pour the sweet milk of concord into Hell' (IV.iii.97–8).

Given that the one-sexed body of a woman was thought to consist of lesser-developed, inverted equivalents of the male sexual and reproductive organs, unsexing in Renaissance Europe could be perceived as both involuntary and instantaneous, occurring with so little provocation as sudden vigorous movement. Montaigne described a particularly striking account of involuntary unsexing in his essay 'Of the Force of Imagination' in the first book of *The Essays: Or Morall, Politike and Millitarie Discourses*, a text that was translated from the French into English by John Florio in 1603 and widely read in England at the time. Seeking to supplement the tales of gendered metamorphoses from female to male told in the writings of Lucian, Ovid and Pontanus with his own eye-witness account, Montaigne proceeds to recount the case of Marie-Germain, the twenty-two-year-old woman who, leaping over a ditch, was, in the same instant, unsexed as a woman and resexed as a man:

> My selfe traveling on a time by Vitry in *France* [Vitry-le-François], happened to see a man, whom the Bishop of Soissons had in confirmation, named *Germane*, and all the inhabitants there about have both knowne and scene to be a woman-childe, until shee was two and twentie yeares of age, called by the name of *Marie*. [...] Hee saith, that upon a time leaping, and straining himself to overleape an other, he wot not how, but where before he was a woman, he sodainly felt the instruments of a man to come out of him; and to this day the maidens of that towne and countrie have a song in use, by which they warne one an other, when they are leaping, not to straine themselves overmuch, or open their legs too wide, for feare they should bee turned to boyes, as *Marie Germane* was.[33]

As Laqueur has pointed out, a version of the story of Marie-Germain also features in Montaigne's *Travel Journal* as well as in the work of French surgeon and anatomist Ambroise Paré, the chief surgeon to Henry II, Francis II, Charles IX and Henry III.[34] Although it is true that Montaigne in the essay is more concerned with asserting the suggestive powers of the imagination than lending credence to the legend of Marie-Germane, his account is nonetheless useful for the insight it gives into early modern perceptions of unsexing. The cold intentionality with which Lady Macbeth approaches the act in I.v could only have enhanced its swiftness and its seamlessness, the transition rendered all the more credible by the masculine body of the boy-actor who would have played the role of the Lady upon the early modern stage.

Unsexing/Unmanning

The case of Marie-Germain is also significant for a reading of *Macbeth* in another respect, for it indicates that unsexing in the period was conceptualized as a danger pertaining exclusively to women, a compromizing process of resexing that was, in effect, a one-way passage, from female to male, with no likelihood of a return. As Laqueur has pointed out, early modern anatomists such as Gaspard Bauhin, Ambroise Paré, Sir Thomas Browne and J. B. Sinibaldi had all rehearsed Pliny's claim concerning the plausibility and likelihood of females being turned into males, all the while doubting that the same process could apply, in reverse, to men.[35] As Bauhin, cited by William Harvey in *Lectures on the Whole of Anatomy* (1616), put it in *Theatrum Anatomicum* (1605), 'we therefore never find in any true story that any man ever became a woman, because Nature tends always toward what is most perfect and not, on the contrary, to perform in such a way that what is perfect should become imperfect'.[36] The limitations that this proviso placed upon the discursive possibilities of unsexing cast an important light on the unmanning of Macbeth himself in the play. Macbeth's lines in III.ii uncannily repeat and echo those of Lady Macbeth's 'unsex me here' speech in so far as both are ushered in by the imperative, 'Come', both invoke the encrypting effects of what Lady Macbeth refers to as 'thick Night' (I.v.47), and both are expressive of masculine political ambition and murderous intent:

> Come, seeling Night,
> Scarf up the tender eye of pitiful Day,
> And, with thy bloody and invisible hand,
> Cancel, and tear to pieces, that great bond
> Which keeps me pale! (III.ii.46–9)

Despite the steely resolve he demonstrates here, it is during the subsequent banquet scene in III.iv that Lady Macbeth accuses her husband of being 'quite unmann'd in folly' (III.iv.73) as he shivers and starts at the horrid, bloody spectacle of Banquo's ghost. 'Are you a man?' she cruelly cajoles, and drawing upon the same coupling of ghostly supernaturalism and femininity that is at work in such plays as *The Winter's Tale*, *The Tempest* and George Peele's *The Old Wife's Tale* (1595), the Lady intensifies her assault by claiming that Macbeth's reactions 'would well become/A woman's story at a winter's fire,/Authoris'd by her grandam' (III.iv.63–65). Ever vulnerable to his wife's suggestions, Macbeth addresses the ghost with the lines 'If trembling I inhabit then, protest me/The baby of a girl' (III.iv.104–5). Macbeth is not the only husband in the play, of course, who is vulnerable to his wife's aspersions of unmanning. At the news of Macduff's desertion, Lady Macduff, in the presence of her son, impugns through the use of an unflattering metaphorical comparison the masculinity of her husband in ways that parallel the words of Lady Macbeth in III.iv: 'He wants the natural touch; for the poor wren,/The most diminutive of birds, will fight,/ Her young ones in her nest, against the owl' (IV.ii.8–11). Later, once the murder of his wife and children has become known to him, the distraught and tearful Macduff himself makes recourse to a similar metaphorical idiom in the anxious pleadings 'All my pretty ones?/Did you say all? – O Hell-kite! – All?/What, all my pretty chickens, and their dam,/At one fell swoop?' (IV.iii.216–19). Malcolm's response to such a feminine use of language replays, from the position of hyper-masculinity, those of Lady Macbeth in relation to Macbeth's reaction to Banquo's ghost: 'Dispute it like a man' (IV.iii.119). At least in the eyes of those who surround them, Macbeth and Macduff appear to have been unmanned, transfigured into women in a movement cognate with the unsexing of Lady Macbeth.

It soon becomes clear, however, that the concept of unmanning as it applies to the action of Macbeth and Macduff is one that is different from the unsexing of the lady in terms of intention, causation, duration, intensity and effect. Unlike unsexing, which appears to be lasting, durable and wholly irreversible in nature, unmanning is a temporary condition from which a man, however deep his distraction, is invariably likely to recover: as the ghost of Banquo disappears, Macbeth claims that 'I am a man again' (III.iv.108), retrospectively making sense of his marvellous return to rationality as if he had been overcome 'like a summer's cloud' (III.iv.110). Figured thus, unmanning is nothing more than a partial eclipse of one's true and essential manly nature, in marked distinction to the permanent and enduring night in which the somnambulistic, unsexed Lady is trapped, a dark state of madness for which physic, having no satisfactory cure, can only be thrown to the dogs. If unsexing, as Lady Macbeth invites it in the lines 'Come, you Spirits/That tend on mortal thoughts' (I.v.40–1), is deliberate and intentional, the unmanning of Macbeth and Macduff is involuntary, the result of both otherwise rational creatures being temporarily overcome by the powerful, feminizing emotions of terror and grief respectively. As testimony to his recovery, Macbeth asserts his irreversible masculinity via the claim that he has fully come to understand and appreciate the difference between true fear and what his wife had earlier dismissed as 'a painted devil' (II.ii.54), 'the very painting of [his] fear' (III.iv.60). And while the unsexed Lady Macbeth, having effected certain irreversible changes in her body, assumes masculine qualities that appear to be absolute, Macduff's responses to Malcolm's criticism that he express his grief and incredulity at the death of his family 'like a man' discloses the conviction that his apparent femininity, far from being essential, has only ever been a performance: 'O! I could play the woman with mine eyes,/And braggart with my tongue' (IV.iii.230–1). Despite his appearance of having been unsexed, the tears of womanhood, it turns out, are nothing other than a mirage, a stylized fiction of repeated acts based, moreover, on the bedrock of a masculinity in which one has no alternative but to 'feel it as a man' (IV.iii.221). Macduff thus recuperates masculinity as an enduring ontological condition from which no man might ever possibly deviate, and to this Malcolm reassuringly replies 'This tune goes manly' (IV.iii.235). If early modern anatomical thought doubted the possibility that men could be unsexed as masculine and resexed as women, this is an assumption that *Macbeth* seems to share. The full extent of Lady Macbeth's turpitude, however, lies in the fact that she breaches, violates and wilfully ignores the important conceptual distinction between unsexing and unmanning, cruelly accusing her husband of having undergone a weird sexual metamorphosis that, in both textual and historical terms, is fundamentally impossible. Her sense of her husband's 'unmanning' is surely founded upon an intimate knowledge of her husband's body, a body that, variously through overt description or tacit metaphorical implication, is consistently signified as sexually underperforming, weak and even literally impotent in the play: as Julie Barmazel has pointed out, the play is in numerous respects an 'elaborate network of puns about and allusions to Macbeth's sexual dysfunction', forms of impotence that have implications for the organic body and the body politic alike.[37]

Coda: Unsexing, 1674–1800

In the years between its first appearance, in print, in the first Folio edition of *The Tragedie of Macbeth* in 1623 and the influential editions, redactions and rewritings of the play undertaken by Edmond Malone, Thomas and Harriet Bowdler and Charles and Mary Lamb in the Romantic period, the category of the unsexed would embark upon a fascinating voyage of widespread cultural appropriation and permeation, one driven as much by performance history and editorial strategy as by the gendered anxieties that it articulated within the play's original historical moment. Sir William Davenant's extensive reworking of the first Folio in *Macbeth, A Tragedy: With All the Alterations, Amendments, Additions, and New Songs* was published in 1674, but first performed in London at the Duke's Theatre in the 1660s. Marked by a conservative Tory political agenda, the play's immediate impact fell upon the newly restored monarchy, for as Christopher Spencer has pointed out, Davenant's Malcolm is a thinly disguised version of Charles II.[38] Equally pertinent to its impact was the admittance of women to the stage as actresses after 1660. Conceivably for the first time, the role of Lady Macbeth was played by a woman in Davenant's musically enhanced version of the play, although the witches, the true focus of its operatic spectacle, continued to be played by men.[39] The effects of this are almost palpable in Davenant's treatment of the category of the unsexed, both as it occurs as a transitive verb in Lady Macbeth's speech and as a conceptual preoccupation throughout the play more generally. In I.i Davenant reworks Lady Macbeth's soliloquy as follows:

> Come all you spirits
> That wait on mortal thoughts: unsex me here:
> Empty my Nature of humanity,
> And fill it up with cruelty: Make thick
> My bloud, and stop all passage to remorse;
> That no relapses into mercy may
> Shake my design, nor make it fall before
> 'Tis ripen'd to effect: you murthering spirits,
> […] come, and fill my breasts
> With gall instead of milk […] (I.i)

What in the first Folio is described as the filling up of the receptacle-like body with the direst cruelty of masculine humour becomes in Davenant's version an emptying out of the Lady's humanity, not her physical sex, an essential, non-gendered core that masks and erases the body's sexed interiors in its entirety: the female pudenda and womb alluded to in the 'accesse, and passage' of the first Folio (I.v.395) disappear as Davenant employs 'passage' as a verb that signifies movement rather than bodily orifice. Thus considerably tempered, unsexing in Davenant is divested of both its urgency and its anatomical specificity: no longer figured as the reversal of the process of sanguine digestion in which the blood of menses is stopped up and the milk of the female breasts returned to its bloody, humorous origins, unsexing becomes more a moderate, metaphorical change in character and sentiment than an instantaneous conversion of physical sex. It is difficult not to see behind this a sense of the limitations of propriety imposed upon theatrical practice by the newfound presence of the actress on stage: unable to effect a convincing metamorphosis through, say, the discarding of the boy-actor's prosthetic breasts or the deliberate defamiliarization of the illusion of feminine performance, the female body of the actress remains present and substantially unchanged after the soliloquy. Although, as in Shakespeare, Davenant's Lady casts familiar aspersions concerning her husband's unmanning (II.i.), she never undergoes the full transition from female to male that attends the act of unsexing in Shakespeare's play. Ever solicitous of her husband's well-being, she remains in Davenant Macbeth's 'Gentle Love' (I.iv), a term of endearment that Shakespeare's continuously goaded husband never uses, but rather has woundingly applied to himself by his virago-like wife in III.ii.28. And while Shakespeare's unsexed creature makes an irreversible journey into madness and death, Davenant's Lady is thoroughly contrite, remaining sufficiently in possession of her faculties to chide her husband, in a moment of tragic insight, on his failure to master and control her more forceful impulses: 'You were a Man./And by the Charter of your Sex you shou'd/Have govern'd me, there was more crime in you/When you obey'd my Councels, then I contracted/By my giving it' (IV.i). Her femininity remaining fundamentally in place, Davenant's

Lady is not immune to seeing the ghost of Banquo herself, the same ghost that she, with considerably less vitriol, had chided Macbeth for imagining in the earlier banquet scene: 'And yet to Me he Lives./His fatal Ghost is now my shadow, and pursues me/Where ere I do' (4.i). Unsexed in sentiment rather than body, and even then, only partially, Davenant's Lady is strategically re-sexed by the end of the play, meeting her death in an affirmation of punishment and tragic inevitability alike.

Davenant's version of the play held the stage for much of the eighteenth century and was only really superseded by David Garrick's fusion of Davenant, the first Folio and some of his own additions in his version of the play in 1744.[40] Of course, the change in Davenant's treatment of the unsexing of Lady Macbeth is not attributable solely to the presence of the actress on the stage, but also to the effects of historical change registered in discursive shifts, scientific experimentation and the slow decline in Galenic conceptualizations of the body. As Laqueur has argued, these changes occurred at different stages throughout the eighteenth century, culminating, after a period of the co-existence of the two, in the eventual replacement of the one-sex model with the two-sex model of sexual difference. With this, the bodily organs and sexual systems and structures that previously both men and women had been thought to share were separated out from one another, each part individuated, identified and named, with the result that two sexes, the one male and the other female, gained independent ontological existence. Across the eighteenth century, in other words, two sexes, each with discreet and distinct sexual organs, reproductive systems and bodily fluids, were discursively invented as a new binaric foundation for gender. Unsurprisingly, the rise of the two-sex model of sexual difference would have considerable implications for conceptualizations of unsexing in the period, changing attitudes towards the concept that, beyond the example of Davenant, are reflected in appropriation and editorial and performance histories of the play across the long eighteenth century. The new historico-discursive context of utterance brought to the term 'unsexed' a host of different cultural meanings and moral values: if, in the early modern period, the underpinnings of Galenic thought meant that unsexing was an instantaneous, often accidental and unpremeditated occurrence that consisted of a folding out of inverted body-parts from inside to out, the implications of the two-sex model were such that unsexing became an extended, drawn-out process of traversal in which a woman deliberately abandoned her natural sex in order to assume the characteristics of an entirely different and discreet masculine other. For the Renaissance, to be unsexed was to be reconciled, by dint of a woman's inverted sexual anatomy, to the masculinity that lay inevitably within; in the eighteenth century, unsexing, somewhat more radically, meant the abandoning of the feminine subject-position altogether so as to assume the opposing characteristics of the masculine pole of the male/female binary. If the former was vertical, the latter was horizontal; if, as the case of Marie-Germain's 'accidental' unfolding attests, unsexing in the early modern period was not necessarily subject to harsh moral censure, it became during the eighteenth century a sure marker of a woman's deliberate and chosen moral turpitude. In a word, unsexing during the eighteenth century became a much more threatening and contentious concept, inscribed, as it was, not only in gender debates of the period but also within the anxious political debates that transpired in Britain in the post-Revolutionary period of the 1790s.

Its genealogy might be plotted in the major editorial endeavours of the eighteenth century. In the years between Nicholas Rowe's edition of the play in *The Works of Mr. William Shakespear; In Six Volumes* (1709) and Pope and Warburton's *Macbeth* in their eight-volume *The Works of Shakespear* (1747), the 'unsexing' soliloquy increasingly became the object of editorial scrutiny.[41] By the time of Samuel Johnson's *The Plays of William Shakespeare* in 1765, editorial interest in the Lady's famous speech had become intense, with Johnson occasionally drawing upon, occasionally interrogating the earlier glosses of Warburton and Pope and adding his own to such phrases as 'mortal thoughts' and 'nor keep peace between/Th'effect, and it'.[42] Throughout, in fact,

Johnson's editorial paraphernalia betrays a deep repugnance for Shakespeare's unsexed Lady, even to the extent of figuring her rebarbativeness as thoroughly in excess of the beauty of Shakespeare's language as he originally intended it: 'The intent of Lady Macbeth evidently is to wish that no womanish tenderness, or conscientious remorse, may hinder her purpose from proceeding to effect; but neither this, nor indeed any other sense, is expressed by the present reading, and therefore it cannot be doubted that Shakespeare wrote [the original lines] differently.'[43] By the end of the play Johnson's distaste is impossible to contain, and he punctuates his edition with an endnote that includes an *ad feminam* attack upon Lady Macbeth: 'Lady *Macbeth* is merely detested; and though the courage of *Macbeth* preserves some esteem, yet every reader rejoices at his fall.'[44] This 'merely detested' Lady had made her unsettling presence felt in Johnson's earlier endeavours as a lexicographer, when, ten years prior to his edition of *Macbeth*, he published *A Dictionary of the English Language* (1755–6). It is in the second volume to the *Dictionary* that Johnson, citing the Lady's speech in *Macbeth* as the term's original source, defines 'unsex' as both a verb and an adjective: '*To* UNSE'X [*sic*]. *v.a.* To make otherwise than the sex commonly is.'[45] Unsexing served as the word and category through which Johnson could condense and punctuate his misgivings about Shakespeare's detestable character. By all accounts, Johnson's disapprobation was founded not only upon a reading of the play but also upon the particular interpretation that the role had been given by Hannah Vaughn Pritchard, the actress who had played Lady Macbeth alongside David Garrick's Macbeth for the twenty-year period between 1748–68.[46] While Garrick cathartically rendered Macbeth the object of the audience's pity and terror, Pritchard emphasized his wife's aggressive, virago-like qualities,[47] initiating a tendency to play the Lady as a threatening, overbearingly masculine force that has persisted to this day. Johnson's *Macbeth*-derived definition of 'UNSE'X' [*sic*] as 'To make otherwise than the sex commonly is' found its epitome in Pritchard's interpretation of the role, an unnatural, somewhat monstrous deviation or departure from the hallowed bounds of womanhood that was made to seem all the more dangerous and extraordinary in the light of the two-sex model of sexual difference. No longer an unfurling of the masculinity within through a performative speech act, unsexing had become, for the eighteenth century, the height of a committed and morally dubious assault upon nature. With the entry of the term into Johnson's *Dictionary* in 1756, the place of the category within the linguistic and cultural systems of the period was assured: the definition Johnson offered there would be repeated in countless other dictionaries, grammars and etymologies, including, *inter alia*, Joseph Nicol Scott's *A New Universal Etymological Dictionary* (1772), John Ash's *The New and Complete Dictionary of the English Language* (1775) (which include separate entries for 'unsex', 'unsexed' and 'unsexing') and Thomas Sheridan's *A General Dictionary of the English Language* (1780). When Sarah Siddons came to the stage as Lady Macbeth in the late 1770s, she continued in the tradition of Pritchard to play the Lady as a powerful virago, wholly overshadowing her brother John Philip Kemble's Macbeth as she did so. Though, in her 'Remarks on the Character of Lady Macbeth' included in Thomas Campbell's *The Life of Mrs. Siddons* (1839), Siddons seems anxious to recuperate the underlying femininity of the Lady, it was her rendition of the role as a terrifying and awe-inspiring creature for which the actress became most renowned. In Siddons, in other words, the category of the unsexed received sublime elevation, serving as a fascinating yet powerfully admonishing example of a woman who traversed the bounds of her sex upon the pain of madness and death.

The frequency with which verbal and adjectival forms of the word 'unsex' occur in advice manuals for young women written and published in the last three decades of the eighteenth century attests to the extent to which the category was wholly amenable to uptake by, and inscription within, the gender politics of the two-sex model. In such texts as Elizabeth Griffith's *Essays Addressed to Young Married Women* (1782),[48] John Stuart's *Travels Over the Most Interesting Parts of the Globe, To Discover the Source of Moral Motion* (1792)[49] George Wright's *The Lady's Miscellany* (1793)[50] and other similar anthologies of instructive reading for women, the category of the unsexed, often excerpted directly from Lady Macbeth's speech, serves as a negative example against which ideal notions of femininity ought to be defined. Presumably for similar reasons Harriet and Thomas Bowdler's *The Family Shakespeare* (1807) left the speech entirely unexpunged, while Charles and Mary Lamb's prose-narrative of the play in *Tales from Shakespeare* (1807) simply described Macbeth's wife as 'a bad ambitious woman', the gendered opposite to which young female readers ought to aspire.[51] In the early modern period, unsexing was a literal anatomical conversion, founded in the biological conversion of a woman's sex; by the end of the eighteenth century, it is a metaphor employed to describe and censure a woman's transgression of the socially constructed codes of gender masquerading as Nature.

But it was in the fourth and final book of T. J. Mathias's *The Pursuits of Literature: A Satirical Poem* (1797), his lengthy indictment of contemporary letters, politics and post-Revolutionary life in general, that the category of the unsexed received its most influential appropriation in late eighteenth-century Britain. Mathias, having accused Matthew Lewis of committing acts of gross obscenity and blasphemy in his outrageous Gothic romance *The Monk* (1796), conservatively turns to assess the Revolutionary spirit that, he fears, is threatening to run amok in Britain in the wake of recent Revolutionary events in France: 'Our peasantry now read the *Rights of Man* on mountains, and moors, and by the way side; and shepherds make the analogy between their occupation and that of their governors. Our *unsexed* female writers now instruct or confuse us and themselves in the labyrinth of politics, or turn us wild with Gallic frenzy.'[52] Unsexing, here, is the consequence of a woman writer who, lured by the call of French-inspired democracy, abandons the place of demure feminine retirement in order to peddle her dangerous ideological wares through the pages of lurid Gothic romance. In the Preface to the First Dialogue in the poem, first published separately in

1794, Mathias had identified the sorts of women writers whom he, in the Fourth Book, seems to have in mind:

> Mrs Charlotte Smith, Mrs Inchbald, Mrs Mary Robinson, Mrs &c. &c. Though all of them are very ingenious ladies, yet they are too frequently whining or striking in novels, till our girls' heads turn wild with impossible adventures, and now and then are tainted with democracy.[53]

For Mathias, women who dare to venture beyond the domestic confines of Nature in order to engage in the masculine realm of radical politics are, as unsexed beings, likely to forfeit all claims to their femininity. Politically rather than biologically conceived, unsexing as Mathias conceives it is informed by the two-sex model of sexual difference and the ideology of separate spheres that superimposes itself upon it. As always, it is the figure of Lady Macbeth that drives and motivates this process, for as E. J. Clery has pointed out, the assaults on literary propriety and respectability mounted by such important late eighteenth-century writers of Gothic romance as Ann Radcliffe, Joanna Baillie and Charlotte Dacre were all self-consciously informed by the sublime inspiration that these writers drew from Sarah Siddons's performance of Lady Macbeth.[54]

Responding to Mathias in *The Pursuits of Literature*, Richard Polwhele published *The Unsex'd Females: A Poem* in 1798, seeking, as the Preface to the American edition of 1800 put it, at once to elaborate upon Mathias's 'animadversions' on those literary ladies who had discarded their feminine modesty in adopting 'the sentiments and the manners of the impious amazons of republican France' and to 'charm them back to the paths from which they have strayed'.[55] Like Mathias's, Polwhele's conceptualization of unsexing is founded upon an appeal to natural femininity and modesty, both traits deeply enshrined within the two-sex model of sexual difference, and compromized, in his estimation, by a woman's dabbling in continental radicalism and fashion-sense alike:

I shudder at the new unpictur'd scene,
Where unsex'd woman vaunts the imperious mien;
Where girls, affecting to dismiss the heart,
Invoke the Proteus of petrific art;
With equal ease, in body or in mind,
To Gallic freaks or Gallic faith resign'd,
The crane-like neck, as Fashion bids, lay bare,
Or frizzle, bold in front, their borrow'd hair [. . .] (8–9)

Polwhele's list of culprits in the scene of widespread cultural unsexing that he surveys before him is more extensive than that of Mathias, extending to include such important writers of the period as Charlotte Smith, Helen Maria Williams, Mary Hays and Mary Robinson. Predictably, it is the figure of the radical feminist Mary Wollstonecraft, the 'hyena in petticoats' of Horace Walpole's infamous designation, that bears the brunt of Polwhele's misogynist rage, the unsexed creature against whom the archly conservative Hannah More appears to be an example of ideal femininity. If Wollstonecraft unsexes herself in championing the rights of women within the broader context of radical agitation and political Revolution, Hannah More embraces wholeheartedly the separate spheres of the two-sex system, and in a lengthy footnote to the poem Polwhele cites, as evidence, the rigid differentiation between men and women that More advances in her own advice manual *Essays on Various Subjects, Principally Designed for Young Ladies* (1776): men are rational and coldly utilitarian while women as naturally perceptive, fanciful and attentive to beauty. The two-sex model informing one particular passage from More's *Essays* that Polwhele cites has an especially powerful resonance within the context of his discussion of unsexing in the poem: 'In short, it appears, that the mind, in each sex, has some natural kind of bias, which constitutes a distinction of character; and that the happiness of both depends, in a great measure, on the preservation and observance of this distinction.'[56] To be unsexed is to turn one's back on Nature, to heap upon oneself, as Wollstonecraft surely did, the misery and eventual death that lies in wait for those who fail to observe the distinctions between the sexes.

In the same year Mary Hays, one of the radical women writers whom Polwhele included in his category of the unsexed, responded to the aspersion in her *Appeal to the Men of Great Britain In Behalf of Women* (1798). If women, Hays – like Wollstonecraft – argues, are rational beings, unsexing remains a fundamental impossibility, not a likelihood or a threat, 'For mind, as has before been fondly quoted, is of no sex; therefore it is not in the power of education or art to unsex it.'[57] Pitting the claim of the seventeenth-century feminist Cartesian philosopher François Poullain de la Barre against conservative appropriations of *Macbeth*, Hays renders the unsexed the site of a reverse discourse. This was by no means an isolated case, for as Adriana Craciun has shown, many of the late eighteenth-century women writers whom patriarchal cultural commentators the likes of Mathias and Polwhele had relegated to the category of the unsexed used this subject position as the site of committed feminist opposition, with figures such as Charlotte Dacre, Anne Bannerman, Laetitia Landon and Mary Lamb actively unsexing themselves, through the graphic articulation of 'unfeminine' sexual desire and the committing of unspeakable acts of violence, so as to trouble and disturb the notion of natural difference between the sexes enshrined in the two sex system. As Craciun explains, though, unsexing in this context is not to be understood as a woman's willful assumption of masculine traits so much as an attempt at rendering subjectivity free of the limitations of the male/female binaric divide: 'Being an "unsexed" Woman [...] is not the same as being male. The unsexed female is *unfemale*, a third term in a non-anomalous position outside the two-sex binary', attesting, as such, to the limitations of modern sexual dimorphism.[58] As resistant to masculine identity as she is to femininity, the unsexed woman of Romanticism anticipates the utopian vision of a subjectivity cut loose from the confines of sexual and gendered identity that is given poignant expression in the work of contemporary Queer theory. Indeed, it is perhaps to Lady Macbeth that Queer theory today ought to turn, finding in her 'unsex me here' soliloquy a call for the unshackling of desire and identity that, in the present, seems not too dissimilar to its own.

CHAPTER FOUR

Macbeth in the Present

TERENCE HAWKES

Sans Everything

A climax in the interpretation of Shakespeare was recently unveiled by a group called the American Synetic Theater. Operating in Washington DC, its performance of *Macbeth* had marvellous reviews and it attracted an enthusiastic audience. Its tale of 'ambition, bloodlust and the supernatural', as one reviewer called it, was apparently riveting. An evening of madness, murder and self-destruction, it fused drama, movement, acrobatics, dance and music in a phenomenon that was lauded 'world-class physical theater'. However, what Shakespeare had to do with it was not clear. This was because the play had no language. It was, literally, wordless.

A 'wordless Shakespeare' has not of course been the first or indeed the sole experiment in what might be called the modern essence of the Bard. There are many variations involving language or its absence. In 2006, the Chekhov International Theatre Company from Moscow, directed by Declan Donnellan, produced an edited and translated version of *Twelfth Night*. It had an all-male cast and it was performed in Russian. The text of the play, displayed in 'surtitles' to the audience in Buenos Aires, was in Spanish. Elsewhere, the edited Russian text could be played, via surtitles, in Turkish, Polish, Finnish, Japanese or presumably any other language. In other words, with English scattered to the winds, it's plain that the effective discourse used in the play really didn't matter. Like the 'wordless' *Macbeth*, this production made clear that its commitment was not, perish the thought, to Shakespeare's language at all. Hence, it's not even surprising that as part of Olympic Games celebrations in London in 2012 it was announced that there would also be a 'Cultural Olympiad' festival featuring Shakespeare. Accordingly, thirty-seven companies from all over the world performed one of Shakespeare's plays at the Globe Theatre, using languages ranging from Armenian to Urdu. There was *Henry IV, Part 2* in Argentine Spanish, *Twelfth Night* in Hindi, *Coriolanus* in Japanese, *All's Well That Ends Well* in Gujarati, *A Midsummer Night's Dream* in Russian, *Troilus and Cressida* in Maori. South Sudan indicated a plan to perform *Cymbeline* in Juba Arabic. There were also, apparently, performances in British Sign Language (for the deaf).[1] Sadly, nobody suggested that a play might even be offered by means of Semaphore.

Could it possibly be true that works written in English have some strange capacity denied to other cultures? Is it the case that they need not be reduced to anyone's puny linguistics to exhibit and renew their potency? Can they override the language in which they were composed? Can they 'mean' to the deaf? Can they discourse whilst being mute? To those in the know, it seems that, with Shakespeare's plays, the commitment is not, perish the thought, to utterance at all, but to something higher, more abstract and wholly engulfing. We can be precise. It seeks to promote the container over what it ought properly to contain. It is called 'Theatre'.

To take a particular example, we might think of a recent stellar performance of Shakespeare in, of all places, Kabul. In 2005 a production of *Love's Labour's Lost*, set in Afghanistan and translated into the Dari language, played in that besieged community to packed audiences. The plot was recast to feature Afghan characters and locations. The local provisions of Muslim patterns of behaviour, not usually allowed beyond the playhouse, scarcely applied in this case. The female actors didn't use veils or wear the burqa and were able to flirt roundly with their colleagues. The performance, which ran for five nights, was sponsored by the British Council, something which perhaps encouraged co-adaptor Stephen Landrigan to remain wholly undismayed, even to welcome the occasion. 'Shakespeare is so adaptable', he claimed, 'because he writes universal truths of human experience.'[2] Perhaps we should not disabuse him. The unveiling of Shakespeare's 'universal truths' presumably aided the war effort in that part of the world. For the Americans, the reports claims, the US Agency for International Development had already started to use troupes of actors in rural areas, staging plays (perhaps the monarchy-defending works of Shakespeare) as a way of educating people concerning forthcoming elections.

In short, these developments seem to mean that we can forget what the plays actually say. To be displaced 'beyond' English, using the language of other nations, even to be 'wordless', seems to be a positive advantage if what we are concerned with is 'Theatre'. We can forget the issues of government, policy, money, crime and retribution that these dramas discuss. It seems, after all, that the words don't matter. Access from some heights beyond language – if there are any – makes all cultures kin. Modern Shakespeare apparently operates in all seasons and for all audiences, in any language, and even without language itself. Who says the Bard doesn't support democracy, or its reverse, or monarchy or republicanism or the rule of Muslim law? You can bet your life that 'Theatre' does. And when it comes to Shakespeare, who needs words when 'Theatre' is king?

However, we can also be sure that in these circumstances real life has its own way of taking command. In Afghanistan, on 19 August 2011, at least six Taliban attackers proceeded to blow their way into the British Council compound in Kabul. Determined and fully armed, they took up positions throughout the buildings and they came for a long fight. There was no announcement that the unveiling of Shakespeare's universal truths had in any way prohibited their action. Quite the reverse. They proclaimed that they had chosen this particular date and target as clearly marking the ninety-second anniversary of Afghanistan's independence from Britain. The British Council seemed an appropriate quarry.

During the operation all the Taliban were killed, and in turn they murdered twelve people.

A Taste of Ambiguity

The truth is that Shakespeare cannot be separated from politics and we ignore that at our peril. Nor can we separate him from his language, which is a paramount concern. As we approach the issue of defining *Macbeth* in the present, these matters come to be more and more important, and we might begin by considering the issues raised by the critic William Empson, who focuses primarily on the play's language as the crucible of its tragedy.

In his major work, *Seven Types of Ambiguity*, Empson describes what he calls Ambiguity of the First Type.[3] This deals with the sort of complexity that derives from questions of Pure Sounds and Atmosphere, in which a particular mode of meaning can be seen to operate in several ways at once. He sketches this effect as one which produces 'a sort of taste in the head', although he also recognizes that for a poet the process of 'putting such a taste in the reader's head involves a great deal of work which does not feel like a taste in the head while it is being done'. In effect, he's talking about what we loosely think of as 'atmosphere' in verse, something which is inevitably implied by how meaning operates in words and 'the consciousness of what is implied by the meaning'. In many cases the 'affective state' embodied in a piece of language is apparently and surprisingly conveyed by 'devices of particular irrelevance'. Yet this apparent lack of relevance turns out to be one of the important ways in which a speech operates. Indeed, 'irrelevance' is a major weapon of meaning, and we need to attend to it.[4]

He offers 'a striking example' from *Macbeth*, where Macbeth speaks of his plan to murder Banquo and Fleance:

> Come, seeling Night,
> Scarf up the tender eye of pitiful Day,
> And, with thy bloody and invisible hand,

> Cancel, and tear to pieces, that great bond
> Which keeps me pale. Light thickens; and the crow
> Makes wing to th'rooky wood.
> Good things of Day begin to droop and drowse,
> Whiles Night's black agents to their preys do rouse.
> Thou marvell'st at my words: but hold thee still;
> Things bad begun make strong themselves by ill.
> So, prithee, go with me.[5] (III.ii. 47–57)

Empson focuses on two almost irrelevant and apparently interchangeable concepts, uttered almost as an afterthought, whilst Macbeth ponders the night sky. They are 'crow' and 'rook'. As 'light thickens', the surprising tartness of that metaphor suddenly releases an image of Macbeth as a single crow, alone in the sky. It's evening so the crow is 'moving towards bed and the other crows'. However, their 'beds' are oddly described as 'rooky' (line 52).[6] Suddenly, two opposite notions start to appear mixed together. Macbeth is momentarily seen as a solitary carrion crow (the sort who normally lives alone). Yet also, in the same signal he presents himself as a peaceful, companionable rook (who normally lives in crowds). As a murderer – as a crow – he will of course appear startlingly different to the other rooks. Yet, as Empson says, he doesn't want to shoulder the burden of that difference even though he now bears his new and illegitimate crown: 'he is anxious, at bottom, to be at one with the other rooks, not to murder them'. Nevertheless, bearing the signs of his murder, he emerges as a single carrion crow, even as he 'makes wing' to the comradeship of the rookery. In a desperate attempt to shield himself from the act's enormity, he wishes (perhaps like all murderers) 'to obtain peace of mind' despite his crime.[7] Yet he also, in due course, aims to kill Banquo and Fleance as well.

Empson's analysis of the complex 'atmosphere' of this tiny part of a particular speech of the play is a very small aspect of his notion of ambiguity as a central feature of language. For him ambiguity implies a dynamic factor of speech which 'stretches' it and so makes it able to enclose new areas of meaning. Such stretching means that mere stability in the area of meaning will not become an overt concern. In fact, there's a sense in which language is wholly entwined and woven in with ambiguity, so that 'opposite' meanings will always shine, illuminate and invade the 'ordinary' features of what happens when we speak. You can't *remove* ambiguity from language: you are forced to embrace it. As Empson says:

> An ambiguity in ordinary speech means something very pronounced, and as a rule witty or deceitful. I propose to use the word in an extended sense, and shall think relevant to my subject any verbal nuance, however slight, which gives room for alternative reactions to the same piece of language.[8]

Empson's ultimate contribution is to recognize that in the use it makes of its stretching capability, ambiguity reveals itself as a language's most dynamic feature. He claims that 'In a sufficiently extended sense any prose statement could be called ambiguous'[9] so that 'what often happens when a piece of writing is felt to offer hidden riches is that one phrase after another lights up and appears as the heart of it; one part after another catches fire' (p. 19).

A Double Sense

In this respect it should be clear that a 'wordless' *Macbeth* offers almost a contradiction in terms. The play throbs with ambiguity and from the witches on it deals in that 'extended sense' of language wholesale. It inhabits a kind of jungle of wild and whirling words, misunderstood vows, half-understood commitments, a maelstrom of language in which the witches' speeches conceal interests never revealed. In the acting profession, even the title of the play is considered unlucky, and despite its overt content, it seems readily to inhabit an alternative world of vivid yet dimly heard tumult. Of course, it's true that the play has evidently been robbed of material. It must be almost half the length of a normal tragedy, and a great deal seems to have been lost. Indeed, some of the language isn't written by Shakespeare at all. The opening scene seems to have been composed by Middleton, and its language and its rhythmic structure have the drastic sweep of an instrument almost deliberately lamed by its own rhymed and end-stopped lines:

> *1st Witch*: When shall we three meet again?
> In thunder, lightning, or in rain?
> *2nd Witch*: When the hurly-burly's done,
> When the battle's lost and won. (I.i.1–4)

The effect of this is to make the rhyming words almost act against the sense which they convey. Their clangour imposes its own drowning measure on the sounds they make and adds its flavour to what they propose. Macbeth's wife may dance attention on his ambition, but the fact that she is played by a male Elizabethan actor means that her forceful reference to her stage sex – 'Come you spirits/That tend on mortal thoughts, unsex me here [...] Come to my woman's breasts,/And take my milk for gall' (1.v.39–47) as well as her admission that 'I have given suck, and know/How tender 'tis to love the babe that milks me' (I.vii.54–5) – raises this acting convention almost in its own right, and so makes dissembling a part of the play's larger reference. Is Lady Macbeth referring to her (female) self in the play or lamely gesturing to her (male) inadequacies on the stage? The same issue is made in the case of the witches. They should be women, 'And yet your beards forbid me to interpret/That you are so' (I. iii.44–5). These broader tensions underlie the hurly-burly of battle and the moral division which start to dominate the stage. They begin to hint at an enormous duplicity which suddenly starts to pervade this spectacle of murder, blood-stained wretched hands, and the sleepwalking of the guilty. Its object is to complicate and mystify communion. Turmoil is promised and delivered, meaning reversed, when 'Fair is foul; and foul is fair'.

And of course witches are traditionally associated with the heart of the hurly burly. Nashe's comment in his *Terrors of the Night* (1594) makes it clear that in this hellish atmosphere 'euery thing must bee interpreted backwards as Witches say their Pater-noster, good being the character of bad, and bad of good'.[10]

As Macbeth discovers, the witches deal entirely with equivocation. This was a topic that had become a major consideration in London at that time and the witches are expert in just that: they are 'juggling fiends' who 'palter with us in a double sense,/ That keep the word of promise to our ear/And break it to our hope' (V.x.20–2). Moreover, at the moment of Macbeth's initial murder, the play introduces through the Porter a famous case of equivocation, which links him precisely with the use of ambiguity and 'double' meaning:

> Knock, knock. Who's there in' th' other devil's name? Faith, here's an equivocator, that cold swear in both the scales against either scale; who committed treason enough for God's sake, yet could not equivocate to heaven. O, come in, equivocator. (II. iii. 7–11)

The passage alludes to the famous trial of Father Garnet (1606) who was charged with others of involvement in the Gunpowder Plot. In his trial, finally realizing that his denial of his relationships with the Plotters had been shown to be false, Garnet replied to his accusers with the scandalous notion that in his case equivocation could be confirmed by oath or sacrament without perjury 'if just necessitie so require'. The idea of a 'double sense', the notion, central to equivocation, of opposed meanings knowingly contained within the same linguistic structure, was – reputedly it seems – a characteristic stratagem in the arguments of Jesuit priests. This conclusion would have outraged a society already disposed to think the worst of Roman Catholics, and it gives to the issue of 'double' meaning a crucial sign that called for moral horror in Jacobean Britain. After all, when he was first presented by his supporters as the so-called 'second' Brutus, it was assumed that King James was destined to reunify the land (i.e. Britain) that the first Brutus founded. And God's divine plan for what James liked to call 'Great Britain' must not, government propaganda indicated, be wrecked by the duplicity and ambiguity of the agents of the Devil, or the Pope. Equivocation could never be tolerated. Certainly not here.

But beyond that denunciation of 'double' meaning there is something in *Macbeth* that pushes it even closer to our own concerns. As Empson notes, ambiguity is deeply rooted in human beings and come what may it fogs our own language. We may hear a person speak, but we can never be sure what he or she actually means. He describes this aspect of equivocation and duplicity as one which uses a standard notion of ambiguity.[11] Empson goes on to say that

> This sort of contradiction is at once understood in literature, because the process of understanding one's friends must always be riddled with such indecisions and the machinery of such hypocrisy; people, often, cannot have done both of two things, but they must have been in some way prepared to have done either; whichever they did, they will have still lingering in their minds the way they would have preserved their self-respect if they had acted differently; they are only to be understood by bearing both possibilities in mind.[12]

Empson's notion that 'Irony in this subdued sense, as a generous scepticism which can believe at once that people are and are not guilty, is a very normal and essential method' remains very interesting.[13] It even suggests, despite King James's claims, that 'double meaning' is still, inevitably, a power in the present.

Britannia

Could it be that 'double meaning' invests all aspects of language in Britain? Perhaps Shakespeare himself stands as the major exponent of an art that wholeheartedly promotes the essence of duplicity in English? In general terms, his plays seem almost to derive from and address themselves to a social way of life which certainly juggles at least two contradictory modes of meaning. A newly capitalist Elizabethan society, for instance, sought to balance an old allegiance to inherited social structures with a new and competing commitment to burgeoning individualism: something which flushes away the past and embraces 'getting on' and iconoclastic 'career'-building. It's a society which has what Marshall McLuhan called a clash between the demands of inherited social 'roles' on the one hand and those of newly established 'goals' on the other. It thus made the newly modern issue of 'playing a part' as opposed to fulfilling stratagems in a divinely ordained scheme a central concern. In the process, it guaranteed plays – those structures which embodied 'playing a part' – the sort of critical purchase on their culture that perhaps they have not enjoyed since.[14]

The two notions of kingship and of acting – the culture's two central performative modes in terms of politics and society – consequently bulk large in Shakespearean drama. Each offers opportunities for a careful probing of the complexities of ambiguity and dualism, the ways in which some entities can concurrently claim to be both 'the same' and 'different', with the paths between the two endlessly changed, deferred or re-routed. Both seem to endorse the silent presuppositions of a way of life in which the polarities of ambiguity, of repetition, (or sameness) and of change (or difference), operate not as mutually exclusive opposites, but in the sort of inclusive tension that challenges our own sequential logic. Thus, a defunct or deposed monarch will always be replaced by a different person, but he or she, although different, will nonetheless always remain 'the same': the King is dead, long live the King. Similarly, an actor cannot avoid being both the same as, and different from, the character whose part he takes: 'This is and is not Cressid', says Troilus in V.ii.144 – ambiguously of a male player – at that astonishing moment in the play when the overt pulse of the story seems to falter and role-playing itself bursts through as its leading subject.[15] Drama of this sort directly challenges a reasoning – say in *Hamlet* – which would say that someone must either be a father or an uncle to the same son, not both, and in so doing it makes possible and fosters those 'leaps' in meaning that seem so central a characteristic of these plays.

If the two roles that embody the essence of that society, in politics the person of the monarch, in culture that of the actor, they seem to fuse as handy symbols of important political and social issues. They do so in the words inscribed over the entrance to the original Globe theatre where they represent a forthright endorsement of 'doubleness'. Ambiguity, repetition, duplicity make us human, they propose. Pretending, counterfeiting, acting, they suggest, are ineluctable and imperative. We live in a world of actors and audiences, spectators and players, a binary 'split' world of essential and necessary opposition. We inhabit not a universe but a duoverse. 'All the world's a stage' is its motto.

As a result, we can expect that Shakespeare's drama engages intimately with a way of life in which the polarities of ambiguity, duality and repetition operate not as mutually exclusive opposites but in creative, inclusive and fruitfully disturbing tension. Does their shifting relationship also provide an index, or even a reflection, of overriding social tendencies? After all, the essence of 'Britishness' itself derives from a sense of each Briton having at least two 'national' identities. We may be Welsh, Scottish or English, but the essence of living in these islands also requires those countries to be drained, to some extent, to further the notion of a state called 'Britain'. Does this hint at an approach to *Macbeth*?

In the Present

Although the tragedy of *Macbeth* is evidently concerned with the figures of Macbeth and his wife, there can be no doubt that its larger focus, beyond the stage, is vested in King James I as he was known in England and James VI as he was called in Scotland. We should remember that the ambiguity of James is either forced upon us immediately by his presence (there is a suggestion that the first performance of *Macbeth* took place at Hampton Court in the presence of James and of his guest King Christian IV of Denmark) or by the context of Britain as a whole.[16] James was a king of Scotland who also became a king of England. So when the play asks us to admire the English king (historically this would have been Edward the Confessor) particularly because of his 'healing' touch, we are meant to note that this gift was passed on 'to the succeeding royalty' (IV. iii. 156). Thus it is James I and VI who is also able to cure the sick (particularly those suffering from scrofula), for 'Such sanctity hath heaven given his hand' (IV.iii. 145). Indeed, his 'most miraculous work' is part of a whole array of wonderful kingly activities, so that 'With this strange virtue,/ He hath a heavenly gift of prophecy;/And sundry blessings hang about his throne,/That speak him full of grace' (IV. iii. 157–60). The opposed horrific 'Evil' pursued in Scotland by Macbeth and the notion that he is impelled to this fate in Scotland by 'juggling fiends' such as the witches is plainly signalled by this. The play clearly offers England as the obvious choice from which an avenging army might thus be recruited. As a result, the setting of England as opposed to Scotland in the play must form the background of my current proposal to talk about *Macbeth* in terms of what has been called 'presentism'.

Presentism in literary criticism simply means that the critic should offer due respect to the present as well as to the past.[17] History lies to us if it seems to offer us any completely realized 'past' which we are able to see independently of what happens in the present. None of us can get beyond time, and time in the present inexhaustibly patterns our notion of what 'used to' or 'did' take place in the past. We can never see the past as it genuinely happened because we can only see the past through, and by means of, the present. In fact, the present is the only means by which it's possible to perceive the past, and it alone provides our means of comprehending it. Football fans, wise in the ways of the slow-motion 'replay', will have that much in common with the student of literature of the past.[18] To see a television 'replay' of a goal that was awarded – or not – earlier can often give rise to serious misgivings about latter-day human perception. To perceive something 'tomorrow' as opposed to 'today', even though it may also be recognized as 'the same', is often to see something rather different. The concern of the nineteenth-century historian Leopold von Ranke to address the past in terms of 'how it really was' (or *wie es eigentlich gewesen*) is spoken of by E. H. Carr as a 'not very profound aphorism' and certainly not in any sense capable of being realized. The terms of the legal notion of *Nunc Pro Tunc* (now for then), where the past may be considered as if it had just occurred, cannot reasonably be applied to literature from a previous age.[19] Neither of these can represent a 'genuine' experience of history.

In short, respect for the *present* obviously militates against those notions that urge us to see a text precisely in terms to which its own society – not ours – has immediate, unthinking access. In effect, we can't. And if we think we can, we ignore the one factor that ensures our failure: our felt, concrete residence in *this* world, where we live and breathe and have our own unthinking being. That present necessarily subverts any sense of the past's distinctness. The one dissipates the other. Given this problem, presentism aims to represent and justify a compromize between these two commitments both to the past and the present. It offers a never-ending dialogue between them – between what we think of as the past and what we know of as the present – and proposes that we recognize both as crucial to our experience of literature. It follows that presentist criticism's engagement with the text should be precisely in terms of those dimensions of the present which most clearly connect with the events of the past. Hence it deliberately employs crucial aspects of the present as a trigger for its investigations: its centre of gravity will necessarily be 'now', rather than 'then'.[20] This means that facts do not speak for themselves. Nor do texts. But we need not wring our hands. To quote an argument I've used before, this doesn't mean that facts or texts don't exist. Of course they do. But it also means that facts and texts are capable of genuinely contradictory meanings, none of which has any independent 'given' or self-evident status. Indeed 'they don't speak at all until they are inserted into and perceived as part of specific discourses which impose their own shaping requirements and agendas [...] Facts and texts, that is to say, don't simply speak, don't merely mean. *We* speak, *we* mean, *by* them.'[21]

This also means that any notion of a play 'in the present' is bound to reveal aspects of itself that the work, viewed in terms of its own history, currently hides. The play cannot simply be mired in its own past and cannot just be held to any plans it seems originally to have laid out. It will always 'mean' more (or less) than it seems to mean.[22] One obvious area of potential presentist interest in *Macbeth* must therefore lie in the recent development of so-called 'devolution' in British politics as a means of meeting the demands of Scottish, Welsh and Irish national sentiment. This principle is reflected nowhere more intensely than in the massive re-negotiation of power relationships that is currently at stake between the four nations comprising Britain. Not for the first time in history, but certainly for the first time concurrently and as aspects of a planned development, separate parliaments or assemblies now exist in Scotland, Wales and Northern Ireland.[23]

The implications of King James's Scottish background, judged by the opinion of some of his latest subjects in London, might originally have been difficult to swallow, but in *Macbeth* these are apparently redeemed by the new heaven-sent virtues which he brings to 'gracious England' (IV. iii. 44). Perhaps this attempts to turn aside some of the sarcasm of such as Ben Jonson, but the embarrassments and awkwardness of certain aspects of James's behaviour persisted. In his play *Eastward Ho* (1605) Jonson, together with his co-authors George Chapman and John Marston, has one of his 'Gentlemen' comment, presumably in an accent hinting firmly at James's own speech patterns, that 'I ken the man weel; he's one of my thirty pound knights'(IV.i.221).[24] The reference to James's promiscuous selling of English honours hardly confirms that he is full of grace and Jonson's punishment for the insult tells much about James's sanctity. His newly found

'British' role, despite his self-appointed guise as the 'hero' of the Gunpowder Plot, makes it appropriate to look at several other developments of James's reign which may raise multiple issues for a modern observer. Within a year of *Macbeth*'s completion, on 14 May 1607, Captain John Smith finally established the first permanent British settlement in North America. In honour of the monarch it was called Jamestown. Just a dozen years later it began the first systematic importation of African slaves to the colony. Also in 1607, two Irish earls named Tyrone and Tyrconnel fled suddenly from Ireland to the Continent. Seizing this opportunity, James took the step of parcelling up that land and offering it for sale to Englishmen and Scotsmen prepared to move to Ireland. It was hoped that the colony this provided – it was also called a 'plantation' – would provide a permanent Protestant bulwark against the native Catholic population and help, in the name of Christianity and of the unity of Great Britain, to subdue it. This area is now called Ulster, and in the last thirty years it has offered to the British many of the horrors it was invented to suppress.

Of course, these developments suggest that the rise of any culture, let alone that of Great Britain, is bound to create horrors as well as peace and prosperity, and any play written by an Englishman and set in Scotland will have enough melancholy of one sort or another to suffice. But the major aspect revealed by *Macbeth* under the flag of presentism is the potential disjunction of that accord which the play's monarch and presumably its first audience sought to secure and perpetuate: the union of Scotland and England. James VI sought to establish this in advance of the official treaty of 1707, and of course it is the case that Scots have been in charge of British affairs not infrequently in the years between. But when it comes to Scottish Nationalism, as a rising tide in current affairs, we seem to have something quite different. One of its concerns is the particular role given to the English language and its literature, to say nothing of the rise to success of the English playwright Shakespeare and his play *Macbeth*.

The English language, English literature, Englishness itself, have never been perceived by the English-born natives as distinctive, something they might possess concretely enough to justify a sense of loss if it were to vanish. In an Anglo-centric, self-contained Britain, that massive project begun over four hundred years ago, to be English, and to speak English, was always meant to be unremarkable and quotidian. In such a context, the central unspoken English belief was that the world in itself was 'English', the language to describe it was 'English' and its use demonstrated that a palpable, homespun, 'English' truth lay beneath everything. Other people have identifiable cultures, distinctive languages, specific cuisines, 'national' dress. The English simply speak, simply eat, simply write, simply live. This unthinking construction of a world finally grounded in Englishness effectively naturalizes its own particular patterns of conventions, characterizations, and modes in literature, making them invisible, effortless, and apparently fully deserving of collusive applause as faithful reflections of a universal 'human nature'. Everybody really speaks English, if they are human. The fish, as Marshall McLuhan liked to say, knows nothing of water.[25]

However, a major irony emerges from this. The dereliction of the English in connection with their own language has meant that the rise of 'English Literature' as an academic subject – and thus the rise of Shakespeare at its helm as a major cultural force in the world – seems to be something for which the English are not primarily responsible. In fact, in a situation fully flushed with irony, those truly liable may well be the Scots. In the last two hundred years, the contradictions implicit in Scotland's dual status have been crucial. Colonized within Britain by the English, they have also acted in the rest of the world as a colonizing force on behalf of the British Empire. Speaking English, Scotland has inevitably drawn attention to the role of the English language as a major ideological and thus a political market place in countries abroad where cultural meanings are often up for grabs. To use Robert Crawford's perceptive words, 'English' has ultimately become an important 'site of negotiation between English and native, non-English voices'. Given Scotland's major export of English teachers, the main proposition of Crawford's book, *The Scottish Invention of English Literature*, reiterated through a number of carefully linked and insistent essays, is starkly revisionist: 'English literature as a university subject is a Scottish invention.'[26] This is not merely a debating point along with other issues in a twenty-first-century drama, where the dismantling of the British Empire will be played out in terms of the break-up of the United Kingdom. It also raises the question of whether Shakespeare will in future rank as the national British Bard. It also poses central questions in connection with *Macbeth* itself.

Passepartout

A presentist view of *Macbeth* is bound to offer to reshape the play. In particular, it makes it not simply, or not only, a drama which concerns itself with metaphysical matters such as evil and regret. Murder, conscience, disharmony and fear all stride the stage, but in the twenty-first century the relationship between Scotland and England is bound to become much more intense. The English king's rather sickly 'touching' for the Evil will have little appeal for Scots. Scotland may be a land stalked by witches, Macbeth and his wife may be involved in the Devil's use of language, but the structure of a newly expanded 'Great Britain' and the problems this engenders must now bulk large. One result will be a change in Macbeth's status. His standing as 'brave Macbeth' and 'Valour's minion' (I.ii.16–19) can hardly be overlooked and his courage will ultimately come to be a major factor when an audience assesses him. A startling grandeur starts to suffuse his role as he's hunted by what's clearly seen as an 'English power' (V.ii.1). As he begins to fortify Dunsinane with 'valiant fury' (V.ii.14), we must begin to admire his stamina and his energy. It's not difficult to view the disdainfully dismissed invading troops as over-civilized and inglorious aliens, foreign to Scotland's shores (V.iii.8). Their pursuit of Macbeth ends not with his stammering hysteria, but with what might be seen as an almost brave and never ignoble death:

I have lived long enough. My way of life
Is fall'n into the sere, the yellow leaf,
And that which should accompany old age,
As honour, love, obedience, troops of friends,
I must not look to have [...] (V.iii.24–8 ff.)

In that death a strange, carnal, fleshly quality starts to replace the humanity with which he began. He commits himself to a physical world and –courageously – takes his chances there: 'Throw physic to the dogs; I'll none of it./Come put my armour on; give me my staff' (V.iii.48–9).

If Macbeth's bravery has estimable qualities, the next line – 'Doctor the Thanes fly from me' (V.iii.51) – gives it more complexity. It resurrects that earlier notion of the crow deserted by the rooks with which he wanted companionship. It offers yet again that ambiguous 'taste in the head' of suddenly awakened yet stoically and coldly dismissed regret. The action of the English soldiers who drape themselves with wooden boughs from Birnam Wood asserts a ramshackle kind of acting that makes Macbeth's more positive assumption of his role rightly clamorous. It's a more tractable sense of valour that runs through his lines, scorning disguise and costume in favour of brazen, 'outward' display:

Hang out our banners on the outward walls.
The cry is still 'They come.' Our castle's strength
Will laugh a siege to scorn. Here let them lie
Till famine and the ague eat them up.
Were they not forced with those that should be ours,
We might have met them dareful, beard to beard,
And beat them backward home. (V.v.1–7)

He is able to rise above mere timidity – 'I have supped full with horrors:/Direness, familiar to my slaughterous thoughts,/Cannot once start me' (V.v.13–15) – and death in battle becomes his choice: 'Ring the alarum bell (*Alarums*) Blow wind, come rack/At least we'll die with harness on our back. (*Exeunt*)' (V.v.49–50).

At the end, Macbeth becomes wholly possessed by a harassed sense of animality wished on him by his enemies: 'They have tied me to a stake: I cannot fly,/But, bear-like I must fight the course' (V.vii.1–2). Set up like a bear for baiting, resolved to 'fight the course', Macbeth nevertheless seems almost to fly freely from the theatre in this speech, audaciously taking up residence in one of the bear-baiting arenas next-door.[27] When he later presents himself as 'a poor player/That struts and frets his hour upon the stage,/And then is heard no more' (V.v.23–5), it's once again as if he suddenly launched himself beyond the theatre into that parallel disturbing world, heard so closely from nearby. It's as if the horrific screams from that arena match those generated in his final battle in this one. Perhaps he himself is even silenced by that shrieking and heard no more.

Yes, of course, Macbeth must be the villain (or one of the villains) of the play. Yet he has much of the best poetry in it, and the 'glamour' he generates becomes readily available to a modern audience well able to think of the English as half-hearted actors in a fumbling military operation beyond their borders. His replacement by Malcolm doesn't inspire confidence. The new administration has a reach-me-down seedy glamour that briskly ushers in its own swift promotions: 'My thanes and kinsmen,/ Henceforth be earls'(V.xi. 28–9); these are confirmed by a hasty scramble to Kingship: 'So thanks to all at once, and to each one,/ Whom we invite to see us crowned at Scone' (V.xi. 40–1). That enervated final couplet sets it own scornful seal on the new order it describes. Probably it also confirms our modern suspicions. As with any new Middle Eastern war, an armed intervention might produce a new regime, but it will necessarily share much with what went before.

There is a sense in which Macbeth's final bear-like lurching beyond the theatre's walls gives some sense of the degree of modern Scotland's animosity concerning the ascendancy of the English language and its way of life. Although the Scots may have 'invented' the subject of 'English', the Nationalist movement is always ready now to go beyond it. Alex Salmond, currently the Scottish First Minister, offered an impeccable post-modern account of Scotland's national identity when he addressed the Scottish Parliament on his reelection on 18 May 2011. He cites his distinguished predecessor:

> When Donald Dewar addressed this parliament in 1999, he evoked Scotland's diverse voices: 'The speak of the Mearns. The shout of the welder above the din of the Clyde shipyard. The battle cries of Bruce and Wallace.' Now these voices of the past are joined in this chamber by the sound of 21st-century Scotland. The lyrical Italian of Marco Biagi. The formal Urdu of Humza Yousaf. The sacred Arabic of Hanzala Malik. We are proud to have those languages spoken here alongside English, Gaelic, Scots and Doric. This land is their land, from the sparkling sands of the islands to the glittering granite of its cities. It belongs to all who choose to call it home. That includes new Scots who have escaped persecution or conflict in Africa or the Middle East. It means Scots whose forebears fled famine in Ireland and elsewhere.[28]

However romanticized the 'sound of 21st century Scotland' may be, it is evidently not the 'English' that was taken up from James's accession and promoted as an academic subject from the eighteenth century onwards.

Of course, we can now see Shakespeare's plays in all their thirty-seven languages presented for 'the world' to relish in 2012 as part of the programme for the Olympic Games perhaps making their own servile claim for the Bard's 'adaptability', even though they fail to shore up the break-down of the United Kingdom. A 'wordless' version of *Macbeth* may sail even closer to those peaks of discernment and good taste. But the quest of the Taliban against the British Council's championship of English certainly indicate a world that is not necessarily in favour of English, or British, or even American preponderance. The notion of a Shakespeare 'adaptable because he writes universal truths of human experience' does not appear to be immediately attractive in Afghanistan or other Muslim countries.

How far any Scottish play written by an Englishman may still be justified remains to be seen, but certain straws in the wind have already become visible in Britain itself.[29] The Irish have long reassembled and reorganized a notion of English, one which does not necessarily include Shakespeare's plays in a cardinal position. The Welsh have their own language, pursued strenuously in their education system, which will not include Shakespeare as its prize possession. Meanwhile the Scottish National Party has recently advertised that, from 2014, elements of Scottish writing and poetry will become compulsory in public examinations. Its current Education Secretary, Mike Russell, has said firmly that 'We want our children and young people to have the chance to learn about our literary tradition and to inspire the future generations of Scottish writers' adding that 'Scotland's contribution to literature is marked down the generations, Burns, Walter Scott and Robert Louis Stevenson have provided work that has lasted the test of time.'[30]

Perhaps we might look once more at the notion of duplicity. 'Doubleness' is rejected by Macbeth as the weapon of the witches. He learns to scorn 'th' equivocation of the fiend,/ That lies like truth' (V.v. 41–2). As I've pointed out, in Jacobean society equivocation was popularly linked to the issue of Roman Catholicism, and it offered believers, and particularly priests, the chance to lie in furtherance of their faith. Not only was this encouraged by their church, it also marked a Catholic's 'double' allegiance: to their own king, and then, on a higher level, to the Pope. But we also have to recognize that duplicity remains a major factor in the whole question of Britishness. To be Scottish as well as British might have been the method by which the Scots deployed 'English' as part of their journey into Empire, but for a modern nationalist – and for non-political citizens too – to be British as well as Scottish might still be insupportable. Macbeth's final rejection of the English troops now invading Scottish borders thus acquires its own kind of magnificent *hauteur*. These soldiers are degenerate 'English epicures' (V.iii.8), despised for feasting on Scottish society. In this way, Shakespeare, who was a proud member of the dramatic company sponsored by James, known as the King's Men, might almost seem to reject his own patron's double crown. Does this presentist reading finally serve to undermine Shakespeare's support of the monarch?

In the last analysis, the slightest tinge of presentism will thus require a change of intellectual gear when we come to *Macbeth*. William Empson's own pious judgment on the play recalls that 'When I was crossing the fighting lines during the siege of Peking, to give my weekly lecture on *Macbeth*, a generous-minded peasant barred my way and said, pointing ahead: "That way lies death."' Empson's reply was immediate: 'Not for me,' he claimed, 'I have a British passport.'[31] Perhaps, as presentists, we ought to agree that this promise now seems at least ironic, at best such stuff as dreams are made on.

Resources

Christy Desmet

Macbeth has long been a staple of secondary school curricula. Children from nineteenth-century England to twenty-first century South Africa have studied, memorized and performed Shakespeare's 'Scottish' play. Many mature artists – some no doubt responding to childhood encounters with Shakespeare – have adapted, appropriated, rewritten and quoted from *Macbeth* in works that self-consciously examine personal and national identity in relation to Shakespeare as a cultural icon. Part of the play's longevity in the critical and popular imagination derives from its ideological malleability. In his introduction to a recent collection of essays, Nick Moschovakis categorizes much criticism of *Macbeth* as being either dualistic – clearly separating good from evil – or problematizing – seeing politics, ethics and even reality as radically unstable. Moschovakis himself makes a sensible plea for interpretations that embrace the full range of the play's rhetorical positioning, a position that is echoed in Bernice Kliman's description of *Macbeth* as a 'chiasmic' play in which opposites metamorphose into one another, where 'fair is foul, and foul is fair'.[1]

No doubt *Macbeth*'s witches and their gory brew have contributed mightily to the play's popularity and, perhaps paradoxically, its purported suitability for young people. Even a cursory glance at the array of *Macbeth* films available through mainstream commercial outlets confirms that directors and viewers lavish considerable imagination on Shakespeare's hags. *Macbeth*'s preoccupation with blood, violence and death, often visualized on screen if only described in the text as we have it, contributes as well to its general appeal. But *Macbeth* is also an artful play, so rhetorically rich that L. C. Knights could argue convincingly that it should be read as a poem. Both stage and film productions have engaged with *Macbeth*'s vivid imagery and poetic flights, sometimes making visible what is only implicit in Shakespeare's script. For university students pursuing a course in Shakespeare or early modern studies, *Macbeth* offers a compact tour guide to a range of topics in early modern culture: early modern history, Jacobean political philosophy, English and Scottish historiography, and the engendering of witches in Scotland and elsewhere. At the same time, as psychoanalytic criticism and gender studies have shown, the play explores basic issues of personal identity, as well as the construction of masculinity and femininity. Finally, the prevalence of *Macbeth* in the popular and literary imagination has resulted in a wide array of appropriations that can be juxtaposed with the source text. As it turns out, there are many ways to explore a world through the axiom 'fair is foul, and foul is fair'.

Texts

The 'text' of *Macbeth* is relatively simple in that only the first Folio version of the play survives. Its brevity (*Macbeth* is the shortest Shakespeare tragedy) has suggested to some scholars that the Folio text is incomplete; others see it as the product of collaboration between Shakespeare and Thomas Middleton. Celia Daileader's comparison of *Macbeth* with Middleton's *The Witch* shows how focusing on the play as a collaborative text enriches critical study.

Print Editions

Macbeth, ed. A. R. Braunmuller, New Cambridge Shakespeare (Cambridge: Cambridge University Press, 1997; updated edition 2008)

Provides an authoritative text with helpful commentary and an extended introduction covering such topics as Macbeth's consideration of legend and history, 'occasional' references in the play and performance history. The section on 'language' is particularly helpful.

Macbeth, ed. Nicholas Brooke (Oxford: Clarendon, 1990)

Based on the Wells–Taylor text of the complete Oxford Shakespeare, this single-play edition has an intelligent introduction that deals specifically with the role of Middleton and revision in the play's textual history.

Macbeth, ed. John Russell Brown, The Shakespeare Handbooks (Houndsmill, Basingstoke: Palgrave Macmillan, 2005)

More of a reader's companion than an edition per se, this handbook provides detailed commentary on the play's action, highlighting such non-textual features as staging and sound effects.

Macbeth, ed. Rex Gibson, Cambridge School Shakespeare (Cambridge: Cambridge University Press, 2005)

Intended for secondary school students, primarily in the UK, this school edition complements the Folger's *Shakespeare Set Free* series. The reader-friendly text offers on the left-hand pages copious exercises for understanding at all levels.

Macbeth, ed. Robert S. Miola, Norton Critical Editions (New York: W. W. Norton, 2004)

This edition includes excerpted criticism and primary documents that deal with the play's sources and cultural contexts, covering topics such as free will, witchcraft and tyrannicide. The attention to dramatic sources in ancient and medieval drama is particularly welcome, as is the section on adaptations such as Welcome Msomi's *uMabatha*. Snippets from *Macbeth* travesties of the nineteenth century are fun to read and relevant to discussion of the play's language.

The Tragedy of Macbeth, eds Barbara Mowat and Paul Werstine, New Folger Library Shakespeare (New York and London: Washington Square Books, 1992)

The Folger edition offers the best balance between scholarly apparatus and cost available among single-play paperbacks. The introductory matter includes information on Shakespeare's life, language and theatre. The 'Modern Perspective' by Susan Snyder analyzes the play as a study in moral decline. A brief, annotated bibliography of Further Reading is included.

William Shakespeare's Macbeth: Texts and Contexts, ed. William C. Carroll (Boston and New York: Bedford/St Martin's, 1999)

Like other volumes in this series, Carroll's Macbeth examines cultural topics ranging from discourses of sovereignty, treason and resistance, witchcraft and prophecy to the role of the feminine. The volume offers excerpts from all the documents you would expect for teaching this play (e.g. Reginald Scot's *Discovery of Witchcraft* and the *Homily Against Disobedience*), plus some you will not find so easily elsewhere (e.g. John Major's and George Buchanan's histories and several texts on Father Garnet's equivocation). The Introduction has a helpful account of the succession question and of Scottish royal genealogy.

Digital Editions

Online print editions have been available for nearly twenty years and now texts are becoming commercially available in formats ranging from Kindle to iPad. Jeremy Hylton's 1993 HTML text in the *MIT Shakespeare*, which proclaims itself the first complete edition of Shakespeare on the Internet, uses the public domain text from the Complete Moby™ Shakespeare. This makes the text's accuracy suspect, but streamlined access and the simple searches enabled by any browser when the play is viewed as one page make word studies possible under the simplest of technological conditions. Project Gutenberg's no-nonsense 'plain vanilla' texts in various digital formats (including plain text for computer analysis, HTML, EPUB, and Kindle) is another resource, although it takes patience to download the texts. Probably the most reputable online text is the version of the first Folio edited by Anthony Dawson for Michael Best's Internet Shakespeare editions. Oxford University Press Canada offers *Macbeth Online*, an interactive 'personal playscript with online registration code' that allows students to annotate the play and gives them access to multimedia content.

We are just beginning to encounter commercial products for other platforms. Oxford University Press markets a Kindle version of the scholarly *Complete Plays of Shakespeare*, edited by Stanley Wells and Gary Taylor. *Shakespeare in Bits* offers a *Macbeth* that seems aimed more at the secondary school than the university student, but is aesthetically pleasing and fun to use. Finally, there is *HyperMacbeth*, more an example of digital performance art than as an edition per se. Accompanied by stylish visuals and music, the site features excerpts from three soliloquies. The text can be read in English and Italian, a reminder, as Bruno Lessard points out, that Shakespeare is experienced globally in many languages. To cope with the application's seemingly random linkages between words, the reader of this hypertext must 'suture' these links with his or her own knowledge of the play.

dlsan, *HyperMacbeth: An Hypertextual Dramatic Piece* <http://www.dlsan.org/macbeth/the_mac.htm> [accessed 25 August 2012]

With 'lyrics by William Shakespeare' and musical accompaniment, this digital performance piece opens with 'The queen, my lord, is dead' in both English and Italian, then offers up three *Macbeth* soliloquies: Lady Macbeth's plea to the spirits to 'unsex her' (I.v), a composite speech from Macbeth (combining text from I.vii and II.i) and Macbeth's pronouncement on the queen's death, 'She should have died hereafter', followed by his musings on 'tomorrow, tomorrow, and tomorrow' (V.v). Hypertext links take the reader in surprising directions.

Macbeth, ed. Anthony Dawson, Internet Shakespeare Editions <http://internetshakespeare.uvic.ca/Library/plays/Mac.html> [accessed 25 August 2012]

Dawson's transcription follows the first Folio closely and includes, as a bonus, five facsimiles of the first four quartos; the facsimiles can be compared with one another and with a transcription in side-by-side displays. There are some performance documents ranging from playbills to postcards, plus a brief bibliography of performances, some of which could be considered appropriations. As of August 2012, the edition was only partially finished, but still serviceable.

Macbeth, ed. Jeremy Hylton, MIT Shakespeare <http://shakespeare.mit.edu/> [accessed 17 June 2012]

Using the public domain text established by Moby Shakespeare, this online edition is useful if the text is checked against a scholarly edition. By making the entire play accessible as a single page, this site makes simple word searches quick and efficient.

Macbeth (F1), Project Gutenberg <http://www.gutenberg.org/ebooks/2264> [accessed 23 August 2012]

The headnote to *Macbeth* notes that this is a third, corrected version of the play, but also states that 'Project Gutenberg Etexts are usually created from multiple editions, all of which are in the Public Domain in the United States, unless a copyright notice is included. Therefore, we usually do NOT keep any of these books in compliance with any particular paper edition.' Like the MIT text, this must be handled with care for classroom use, but this is a reputable scholarly site offering text in a range of formats.

Macbeth (for iPad and iPhone), Animation Jeremy McAuliffe and Sara Healy, Art Design Jeremy McAuliffe, Audio Naxos Books, Shakespeare in Bits <http://www.MindConnex.com> [accessed 23 August 2012]

In addition to the playtext and a compelling animated performance, this version offers plot and scene synopses, information on themes, imagery and language, a list of well-known quotations with translation into 'ordinary English', character portraits and a handy map of 'Character Relationships'. The soundtrack is taken from the venerable Naxos Audiobooks; viewers and readers can navigate easily between sections and scenes, while word glosses, historical tidbits and study questions are available at a touch without obscuring the text.

Macbeth Online (Oxford: Oxford University Press, 2010)

Intended primarily for secondary school students and available only in Canada, this resource combines a portable electronic playscript with website access to rich multimedia.

Macbeth, in *The Oxford Shakespeare: The Complete Works*, second edition (Oxford: Oxford University Press, 2005; The Complete Works Collection, distributed by Kindle Books, 2011)

A handy, portable version of the play's most authoritative edition that lacks glosses and navigation tools.

Approaches to Teaching *Macbeth*

Teaching *Macbeth* through Cultural and Critical Contexts

History and Intellectual Topics

Set in ancient Scotland, *Macbeth* recreates from Holinshed's *Chronicles* and other sources a vivid picture of an imagined warrior culture. James I claimed Banquo as an ancestor to support his claim to the English throne and to further his project of unifying England and Scotland, so not surprisingly the play resonates with both history and references to events and ideas of the early Jacobean period. Critics remain divided on whether or not

Shakespeare's treatment of his historical and occasional material supports a pro-James reading of the play: Elliott argues that the play represents divine providence at work, which would support James's concept of kingship, while Norbrook and Sinfield offer a more sceptical reading of Shakespeare's use of history. Crucial to the evaluation of moral opposites in *Macbeth* is the figure of the Porter, alternately seen as St Peter guarding Heaven's Gate, the Keeper of Hell and an evil genius (Allen, Baker, and Wickham).

Macbeth also addresses more generally the nature of kingship and the problem of tyranny. James himself contributed to the debate in *De Monarchia*, where he argued the strong version of divine right monarchy, proclaiming that kings are not only God's lieutenants on earth, but are themselves 'little gods'. From this perspective, a people burdened with a tyrant could do no more than endure patiently; no measure of resistance is justified. Other writers, such as Jean Bodin, distinguished between lawful kings and usurpers, legitimating resistance against tyrants. This intellectual background is relevant to *Macbeth*, a play in which, as Rebecca Lemon tells us, the relationship between legitimate king and tyrant is complicated by the fact that both Macbeth and Malcolm, Scotland's saviour, technically become king through treason.

A specific current event referenced by *Macbeth* is the failed Gunpowder Plot, in which English Catholic dissidents, supported by Jesuit activists, attempted to blow up the king and members of both houses of parliament. Again, critics are divided about whether Shakespeare supports a Jamesian reading of the outcome as the work of providence.

While Henry Paul's argument that *Macbeth* was written as an occasional play celebrating the failure of the Gunpowder Plot has been questioned, Alvin Kernan also investigates the play as Jamesian propaganda through its first court performance. Gary Wills offers the most complete, if totalizing, account of the Gunpowder Plot's relevance to *Macbeth*, and Arthur Kinney's *Lies Like Truth* provides a lively and probably the best compact introduction to the intellectual topics surrounding the play.

Witchcraft and the Supernatural

Macbeth's tantalizing 'Weird Sisters' have been the focus for several centuries of schoolchildren otherwise immune to Shakespeare's charms. Beginning with their choric chanting of the cauldron's contents (the Folger Shakespeare Library's *Shakespeare Set Free* provides a compelling classroom exercise), the witches and their rhetoric are attractive to even young children, while the Gothic details of how early modern culture constructed the witch can grab the imagination of older students. Debate continues over whether or not *Macbeth*'s depiction of witchcraft reflects cultural realities of the early modern period. Stephen Greenblatt is sceptical, arguing that Shakespeare saw witchcraft as a kind of theatre. Deborah Willis finds in the witches' treatment a critique of patriarchal rule. Laura Kolb provides an analysis of how *Macbeth* interrogates the narrative practice of witchcraft narratives, in particular their tendency to use single exempla to prove general 'truths'. Finally, Peter Stallybrass generalizes broadly to argue that *Macbeth*'s exploration of witchcraft, as part of the creation of the early modern state, serves to legitimate 'the hegemony of patriarchy'.

Character, Gender and the Human

As one of Shakespeare's 'great tragedies', *Macbeth* offers us the paradox of a tragic hero who is also a tyrant and criminal. Combined with Macbeth's own ambiguous morality are his and Lady Macbeth's meditations on what it means to be human. Harry Berger, G. R. Elliott and Howard Felperin explore this topic through the play's rhetorical manipulation of moral oppositions, Mary Floyd-Wilson through an historical analysis of the Scots and English grounded in early modern humoural theory. The play also engages with the nature of identity itself, largely though not exclusively through the conceptual opposition of masculinity and femininity. Janet Adelman offers the most influential reading of this subject, arguing that *Macbeth* explores the crucial psychoanalytic premise that male identity depends on a violent separation from the problematic maternal body (see also Ramsey and Asp); feminist Joan Larsen Klein focuses on Lady Macbeth's relation to Renaissance discourse about marriage; McDonald, Rosenberg and Ziegler take the discussion of Lady Macbeth into later centuries by examining her representations on stage and in visual art.

Language, Rhetoric and Poetry

L. C. Knights in his famous attack on Bradleyian character criticism – 'How Many Children Had Lady Macbeth?' – declared *Macbeth* to be a poem organized around oppositions of powerful image pairs: black and white, good and evil, heaven and hell. Other readers have seen *Macbeth*'s language as darker, more ambiguous, demonically misleading. A particular rhetorical feature of *Macbeth* is its exploration and practice of the art of equivocation. Steven Mullaney discusses the role played by equivocation through the rhetorical trope of amphibology, the act of 'lying like truth' that links *Macbeth* to the discourse of treason in the aftermath of the Gowrie and Gunpowder Plots against James (see also Huntley and Scott). Richard McCoy explores the paradoxical importance of acting, rhetoric and dissimulation to Malcolm as Scotland's redeemer. David Krantz analyzes how the witches' characteristic poetry both differentiates them from the human realm but also signifies the diffusion of their power and influence throughout the play world. Other more general explorations of *Macbeth*'s rhetoric can be found in Berger, Calderwood and Jorgensen.

Teaching *Macbeth* through Performance

Writing about live performances can be a challenge, simply because performance is ephemeral. Interpreting the play through performance history works particularly well in the case of *Macbeth*, however, because we have performance histories detailing important productions (see Kliman, McDonald and Wilders) and because there is a rich tradition of visual representations for Macbeth and Lady Macbeth, both on and off the stage, from the eighteenth through the twentieth centuries that are readily available through the internet and the Shakespeare Illustrated website. The Henri Fuseli portrayals of David Garrick and Sarah Siddons in these roles and John Singer Sargent's famous portrait of Ellen Terry as Lady Macbeth are perhaps the best known of these iconic portrayals. 'Galleries' of Shakespeare's heroines also give insight into how Lady Macbeth, in particular, was typed and characterized (Ziegler). Lady Macbeth, as represented by stellar actors from Siddons and Terry to Judi Dench, also has a long and well-documented performance tradition of her own (McDonald). Another topic of recent interest is colour-blind casting, which is discussed by Lisa Anderson and by some essays in *Weyward Macbeth*. For teachers interested in contemporary performances, the websites of Shakespeare's Globe Theatre, London and the Royal Shakespeare Company are useful, providing production details, pictures and sometimes character and actor blogs:

Royal Shakespeare Company, http://www.rsc.org.uk/ [accessed 22 September 2012].

Shakespeare's Globe, http://www.shakespearesglobe.com/ [accessed 22 September 2012].

Shakespeare Illustrated, http://shakespeare.emory.edu/illustrated_index.cfm [accessed 22 September 2012].

Teaching *Macbeth* through Film

Teachers have long relied on film interpretations to make *Macbeth* come alive for students and recently Shakespeare on film has become a subject in its own right. Comparing different ways of casting the witches, the Porter scene, the appearance of Banquo's spectre at Macbeth's feast and the final battle provides a good entrée into the play as well into different directors' choices and cinematic technique. The films included here are generally available through Amazon.com, Netflix and other accessible venues. They are listed in chronological order.

Macbeth, dir. Orson Welles, perf. Orson Welles, Jeanette Nolan (Mercury Productions, 1948; restored version available on DVD. 107 min.

Filmed in a misty, desolate setting, Welles's *Macbeth* features an allegorical struggle between the (Christian) forces of good, epitomized by Duncan's association with the cross, and (pagan) evil, epitomized by Welles's fateful crones with forked, druidical staffs. The witches manipulate Macbeth through a voodoo doll; at the film's end they face the mist-enshrouded castle of which Malcolm has taken charge and chant once again, 'Peace, the charm's wound up.' Lady Macbeth, too, is active to an extra-textual degree: she is Lady Macduff's confidante, is present with her husband at the slaughter of Macduff's family and commits suicide by throwing herself from the castle wall. Dan Juan Gil analyzes Welles's cinematic technique as congenial to the 'asocial sexuality' of Shakespeare's plays. (See Catania, Donaldson, Gil, Hatchuel, Holland and Jorgens.)

Macbeth, dir. Roman Polanski, perf. Jon Finch, Francesca Annis (UK, Caliban Films, US Playboy Production, 1971). DVD. 140 min.

Notorious in its time for a plethora of pre-pubescent nude witches, the Polanski *Macbeth* nevertheless has aged well and is useful in the classroom. Set in a vaguely defined medieval Scotland, the film makes good use of wild crags, a stone castle and a courtyard teeming with chickens and large dogs. The witches, threatening in their femininity, are both deformed old women and pretty girls who swarm around Macbeth. Duncan is saintly, old and weak, Macbeth and Lady Macbeth young and sexy and do their plotting together in bed. The film also has a powerful banquet scene, with Banquo appearing quietly in Macbeth's chair, decomposing before our eyes and finally lunging at his murderer. Polanski adds a twist to Shakespeare's plot by having Donalbain, absenting himself from Malcolm's coronation, seek out the witches of his own volition; the cycle of betrayal and violence inexorably repeats itself. (See Holland, Kliman and Reynolds.)

Macbeth, dir. Trevor Nunn, perf. Ian McKellen, Judi Dench (UK, Royal Shakespeare Company); television film directed by John Casson (UK, Thames Television, 1979). DVD. 145 min.

This filmed version of the stage production is both powerful and pedagogically useful in that it demonstrates how witchcraft and mystery can be created on a bare stage. Lady Macbeth, like her husband, is middle aged and so beyond child-bearing, adding poignancy to the couple's childlessness. The final battle is prolonged and beautifully choreographed, made almost unbearable not through visual excess but through the resounding, almost deafening sound of the organ. (See Hatchuel.)

Macbeth, dir. Jack Gold, perf. Nigel Williamson, Jane Lapotaire (BBC/Time-Life films, 1983). DVD. 148 min.

Largely overshadowed now in production values by the commercial films available on DVD, the BBC television *Macbeth* nevertheless is still available in a DVD five-pack of the principal tragedies. Claiming to offer a 'word-for-word' rendition of Shakespeare's text, it provides a good reader's companion to the play. (For discussion, see Kliman.)

Macbeth, dir. Rupert Goold, perf. Patrick Stewart, Kate Fleetwood (Chichester Festival Theatre, 2007; television series BBC 4, 2010; PBS, 2010). DVD. 180 min.

Heralded as the '*Macbeth* of the Century' when it played in New York, this masterful performance is expertly adapted to television and then packaged on DVD. Most striking and chilling, perhaps, are the witches, imagined here as sadistic hospital nurses. The Macbeth–Banquo relationship is rich and vexed. In the appearance of Banquo's ghost at the banquet, Banquo points an accusatory finger at Macbeth while striding purposefully down the banquet table. The scene ends, however, with Macbeth astride the table in Banquo's place, becoming his victim's double. Kate Fleetwood is a splendid Lady Macbeth, emotional and sexy; she gives a strong performance in the sleepwalking scene and is equally lovely in her on-screen death, laid out nude in the bathtub, her slit wrists 'lacing' Lady Macbeth's alabaster skin with 'golden' blood.

Macbeth, dir. Geoffrey Wright, perf. Sam Worthington, Victoria Hill (Palace Films, 2006). DVD. 105 min.

Set in contemporary Melbourne's drug-gangster culture, this version matches film noir ambience with a precisely enunciated first Folio script. The witches are scary goth teens who make their first appearance desecrating monuments in a graveyard, later concocting their ghastly hallucinogenic brew in Macbeth's suburban compound, then engaging with him in wild, drug-fueled sex. Lady Macbeth, with maternal longings lurking beneath her voluptuous appearance, is caught looking wistfully at an empty child's swing moving in the night breeze. The film is rated 'mature' for violence and sexuality.

Macbeth, dir. Aaron Posner and Teller, perf. Ian Merrill Peakes, Kate Eastwood Norris (Folger Theatre/Two Rivers Company, 2008). 124 min.

A filmed version of a live performance that has been packaged for classroom use with the Folger Shakespeare Library edition. Macbeth, Lady Macbeth and the Porter all interact extensively with the audience through the Folger Theatre's central aisle, and the Porter's scene is particularly effective for its raunchy humour. This production shows how a minimalist live performance can be staged.

Teaching *Macbeth* through Appropriation

A key text for both colonizers and colonized within replications of the British curriculum globally, *Macbeth* has been subject to appropriation, read differently by readers situated in locales outside what Martin Orkin has called the 'Shakespeare metropolis'.[2] Lacking a figure for the native such as *The Tempest's* Caliban, *Macbeth* is reconfigured most frequently not as a parable of colonization itself but as a study in either tyranny or criminality. Welcome Msomi's *uMabatha*, published in Fischlin and Fortier's *Adaptations of Shakespeare*, provides a good example. *Macbeth* has also found its way into a number of relatively lowbrow genres such as the detective story, informing such examples as Simon Brett's *What Bloody Man is That?* (1987), Agatha Christie's *By the Pricking of My Thumbs* (1968), Josephine Tey's *The Daughter of Time* (1951) and Simon Shaw's *Bloody Instructions* (1991) (see Hateley). Some *Macbeth* films stray so far from their model that they must be counted as appropriations. Particularly appealing and teachable films of this kind include Peter Moffat's *Macbeth* in the BBC's 'Shakespeare Retold' series, the black comedy *Scotland, PA* and Akira Kurosawa's artistic masterpiece *Throne of Blood*.

Macbeth, dir. Mark Brozel, perf. James McAvoy (Joe Macbeth), Keeley Hawes (Ella Macbeth), *Shakespeare Retold: Four Modern Interpretations of Shakespeare Plays* (Acorn Media, 2005). DVD. 320 min.

This contemporary reworking of *Macbeth*, written by Peter Moffat and directed by Mark Brozel, first aired on BBC 1 in 2005 as part of the greatly successful Shakespeare Retold series. Duncan Docherty (Vincent Regan), a famous celebrity chef with his own television cookery programme, is the owner of an up-market Glasgow restaurant. The ambitions of Joe Macbeth (James McAvoy), the head chef in Duncan's kitchen, are roused when he is made privy to some seemingly prophetic information imparted by three garbage disposal workers clearing waste in an alley behind the restaurant: that Duncan's establishment is about to be awarded three coveted Michelin Stars; that Joe himself will come to own Duncan's restaurant; but also that, in time, its proprietorship will ultimately devolve to the sons of one of his co-chefs, Billy. When the Michelin stars are shortly thereafter rewarded, Joe Macbeth's vaulting ambitions are stirred, and having shared the terms of the prophecy with his wife Ella (Keeley Hawes), the restaurant's front-of-house manageress, the couple plot and conspire to murder their boss as well as all others perceived as standing in the way of their success. For all its creative appropriation of Shakespeare's play, several iconic dramatic elements remain, including the ghostly appearance of Billy/Banquo (Joseph Millson) as a video message on the mobile phone of the guilt-stricken Joe Macbeth and the recasting of the Birnam Wood/Dunsinane conundrum as the proviso that Joe's success and safety are secured so long as 'pigs don't fly' – cold comfort, indeed, as policemen in helicopters eventually swoop in on the 'dead butcher' in the film's final scenes. Tragic chaos has been replaced by order in the film's closing moments as Duncan Docherty's son, Malcolm, is shown to have taken over his father's restaurant and his television programme alike.

Maqbool, dir. Vishal Bhardwaj, perf. Irfan Khan, Tabu (Kaleidoscope Entertainment, 2004). DVD. 129 min.

Set in Mumbai's underworld, the film combines *Macbeth*'s plot with Bollywood gangster film conventions. Corrupt policemen stand in for the weird sisters, and in an added twist Lady Macbeth is not only the lover of the underworld's boss, but also secretly carries Maqbool's child.

Msomi, Welcome, *uMabatha*, in *Adaptations of Shakespeare: A Critical Anthology*, (eds) Daniel Fischlin and Mark Fortier (London: Routledge, 2000), pp. 164–87.

This South African adaptation transforms *Macbeth* into the story of Shaka, 'an early nineteenth-century Zulu chief made legendary by his martial skills, brutality, and aristocratic rule' whose political trajectory is also foretold by a witch (Isongoma) (Fischlin and Fortier, *Adaptations of Shakespeare*, p. 164). For opposed opinions on the 1997 London production, see McLuskie and Wright; see also Newstok's interview with Msomi.

Scotland, PA, dir. Billy Morrissette, perf. James LeGros (Joe 'Mac' McBeth), Maura Tierney ('Pat' McBeth), Christopher Walken (Lieutenant McDuff) (Abandon Pictures, 2001). DVD. 104 min.

This film imports *Macbeth* into suburban America during the 1970s, where 'Mac' is a fast food worker with an ambitious wife and doughnut king Duncan's plunge into an oil vat makes room for 'McBeth's' hamburger and fries emporium. Despite its heavy-handed allegory and generally parodic tone, the film elicits strong and poignant performances from its tragic protagonists. (See Shohet for a critical discussion.)

Throne of Blood (Kumonosu-jō, or literally *Spider Web Castle*), dir. Akira Kurosawa, perf. Toshiro Mifune (Washizu, aka Macbeth), Isuzu Yamada (Lady Asaji, aka Lady Macbeth), Minoru Chiaki, (Miki, aka Banquo) (Kurosawa Production Company, 1957). DVD. 110 min.

This classic film engages intensively with *Macbeth* as source text to highlight cultural differences in worldview and character motivation. Washizu (Macbeth) is consumed with ambition and the Lady Asaji (Lady Macbeth) exerts strong pressure on him to realize the honours promised to him. At the same time, Kurosawa makes it clear that in the feudal culture of this film the players are caught in an endless cycle of ambition and treason: the Duncan figure had achieved his position by betraying his own lord. The eerie Forest Spirit who stands in for *Macbeth*'s witches sits at the centre of the forest, calmly spinning her web and entrapping her prey with nothing but the truth of her prophecies. (For critical discussion, see Catania, Donaldson, Gil, Hatchuel and Jorgens.)

Teaching *Macbeth* through Social Media

Not surprisingly, considering the play's prominence in secondary school and college curricula, *Macbeth* has found a place in social media and particularly on YouTube, the video-sharing website.

Both professional and amateur efforts (the latter largely the product of US schoolchildren) can be found there. Because the landscape changes so rapidly in social media, it is impossible to pinpoint *Macbeth*'s status there at any given time. Between 2008 and 2012, however, *Macbeth* parodies and remakes were second in popularity only to *Hamlet* remakes. Among the principal genres available were *Macbeth* raps, Lego productions of individual scenes, comic translations of the play's plot into television shows and adaptations of its language to popular songs. The parodies can be evoked in class to discuss topics ranging from character to staging and offered as models for students' own productions. It is now possible, furthermore, to analyze YouTube Shakespeare 'genres' as art forms in their own right.

Bibliography

The bibliography of critical resources is organized into three sections: books, essay collections, and essays and articles. Critical works were chosen for their intelligence, clarity, availability and focus on key issues.

Books

Calderwood, James L., *If It Were Done: Macbeth and Tragic Action* (Amherst: University of Massachusetts Press, 1986)

A deconstructive reading of *Macbeth* and the 'undoing' of its tragic action, this book is divided into small sections devoted to separate portions of text, while the opening chapter contrasts *Macbeth* to *Hamlet*.

Jorgensen, Paul A., *Our Naked Frailties: Sensational Art and Meaning in Macbeth* (Berkeley and Los Angeles: University of California Press, 1971)

This study of 'sensation' or feeling in *Macbeth* focuses on violent imagery as a window on this drama of crime and punishment,

Shakespeare's construction of a hell on earth. Among the topics discussed are nature and the mystery of evil; murder; blood; the figure of the slaughtered babe; the witches as agents of evil; and labour.

Kinney, Arthur F., *Lies Like Truth: Shakespeare, Macbeth, and the Cultural Moment* (Detroit: Wayne State University Press, 2001)

Imagining *Macbeth* as an inherently equivocal play, this book provides a treasure trove of short chapters discussing a series of topics from varied perspectives in order to define Shakespeare's play in terms of its 'cultural moment'. Each unit or 'lexia' addresses a different chain of circumstances and discourses informing the play, ranging from resistance and justice to family, household and disease.

Kliman, Bernice W., *Shakespeare in Performance: Macbeth*, second edition (Manchester and New York: Manchester University Press, 2004)

Covers select monuments in the history of *Macbeth* on stage, in opera, on television and in film. Discusses Verdi's *Macbeth* and Orson Welles's Voodoo *Macbeth*.

McDonald, Russ, *Look to the Lady: Sarah Siddons, Ellen Terry, and Judi Dench on the Shakespearean Stage* (Athens: University of Georgia Press, 2005)

A wide-ranging and readable introduction to the three actresses of the title and their portrayals of Lady Macbeth. Although the section on Dench discusses the Trevor Nunn stage production, it is also useful for teaching the filmed version.

Paul, Henry N., *The Royal Play of Macbeth: When, Why, and How it was Written by Shakespeare* (New York: Macmillan Company, 1950)

Although Paul's thesis that *Macbeth* was written especially for King James is now considered to be overstated, the book remains a useful source of information about historical contexts informing *Macbeth*, covering topics ranging from James's involvement in writing about and persecuting witches to the Gunpowder Plot and the King's Touch.

Shakespeare Set Free: Teaching Romeo & Juliet, Macbeth, & A Midsummer Night's Dream, ed. Peggy O'Brien (New York: Washington Square Press, 1993)

Aimed primarily at secondary school teachers, this pedagogical programme nevertheless can be used profitably at college or university level, focusing largely on language and performance.

Wilders, John, ed., *Macbeth*, Shakespeare in Production (Cambridge: Cambridge University Press, 2004)

With a strong introduction that outlines succinctly *Macbeth*'s performance history, this volume provides useful information about particular landmark performances. Wilders's notes provide teachers with information about staging, props and actors' mannerisms.

Wills, Gary, *Witches and Jesuits: Shakespeare's Macbeth* (Oxford and New York: Oxford University Press, 1995)

Studying *Macbeth* as a 'Gunpowder Plot' play and therefore as Jamesian propaganda, this brief book offers in Chapter 1 a summary of the Plot and its ideological aftermath. Subsequent chapters argue for the Gunpowder Plot as a central cultural context for Shakespeare's play.

Essay Collections

Asian Shakespeares on Screen: Two Films in Perspective, special issue ed. Alexander C. Y. Huang, *Borrowers and Lenders: The Journal of Shakespeare and Appropriation,* 4.2 (Spring/Summer 2009) http://www.borrowers.uga.edu [accessed 3 October 2012]

Discussing *Maqbool* along with *The Banquet*, this cluster of short essays is designed to help teachers and students see how in Asian film 'visceral and political experiences' are enabled through transcultural re-writings of Shakespearean tragedy. The essays are particularly helpful to viewers not well versed in Asian film traditions.

Macbeth: New Critical Essays, ed. Nick Moschovakis (London and New York: Routledge, 2008)

An excellent recent collection with essays ranging in subject matter from politics to history, social context and identity; includes a generous number of pieces on global appropriations, film and *Macbeth* in the digital age.

Focus on Macbeth, ed. John Russell Brown (London: Routledge & Kegan Paul, 1982)

A high-quality collection of essays on a range of topics, including the 'Director's View' of Peter Hall.

Weyward Macbeth: Intersections of Race and Performance, ed. Scott L. Newstok and Ayanna Thompson (New York: Palgrave Macmillan, 2010)

As the Introduction explains, the volume is concerned with the 'ambivalent nature of racialized re-stagings, adaptations, and allusions to "*Macbeth*"' (p. 3). The book will be of particular interest to instructors of classes in global Shakespeare, Shakespearean appropriation and performance history – it includes a selected list of productions using non-traditional casting.

Essays and Articles

Adelman, Janet, 'Escaping the Matrix: The Construction of Masculinity in *Macbeth* and *Coriolanus*', in *Suffocating Mothers: Fantasies of Maternal Origin in Shakespeare's Plays, Hamlet to The Tempest* (London and New York: Routledge, 1992), pp. 130–64

Part of the author's larger examination of how masculine identity is rooted in the 'problematic maternal body' (p. 2), this chapter analyses *Macbeth*'s simultaneous representation of the 'fantasy of virtually absolute and destructive maternal power' and of 'the fantasy of absolute escape from this power' (p. 131). With Macduff's ascendance at the end of the play, *Macbeth* both denies the possibility of a self-sufficient male identity (Macduff did have a mother) and confirms that functional masculinity requires a brutal separation from the mother (Macduff is 'untimely ripped' from the womb [*Macbeth*, V.x.16]).

Allen, Michael J. B., '*Macbeth's* Genial Porter', *English Literary Renaissance,* 4 (1974), pp. 325–34.

While the porter is a gatekeeper, whether to heaven or hell, the 'genius' is a more complex figure, equally a representation of the divine nature in humans and a conductor between life and death. *Macbeth*'s porter turns out to be an evil genius, a perversion of the porter's social function.

Anderson, Lisa M., '*When Race Matters: Reading Race in Richard III and Macbeth*', in *Colorblind Shakespeare: New Perspectives on Race and Performance*, ed. Ayanna Thompson (New York and London: Routledge, 2006), pp. 89–102.

Analyses the Red Company's production at Shakespeare's Globe Theatre in 2001, which cast Duncan as white and both of his sons as black.

Asp, Carolyn, 'Be Bloody, Bold, and Resolute': Tragic Action and Sexual Stereotyping in *Macbeth*', *Studies in Philology*, 78, 2 (2001), pp. 153–69

Argues that both Macbeth and Lady Macbeth are undone by their entanglement in sexual stereotypes. In the play world, masculinity is associated with the violence and brutality of warfare, femininity with weakness and helplessness. Macbeth finds himself unable to be a 'man' except through violence, while Lady Macbeth adopts the masculine stereotype of cruel violence to compensate for Macbeth's humane impulses. She becomes further isolated and alienated, however, by Macbeth's perception of her in terms of feminine stereotypes.

Baker, Christopher, 'St. Peter and *Macbeth's* Porter', *Ben Jonson Journal,* 18, 2 (2011), pp. 233–53

Examines the symbolic relationship linking *Macbeth*'s Porter, Henry Garnet as equivocator and the figure of St Peter as interpreted through Calvinist theology and medieval drama.

Berger, Harry, Jr, 'The Early Scenes of *Macbeth:* Preface to a New Interpretation', in *Making Trifles of Terror: Redistributing Complexities in Shakespeare* (Stanford: Stanford University Press, 1997), pp. 78–97

An analysis of the play's early scenes (I.i–II.iii), this essay argues against the traditional interpretation of *Macbeth* as a play of restoration by uncovering instabilities in the Scottish court. In a warrior society based on bloodshed and violence, competition for primacy between ruler and thane is inevitable.

Catania, Saviour, 'The Haiku *Macbeth:* Shakespearean Antithetical Minimalism in Kurosawa's *Komonosu-jō'*, in *World-wide Shakespeares: Local Appropriations in Film and Performance*, ed. Sonia Massai (London and New York: Routledge, 2005), pp. 149––56.

This essay discusses Kurosawa's understanding of *Macbeth*'s central paradox, that 'nothing is but what is not', in terms of the haiku's principle of 'antithetical minimalism', offering as well an elegant analysis of circular patterns in the play.

Daileader, Ceilia R., 'Weird Brothers: What Thomas Middleton's *The Witch* Can Tell Us about Race, Sex, and Gender in *Macbeth*', in *Weyward Macbeth: Intersections of Race and Performance*, eds Scott L. Newstok and Ayanna Thompson (New York: Palgrave Macmillan, 2010), pp. 11–20

Argues that Middleton's adaptation of *Macbeth* makes the play subversive because his witches are a morally beneficent community of women outside of the patriarchal order.

Donaldson, Peter S., 'Surface and Depth: *Throne of Blood* as Cinematic Allegory', in *Shakespearean Films/Shakespearean Directors* (Boston: Unwin Hyman, 1990), pp. 69–91

Donaldson analyses the film as allegorizing its own position between traditional Japanese cinema and Western, 'realistic' film. The camera's exploration of the paradoxical relation of narrative depth to the flat cinematic screen image exposes the illusoriness of Macbeth's ambition to control his own narrative and fate.

Elliott, G. R., *Dramatic Providence in Macbeth: A Study of Shakespeare's Tragic Theme of Humanity and Grace* (Princeton: Princeton University Press, 1958)

Offers a classic reading of *Macbeth* as a dualistic play that dramatizes how active evil, without the intervening power of God's grace, can ruin humanity and concludes that Malcolm's triumph re-establishes order and grace in Scotland.

Felperin, Howard, 'A Painted Devil: *Macbeth*', in *Shakespearean Representation: Mimesis and Modernity in Elizabethan Tragedy* (Princeton: Princeton University Press 1977), pp. 118–44

Arguing that *Macbeth* follows more closely the structure of its sources than some other Shakespeare tragedies, Felperin links *Macbeth* to the *Massacre of the Innocents* from the medieval cycle plays. Macbeth, like Herod, is a tyrant plagued by a prophecy of a king to succeed and supplant him; but Macbeth follows his predetermined plot in a world where meaning has, paradoxically ceased to be simple and stable.

Floyd-Wilson, Mary, 'English Epicures and Scottish Witches', *Shakespeare Quarterly*, 57, 2 (2006), pp. 131–61.

With the influx of Scots into England after the coronation of James I, both cultures are confronted with anxieties about their differences. Analyzing the play from a humoural and environmental perspective, Floyd-Wilson shows that the Scots see themselves as naturally temperate, but the south associates them with elemental witchcraft; the English are stereotyped in turn by their northern neighbours as epicures.

Gil, Dan Juan, 'Avant-Garde Technique and the Visual Grammar of Sexuality in Orson Welles's Shakespeare Films', *Borrowers and Lenders: The Journal of Shakespeare and Appropriation,* 1, 2 (2005) http://www.borrowers.uga.edu [accessed 24 September 2012]

Although the essay does not deal exclusively with *Macbeth*, it explains accurately the asocial sexuality that runs through both Shakespeare's play and Welles's film, particularly through alternations of shot-reverse shot.

Greenblatt, Stephen, 'Shakespeare Bewitched', in *New Historical Literary Study: Essays on Reproducing Texts, Representing History,* eds Jeffrey N. Cox and Larry J. Reynolds (Princeton: Princeton University Press, 1993), pp. 108–35

Macbeth does not engage with the legal or theological foundations of witch-hunting, much less with James's personal take on the subject. Rather, *Macbeth*, like Reginald Scot's *Discoverie*, sees witchcraft as an illusion – illicit theatre – grounded in figurative language that can only counterfeit the power of the divine Word.

Hatchuel, Sarah, '"Prithee, See There! Behold! Look!" (3.4.69): The Gift or Denial of Sight in Screen Adaptations of Shakespeare's *Macbeth*', *Borrowers and Lenders: The Journal of Shakespeare and Appropriation*, 1.2 (2005) http://www.borrowers.uga.edu [accessed 24 September 2012]

Examining vision as a theme and filmic convention in four *Macbeths* (directed by Trevor Nunn, Roman Polanski, Orson Welles and Jeremy Freeston), this essay provides sharply focused comparisons of their different approaches to Macbeth's vision of the dagger, Banquo's ghost and Macbeth's encounters with the witches.

Hateley, Erica, 'Lady Macbeth in Detective Fiction: Criminalizing the Female Reader', *Clues: A Journal of Detection, 24, 2* (Summer *2006*), pp. 31–46

This essay analyses a series of detective novels that use Lady Macbeth as a negative model of femininity to criminalize both innocent female characters and the female reader in order to redeem social order through the exercise of male intellect.

Holland, Peter, '"Stands Scotland Where It Did?": The Location of *Macbeth* on Film', in William Shakespeare, *Macbeth,* ed. Robert S. Miola (New York: W. W. Norton, 2004), pp. 357–80.

Provides a good perspective on the relation of film locale to Scotland as a symbolic place in films both familiar (e.g., Polanksi, Welles, Kurosawa) and less well-known (e.g., *Joe Macbeth, Men of Respect*). The essay argues that *Macbeths* on film re-locate the action to varied locales but use setting to define Scotland as a place adjacent to sources of political power, both outside the norm and vulnerable to penetration.

Huntley, Frank L., '*Macbeth* and the Background of Jesuitical Equivocation', *PMLA*, 79, 4 (1964), pp. 390–400.

Gives a thorough account of equivocation as a means of preserving the speaker's life and soul under nearly impossible circumstances and analyses its thematic role in *Macbeth*.

Jorgens, Jack, 'Kurosawa's *Throne of Blood:* Washizu and Miki Meet the Forest Spirit', *Literature/Film Quarterly,* 11 (1983), 167–73

Offers a convincing close reading of the film's opening scene, in which Washizu (Macbeth) and Miki (Banquo) meet the Forest Spirit. Jorgens offers useful observations on Shakespeare's and Kurosawa's different understandings of the tragic hero's relation to supernatural forces.

Kernan, Alvin, 'The Politics of Madness and Demonism: *Macbeth*, Hampton Court, August 7, 1606', in *Shakespeare, The King's Playwright: Theatre in the Stuart Court, 1603–1613* (New Haven: Yale University Press, 1995), pp. 71–88

Macbeth was performed for James I's entertainment of King Christian of Denmark at Hampton Court in 1606, which provides the impetus for this book's comparison of Shakespeare's politics with those of his king and royal patron.

Klein, Joan Larsen, 'Lady Macbeth: "Infirm of Purpose"', in *The Woman's Part: Feminist Criticism of Shakespeare,* eds Ruth Swift Lenz, Gayle Greene and Carol Thomas Neely (Urbana: University of Illinois Press, 1980), pp. 240–55

This feminist essay argues that although Lady Macbeth embodies the early modern belief in women's weakness in reason, she also thinks of herself primarily as a wife. Even in murder, she acts as Macbeth's helpmeet; after Duncan's murder, however, Lady Macbeth loses her place in both society and the home.

Knights, L. C., 'How Many Children Had Lady Macbeth?' in *Explorations: An Essay in the Theory and Practice of Shakespeare Criticism* (New York: G. W. Stewart, 1947), pp. 15–54

A polemical piece, this essay argues against A. C. Bradley's character-oriented criticism of Shakespeare, contending that *Macbeth* can be read as a poem whose language deserves close scrutiny.

Kolb, Laura, 'Playing with Demons: Interrogating the Supernatural in Jacobean Drama', *Forum for Modern Language Studies*, 43, 1 (2007), pp. 337–50

Relating *Macbeth* to the North Berwick witch trials, this essay offers an excellent analysis of how witchcraft is constructed narratively through comparison with the pamphlet *Newes from Scotland* and James I's tract *Daemonologie*. The essay argues that drama exposes the imperfect conjunction of examples and the general principles they supposedly illustrate in the narrative construction of witchcraft.

Kranz, David L., 'The Sounds of Supernatural Soliciting in *Macbeth*', *Studies in Philology*, 100, 3 (2003), pp. 346–83

Connections between Macbeth and the Weird Sisters are established by 'poetic continuities' linking the human and supernatural realms. These verbal echoes show the witches' penetration into not only the inner thoughts of key characters, but also into public Christian discourse. While the witches possess their own verbal style, distinct from the iambic pentameter of the Scottish court, *Macbeth* becomes saturated with the witches' influence through the porous medium of sound.

Lemon, Rebecca, 'Sovereignty and Treason in *Macbeth*', in *Macbeth: New Critical Essays*, ed. Nick Moschovakis (London and New York: Routledge, 2008), pp. 73–87

Rehearsing the period's arguments for and against tyrannicide, Lemon suggests that *Macbeth* shows ambivalence towards the concept of absolute sovereignty by establishing important similarities between 'good' and 'bad' monarchs. Malcolm, although represented as being motivated by love for the common good, nevertheless parallels *Macbeth* in that he gains the throne by treason.

Lessard, Bruno, 'Hypermedia *Macbeth:* Cognition and Performance', in *Macbeth: New Critical Essays,* ed. Nick Moschovakis (London and New York: Routledge, 2008), pp. 318–34

Arguing that hypermedia texts entail active cognitive work on the part of interactors, Lessard discusses at length performance artist dlsan's *HyperMacbeth* and the Voyager CD-ROM Macbeth, now rendered inaccessible by its legacy platform.

McCoy, Richard, ' "The Grace of Grace" and Double-Talk in *Macbeth', Shakespeare Survey,* 57 (2004), 27–37

Conventionally opposed to Macbeth the equivocator, Malcolm is actually an actor skilled at dissimulation. Paradoxically, the 'grace of grace' that he returns to Scotland is a matter of rhetoric and artful language use.

McLuskie, Kate, '*Macbeth/uMabatha*: Global Shakespeare in a Post-Colonial Market', *Shakespeare Survey*, 52 (1999), 154–65

Explores *uMabatha*'s cultural significance from the perspective of a British spectator at the Globe production of 1997. Part performance review, part theatre history, this essay examines the play's complex positioning in South African and English theatrical culture. Lawrence Wright offers a rebuttal.

Mullaney, Steven, 'Lying Like Truth: Riddle, Representation, and Treason in Renaissance England', *ELH*, 47, 1 (1980), pp. 32–47

Focusing on the rhetorical trope of amphibology and its relationship to discourses of treason (lying) and equivocation (church-sanctioned evasions when secular and sacred authority are in conflict), this essay talks about amphibology's power not only to obscure the truth, but also to generate reality actively. The witches' prophecies are creative because the improbable events they prophesy come true, albeit in an unruly, indirect way.

Newstok, Scott L. '"Why *Macbeth?*" Looking Back on *uMabatha* after Forty Years: An Interview with Welcome Msomi', *Shakespeare in South Africa*, 21 (2009), 74–80

Discusses Msomi's life-long familiarity with Shakespeare and the rationale of his choice of *Macbeth* as a Shakespearean source-text.

Norbrook, David, '*Macbeth* and the Politics of Historiography', in *Politics of Discourse: The Literature and History of Seventeenth-Century England,* eds Kevin Sharpe and Stephen Zwicker (Berkeley: University of California Press, 1987), pp. 78–116

Some of the contradictions in *Macbeth* can be traced back to its historical sources, as historians from humanism up through James's ascension to the throne moved between republican and constitutional approaches to kingship to the more absolutist position represented by James I in his own writings. The central question in this debate was where tyrannicide is a monstrous crime or a reasonable, even 'virtuous action' (p. 91); Shakespeare occupies a medial position.

Ramsay, Jerold, 'The Perversion of Manliness in *Macbeth*', *Studies in English Literature,* 13, 2 (1973), pp. 285–300

At the beginning of the play Macbeth fulfills a legitimate definition of martial masculinity but then loses the 'humane' qualities that are an essential part of complete manhood.

Reynolds, Bryan, '"Untimely Ripped": Mediating Witchcraft in Polanski and Shakespeare', in *Performing Transversally:*

Reimagining Shakespeare and the Critical Future (New York: Palgrave Macmillan, 2003), pp. 111–35

Reynolds draws theoretical parallels between the historical moments of *Macbeth* and of Polanski's film, comparing early modern fears of witchcraft and preoccupation with gruesome murder to public response to the murders of Polanski's wife and others by followers of Charles Manson. The essay argues that both play and film engage in Theatre of Cruelty.

Rosenberg, Marvin, 'Macbeth and Lady Macbeth in the Eighteenth and Nineteenth Centuries', in *Focus on Macbeth,* ed. John Russell Brown (London: Routledge & Kegan Paul, 1982), pp. 73–86

A brief history of how the play was performed during these centuries, with particular attention to the performances of David Garrick and Hannah Pritchard, Sarah Siddons and John Philip Kemble, and Henry Irving and Ellen Terry.

Scott, William O., 'Macbeth's – and Our – Self-Equivocations', *Shakespeare Quarterly,* 37, 2 (1986), pp. 160–74

Examining the nature of speech acts in *Macbeth*, this essay argues that the slippery truth-value of even simple statements characterizes not only the special case of Jesuitical equivocation, but all communication. The audience, like Macbeth himself, contributes to its own delusion.

Shohet, Lauren, 'The Banquet of *Scotland (PA)*', *Shakespeare Survey,* 57 (2004), pp. 186–95

Scotland, PA playfully literalizes the banquet metaphor of *Macbeth*, which represents the ideal relationship between lord and thane as a mutual exchange of nourishment. Within the 1970s ethos of fast food, people and places are both homogenized, reducing agency and rendering both symbolic fathers and mothers ineffective. Neither Scotland (associated with meat) nor England (associated with McDuff's vegetarianism) wins in the end, as we see McDuff offering veggie-burgers to non-existent customers.

Sinfield, Alan, '*Macbeth*: History, Ideology, and Intellectuals', *Critical Quarterly*, 28 (1986), pp. 3–77

Sinfield's essay re-reads *Macbeth* as dramatizing the formulation of the modern absolutist state. He examines the paradox of the tyrant's relation to the legitimate monarch, the difference between them being a matter of motive rather than behavior. But while violence is 'good' when it supports the dominant power structure and 'evil' when it disrupts that power dynamic, in fact the paradoxical status of violence in governance is a 'dysfunction of the absolutist state' (p. 65) that *Macbeth* both replicates and uncovers.

Stallybrass, Peter, '*Macbeth* and Witchcraft', in *Focus on Macbeth,* ed. John Russell Brown (London: Routledge & Kegan Paul, 1982), pp. 189–209

Offers an anthropological perspective on *Macbeth*'s witchcraft, arguing that such beliefs define both a particular social order and the threats against it. The essay argues further that the witches are aligned dramatically and structurally with Lady Macbeth, so that the 'mother' is identified as a threat to both family and crown.

Wickham, Glynne, 'Hell-Castle and Its Door-Keeper', *Shakespeare Survey*, 19 (1966), pp. 68–74

Pointing to the medieval trope of Hell as a castle, this essay reads the Porter scene through the Harrowing of Hell in medieval theology and drama. Malcolm rescues the Scottish as Christ rescues the souls from Hell.

Willis, Deborah, 'Strange Brew', in *Malevolent Nurture: Witch-Hunting and Maternal Power in Early Modern England* (Ithaca: Cornell University Press, 1995), pp. 209–37

Argues that the witches represent lower-class, village witchcraft while Lady Macbeth stands for an aristocratic perversion of nurturing maternity. The association of the witches with Macbeth, however, points to inherent weaknesses of patriarchal rule. The witches themselves are 'egalitarian and cooperative' (p. 217) when tormenting the pilot, highlighting further the inherent flaws in a society founded on the father's prerogative.

Wilson, Richard, 'The Pilot's Thumb: *Macbeth* and the Martyrs', in *Secret Shakespeare: Studies in Theatre, Religion, and Resistance* (Manchester: Manchester University Press, 2004), pp. 186–205

As part of Wilson's larger argument about Shakespeare's imaginative engagement with Catholic resistance and martyrdom, this essay reads *Macbeth* as a sequel to *Henry VI, Part 2*; *Macbeth* extends the earlier play's ideological trajectory by transferring blame for the treason of English Catholics treason to (foreign) Jesuit influence and the 'female demoniac' (p. 196).

Wright, Lawrence, '*uMabatha*: Global and Local', *English Studies in Africa*, 47, 2 (2004), pp. 97–116

In a response to McLuskie's assessment of the 1997 Globe Theatre performance of *uMabatha*, Wright contests some of her emphases to argue that the globalization of theatre erases local theatrical and ideological elements.

Ziegler, Georgianna, 'Accommodating the Virago: Nineteenth-Century Representations of Lady Macbeth', in *Shakespeare and Appropriation*, eds Christy Desmet and Robert Sawyer (London: Routledge, 1999), pp. 119–41.

Discusses the full range of ideological approaches to Lady Macbeth during the period through the history of illustration.

NOTES

Introduction

1 Ronald Black, ed., *To The Hebrides: Samuel Johnson's Journey to the Western Islands of Scotland and James Boswell's Journal of a Tour to the Hebrides*, 2nd edition (Edinburgh: Birlinn, 2011), p. 17.
2 Ibid., p. 20.
3 Ibid., p. 21.
4 Ibid., p. 53.
5 See W. K. Wimsatt, ed., *Dr Johnson on Shakespeare* (Harmondsworth: Penguin, 1969), p. 131.
6 Ibid., p. 131.
7 Ibid., p. 132.
8 Ibid.
9 Ibid., p. 133.
10 Ibid., p. 134.
11 Terence Hawkes, ed., *Twentieth Century Interpretations of Macbeth* (New Jersey: Englewood Cliffs, 1977), p. 1.
12 Ibid., p. 2.
13 Ibid., p. 3.
14 New York: Macmillan, 1950.
15 See A. R. Braunmuller, ed., *Macbeth*, The New Cambridge Shakespeare (Cambridge: Cambridge University Press, 2008), pp. 5–15 for a succinct account of the differences between the two approaches and to the dating of the play.
16 Kenneth Muir, ed., *Macbeth*, Arden 2 series (London: Methuen, 1964), p. xx.
17 Ibid. See also Braunmuller, *Macbeth*, pp. 5–6, where he concludes that such analogies are 'vague, circumstantial, or undatable' (p. 6).
18 See Geoffrey Bullough, *Narrative and Dramatic Sources of Shakespeare*, vol. VII, (London: Routledge, 1973), pp. 423 and following.
19 Ibid., p. 488.
20 Ibid.
21 Ibid.

22 All references to *Macbeth* in this Introduction are taken from Kenneth Muir, ed., *Macbeth*, Arden 2 (London: Methuen, 1951; London and New York: Routledge, 1984). All further Act, scene and line references will occur parenthetically within the body of the text.
23 Bullough, *Narrative*, p. 489.
24 Ibid., pp. 490–91.
25 Ibid., pp. 470–71.
26 Ibid., pp. 494–5.
27 Ibid., p. 495.
28 Ibid., p. 496.
29 Wimsatt, *Dr Johnson*, p. 134.
30 Bullough, *Narrative*, p. 496.
31 Terry Eagleton, *William Shakespeare* (Oxford and New York: Blackwell 1986), p. 2 and following. Of the Weird Sisters, Eagleton observed: 'Their words and bodies mock rigorous boundaries and make sport of fixed positions, unhinging received meanings as they dance, dissolve and re-materialise' (p. 2). He goes on to suggest that society can only envisage their 'creativity' as 'chaos' (p. 3), although more recently Eagleton has revised this view: see Terry Eagleton, *On Evil* (New Haven and London: Yale University Press, 2010), p. 81 and following, where the witches are characterized as 'a threat to any conceivable social order' and are 'toothless old hexes [who] are the enemies of political society as such' (p. 81).
32 Cf. Brian Vickers, *Shakespeare, Co-Author: A Historical Study of Five Collaborative Plays* (Oxford: Oxford University Press, 2002), pp. 96–9. See also Gary Taylor and John Lavagnino, eds, *Thomas Middleton: The Collected Works* (Oxford: Oxford University Press, 2010), pp. 1188–9, where they extend the influence of Middleton into the dialogue of *Macbeth* and print the play as a whole as part of the Middleton *oeuvre* (pp. 1165–201).
33 Braunmuller, *Macbeth*, p. 112 and following.
34 William Hazlitt, *Characters of Shakespeare's Plays* (London: Dent, 1906), p. 12.
35 See John Wain, ed., *Shakespeare: Macbeth: A Casebook* (London and Basingstoke: Macmillan, 1984), p. 93.
36 London: Chatto & Windus, 1937; Harmondsworth: Penguin, 1962.
37 Cambridge: Cambridge University Press, 1935.
38 See John Drakakis, ed., *Alternative Shakespeares* (London: Methuen, 1985), pp. 1–25 for an overview.
39 Jan Kott, *Shakespeare Our Contemporary* (London: Methuen, 1967), pp. 99–133.
40 Ibid., p. 72.
41 Ibid., p. 74.
42 See Peter Stallybrass, '*Macbeth* and Witchcraft' in John Russell Brown, ed., *Focus on Macbeth* (London: Routledge & Kegan Paul, 1982), pp. 189–209.

43 See Naomi Conn Liebler, *Shakespeare's Festive Tragedy: The Ritual Foundations of Genre* (London and New York: Routledge, 1995), pp. 206–23.

44 See Terence Hawkes, *Shakespeare and the Reason: A Study of the Tragedies and the Problem Plays* (London: Routledge and Kegan Paul, 1964) and *Shakespeare's Talking Animals* (London: Edward Arnold, 1973). In the latter we can detect the first steps towards a 'presentism' that *mutatis mutandis* remains of direct relevance to the twenty-first century.

The Critical Backstory

1 As quoted from Simon Forman, *Book of Plaies*, by A. L. Braunmuller in his edition of *Macbeth*, New Cambridge Shakespeare (Cambridge: Cambridge University Press, 1997), p. 58. All quotations from *Macbeth* in this chapter are taken from this edition and referred to as Braunmuller.

2 For details, see G. Blakemore Evans, *Shakespearean Prompt-Books of the Seventeenth Century*, 7 vols (Charlottesville: Bibliographical Society of the University of Virginia, 1960–89), vol. 1, pt 1 http://etext.virginia.edu/bsuva/promptbook/ [accessed 6 June 2012].

3 Ibid., vol. 5, pts 1 and 2.

4 Ibid., vol. 5, pt 1, p. 7.

5 In his *Essay on the Dramatique Poetry of the Last Age* (1672), in Brian Vickers, ed., *Shakespeare: The Critical Heritage*, 6 vols (London and Boston: Routledge & Kegan Paul, 1974–81) and subsequently referred to as Vickers, Dryden refers to 'some bombast speeches of Macbeth, which are not to be understood' (vol. 1, p. 174).

6 *The Grounds of Criticism in Tragedy* (1679), in ibid., vol. 1, p. 250.

7 All references to Davenant's reworking of *Macbeth* are taken from the version of the text printed in Christopher Spencer, ed., *Five Restoration Adaptations of 'Macbeth'* (Urbana: University of Illinois Press, 1965), pp. 33–107.

8 As advocated by Thomas Sprat in his *History of the Royal Society, For the Improving of Natural Knowledge* (London: Printed by T. R. for J. Martyn, 1667), p. 113.

9 For a Garrick's version of the play, see David Garrick, *The Plays of David Garrick*, eds Harry William Pedicord and Frederick Louis Bergmann, 4 vols (Carbondale: Southern Illinois University Press, 1981).

10 John Dennis, *An Essay upon the Genius and Writings of Shakespeare* (1712) in Vickers, *Shakespeare*, vol. 2, p. 285.

11 Ibid., vol. 2, p. 25.

12 Ibid., vol. 3, p. 98.

13 Ibid., vol. 5, p. 288.

14 Ibid., vol. 2, p. 79.

15 James Beattie, *Essays: On Poetry and Music* (1776) in ibid., vol. 6, p. 152.

16 N. S., 'Remarks on the Tragedy of the *Orphan*', in *The Gentleman's Magazine* 18 (1748) in Vickers, *Shakespeare* vol. 3, p. 329.

17 Ibid., vol. 6, p. 121.

18 Elizabeth Montagu, *An Essay on the Writings and Genius of Shakespeare* (1769), in ibid., vol. 5, p. 337.

19 Unsigned notices in the *Universal Museum*, 1 (1762), in ibid., vol. 4, p. 461.

20 Francis Gentleman, *The Dramatic Censor; or, Critical Companion* (1770), in ibid., vol. 5, p. 394.

21 John Upton, *Critical Observations on Shakespeare* (1748), in ibid., vol. 3, p. 294.

22 Joseph Donohue, *Dramatic Character in the English Romantic Age* (Princeton: Princeton University Press, 1970), p. 192.

23 Arthur Murphy, *The London Chronicle: or Universal Evening Post* (1757), in Vickers, *Shakespeare*, vol. 4, p. 281.

24 T. W., 'Observations upon the Tragedy of *Macbeth*' (1767), in ibid., vol. 5, p. 288.

25 Ibid., vol. 5, p. 338.

26 Nicholas Rowe, *Some Account of the Life, &c of Mr. William Shakespeare* (1709), in ibid., vol. 2, p. 199.

27 William Duff, *Critical Observations on the Writings of the Most Celebrated Original Geniuses in Poetry* (1770), in ibid., vol. 5, p. 368.

28 Ibid., vol. 5, p. 336.

29 Horace Walpole, from his manuscript 'Book of Materials', in ibid., vol. 5, p. 485.

30 Dennis Bartholomeusz, *Macbeth and the Players* (London: Cambridge University Press, 1969), p. 95.

31 Thomas Davies, *Dramatic Miscellanies* (1784), in Vickers, *Shakespeare*, vol. 6, p. 375.

32 Maurice Morgann, *An Essay on the Dramatic Character of Sir John Falstaff* (1777), ibid., vol. 6, p. 172.

33 Ibid., vol. 5, p. 391.

34 Sir Richard Steele, *Spectator* 208 (1711), in ibid., vol. 2, p. 270. See also Bartholomeusz, *Macbeth*, pp. 65–6.

35 Peter Holland, 'The Age of Garrick', in *Shakespeare: An Illustrated Stage History*, eds Jonathan Bate and Russell Jackson (Oxford: Oxford University Press, 1996), p. 87.

36 *The Plays of David Garrick*, eds Harry William Pedicord and Frederick Louis Bergmann, 4 vols (Carbondale: Southern Illinois University Press, 1981), 3, p. 399.

37 Until Gary Taylor in his edition of *Macbeth* in *Thomas Middleton: The Collected Works*, (eds) Gary Taylor and John Lavagnino (Oxford: Clarendon Press, 2007), pp. 1165–201.

38 H. R. Woudhuysen, ed., *Samuel Johnson on Shakespeare* (Harmondsworth: Penguin Books, 1989), p. 160.

39 Ibid., p. 70.

40 Ibid., pp. 1–2.

41 Johnson's comment on II.i.25.

42 *The Rambler* 168, in Woudhuysen, *Samuel Johnson*, pp. 92–3.

43 Ibid., p. 229.

44 Arthur Murphy, *The London Chronicle* (1757), in Vickers, *Shakespeare*, vol. 4, p. 279.

45 Edward Capell, *Notes and Various Readings to Shakespeare* (1783), in Vickers, *Shakespeare*, vol. 6, p. 233.

46 George Steevens, *The Plays of Shakespeare* (1793), in Vickers, *Shakespeare*, vol. 6, p. 593.

47 Horace Howard Furness, ed., *Macbeth: A New Variorum Edition* (Philadelphia: Lippincott, 1873), pp. 361–2.

48 Vickers, *Shakespeare*, vol. 6, p. 217.

49 See Charles Gildon on Kemble and Siddons, 1793, in Gāmini Salgādo, ed., *Eyewitnesses of Shakespeare: First Hand Accounts of Performances of Shakespeare, 1590–1890* (London: Chatto and Windus, 1975), p. 299.

50 William Richardson as quoted in Nicholas Tredell, ed., *Shakespeare: Macbeth* (Houndmills, Basingstoke: Palgrave Macmillan, 2006), p. 19.

51 Vickers, *Shakespeare*, vol. 5, p. 340.

52 Thomas Whately, *Remarks on Some of the Characters of Shakespeare* (1785), in Vickers, *Shakespeare*, vol. 6, p. 427.

53 Richard Cumberland, *The Observer* (1785–91), in Vickers, *Shakespeare*, vol. 6. pp. 453–4.

54 Ibid., vol. 6, p. 449.

55 William Hazlitt, *Characters of Shakespeare's Plays* (1817) (Oxford: Oxford University Press, 1917), Preface, pp. xxxv–xxxvii.

56 As quoted in ibid., p. xxxiv.

57 Ibid., pp. 12–13.

58 Jonathan Bate, ed., *The Romantics on Shakespeare* (London: Penguin Books, 1992), p. 33.

59 Jonathan Bate, *Shakespeare and the English Romantic Imagination* (Oxford: Clarendon Press, 1992), pp. 228–9.

60 Bate, *Romantics*, p. 424

61 Charles Lamb, 'On the Tragedies of Shakespeare, considered with Reference to their Fitness for Stage Representation', in *English Critical*

Essays: Nineteenth Century, ed. Edmund D. Jones (Oxford: Oxford University Press, 1919), p. 109.

62 Bate, *Romantics*, pp. 429–30.

63 Samuel Taylor Coleridge, *Shakespearean Criticism*, ed. T. M. Raysor, 2 vols (London: Dent, 1907; reprinted 1974), vol. 2, p. 220.

64 Bate, *Romantics*, p. 411.

65 See John Wilders, ed., *Macbeth*, Shakespeare in Production (Cambridge: Cambridge University Press, 2004), pp. 21–3.

66 Coleridge, *Shakespearean Criticism,* vol. 1, p. 64.

67 Anna Jameson, *Shakespeare's Heroines: Characteristics of Women, Moral, Poetical and Historical* (London: G. Bell and Sons, 1913), p. 323.

68 Ibid., p. 323.

69 Ibid., p. 329.

70 Bate, *Romantics*, pp. 435–40.

71 Ibid., pp. 439–40.

72 Ibid., p. 426.

73 Bate, *Shakespeare*, p. 45.

74 Coleridge, *Shakespearean Criticism* vol. 2, p. 220.

75 Ibid. vol. 1, p. 67.

76 Jones, *English Critical Essays*, pp. 98–9.

77 Ibid., p. 115.

78 From Blake's description of the painting 'Sir Jeffery Chaucer and the nine and twenty Pilgrims on their Journey to Canterbury' quoted in Bate, *Shakespeare*, p. 127.

79 Bate, *Romantics*, p. 449.

80 Ibid., pp. 434–5.

81 George Fletcher, *Studies of Shakespeare* (London: Longman, 1847), pp. 119, 194, 152.

82 J. W. Comyns Carr, *Macbeth and Lady Macbeth: An Essay* (London: Bickers and Son, 1889), pp. 17, 13, 24, 32.

83 Oxford: Clarendon Press, 1885.

84 London: 1856.

85 Fletcher, *Studies*, p. 110.

86 Edward Dowden, *Shakspere. A Critical Study of his Mind and Art* (London: Routledge and Kegan Paul, 1857; reprinted 1953), p. 245.

87 Fletcher, *Studies*, p. 167.

88 *The Windsor Shakespeare*, ed. Henry H. Hudson, 20 vols (London: Blackwood, Le Bas and Co., n.d.). *Macbeth* is in vol. 17.

89 E. A. Abbott, *A Shakespearian Grammar: An Attempt to Illustrate some of the Differences between Elizabethan and Modern English* (London and New York: Macmillan and Co., 1869).

90 A. C. Bradley, *Shakespearean Tragedy* (London: Macmillan and Co. Ltd, 1904, 1963), pp. 295, 298, 319.

91 Caroline Spurgeon, *Shakespeare's Imagery and What it Tells Us* (Cambridge: Cambridge University Press, 1935, 1968), p. 326.

92 Lily B. Campbell, *Shakespeare's Tragic Heroes: Slaves of Passion* (Cambridge: Cambridge University Press, 1930).

93 William Empson, *Seven Types of Ambiguity* (Harmondsworth: Penguin Books, 1965, 2nd edition), pp. 18–19.

94 M. M. Mahood, *Shakespeare's Wordplay* (London: Methuen and Co., 1968), pp. 130–45.

95 Francis Berry, *Poets' Grammar: Person, Time and Mood in Poetry* (London: Routledge and Kegan Paul, 1958).

96 Hilda Hulme, *Explorations in Shakespeare's Language: Some Problems of Word Meaning in the Dramatic Text* (London: Longman, 1962, 1977).

97 Laurence Danson, *Tragic Alphabet: Shakespeare's Drama of Language* (Yale: Yale University Press, 1974), pp. 124, 132, 138.

98 Michael Goldman, *Acting and Action in Shakespearean Tragedy* (Princeton: Princeton University Press, 1985), p. 102.

99 James L. Calderwood, *'If It Were Done': Macbeth and Tragic Action* (Amherst: University of Massachusetts Press, 1986).

100 Kenneth Muir, ed., *Macbeth* (London: Methuen and Co., 1951, revised edition 1984).

101 A. R. Braunmuller, ed., *Macbeth* (Cambridge: Cambridge University Press, 1997).

102 George Wilson Knight, *The Imperial Theme* (London: Methuen and Co., 1931, reprinted 1968), p. 153.

103 L. C. Knights, *Some Shakespearean Themes and an Approach to Hamlet* (London: Chatto & Windus, 1959), p. 9.

104 Cleanth Brooks, 'The Naked Babe and the Cloak of Manliness', in *The Well Wrought Urn: Studies in the Structure of Poetry* (New York: Harcourt, 1947), pp. 22–49.

105 Helen Gardner, *The Business of Criticism* (Oxford: Clarendon Press, 1956).

106 John Holloway, *The Story of the Night: Studies in Shakespeare's Major Tragedies* (London: Routledge and Kegan Paul, 1961), pp. 63–6.

107 Paul A. Jorgensen, *Our Naked Frailties: Sensational Art and Meaning in Macbeth* (Berkeley: University of California Press, 1971).

108 E. M. W. Tillyard, *Shakespeare's History Plays* (Harmondsworth: Penguin Books, 1944, 1989), p. 321.

109 Nick Moschovakis, ed., *Macbeth: New Critical Essays* (New York and London: Routledge, 2008), p. 29.

110 Princeton: Princeton University Press, 1958.

111 G. R. Elliott, *Dramatic Providence in Macbeth: A Study of Shakespeare's Tragic Theme of Humanity and Grace* (Princeton: Princeton University Press, 1958), p. 16.

112 Roy Walker, *The Time is Free: A Study of Macbeth* (London: Andrew Dakers Ltd., 1949).

113 Hebert R. Coursen, 'In Deepest Consequence: *Macbeth*', *Shakespeare Quarterly* 18.4 (1967), pp. 375–88 (375, 387).

114 Leonard F. Dean, '*Macbeth* and Modern Criticism', *The English Journal* 47.2 (1958), pp. 57–67; G. K. Hunter, '*Macbeth* in the Twentieth Century', *Shakespeare Survey* 19 (1966), pp. 1–11.

115 Sigmund Freud, 'Some Character-Types met with in Psychoanalytic Work', in *The Pelican Freud Library* vol. 14, ed. Albert Dickson (Harmondsworth: Penguin Books, 1985), p. 308.

116 Eugene M. Waith, 'Manhood and Valour in Two Shakespearean Tragedies', *ELH* 17.4 (1950), pp. 262–73.

117 Matthew N. Proser, *The Heroic Image in Five Shakespearean Tragedies* (Princeton: Princeton University Press, 1965).

118 D. W. Harding, 'Woman's Fantasy of Manhood: A Shakespearian Theme', *Shakespeare Quarterly* 20.3 (1969), 245–53.

119 Coppélia Kahn, *Man's Estate: Masculinity on Shakespeare* (Berkeley and London: University of California Press, 1981), pp. 172, 173.

120 Janet Adelman, *Suffocating Mothers: Fantasies of Maternal Origin in Shakespeare's Plays, from Hamlet to The Tempest* (New York and London: Routledge, 1992).

121 Ibid., pp. 1, 131, 139, 145, 144.

122 Berger, Harry Jr., 'The Early Scenes of *Macbeth*: Preface to a New Interpretation', *ELH* 47.1 (1980), pp. 1–31; Berger, Harry Jr, 'Text Against Performance: The Example of *Macbeth*', *Genre* 15 (1892), pp. 49–79.

123 Berger, 'Text Against Performance', pp. 49–79 (70, 71). Richard Levin mounts a strong challenge to Berger's critical procedures in this article and his reading of the play in 'The New Refutation of Shakespeare', *MP* 83.2 (1985), pp. 123–41.

124 Wilson Knight, *The Imperial Theme*, p. 129.

125 Berger, 'The Early Scenes of *Macbeth*', pp. 3, 5, 25, 4.

126 Stephen Booth, *King Lear, Macbeth, and Tragedy* (New Haven, London: Yale University Press, 1983), p. 96.

127 Ibid., p. 99.

128 Jan Kott, *Shakespeare our Contemporary* (London: Methuen and Co., 1964), p. 89.

129 Tredell, *Shakespeare: Macbeth*, p. 73.

130 Henry N. Paul, *The Royal Play of Macbeth: When, Why, and How it was Written by Shakespeare* (New York: Macmillan, 1950).

131 Alvin Kernan, *Shakespeare, the King's Playwright: Theater in the Stuart Court 1603–1613* (New Haven: Yale University Press, 1995), p. 88.

132 Walter Clyde Curry, *Shakespeare's Philosophical Patterns* (Baton Rouge: Louisiana State University, 1937).

133 Wilbur Sanders, *The Dramatist and the Received Idea: Studies in the Plays of Marlowe and Shakespeare* (Cambridge: Cambridge University Press, 1968), p. 285.

134 Arthur Melville Clark, *Murder under Trust, or, The Topical Macbeth and other Jacobean Matters* (Edinburgh: Scottish Academic Press, 1981), p. ix.

135 Michael Hawkins, 'History, Politics and *Macbeth*', in *Focus on Macbeth*, ed. John Russell Brown (London: Routledge and Kegan Paul, 1982), pp. 155–88 (166, 165).

136 Ibid., p. 175.

137 Ibid., p. 178.

138 David Norbrook, '*Macbeth* and the Politics of Historiography' in *The Politics of Discourse: The Literature and History of Seventeenth-Century England*, eds Kevin Sharpe and Steven N. Zwicker (Berkeley: University of California Press, 1987), pp. 78–116 (98, 116).

139 Alan Sinfield, '*Macbeth*: History, Ideology and Intellectuals' in *Faultlines: Cultural Materialism and the Politics of Dissident Reading* (Oxford: Clarendon Press, 1992), pp. 96, 102.

140 Garry Wills, *Witches and Jesuits: Shakespeare's 'Macbeth'* (Oxford: Oxford University Press, 1996.

141 Arthur F. Kinney, 'Shakespeare's *Macbeth* and the Question of Nationalism', in *Literature and Nationalism*, (eds) Vincent Newey and Ann Thompson (Liverpool: Liverpool University Press, 1991), pp. 56–75 (72).

142 Arthur F. Kinney, 'Scottish History, the Union of the Crowns and the Issue of Right Rule: The Case of Shakespeare's *Macbeth*', in *Renaissance Culture in Context: Theory and Practice*, (eds) Jean R. Brink and William F. Gentrup (Aldershot: Scolar, 1993), pp. 18–53 (39).

143 Kinney, 'Scottish History', p. 51.

144 Calderwood, *'If It Were Done'*, p. 113.

145 Sally Mapstone, 'Shakespeare and Scottish Kingship: A Case History', in *The Rose and the Thistle: Essays on the Culture of Late Medieval and Renaissance Scotland*, (eds) Sally Mapstone and Juliette Wood (East Linton: Tuckwell Press, 1998), pp. 158–93 (168).

146 Nick Aitchison, *Macbeth: Man and Myth* (Thrupp: Sutton Publishing, 1999).

147 Peter Stallybrass, '*Macbeth* and Witchcraft', in *Focus on Macbeth*, ed. Russell Brown, pp. 189–209.

148 Ibid., pp. 198, 190.

149 Terry Eagleton, *William Shakespeare* (Oxford: Basil Blackwell, 1986), pp. 1–2. Eagleton has recently modified this view in *On Evil* (New Haven and London: Yale University Press, 2010), pp. 84–86.

150 Stephen Greenblatt, 'Shakespeare Bewitched', in *New Historical Literary Study: Essays on Reproducing Texts, Representing History*, (eds) Jeffery N. Cox and Larry J. Reynolds (Princeton: Princeton University Press, 1993), pp. 108–35 (121, 124).

151 Diane Purkiss, *The Witch in History* (London and New York: Routledge, 1996), pp. 207, 214.

152 Stephen Orgel, '*Macbeth* and the Antic Round', *Shakespeare Survey* 52 (1999), pp. 143–53.

153 Ibid., pp. 148, 150.

154 John Dover Wilson, ed. *Macbeth*, The New Shakespeare (Cambridge: Cambridge University Press, 1947), p. xxvi.

155 Richard Flatter, *Shakespeare's Producing Hand* (New York: W. W. Norton and Co., 1948), p. 94.

156 G. K. Hunter, ed., *Macbeth* (London: Penguin Books, 1967; reprinted 2005).

157 J. M. Nosworthy, *Shakespeare's Occasional Plays* (London: Edward Arnold, 1965).

158 Nicholas Brooke, ed., *Macbeth* (Oxford: Oxford University Press, 1990), p. 56.

159 Braunmuller, *Macbeth*, p. 259.

Performance History

1 The opening paragraph of this chapter was largely written by Bernice W. Kliman, my very dear friend and colleague of many years, who became ill and died before we had a chance to carry out our original plan of writing the chapter together. The whole chapter is deeply indebted to her. Kliman left notes, we worked on an outline, and I draw heavily on her extensive publications on *Macbeth* and directly from her reviews of performances of the play in *The Shakespeare Newsletter* (as indicated below, in note 59 of the present chapter).

2 Dennis Bartholomeusz, *Macbeth and The Players* (Cambridge: Cambridge University Press, 1969).

3 Marvin Rosenberg, *The Masks of Macbeth* (Newark: University of Delaware Press, 1993).

4 Ibid., Appendix 2, pp. 769–85.

5 Ibid., p. ix.

6 Gordon Williams, *Macbeth: Text and Performance* (London: Macmillan, 1985).

7 Ibid., p. 66.
8 Ibid., p. 65.
9 Ibid., p. 66.
10 Ibid.
11 Bernice W. Kliman, *Shakespeare in Performance: Macbeth* (Manchester: Manchester University Press, 2004).
12 Ibid., p. xiii.
13 Ibid.
14 Ibid., p. 120.
15 'Original practices' refers to the reconstruction of original playing conditions as embodied in the performance ideals of the New Globe and of the American Shakespeare Center at the Blackfriars Playhouse in Staunton, Virginia. See Paul Menzer's *Inside Shakespeare: Studies on the Blackfriars Stage* (Selinsgrove, Pennsylvania: Susquehanna University Press, 2006) and Jeremy Lopez's 'A Partial Theory of Original Practice', *Shakespeare Survey* 61 (2008), pp. 302–17.
16 The discovery of walls of the actual Curtain Theatre in June 2012 promises further to enhance our knowledge of original performance as well.
17 For a discussion of the varying dynamics of hearing, overhearing, eavesdropping and stage whispering on the early modern stage, see Laury Magnus and Walter W. Cannon (eds), *Who Hears in Shakespeare? Auditory Worlds on Stage and Screen* (Madison, New Jersey: Fairleigh Dickinson University Press; Lanham, Maryland: The Roman & Littlefield Publishing Group, 2012).
18 Kliman, *Shakespeare in Performance*, p. 2.
19 Ibid., p. 14.
20 Gary Taylor and John Lavagnino explain in the introduction to their edition of *Macbeth* in *Thomas Middleton: The Collected Works* (Oxford: Clarendon Press, 2007) that Middleton also produced some dialogue around the sections that include the songs from *The Witch* and that Middleton was either a collaborator or a reviser of the Folio text, accounting, in this way, for the mixed style of the play. Middleton, they argue, added 'to a text of *Macbeth* which already had the weird sisters and a cauldron scene (4.1)', and that to 'motivate' both the witch's songs and 'the appearance of Hecate in these, he added the rest of what is now 3.5 and some lines in 4.1 (39–43; 143–50)' (p. 1166).
21 Ibid.
22 Kliman, *Shakespeare in Performance*, p. 28.
23 It might be stressed, however, that modern conditions can nevertheless considerably sharpen the reversal of the gender roles of Macbeth and the Lady in the early scenes of the play. There is a wonderful moment in William Reilly's film *Men of Respect* (1990) in which the Macbeth figure

(John Turturro) lies decorously naked on a bed after the murder, while his wife Ruthie (Katherine Borowitz) sits fully clothed on the bed beside him.

24 The early *Romeo and Juliet* and the late *Anthony and Cleopatra* are the only tragic plays with parallel top-billing.

25 Quoted in Jonathan Bate and Russell Jackson (eds), *The Oxford Illustrated History of Shakespeare on Stage* (Oxford: Oxford University Press, 2001), p. 52.

26 Ibid., p. 53.

27 Ibid., p. 56.

28 Quoted in Blanca Lopez Roman, 'Sir William D'Avenant's So-Called Improvements of *Macbeth* (1674)', *Actas del I congreso nacional* (1990), pp. 211–22.

29 David Roberts, *Thomas Betterton: The Greatest Actor of the Restoration Stage* (Cambridge: Cambridge University Press, 2010), p. 1.

30 Bartholomeusz, *Macbeth and The Players*, pp. 41–4.

31 Rosenberg, *The Masks of Macbeth*, p. 563.

32 Kliman, *Shakespeare in Performance*, p. 28.

33 Sarah Siddons, 'Remarks on the Character of Lady Macbeth' from volume II of Campbell's *Life of Mrs. Siddons*, reproduced in *William Shakespeare: A New Variorum Edition of Shakespeare – Macbeth*, Horace Howard Furness, Jr, ed. (New York: Dover Publications, 1963), pp. 472–7.

34 Siddons, 'Remarks', p. 474.

35 Ibid., p. 475.

36 'Tickling commodity' and the notion of what directors and producers must do to accommodate financial constraints is a key term throughout Kenneth Rothwell's *A History of Shakespeare on Screen* (Cambridge: Cambridge University Press, 2004), p. 3.

37 *Macbeth*, dir. Orson Welles, perf. Orson Welles and Jeanette Nolan (Mercury Productions, 1948), restored version available on DVD. 107 min.

38 *Throne of Blood* (Kumonosu-jō, or, literally, *Spider Web Castle*), dir. Akira Kurosawa, perf. Toshiro Mifune (Washizu, aka Macbeth), Isuzu Yamada (Lady Asaji, aka Lady Macbeth), Minoru Chiaki, (Miki, aka Banquo) (Kurosawa Production Company, 1957). DVD. 110 min.

39 As a youth, Kurosawa worked in his brother's film studio, where his brother's voice and piano playing accompanied films' silent images. The non-diegetic use of sound, a disjunction and re-assemblage of voice and image, is the likely source of Kurosawa's ideas for creating spooky mediums who are women but whose voices are male. A medium who speaks for a dead samurai appears earlier in his film *Rashomon*, but the same mocking voice in the Spirit of the Forest is certainly an effective equivalent of 'women with beards'.

40 Rothwell, *A History*, p. 196.

41 Kliman, *Shakespeare in Performance*, p. 190.

42 *Macbeth*, dir. Roman Polanski, perf. Jon Finch, Francesca Annis (UK, Caliban Films, US, Playboy Production, 1971). DVD. 140 min.
43 Rothwell explains the odd genesis of the character of Rosse in an 'obscure Victorian essay' and shows in detail Polanski's camerawork portraying Rosse as a 'smirking sociopath' (*A History*, p. 158).
44 Antonin Artaud, *The Theatre and Its Double*, trans Mary C. Richards (New York: Grove Press, 1994), p. 13.
45 Kliman, *Shakespeare in Performance*, p. 206.
46 Maslin, Janet, '*Men of Respect*: Car Bomb and Chianti in "Macbeth" Variation', *The New York Times*, 18 January 1991 http://movies.nytimes.com/movie/review?res=9D0CE7D81230F93BA25752C0A967958260 [accessed 1 September 2012].
47 *Scotland, PA*, dir. Billy Morrissette, perf. James LeGros (Joe 'Mac' McBeth), Maura Tierney ('Pat' McBeth), Christopher Walken (Lieutenant McDuff) (Abandon Pictures, 2001). DVD. 104 min.
48 See Kliman, *Shakespeare in Performance*, p. 62.
49 Ibid., p. 62.
50 Rosenberg, *The Masks of Macbeth*, p. 482.
51 Ibid., p. 564.
52 Quoted in Kliman, *Shakespeare in Performance*, p. 72.
53 Ibid., p. 77.
54 Peter Donaldson, *Shakespearean Films, Shakespearean Directors* (London: Routledge, 1990).
55 See Andrew Gurr's 'Why was the Globe Round?' for an interesting discussion of the auditory nature of Shakespearean stagecraft that frequently dictates a 'surround' of a character, mediating the space between him and the audience, in Magnus and Cannon, *Who Hears*, pp. 3–16.
56 All references to *Macbeth* in this chapter are taken from Kenneth Muir, ed., *Macbeth*, Arden Edition (London: Methuen and Co., 1951; London and New York: Routledge, 1984). All further Act, scene and line references will occur parenthetically within the body of the text.
57 Richard Armitage, 'Macbeth (RSC)' http://www.richardarmitageonline.com/macbeth-rsc/macbeth-introduction.html [accessed 1 September 2012].
58 Ben Brantley, 'Fierce Kindred Spirits, Burning for a Throne', *The New York Times*, 22 June 2002 http://www.nytimes.com/2000/06/22/theater/theater-review-fierce-kindred-spirits-burning-for-a-throne.html?n=Top%2fReference%2fTimes%20Topics%2fSubjects%2fT%2fTheater [accessed 1 September 2012].
59 In this section on twenty-first-century stage productions, I am highly indebted to Professors Thomas Pendleton and John Mahon, editors of *The Shakespeare Newsletter*, for their generous permission to reproduce portions of previously published reviews: Bernice W. Kliman's 'Another

Ninagawa *Macbeth*', *The Shakespeare Newsletter* 52.4 (2002/3), pp. 93–106; and my own reviews, '"Bearing the Weight of this Sad Time": *Macbeth* at the Delacorte, *Lear* at LaMama', *The Shakespeare Newsletter* 56.1, No. 268 (Spring/Summer 2006), pp. 11–35; and 'Playing the Moments: *Macbeth* at the Theatre for a New Audience' in *The Shakespeare Newsletter* 61.1 (Spring/Summer 2011), pp. 3–14.

60 One major exception to this was *Cahoot's Macbeth*, Tom Stoppard's framed piece in which a stage audience watches and interacts with a radically shortened version of the play. *Cahoot's Macbeth* is a tribute to the dissident Czech playwright Pavel Kohout, who illegally performed plays in people's living rooms to escape the secret police after his theatre had been closed by the authorities.

61 Quoted in Kliman, *Shakespeare in Performance*, p. 159.

62 Quoted in Paul A. S. Harvey and Bernice W. Kliman, 'Ninagawa *Macbeth*: Fusion of Japanese and Western Theatrical Styles', in Kliman, *Shakespeare in Performance*, pp. 159–82 (162).

63 Ezra Pound, 'Hugh Selwyn Mauberley', in *Selected Poems, 1908–1959* (London and Boston: Faber and Faber, 1975), pp. 98–112 (101, Canto V).

64 Ben Brantley, 'Something Wicked This Way Comes', *The New York Times*, 15 February 2008 http://theater2.nytimes.com/2008/02/15/theater/reviews/15macb.html?pagewanted=all&_r=0 [accessed 1 September 2012].

65 Ben Brantley, 'The Deed is Done, the Doers Undone', *The New York Times*, 25 March 2011 http://theater.nytimes.com/2011/03/26/theater/reviews/macbeth-opens-at-the-duke-on-42nd-street-review.html [accessed 1 September 2012].

66 See Laury Magnus, 'An Interview with Arin Arbus of the Theatre for a New Audience' in *The Shakespeare Newsletter* (Spring/Summer 2011), pp. 10–14, where Arbus discusses the pervasiveness of the motif of the child and her unrealized plan to have the witches played by children.

67 Until its new theatre opens at the Brooklyn Academy of Music (it is being completed), the Duke Theatre on Broadway has been the venue for most TFANA productions.

68 Jan Kott, *Shakespeare Our Contemporary* (New York: W. W. Norton, 1974), p. 86.

Macbeth: The State of the Art

1 Kent Cartwright, 'Scepticism and Theatre in *Macbeth*', *Shakespeare Survey* 55 (2002), pp. 219–36 (p. 220).

2 Ibid., p. 222.

3 Ibid., p. 236.

4 Sean H. McDowell, 'Macbeth and the Perils of Conjecture', in *Knowing Shakespeare: Senses, Embodiment, and Cognition*, eds Lowell Gallagher and Shankar Raman (Basingstoke and London: Palgrave Macmillan, 2010), pp. 30–49 (p. 30).

5 Ibid., p. 31.

6 Arthur F. Kinney, 'Macbeth's Knowledge', *Shakespeare Studies* 57 (2004), pp. 11–26.

7 Ibid., p. 26.

8 Stuart Clark, *Vanities of the Eye: Vision in Early Modern European Culture* (Oxford: Oxford University Press, 2007), pp. 242, 1.

9 Ibid., p. 236.

10 Ibid., p. 255.

11 Ibid.

12 Mary Thomas Crane, '"Fair is Foul": *Macbeth* and Binary Logic', in *The Work of Fiction: Cognition, Culture, and Complexity*, eds Alan Richardson and Ellen Spolsky (Aldershot, Hampshire and Burlington, VT: Ashgate, 2004), pp. 107–26 (p. 108).

13 Ibid., p. 115.

14 Richard Kerridge, 'An Ecocritic's *Macbeth*', in *Ecocritical Shakespeare*, eds Lynne Bruckner and Dan Brayton (Farnham, Surrey and Burlington, VT: Ashgate, 2011), pp. 193–210 (p. 194).

15 Ibid., p. 195.

16 Ibid., p. 201.

17 Kristen Poole, *Supernatural Environments in Shakespeare's England: Spaces of Demonism, Divinity, and Drama* (Cambridge: Cambridge University Press, 2011), p. 158.

18 Ibid., p. 136.

19 Ibid.

20 Ibid., p. 157.

21 Robert Weimann, 'Theatrical Space in Shakespeare's Playhouse: Revisiting *locus* and *platea* in *Timon* and *Macbeth*', *Shakespeare International Yearbook* 2 (2002), pp. 203–17 (205).

22 Ibid., p. 211.

23 Ibid., pp. 215–16.

24 Ibid., p. 209. Weimann is here engaging Martin Heidegger's notion of 'picturing' space in modern projects of mastery.

25 Martin Orkin, '"It will have blood they say; blood will have blood" – Proverb Usage and the Vague and Undetermined Places of *Macbeth*', in *Shakespeare Without Boundaries: Essays in Honor of Dieter Mehl*, eds Christa Jansohn, Lena Cowen Orlin and Stanley Wells (Newark: University of Delaware Press, 2011), pp. 189–202 (190, 191, 191–2).

26 Jonathan Gil Harris, *Untimely Matter in the Time of Shakespeare* (Philadelphia: University of Pennsylvania Press, 2009), p. 22.
27 Ibid., p. 121.
28 Ibid., p. 138.
29 Ibid., p. 137.
30 Ibid., p. 138.
31 Ibid., p. 139.
32 Brayton Polka, *Shakespeare and Interpretation, Or, What You Will* (Newark: University of Delaware Press, 2011), p. 51.
33 Heather Love, 'Milk', in *Shakesqueer: A Queer Companion to the Complete Works of Shakespeare*, ed. Madhavi Menon (Durham and London: Duke University Press, 2011), pp. 201–8 (p. 201).
34 Ibid., p. 201.
35 Ibid., p. 202. All references to *Macbeth* in this chapter are taken from Kenneth Muir, ed., *Macbeth*, Arden Edition (London: Methuen and Co., 1951; London and New York: Routledge, 1984). Further Act, scene and line references will occur parenthetically within the body of the text.
36 Love, 'Milk', p. 202. On '*sinthomo*sexual', see Lee Edelman, *No Future: Queer Theory and the Death Drive* (Durham and London: Duke University Press, 2004). Edelman develops the term from Lacan's '*sinthome*'.
37 Love, 'Milk', p. 204.
38 Jennifer Lewin, 'Murdering Sleep in *Macbeth*: The Mental World of the Protagonist', *Shakespeare International Yearbook* 5 (2005), pp. 181–8 (p. 181).
39 Derek Cohen, *Searching Shakespeare: Studies in Culture and Authority* (Toronto: University of Toronto Press 2003), pp. 137, 138, 127.
40 Lynne Dickson Bruckner, '"Let Grief Convert to Anger": Authority and Affect in *Macbeth*', in *Macbeth: New Critical Essays*, ed. Nick Moschovakis (London and New York: Routledge, 2008), pp. 192–207 (p. 192).
41 Steven J. Brams, *Game Theory and the Humanities: Bridging Two Worlds* (Cambridge, MA: MIT Press, 2011), p. 159.
42 Ibid., p. 180.
43 Katherine A. Rowe, 'Humoral Knowledge and Liberal Cognition in Davenant's *Macbeth*', in *Reading the Early Modern Passions: Essays in the Cultural History of Emotion*, eds Gail Kern Paster, Katherine Rowe and Mary Floyd-Wilson (Philadelphia: University of Pennsylvania Press, 2004), pp. 169–91 (170).
44 Ibid., p. 172.
45 Ibid., p. 171; William Davenant, *Proposition for Advancement of Moralitie by a New Way of Entertainment of the People* (London, 1653).
46 Rowe, 'Humoral', p. 173.
47 Ibid., p. 174.

48 Ibid., p. 187.
49 Ibid., p. 190.
50 Abraham Stoll, '*Macbeth*'s equivocal conscience', in Moschovakis, *Macbeth*, pp. 132–50 (132).
51 Ibid., p. 145.
52 Ibid., p. 134.
53 Richard C. McCoy, '"The Grace of Grace" and Double-Talk in *Macbeth*', *Shakespeare Survey* 57 (2004), pp. 27–37 (28, 29).
54 Ibid., p. 29.
55 Lina Perkins Wilder, *Shakespeare's Memory Theatre: Recollection, Properties, and Character* (Cambridge: Cambridge University Press, 2010), p. 22.
56 Ibid., p. 160.
57 Ibid., p. 157.
58 Ibid., p. 165.
59 Rebecca Ann Bach, 'The "Peerless" Macbeth: Friendship and Family in *Macbeth*', in Moschovakis, *Macbeth*, pp. 104–17 (105).
60 Fred B. Tromly, *Fathers and Sons in Shakespeare: The Debt Never Promised* (Toronto: University of Toronto Press, 2010), p. 218.
61 Carol Thomas Neely, *Distracted Subjects: Madness and Gender in Shakespeare and Early Modern Culture* (Ithaca: Cornell University Press, 2004), p. 56.
62 Jonathan Baldo, '"A Rooted Sorrow': Scotland's Unusable Past', in Moschovakis, *Macbeth*, pp. 88–103 (99).
63 Malcolm Smuts, 'Banquo's Progeny: Hereditary Monarchy, the Stuart Lineage, and *Macbeth*', in *Renaissance Historicisms: Essays in Honor of Arthur F. Kinney*, (eds) James M. Dutcher and Anne Lake Prescott (Newark: University of Delaware Press, 2008), pp. 225–46 (226).
64 Rebecca Rogers, 'How Scottish was "the Scottish Play"? *Macbeth*'s National Identity in the Eighteenth Century', in *Shakespeare and Scotland*, eds Willy Maley and Andrew Murphy (Manchester and New York: Manchester University Press, 2004), pp. 104–23 (104).
65 Ibid., p. 104.
66 Kathleen McLuskie, 'Humane Statute and the Gentle Weal: Historical Reading and Historical Allegory', *Shakespeare Survey* 57 (2004), pp. 1–10.
67 Paul Innes, 'Harming *Macbeth*: A British Translation', in *Shakespeare and the Translation of Identity in Early Modern England*, ed. Liz Oakley-Brown (London and New York: Continuum, 2011), pp. 103–30 (104).
68 Ibid., p. 115.
69 Ibid., p. 104.
70 Olga Valbuena, *Subjects to the King's Divorce: Equivocation, Infidelity, and Resistance in Early Modern England* (Bloomington: Indiana University Press, 2003), p. 80.
71 Ibid., p. 81.

72 Mary Floyd-Wilson, 'English Epicures and Scottish Witches', *Shakespeare Quarterly* 57, 2 (2006), pp. 131–61 (140, 161).

73 Floyd-Wilson contends that the play's hardy view of ancestral Scots can be traced to John Bellenden's introduction to the 1540 Scots translation of Hector Boece's *History and Chronicles of Scotland* (ibid., p. 132).

74 Ibid., p. 135.

75 Ibid., p. 161.

76 Rebecca Lemon, *Treason by Words: Literature, Law, and Rebellion in Shakespeare's England* (Ithaca: Cornell University Press, 2006), p. 74.

77 Ibid., p. 74.

78 Ibid., p. 84.

79 Ibid.

80 Peter C. Herman, '*Macbeth*: Absolutism, the Ancient Constitution, and the Aporia of Politics', in *The Law in Shakespeare*, (eds) Constance Jordan and Karen Cunningham (New York and Basingstoke: Palgrave, 2007), pp. 208–32 (209).

81 Judith Weil, *Service and Dependency in Shakespeare's Plays* (Cambridge: Cambridge University Press, 2005). Weil remarks the failure to value individual liberties common to all of the political orders Michael Hawkins taxonomizes in the play, the non-integration of women and the populace remarked by Alan Sinfield, and the conservatism of the republicanism discussed by David Norbrook. On all of these, see 'The Critical Backstory' in the present volume.

82 Ibid., p. 133.

83 Ibid., p. 134.

84 Ibid.

85 Elizabeth Fowler, '*Macbeth* and the Rhetoric of Political Forms', in Maley and Murphy, *Shakespeare and Scotland*, pp. 67–86 (p. 74).

86 Ibid., p. 73.

87 Ibid. p. 79.

88 Anselm Haverkamp, *Shakespearean Genealogies of Power: A Whispering of Nothing in Hamlet, Richard II, Julius Caesar, Macbeth, The Merchant of Venice, and The Winter's Tale* (London: Routledge, 2011), pp. 73, 75.

89 Ibid., p. 74.

90 Ibid., p. 76.

91 Ibid., p. 82.

92 Ibid., p. 84.

93 William C. Carroll, '"Two Truths are Told": Afterlives and Histories of Macbeths', *Shakespeare Survey* 57 (2004), pp. 69–80.

94 John H. Astington, '*Macbeth* and Modern Politics', in *Shakespeare/Adaptation/Modern Drama: Essays in Honour of Jill L. Levenson*, (eds) Randall Martin and Katherine Scheil (Toronto: University of Toronto Press, 2011), pp. 93–109.

95 Stephen M. Buhler, 'Politicizing *Macbeth* on U.S. Stages: Garson's *MacBird!* and Greenland's *Jungle Rot*', in Moschovakis, *Macbeth*, pp. 258–75.

96 Katherine A. Rowe, 'The Politics of Sleepwalking: American Lady Macbeths', *Shakespeare Survey* 57 (2004), pp. 126–36 (128, 135).

97 Gay Smith, *Lady Macbeth in America: From the Stage to the White House* (New York: Palgrave, 2010), p. 1.

98 Pamela Mason, 'Sunshine in *Macbeth*', in Moschovakis, *Macbeth*, pp. 335–49. For another intriguing recent textual study, see Graham Holderness, ' "To be Observed": Cue One *Macbeth*', in *Re-Visions of Shakespeare: Essays in Honor of Robert Ornstein*, ed. Evelyn Gajowski (Newark: University of Delaware Press, 2004), pp. 165–86, which, after remarking that *Macbeth* is extant only in folio, triangulates the Folio, Simon Forman's performance account of 1611 and Davenant's adaptation to surmise what one of the lost versions of the play would have looked like.

99 Simon Williams, 'Taking Macbeth out of Himself: Davenant, Garrick, Schiller, and Verdi', *Shakespeare Survey* 57 (2004), pp. 54–68.

100 Paul Prescott, 'Doing All that Becomes a Man: The Reception and Afterlife of the Macbeth Actor, 1744–1889', *Shakespeare Survey* 57 (2004), pp. 81–95.

101 Ruth Morse, 'Monsieur Macbeth: From Jarry to Ionesco', *Shakespeare Survey* 57 (2004), pp. 112–25.

102 Juliet Dusinberre, 'Wilfred Owen and *Macbeth*', *Borrowers and Lenders: The Journal of Shakespeare and Appropriation* 6.2 (Fall/Winter 2011) http://www.borrowers.uga.edu/cocoon/borrowers/pdf?id=782958 [accessed 1 September 2012].

103 Natasha Distiller, ' "The Zulu *Macbeth*": The Value of an "African Shakespeare" ', *Shakespeare Survey* 57 (2004), pp. 159–68 (162).

104 Ruru Li, ' "A Drum, A Drum – Macbeth doth come": When Birnam Wood Moved to China', *Shakespeare Survey* 57 (2004), pp. 169–85; Beatrice Bi-qi Lei, '*Macbeth* in Chinese Opera', in Moschovakis, *Macbeth*, pp. 276–99.

105 Stephen Purcell, *Popular Shakespeare: Simulation and Subversion on the Modern Stage* (Basingstoke and New York: Palgrave, 2009), p. 112.

106 Sarah Hatchuel, ' "Prithee, see there! Behold! Look!" (3.4.69): The Gift or the Denial of Sight in Screen Adaptations of Shakespeare's *Macbeth*', *Borrowers and Lenders* 1.2 (Fall/Winter 2005), p. 3 http://www.borrowers.uga.edu/cocoon/borrowers/request?id=781443 [accessed 1 September 2012].

107 Peter D. Holland, ' "Stands Scotland Where it Did?": The Location of *Macbeth* on Film', in *Macbeth: Authoritative Text, Sources, and Contexts*, ed. Robert S. Miola (New York: Norton, 2004), pp. 357–80 (359).

108 Ibid., p. 360.

109 Mark Thornton Burnett, 'Local *Macbeth*/Global Shakespeare: Scotland's Screen Destiny', in Maley and Murphy, *Shakespeare and Scotland*, pp. 189–206 (191).

110 Kim Fedderson and J. Michale Richardson, '*Macbeth*: Recent Migrations of the Cinematic Brand', in Moschovakis, *Shakespeare and Scotland*, pp. 300–317 (301).

111 Ibid., p. 307.

112 Courtney Lehmann, 'Out Damned Scot: Dislocating *Macbeth* in Transnational Film and Media Culture', in *Shakespeare, the Movie, II: Popularizing the Plays on Film, TV, Video, and DVD*, (eds) Richard Burt and Lynda E. Boose (London and New York: Routledge, 2003), pp. 231–51 (231).

113 Ibid., p. 232.

114 Ayanna Thompson, 'What is a "Weyward" *Macbeth*?', in *Weyward Macbeth: Intersections of Race and Performance*, (eds) Scott L. Newstok and Ayanna Thompson (New York: Palgrave, 2010), pp. 3–10 (3).

115 Ibid., p. 4.

116 Francesca Royster, 'Riddling Whiteness, Riddling Certainty: Roman Polanski's *Macbeth*', in Newstok and Thompson, *Weyward Macbeth*, pp. 173–82 (176).

117 Thompson, 'What is a "Weyward" *Macbeth*?', p. 4.

118 Thompson cites Frances Teague's documentation of a *Macbeth* text in the library of a Virginia plantation owner in 1699. See Teague's *Shakespeare and the American Popular Stage* (Cambridge: Cambridge University Press, 2006), p. 14.

119 Heather S. Nathans, '"Blood Will Have Blood": Violence, Slavery and *Macbeth* in the Antebellum American Imagination', in Newstok and Thompson, *Weyward Macbeth*, pp. 23–34.

120 John C. Briggs, 'The Exorcism of *Macbeth*: Frederick Douglass's Appropriation of Shakespeare', in Newstok and Thompson, *Weyward Macbeth*, pp. 35–44.

121 Bernth Lindfors, 'Ira Aldridge as Macbeth', in Newstok and Thompson, *Weyward Macbeth*, pp. 45–54.

122 Joyce Green MacDonald, 'Minstrel Show *Macbeth*', in Newstok and Thompson, *Weyward Macbeth*, pp. 55–64.

123 Charita Gainey-O'Toole and Elizabeth Alexander, '"Three Weyward Sisters": African-American Female Poets Conjure with *Macbeth*', in Newstok and Thompson, Weyward Macbeth, pp. 205–10 (206).

124 Alexander Nemerov, *Acting in the Night: Macbeth and the Places of the Civil War* (Berkeley: University of California Press, 2010).

125 Bruno Lessard, 'Hypermedia *Macbeth*: Cognition and Performance', in Moschovakis, *Macbeth*, pp. 318–34 (318).

126 Ibid., p. 321.
127 Ibid., p. 330.
128 See *Macbeth*, dir. Rupert Goold, perf. Patrick Stewart and Kate Fleetwood (PBS, 2009) http://www.pbs.org/wnet/gperf/episodes/macbeth/watch-the-full-program/1030/ [accessed 1 September 2012].
129 *Macbeth*, dir. Geoffrey Wright, perf. Sam Worthington, Victoria Hill and Lachy Hulme (Revolver Entertainment, 2007). DVD.
130 Alexander C. Y. Huang, 'Introduction', *Borrowers and Lenders* 4.2, special issue on 'Asian Shakespeares on Screen: Two Films in Perspective', ed. A. C. Y. Huang (Spring/Summer 2009) http://www.borrowers.uga.edu/cocoon/borrowers/request?id=782328 [accessed 1 September 2012].
131 On *Maqbool*'s self-referentially remarking 'the notorious nexus between the underworld and the film industry in Mumbai', see Poonam Trivedi, '"Mak[ing] ... Strange/Even to the disposition that I owe": Vishal Bhardwaj's *Maqbool*', *Borrowers and Lenders* 4.2 (Spring/Summer 2009), p. 2 http://www.borrowers.uga.edu/cocoon/borrowers/pdf?id=782301 [accessed 1 September 2012].
132 On paternal inheritance in *Scotland, PA*, see Lauren Shohet, 'The Banquet of Scotland (PA)', *Shakespeare Survey* 57 (2004), pp. 186–95.
133 David Mason, 'Dharma and Violence in Mumbai', in *Borrowers and Lenders* 4.2 (Spring/Summer 2009), pp. 1, 2 http://www.borrowers.uga.edu/cocoon/borrowers/pdf?id=782302 [accessed 1 September 2012].
134 *Scotland, PA*, dir. Billy Morrissette, perf. James LeGros (Joe 'Mac' McBeth), Maura Tierney ('Pat' McBeth), Christopher Walken (Lieutenant McDuff) (Abandon Pictures, 2001). DVD. 104 min.
135 The analysis imaginatively presented by *Scotland, PA* is remarkably congruent with Eric Schlosser's conclusions in *Fast Food Nation: The Dark Side of the All-American Meal* (New York: Houghton Mifflin, 2001). The two works were produced at the same time and exemplify the potential for narrative and analytic forms to undertake complementary examinations.
136 Arthur Byron Cover and Tony Leonard Tamai, *William Shakespeare's Macbeth: The Graphic Novel* (New York: Byron Preiss, 2005), pp. 85–93, 132.
137 Ibid., p. 5.
138 Ibid., p. 6.
139 Ibid.
140 Ibid., p. 7.
141 Alexander McCall Smith and Tom Cunningham, *The Okavango Macbeth*, conducted by Michael Bawtree (Delphian, 2011). All further references will occur parenthetically within the body of the text. There is not as of this printing any licensed downloadable film of the opera, although portions can be viewed on YouTube.

142 Smith cites Dorothy Chaney and Robert Seyfarth's *Baboon Metaphysics: The Evolution of a Social Mind* (Chicago: University of Chicago Press, 2008) as inspiration. He writes that this account of status-conscious female baboons, in a hierarchical society, who prove 'very ambitious for their males', is 'the *Macbeth* story'. 'What if an ambitious female baboon wanted her mate to become the alpha male and persuaded him to kill the leader of the troop?' See Alexander Mc Call Smith, 'Baboons with Bassoons: Why Alexander McCall Smith Monkeyed with *Macbeth*', *The Daily Mail*, 14 July 2012 http://www.dailymail.co.uk/tvshowbiz/article-2173484/The-Okavango-Macbeth-Alexander-McCall-Smith-unusual-opera.html [accessed 10 September 2012].

1: *Macbeth* and 'Sovereign Process'

1 Thomas Smith, *De Republica Anglorum: The Maner of Government or Policie of the Realme of England* (London: Printed by Henrie Midleton for Gregorie Seton, 1583), p. 44.

2 Ibid.

3 Carl Schmitt, *The Concept of The Political*, trans. George Schwab (Chicago and London: University of Chicago Press, 2007), p. 33.

4 Cf. Xenophon, *The Polity of The Athenians and The Lacedaemonians*, trans. H. G. Dakyns http://www.gutenberg.org/files/1178/1178-h/1178-htm [accessed 3 April 2012], pp. 35–6.

5 Where emphasis is placed on 'the covenant between king and state as instituted by Lycurgus' (p. 35), that is conditional upon the monarch's abiding 'by his oaths' (p. 36) and the curbs designed to neutralize 'the pride of the despotic monarch', but also to minimize 'in the heart of the citizen envy of their power' (p. 36), Xenophon's Lacedaemonian kings 'are not mere mortals but heroic beings' whose authority is underwritten by the gods.

6 All references to *Hamlet* in this chapter are taken from William Shakespeare, *Hamlet*, ed. Harold Jenkins, Arden 2 (London and New York: Methuen, 1982). All further Act, scene and line references will occur parenthetically within the body of the text.

7 Gilles Deleuze, *Difference and Repetition*, trans. Paul Patton (London: Continuum, 1997), p. 90.

8 Carl Schmitt, *Political Theology: Four Chapters on the Concept of Sovereignty*, trans. George Schwab (Chicago: University of Chicago Press, 1985), p. 5.

9 Giorgio Agamben, *Homo Sacer*, trans. Daniel Heller-Roazen (Stanford: Stanford University Press, 1988), p. 25.

10 Ibid., pp. 24–5.

11 Ibid., p. 25.

12 Ibid., p. 27.
13 Ibid., p. 28.
14 Aristotle, *The Politics*, trans. T. A. Sinclair (Harmondsworth: Penguin, 1992), p. 224.
15 Jonathan Dollimore, *Sex, Literature and Censorship* (Oxford: Polity Press, 2001), pp. 73–4.
16 Agamben, *Homo Sacer*, pp. 28–9.
17 Smith, *De Republica Anglorum*, p. 44.
18 Schmitt, *The Concept*, p. 17.
19 See Georges Bataille, *The Accursed Share: An Essay on General Economy Vols 2 and 3*, trans. Robert Hurley (New York: Zone Books, 1993). Bataille defines 'sovereign' as the preference 'for an unproductive use of wealth' compared to 'the preference of the bourgeois world' for 'accumulation' (p. 280).
20 Bataille, *The Accursed Share* p. 199.
21 All references to *Macbeth* in this chapter are taken from Kenneth Muir, ed,, *Macbeth*, Arden edition (London: Methuen and Co., 1951; London and New York: Routledge, 1984). All further Act, scene and line references will occur parenthetically within the body of the text.
22 Henry. N. Paul, *The Royal Play of Macbeth: When, Why, and How it was Written by Shakespeare* (New York: Macmillan, 1950), p. 24.
23 Ibid., p. 401.
24 Jacques Derrida, 'Plato's Pharmacy' in *Dissemination*, trans. Barbara Johnson (Chicago: University of Chicago Press, 1981), p. 99.
25 Agamben, *Homo Sacer*, p. 28.
26 Ibid., p. 83.
27 Ibid., pp. 142, 28.
28 Ibid., p. 32.
29 Ibid., p. 37.
30 Bataille, *The Accursed Share*, p. 237.
31 Agamben, *Homo Sacer*, p. 211.
32 Ibid., p. 16.
33 Ibid., pp. 17–18.
34 Cf. Schmitt, *Political Theology* and Carl Schmitt, *Political Theology II: The Myth of the Closure of Any Political Theology*, trans and intro. Michael Hoelzl and Graham Ward (Cambridge: Polity Press, 2008) for an extensive analysis of the implications of a 'political theology'.
35 Agamben, *Homo Sacer*, p. 18.
36 Ibid., p. 83.
37 Ibid.
38 Ibid., p. 19.
39 Ibid.
40 Ibid., p. 28.

41 Walter Benjamin, 'Critique of Violence', in *Reflections: Essays, Aphorisms, Autobiographical Writings*, ed. Peter Demetz, trans. Edmund Jephcott (New York: Schocken Books, 1978), pp. 276–300 (300).

42 Ibid., p. 300.

43 Terry Eagleton, *William Shakespeare* (Oxford: Blackwell, 1986), p. 2. Eagleton has since revised this view in *On Evil* (New Haven and London: Yale University Press, 2010), pp. 79–85.

44 Ibid., p. 2.

45 *Oxford English Dictionary*, http://www.oed.com/, 1a [accessed 6 June 2012]. Hereafter referenced as *OED* within the body of the text.

46 Agamben, *Homo Sacer*, p. 27.

47 Cf. Alain Badiou, *Ethics: An Essay on the Understanding of Evil*, trans. Peter Hallward (London: Verso Press, 2001), p. 81.

48 Ibid., p. 91.

49 Folio, 576–85; emphasis mine: *The Norton Facsimile: The First Folio of Shakespeare, Based on Folios in the Folger Shakespeare Library Collection, prepared by Charlton Hinman*, 2nd edition, intro. Peter W. M. Blayney (New York and London: W. W. Norton & Co., 1996), pp. 135–6. Since Rowe, editors have tampered with the lineation of this speech. For instance, Kenneth Muir's Arden 2 edition (1964) produces the following emendation: 'Hold, take my sword. – There's husbandry in heaven;/Their candles all are out – Take thee that too'.

50 Fulke Greville, Lord Brooke, *The Remains Being Poems of Monarchy and Religion*, ed. G. A.Wilkes (Oxford: Oxford University Press, 1965), p. 43.

51 Ibid., p. 6.

52 Ibid., p. 43.

53 Ibid., p. 46. But see also p. 45 where the temptations and the 'dreames' of unlimited power are dispersed by its 'contrary windes' in the quasi-biblical realization that human freedom is limited: 'And make men see their freedome bound so fast,/As it of noe forbidden fruite dare tast'.

54 Ibid., p. 49.

55 Timothy Bright, *A Treatise of Melancholie* (London, 1586), p. 119.

56 Paul, *The Royal Play*, p. 136.

57 J. Craigie, ed., *Minor Prose Works of James VI and I* (Edinburgh: Edinburgh University Press, 1982), pp. 2–3.

58 Agamben, *Homo Sacer*, p. 27.

2: Rooting for *Macbeth*: Parable Ethics in Scotland

1 William Shakespeare, *The Two Gentlemen of Verona*, in *The Norton Shakespeare*, ed. Stephen Greenblatt et al. (New York and London: W. W. Norton & Co.,

1997). Lance says that any response from his dog means that Proteus and Julia will be matched: the scene probably offered the opportunity for a trained dog to participate in the comedy by barking and wagging his tail.

2 The relevant chapters of the Gospels are Matthew 13, Mark 4 and Luke 8.

3 All biblical references are to the Geneva Bible. *The Bible, That Is, The Holy Scriptures Conteined in The Olde and Newe Testament* (London: Christopher Barker, 1599). Typologically this verse is a restatement of Psalm 78.2, which is a prophecy made by Asaph, one of David's musicians. See also Mark 5.1–20.

4 For discussion of how biblical allusions might work in Shakespeare and early modern drama, see for example Stephen Marx, *Shakespeare and the Bible* (Oxford: Oxford University Press, 2000); Beatrice Groves, *Texts and Traditions: Religion in Shakespeare 1592–1604* (Oxford: Oxford University Press, 2007); and Adrian Streete, ed., *Early Modern Drama and the Bible: Contexts and Readings, 1570–1625* (Basingstoke: Palgrave Macmillan, 2012). See also Debora Shuger, *The Renaissance Bible: Scholarship, Sacrifice and Subjectivity* (Berkeley: University of California Press, 1994).

5 On midrash and its applicability to biblical interpretation, see Marx, *Shakespeare and the Bible*, pp. 14–16.

6 Clearly this is not to suggest that the Parable of the Sower is the *only* source for such imagery. However, by isolating this parable and its use in *Macbeth*, Shakespeare's complex use of the story becomes apparent.

7 G. Wilson Knight, *The Wheel of Fire: Interpretations of Shakespearian Tragedy With Three New Essays* (London: Methuen and Co., 1954), p. 73.

8 Marx, *Shakespeare and the Bible*, p. 15.

9 This is not to dismiss the centrality of classical literature as a storehouse of natural imagery, especially the pastoral tradition inspired by texts like Virgil's *Eclogues* and *Georgics* and Ovid's *Metamorphoses*. There is also an important strand in recent ecocritical work that has begun to explore the relationship between Scripture and 'green' issues in the early modern period: see, for example, the essays in part two of *Early Modern Ecostudies: From the Florentine Codex to Shakespeare*, eds Thomas Hallock, Ivo Kamps and Karen Raber (Basingstoke: Palgrave Macmillan, 2008); Todd Borlik, *Ecocriticism and Early Modern Literature: Green Pastures* (New York and London: Routledge, 2011); and *The Indistinct Human in Renaissance Literature*, eds Jean E. Feerick and Vin Nardizzi (Basingstoke: Palgrave Macmillan, 2012).

10 Levinus Lemnius, *An Herbal for the Bible*, trans. Thomas Newton (London: Edmund Bollifant, 1587), p. 6.

11 See Groves, *Texts and Traditions*, pp. 10–25. On literacy in the early modern period, see Ian Green, *The Christian's ABC: Catechisms and Catechising in England c. 1530–1740* (Oxford: Clarendon Press, 1996).

12 Lemnius, *An Herbal*, p. 1.

13 All references to *Macbeth* in this chapter are taken from Kenneth Muir, ed., *Macbeth*, Arden 2 Edition (London: Methuen & Co., 1951; London and New York: Routledge, 1984). All further Act, line and scene references will occur parenthetically within the body of the text.

14 Lemnius, *An Herbal*, p. 229.

15 As the *OED* makes clear (definitions 1a, 1b and 20), 'infold' or 'enfold' often has horticultural usages. *Oxford English Dictionary*, Online edition (Oxford: Oxford University Press, 2012) [accessed 10 September 2012].

16 For a fascinating materialist analysis of time and the untimely in *Macbeth*, see chapter four of Jonathan Gil Harris, *Untimely Matter in the Time of Shakespeare* (Philadelphia: University of Pennsylvania Press, 2009), pp. 119–39.

17 *Oxford English Dictionary* [accessed 10 September 2012].

18 Harris, *Untimely Matter*, p. 139.

19 The notes to this chapter in the Geneva Bible point the reader to Daniel 11:3 and Revelation 14:25, two key apocalyptic texts in the Old and New Testaments.

20 See also Macbeth's demand to the witches: 'though the treasure/Of Nature's germens [seeds] tumble all together,/Even till destruction sicken, answer me/To what I ask you' (IV.i.59–61).

21 See Donalbain's comment at II.iii.125 and Malcolm's words at IV.iii.1–2.

22 Arthur Kinney, *Lies Like Truth: Shakespeare, Macbeth, and the Cultural Moment* (Detroit: Wayne State University Press, 2001), p. 203. For a fuller explication of the play's apocalyptic language, see Adrian Streete, '"What Bloody Man is That?": Questioning Biblical Typology in *Macbeth*', *Shakespeare* 5, 1 (2009), pp. 18–35.

23 On the burdens and costs accrued by householders when early modern monarchs came to visit, and of the general cost of maintain an aristocratic household generally, see Lawrence Stone, *The Crisis of the Aristocracy, 1558–1641* (Oxford: Oxford University Press, 1967), pp. 208–12, 249–67.

24 She also says to Duncan, 'We rest your hermits' (I.vii.20). It is worth noting that, as John Florio points out, the term 'hermit' connotes 'a solitarinesse', and the word's Greek root, 'desert', casts Lady Macbeth's assurance in the decidedly anti-fecund light that we often also see used in the Bible. John Florio, *Queen Anna's New World of Wordes* (London: Melchior Bradwood, 1611), p. 228.

25 The etymology of 'sacrilegious' and 'sacrifice' is related: '*sacer*' – 'sacred'.

26 For more on the book of nature metaphor in early modern theology and philosophy, see Peter Harrison, *The Bible, Protestantism and the Rise of Natural Science* (Cambridge: Cambridge University Press, 2001), pp. 193–204. For more on Calvin's doctrine of nature, see François Wendel, *Calvin: The Origin and Development of his Religious Thought*, trans. Philip Mairet (London and New York: Collins/Fontana, 1973), pp. 150–84.

27 John Calvin, *Institutes of the Christian Religion*, ed. John T. McNeill, trans. Ford Lewis Battles (London: Westminster, 1961), p. 254. For an important reading of *Macbeth* and Calvinism, especially Perkins, see John Stachniewski, 'Calvinist Psychology in *Macbeth*', *Shakespeare Studies* 20 (1988), pp. 169–89.
28 Calvin, *Institutes*, p. 254.
29 See Alexandra Walsham, *Providence in Early Modern England* (Oxford: Oxford University Press, 2001), esp. pp. 167–224.
30 Desiderius Erasmus, *Collected Works of Erasmus, Paraphrase on Matthew*, trans. Dean Simpson (Toronto and London: University of Toronto Press, 2008), p. 211.
31 John Calvin, *A Harmony of the Gospels, Matthew, Mark and Luke*, vol. 2, trans. T. H. L. Parker (Michigan: William Eerdmans, 1995), pp. 71–3.
32 Ibid., p. 71.
33 See Adrian Streete, *Protestantism and Drama in Early Modern England* (Cambridge: Cambridge University Press, 2009), pp. 98–9. See, too, Kristen Poole, *Supernatural Environments in Shakespeare's England: Spaces of Demonism, Divinity, and Drama* (Cambridge: Cambridge University Press, 2011), pp. 156–7.
34 Calvin, *Institutes*, p. 242.
35 On the doctrine of temporary faith in Calvin, Beza and Perkins, see R. T. Kendall, *Calvin and English Calvinism to 1649* (Carlisle: Paternoster Press, 1997), pp. 21–5, 36, 67–75. See, too, Brian Cummings, *The Literary Culture of the Reformation: Grammar and Grace* (Oxford: Oxford University Press, 2007), pp. 261–4.
36 William Perkins, *A treatise tending vnto a declaration whether a man be in the estate of damnation or in the estate of grace: and if he be in the first, how he may in time come out of it: if in the second, how he maie discerne it, and perseuere in the same to the end* (London: R. Robinson, 1590), sig. A5r–A6v.
37 Ibid., A6r.
38 Ibid., C4v.
39 Ibid., C5r. See also George Gifford's popular *A Sermon on the Parable of the Sower* (London: Roger Warde, 1583): 'we see that a man may proceede thus far in religion and yet be damned', sig. B3r.
40 It is highly probable that, as the foremost Calvinist theologian during Shakespeare's day, the playwright was aware of Perkins's work. A number of Perkins's books were published by Shakespeare's Stratford contemporary, Richard Field. On Field as a possible source of books for Shakespeare, see Park Honan, *Shakespeare: A Life* (Oxford: Oxford University Press, 1999), pp. 202, 332.
41 A number of scholars have drawn attention to Shakespeare's use of the story of Saul in *Macbeth*. See Jane H. Jack, 'Macbeth, King James and the Bible',

ELH, 22.3 (1955), pp. 173–93; Peter Stallybrass, '*Macbeth* and Witchcraft', in *Macbeth*: *New Casebooks*, ed. Alan Sinfield (Basingstoke: Macmillan, 1992), pp. 25–38; and Streete, '"What Bloody Man is That?"

42 Poole, *Supernatural Environments*, p. 157.

43 Gifford, *A Sermon*, sig. B7r.

44 There may also be an ironical allusion here to Christ's words in Matthew 16:18, 'thou are Peter, and vpon this rocke will I build my Church', an allusion that adds to Macbeth's decidedly anti-Christian representation throughout the play.

45 In his exegesis of this passage, Calvin argues that the story is told because 'it is often very hard to tell the true professors of the Gospel from the false'. John Calvin, *A Harmony of the Gospels, Matthew, Mark and Luke*, vol. 1, trans. A. W. Morrison (Michigan: William Eerdmans, 1994), p. 241.

46 As outlined in Mark's Gospel, after sowing his seed, the sower goes to 'sleepe' (Mark 4.27).

47 It is worth noting that a sermon was preached before King James in 1604 by John Hopkins that drew extensively on the parable of the sower. He uses ideas of sowing and planting to discuss the plantations in Ireland, arguing at one point: 'Were carefull Bishopyes and faythfull teachers planted, seducers remooued, and compulsion to heare established, no doubt in short time a happy effect would follow.' John Hopkins, *A Sermon preached before the Kinges Maiestie* (London: W. W., 1604), sig. C6r.

48 Perkins, *A treatise tending*, sigs. A3r–A4v.

3: Unsexing *Macbeth*, 1623–1800

1 All references to *Macbeth* in this chapter are taken from Kenneth Muir, ed., *Macbeth*, Arden 2 Edition (London: Methuen and Co., 1951; London and New York: Routledge, 1984). All further Act, scene and line references will occur parenthetically within the body of the text.

2 *Oxford English Dictionary*, http://www.oed.com/ [accessed 23 June 2012]. Hereafter referenced as *OED* within the body of the text.

3 Alice Fox, 'Obstetrics and Gynaecology in *Macbeth*', *Shakespeare Studies*, 12 (1979), pp. 127–41.

4 Jenijoy La Belle, '"A Strange Infirmity": Lady Macbeth's Amenorrhea', *Shakespeare Quarterly*, 31 (1980), pp. 381–86.

5 Joanna Levin, 'Lady Macbeth and the Daemonologie of Hysteria', *ELH*, 69 (2002), pp. 21–55.

6 Michel Foucault, 'Nietzsche, Genealogy, History', in *The Foucault Reader*, ed. Paul Rabinow (London: Penguin Books, 1984), pp. 76–100 (83).

7 All references to the first Folio of *Macbeth* are taken from *The Norton Facsimile: The First Folio of Shakespeare, Based on Folios in the Folger*

Shakespeare Library Collection, prep. Charlton Hinman, intro. Peter W. M. Blayney, 2nd edition (New York and London: W. W. Norton & Co., 1996).

8 Edmond Malone, ed., *The Plays and Poems of William Shakspeare: Volume the Fourth* (London, 1790), p. 295.

9 But see Kathleen M. E. McLuskie's reading of the corporeal implications to the term 'Spirits' in *William Shakespeare: Macbeth*, Writers and their Work (Horndon: Northcote House Publishing, 2009), p. 22.

10 Mark Rose, *Shakespearean Design* (Cambridge, MA: Belknap Press of Harvard University Press, 1972), p. 88.

11 William Harvey, *Two Anatomical Exercitations Concerning The Circulation of the Blood* (London, 1653), p. 42.

12 Ibid., p. 44.

13 Ibid., p. 45.

14 Ibid.

15 See Judith Butler, *Gender Trouble: Feminism and the Subversion of Identity* (London: Routledge, 1990).

16 Robert Boyle, *Memoirs for the Natural History of Humane Blood, Especially the Spirit of that Liquor* (London, 1683), p. 125.

17 Alexander Ross, *Arcana Microcosmi: Or, The hid Secrets of MAN'S Body discovered; In an Anatomical Duel Between Aristotle and Galen concerning the Parts thereof* (London, 1652), p. 44.

18 See the extended argument in Thomas Laqueur, *Making Sex: Body and Gender from the Greeks to Freud* (Cambridge, MA and London: Harvard University Press, 1992).

19 Thomas Vicary, *A Profitable Treatise of the Anatomie of Mans Body* (London, 1577). Vicary's tract contains neither chapter divisions nor page numbers.

20 Thomas Cogan, *The Haven of Health* (London, 1596), p. 152.

21 Ibid., p. 240.

22 Ross, *Arcana Microcosmi*, p. 48.

23 Vicary, *A Profitable Treatise*.

24 Ross, *Arcana Microcosmi*, p. 47.

25 La Belle, '"A Strange Infirmity"', p. 383.

26 See Terence Hawkes, 'Introduction', in *Macbeth: Twentieth Century Interpretations*, ed. Terence Hawkes (Englewood Cliffs, NJ: Prentice Hall, 1977), pp. 1–2 (8).

27 Baldassar Castiglione, *The Book of the Courtier*, trans. George Bull (London: Penguin, 1967), p. 211.

28 Laqueur, *Making Sex*, p. 103.

29 Ibid., p. 106.

30 Ross, *Arcana Microcosmi*, p. 88.

31 Ibid., p. 85.

32 See the extract from Moulton's *Shakespeare as a Dramatic Artist* reprinted in S. Schoenbaum, ed., *Macbeth: Critical Essays* (New York and London: Garland Publishing, 1991), p. 64.

33 Michel de Montaigne, *The Essayes: Or Morall, Politike and Millitary Discourses of Lo: Michaell de Montaigne*, trans. John Florio (London, 1603), pp. 41–2.

34 Laqueur, *Making Sex*, p. 126.

35 Ibid., pp. 127–8.

36 Quoted in ibid., p. 127.

37 Julie Barmazel, '"The Servant to Defect": Macbeth, Impotence, and the Body Politic', in *Macbeth: New Critical Essays*, ed. Nick Moschovakis (London and New York: Routledge, 2008), pp. 118–31 (119).

38 Christopher Spencer, *Davenant's Macbeth from the Yale Manuscript: An Edition, With a Discussion of the Relation of Davenant's Text to Shakespeare's* (New Haven: Yale University Press, 1961), p. 2.

39 Bernice W. Kliman, *Shakespeare in Performance: Macbeth*, 2nd edition (Manchester and New York: Manchester University Press, 2004), p. 17.

40 Ibid., p. 23.

41 See the various editorial glosses of the unsexing speech in Nicholas Rowe, ed., *The Works of Mr. William Shakespear, Volume the Fifth* (London, 1709), pp. 2300–365; Alexander Pope, ed., *The Works of Shakespear* (London, 1725); and Alexander Pope and William Warburton (eds), *The Works of Shakespear in Eight Volumes* (London, 1747).

42 Samuel Johnson, ed., *Plays of Willliam Shakespeare: Volume the Sixth* (London, 1765), p. 394.

43 Ibid., p. 394.

44 Ibid., p. 484.

45 Samuel Johnson, *A Dictionary of the English Language*, 2 vols (London: 1755–6), II (1756). Dr Johnson's *Dictionary* does not include page numbers.

46 Nick Moschovakis, 'Introduction: Dualistic *Macbeth*? Problematic *Macbeth*?' in Moschovakis, ed., *Macbeth*, pp. 1–73 (9–10).

47 Kliman, *Shakespeare in Performance*, pp. 24–5.

48 Elizabeth Griffith, *Essays Addressed to Young Married Women* (London, 1782), p. 51.

49 John Stewart, *Travels Over the most Interesting Parts of the Globe, to Discover the Source of Moral Motion* (London, 1792), p. 32.

50 George Wright, *The Lady's Miscellany; Or, Pleasing Essays, Poems, Stories, and Examples, for the Instruction and Entertainment of the Female Sex in General, in Every Station of Life* (London, 1793), p. 105.

51 Charles Lamb, *Tales from Shakespeare: Designed for the Use of Young Persons*, 2 vols (London, 1807), I, 217.

52 T. J. Mathias, *The Pursuits of Literature: A Satirical Dialogue. With Notes: Part the Fourth and Last* (London, 1797), p. ii.

53 Reference taken from a later reprint of all four books of the poem in T. J. Mathias, *The Pursuits of Literature, A Satirical Poem in Four Dialogues* (Dublin, 1799), p. 58.

54 See E. J. Clery's argument in *Women's Gothic: From Clara Reeve to Mary Shelley* (Tavistock: Northcote House and the British Council, 2000).

55 Richard Polwhele, *The Unsex'd Females; A Poem, Addressed to the Author of The Pursuits of Literature* (London, 1798), p. v.

56 Ibid., p. 48.

57 Mary Hays, *Appeal to the Men of Great Britain in Behalf of Women* (London, 1798), p. 187.

58 Adriana Craciun, *Fatal Women of Romanticism* (Cambridge: Cambridge University Press, 2003), p. 58.

4: *Macbeth* in the Present

1 See Alex Needham, 'Taking South Sudan to the Globe: Shakespeare from the Newest Nation', *The Guardian*, 21 March 2012 http://www.guardian.co.uk/stage/2012/mar/20/south-sudan-globe-shakespeare-cymbelin [accessed 27 May 2012]. The day before the anniversary of Shakespeare's birthday, an editorial entitled 'In Praise of ... Shakespeare's Sonnet 18' in *The Guardian* on Sunday 22 April 2012 commemorated the Globe Theatre's multilingual celebration of Shakespeare's works with the following reworking of his most famous sonnet:

> Skal jeg sammenligne deg med en sommers dag?
> Veel zachter en veel zonniger ben jij
> Der Sturm zerreißt des Maien Blüthen-Kränze,
> Och sommarns fröjd hvad är så kort som den?
> As vezes em calor e brilho o Sol se excede
> Interdum, aut hebes est aureus ille color;
> Toute beauté parfois diminue de beauté,
> Sciupata dal caso o dal mutevole corso di natura;
> Mas tu eterno estío no decaerá
> Ty nikdy neztratíš nynejší jas své krásy,
> Kuolemakaan ei kersku; vaikka vaellat sen varjossa,
> Sen esitken ebedi misralarla zamana
> Mentre els homes respirin i els ulls puguin mirar,
> So long lives this and this gives life to thee.

2 BBC News, 'Shakespeare Play Staged in Kabul, 08/09/2005' http://news.bbc.co.uk/go/em/fr/-/1/hi/entertainment/arts/4226652.stm [accessed 20 September 2012]. See also Stephen Landrigan and Qais Akbar Omar, *Shakespeare in Kabul* (London, Haus Publishing, 2012).

3 William Empson, *Seven Types of Ambiguity* (London: Chatto & Windus, 1930; Harmondsworth: Penguin Books, 1965), pp. 19–68.

4 Ibid., pp. 36–7.

5 Kenneth Muir, ed., *Macbeth*, Arden 2 edition (London and New York: Routledge, 1984). All references to *Macbeth* in this chapter are taken from this edition. All further Act, scene and line references will occur parenthetically within the body of the text.

6 As Kenneth Muir notes, there 'have been many attempts to save Shakespeare from writing this excellent line' with suggestions of 'roky', 'reeky', 'rucky', etc. Nonetheless, 'rooky' stands supreme. Ibid., pp. 85–6.

7 Empson, *Seven Types of Ambiguity*, p. 39. See also Empson's footnote.

8 Ibid., p. 19.

9 Ibid., p. 11.

10 Muir, *Macbeth*, p. 4

11 See Neil Hertz, 'More Lurid Figures: De Man Reading Empson', cited in Jacqueline Rose, 'The Iron Rule', *London Review of Books*, Vol. 30, No. 15 (31 July 2008), p. 23. This is an important essay on the issue of equivocation and lying in the case of Paul de Man.

12 Empson, *Seven Types of Ambiguity*, p. 66.

13 Ibid., p. 65.

14 See Marshall McLuhan, *The Gutenberg Galaxy* (London: Routledge 1962), pp. 14–18.

15 William Shakespeare, *Troilus and Cressida*, ed. Kenneth Palmer, Arden 2 edition (London and New York: Routledge, 1991).

16 See the information in Henry N. Paul, *The Royal Play of Macbeth: When, Why, and How it was Written by Shakespeare* (New York: Macmillan, 1950) concerning Macbeth's first performance.

17 A good summary of present notions of presentism appears in Cary DiPietro and Hugh Grady, 'Presentism, Anachronism and the Case of *Titus Andronicus*', *Shakespeare*, 8.1 (2012), pp. 44–73.

18 To say nothing of admirers of Jorge Borges' story 'Pierre Menard, author of *Don Quixote*', trans. Anthony Bonner in Jorge Luis Borges, *Fictions* (London: Calder, 1965).

19 See E. H. Carr, *What is History* (London: Macmillan, 1961; Harmondsworth: Penguin Books, 1985), p. 8.

20 See my own *Shakespeare in the Present* (London and New York: Routledge, 2002), pp. 61–2.

21 Ibid., p. 3.

22 Empson speaks, for instance, of the 'fog' enveloping all experience as Macbeth starts to rule in Scotland, and he relates this to his own experience of international and of civil war in the twentieth century (he resided in China in the 1930s and took part in the revolution of Mao Tse-tung). See William Empson, *Essays on Shakespeare*, ed. David B. Pirie (Cambridge: Cambridge University Press, 1986). This 'fog' is exactly what 'what people really do feel in times of civil war', he says (p. 143). It provokes lying as standard practice, and it is part of the genuine confusion, of 'a fatal decision made hurriedly

in confusion' (p. 149) and of a 'horrified determination in which a crucial decision is scrambled through hurriedly and confusedly' (p. 150) Speaking of lines which in some commentaries are said to have 'no sense', where the pay describes that we 'float upon a wild and violent sea', Empson claims that 'no one who had experienced civil war could say it had no sense' (p. 157).

23 At present, the question of an 'English' parliament remains, significantly, unresolved.

24 Ben Jonson et al., *Eastward Ho*, ed. R. W. Van Fossen (Manchester: Manchester University Press, 1979).

25 Marshall McLuhan and Quentin Fiore, *War and Death in the Global Village* (California: Ginko Press, 1977), p. 175

26 Robert Crawford, ed., *The Scottish Invention of English Literature* (Cambridge: Cambridge University Press, 1998), p. 1. See my review 'Dr. Blair, the Leavis of the North' in the *London Review of Books*, vol. 21, no. 4 (1999), pp. 23–4.

27 'Course' was a technical term used in this sport.

28 Cited in Hamish Macdonell, 'Alex Salmond's Holyrood Address on Being Re-Elected First Minister', *Caledonian Mercury*, 18 May 2011 http://caledonianmercury.com/2011/05/18/alex-salmonds-holyrood-address-on-being-re-elected-first-minister/0020027 [accessed 12 May 2012].

29 My previous concern with Shakespeare's position in a nationalized Scotland is raised by Willy Maley and Andrew Murphy, eds, *Shakespeare and Scotland* (Manchester: Manchester University Press, 2004), p. 9. They claim that the broader question of the 'Americanization' of British culture needs to be addressed and that 'there is more to breaking the mould of British politics than arresting an incorporating Englishness. Moreover, why throw out the Bardic baby with the British bathwater?' The first question raises an issue that England as well as Scotland has to confront. My answer to the second question – at least for Welsh speakers – might be 'Why not?'

30 Statement made on Burns Night, 25 January 2012. See 'Exams to Include Scottish Texts', in *The Scottish Government News* http://www.scotland.gov.uk/News/Releases/2012/01/exams25012012 [accessed 15 May 2012].

31 John Haffenden, ed., *Selected Letters of William Empson* (Oxford: Oxford University Press, 2006), p. 550.

Resources

1 Unless otherwise stated, all references to *Macbeth* in this chapter are taken from Kenneth Muir, ed., *Macbeth*, Arden 2 edition (London: Methuen and Co., 1951; London and New York: Routledge, 1984).

2 Martin Orkin, 'Shifting Shakespeare', *PMLA*, 118 (2003), pp. 134–6.

REFERENCES

Abbott, E. A., *A Shakespearian Grammar [. . .] for the Use of Schools* (London and New York: Macmillan and Co., 1869).

Adelman, Janet, 'Escaping the Matrix: The Construction of Masculinity in *Macbeth* and *Coriolanus*', in *Suffocating Mothers: Fantasies of Maternal Origin in Shakespeare's Plays, 'Hamlet' to 'The Tempest'* (London and New York: Routledge, 1992), pp. 130–64.

Adelman, Janet, *Suffocating Mothers: Fantasies of Maternal Origin in Shakespeare's Plays, from 'Hamlet' to 'The Tempest'* (New York and London: Routledge, 1992).

Agamben, Giorgio, *Homo Sacer*, trans. by Daniel Heller-Roazen, (Stanford: Stanford University Press, 1988)

Aitchison, Nick, *Macbeth: Man and Myth* (Thrupp, Gloucs.: Sutton Publishing, 1999).

Allen, Michael J. B., '*Macbeth*'s Genial Porter', *English Literary Renaissance*, 4 (1974), 325–34.

Anderson, Lisa M., 'When Race Matters: Reading Race in *Richard III* and *Macbeth*', in *Colorblind Shakespeare: New Perspectives on Race and Performance*, ed. by Ayanna Thompson (New York and London: Routledge, 2006), 89–102.

Aristotle, *The Politics*, trans. by T. A. Sinclair, (Harmondsworth: Penguin, 1992).

Armitage, Richard. 'Macbeth (RSC)' http://www.richardarmitageonline.com/macbeth-rsc/macbeth-introduction.html [accessed 1 September 2012].

Artaud, Antonin, *The Theater and Its Double*, trans. by Mary C. Richard (New York: Grove Press, 1994).

Asian Shakespeares on Screen: Two Films in Perspective, ed. by Alexander C. Y. Huang, *Borrowers and Lenders: The Journal of Shakespeare and Appropriation*, 4.2 (Spring/Summer 2009) http://www.borrowers.uga.edu [accessed 3 October 2012].

Asp, Carolyn, 'Be bloody, bold, and resolute': Tragic Action and Sexual Stereotyping in *Macbeth*', *Studies in Philology*, 78, 2 (2001), 153–69.

Astington, John H., '*Macbeth* and Modern Politics', in *Shakespeare/Adaptation/Modern Drama: Essays in Honour of Jill L. Levenson*, ed. by Randall Martin and Katherine Scheil (Toronto: University of Toronto Press, 2011), pp. 93–109.

Bach, Rebecca Ann, 'The "peerless" Macbeth: Friendship and Family in *Macbeth*', in *'Macbeth': New Critical Essays*, ed. by Nick Moschovakis (London and New York: Routledge, 2008), pp. 104–17.

Badiou, Alain, *Ethics: An Essay on the Understanding of Evil*, trans. by Peter Hallward (London: Verso Press, 2001).

Baker, Christopher, 'St. Peter and *Macbeth*'s Porter', *Ben Jonson Journal*, 18, 2 (2011), 233–53.

Baldo, Jonathan, '"A rooted sorrow": Scotland's unusable past', in *'Macbeth': New Critical Essays*, ed. by Nick Moschovakis (London and New York: Routledge, 2008), pp. 88–103.

Barmazel, Julie, '"The servant to defect": Macbeth, impotence, and the body politic', in *'Macbeth': New Critical Essays*, ed. by Nick Moschovakis (London and New York: Routledge, 2008), pp. 118–131.

Bartholomeusz, Dennis, *'Macbeth' and the Players* (London: Cambridge University Press, 1969).

Bataille, Georges, *The Accursed Share: An Essay on General Economy, Vols 2 & 3*, trans. by Robert Hurley (New York: Zone Books, 1993).

Bate, Jonathan, *Shakespeare and the English Romantic Imagination* (Oxford: Clarendon Press, 1992).

—ed., *The Romantics on Shakespeare* (London: Penguin Books, 1992).

—and Russell Jackson, eds, *The Oxford Illustrated History of Shakespeare on Stage* (Oxford: Oxford University Press, 2001).

BBC News, 'Shakespeare play staged in Kabul, 08/ 09/2005' http://news.bbc.co.uk/go/em/fr/-/1/hi/entertainment/arts/4226652.stm [accessed 20 September 2012].

Benjamin, 'Critique ofViolence', in *Reflections: Essays, Aphorisms, Autobiographical Writings*, ed. by Peter Demetz and trans. by Edmund Jephcott (New York: Schocken Books, 1978), pp. 276–300.

Berger, Harry, Jr., 'The Early Scenes of *Macbeth*: Preface to a New Interpretation', *ELH* 47.1 (1980), 1–31.

—'The Early Scenes of "Macbeth": Preface to a New Interpretation', in *Making Trifles of Terror: Redistributing Complexities in Shakespeare* (Stanford: Stanford University Press, 1997), pp. 78–97.

—'Text Against Performance The Example of *Macbeth*', *Genre* 15 (1892), 49–79.

Berry, Francis, *Poets' Grammar: Person, Time and Mood in Poetry* (London: Routledge and Kegan Paul, 1958) *The Bible, That Is, The Holy Scriptures* [...] (London: Christopher Barker, 1599).

Black, Ronald, ed., *To The Hebrides: Samuel Johnson's 'Journey to the Western Islands of Scotland' and James Boswell's 'Journal of a Tour to the Hebrides'*, 2nd edition. (Edinburgh: Birlinn, 2011).

Blakemore Evans, G., *Shakespearean Prompt-Books of the Seventeenth Century*, 7 vols. (Charlottesville, Virginia: Bibliographical Society of the University of Virginia, 1960–89), vol. 1.pt 1. http://etext.virginia.edu/bsuva/promptbook/ [accessed 6 June, 2012]

Booth, Stephen, *'King Lear', 'Macbeth', Indefinition, and Tragedy* (1983; repr. Cyberedition, 2001).

Borges, Jorge Luis, *Fictions* (London: Calder, 1965).

Borlik, Todd, *Ecocriticism and Early Modern Literature: Green Pastures* (New York and London: Routledge, 2011).

Boyle, Robert, *Memoirs for the Natural History of Humane Blood, Especially The Spirit of that Liquor* (London, 1683).

Bradley, A. C., *Shakespearean Tragedy* (London: Macmillan and Co. Ltd, 1904; repr. 1963).

Brams, Steven J., *Game Theory and the Humanities: Bridging Two Worlds* (Cambridge, Mass.: MIT Press, 2011).

Brantley, Ben, 'The Deed is Done, the Doers Undone', *The New York Times*, 15 March 2011 < http://theater.nytimes.com/2011/03/26/theater/reviews/macbeth-opens-at-the-duke-on-42nd-street-review.html> [accessed 1 September 2012].

—'Fierce Kindred Spirits, Burning for a Throne', *The New York Times*, 22 June 2002. < http://www.nytimes.com/2000/06/22/theater/theater-review-fierce-kindred-spirits-burning-for-a throne.html?n=Top%2fReference%2fTimes%20Topics%2fSubjects%2fT%2fTheater> [accessed 1 September 2012].

—'Something Wicked This Way Comes', *The New York Times*, 15 February 2008 <http://theater2.nytimes.com/2008/02/15/theater/reviews/15macb.html?pagewanted=all&_r=0> [accessed 1 September 2012].

Braunmuller, A. L., ed., *Macbeth*, New Cambridge Shakespeare (Cambridge: Cambridge University Press, 1997).

Briggs, John C., 'The Exorcism of *Macbeth*: Frederick Douglass's Appropriation of Shakespeare', in *Weyward 'Macbeth': Intersections of Race and Performance*, ed. by Scott L. Newstok and Ayanna Thompson (New York: Palgrave, 2010), pp. 35–44.

Bright, Timothy, *A Treatise of Melancholie* [. . .] (London, 1586).

Brooke, Nicholas, ed., *Macbeth* (Oxford: Oxford University Press, 1990).

Brooks, Cleanth, 'The Naked Babe and the Cloak of Manliness', in *The Well Wrought Urn: Studies in the Structure of Poetry* (New York: Harcourt, 1947), pp. 22–49.

Bruckner, Lynne Dickson, '"Let grief convert to anger": Authority and Affect in *Macbeth*', in *'Macbeth': New Critical Essays*, ed. by Nick Moschovakis (London and New York: Routledge, 2008), pp. 192–207

Buhler, Stephen M., 'Politicizing *Macbeth* on U.S. stages: Garson's *MacBird!'* and Greenland's *Jungle Rot*', in *'Macbeth': New Critical Essays*, ed. by Nick Moschovakis (London and New York: Routledge, 2008), pp. 258–75.

Bullough, Geoffrey, *Narrative and Dramatic Sources of Shakespeare*, vol. VII, (London: Routledge, 1973).

Burnett, Mark Thornton, 'Local *Macbeth*/global Shakespeare: Scotland's screen destiny', in *Shakespeare and Scotland*, ed. by Willy Maley and Andrew Murphy (Manchester and New York: Manchester University Press, 2004), pp. 189–206.

Butler, Judith, *Gender Trouble: Feminism and the Subversion of Identity* (London: Routledge, 1990).

Calderwood, James L., *'If It Were Done': 'Macbeth' and Tragic* Action (Amherst: University of Massachussetts Press, 1986).

Calvin, John, *A Harmony of the Gospels, Matthew, Mark and Luke*, vol. 1, trans. by A. W. Morrison (Michigan: William Eerdmans, 1994).

—*A Harmony of the Gospels, Matthew, Mark and Luke*, vol. 2, trans. by T. H. L. Parker (Michigan: William Eerdmans, 1995).

—*Institutes of the Christian Religion*, ed. by John T. McNeill and trans. by Ford Lewis Battles (London: Westminster, 1961).

Campbell, Lily B., *Shakespeare's Tragic Heroes: Slaves of Passion* (Cambridge: Cambridge University Press, 1930).

Carr, E. H., *What is History* (London: Macmillan 1961; Harmondsworth: Penguin Books, 1985).

Carr, J. W. Comyns, *Macbeth and Lady Macbeth: An Essay* (London: Bickers and Son, Leicester Square, 1889).

William C. Carroll, '"Two Truths are Told": Afterlives and Histories of Macbeths', *Shakespeare Survey* 57 (2004), 69–80.

Cartwright, Kent, 'Scepticism and Theatre in *Macbeth*,' *Shakespeare Survey* 55 (2002), 219–36.

Castiglione, Baldassar, *The Book of the Courtier*, trans. by George Bull (London: Penguin, 1967)

Catania, Saviour, 'The Haiku *Macbeth*: Shakespearean Antithetical Minimalism in Kurosawa's *Komonosu-jo*', in *World-wide Shakespeares: Local Appropriations in Film and Performance*, ed. by Sonia Massai (London and New York: Routledge, 2005), pp. 149–56.

Chaney, Dorothy, and Robert Seyfarth, *Baboon Metaphysics: The Evolution of a Social Mind* (Chicago: University of Chicago Press, 2008)

Clark, Arthur Melville, *Murder under Trust, or, The Topical 'Macbeth' and other Jacobean Matters* (Edinburgh: Scottish Academic Press, 1981).

Clark, Stuart, *Vanities of the Eye: Vision in Early Modern European Culture* (Oxford: Oxford University Press, 2007).

Clery, E. J., *Women's Gothic: From Clara Reeve to Mary Shelley* (Tavistock: Northcote House and the British Council, 2000).

Cogan, Thomas, *The Haven of Health [. . .]* (London, 1596).

Cohen, Derek, *Searching Shakespeare: Studies in Culture and Authority* (Toronto: University of Toronto Press 2003).

Coleridge, Samuel Taylor, *Shakespearean Criticism*, ed. by T. M. Raysor, 2 vols (London: Dent, 1907; repr. 1974).

Coursen, Herbert R., 'In Deepest Consequence: *Macbeth*', *Shakespeare Quarterly* 18.4 (1967), 375–88.

Cover, Arthur Byron, and Tony Leonard Tamai, *William Shakespeare's Macbeth: The Graphic Novel* (New York: Byron Preiss, 2005).

Craciun, Adriana, *Fatal Women of Romanticism* (Cambridge: Cambridge University Press, 2003).

Craigie, J, ed., *Minor Prose Works of James VI and I* (Edinburgh: Edinburgh University Press, 1982).

Crane, Mary Thomas, '"Fair is Foul": *Macbeth* and Binary Logic', in *The Work of Fiction: Cognition, Culture, and Complexity*, ed. by Alan Richardson and Ellen Spolsky (Aldershot, Hampshire, and Burlington, Vermont: Ashgate, 2004), pp. 107–126

Crawford, Robert, ed., *The Scottish Invention of English Literature* (Cambridge: Cambridge University Press, 1998).

Cummings, Brian, *The Literary Culture of the Reformation: Grammar and Grace* (Oxford: Oxford University Press, 2007).

Curry, Walter Clyde, *Shakespeare's Philosophical Patterns* (Baton Rouge, La.: Louisiana State University, 1937)

Daemonologie, In Forme of a Dialogue, Divided into three Bookes (Edinburgh, 1597)

Daileader, Ceilia R., 'Weird Brothers: What Thomas Middleton's *The Witch* Can Tell Us about Race, Sex, and Gender in *Macbeth*', in *Weyward 'Macbeth': Intersections of Race and Performance*, ed. by Scott L. Newstok and Ayanna Thompson (New York: Palgrave Macmillan, 2010), pp. 11–20.

Danson, Laurence, *Tragic Alphabet: Shakespeare's Drama of Language* (Yale: Yale University Press, 1974).

Davenant, William, *Macbeth, A Tragedy. With all the Alterations, Amendments, Additions, and New Songs* (London, 1674).

—*Proposition for Advancement of Moralitie by a New Way of Entertainment of the People* (London, 1653).

Dean, Leonard F., '*Macbeth* and Modern Criticism', *The English Journal* 47.2 (1958), 57–67.

Deleuze, Gilles, *Difference and Repetition*, trans. by Paul Patton (London: Continuum, 1997).

Derrida, Jacques, 'Plato's Pharmacy' in *Dissemination*, trans. by Barbara Johnson (Chicago: University of Chicago Press, 1981), pp. 61–172.

DiPietro, Cary and Hugh Grady, 'Presentism, Anachronism and the Case of *Titus Andronicus*', *Shakespeare*, 8:1 (2012), 44–73.

Distiller, Natasha, '"The Zulu *Macbeth*": The Value of an "African Shakespeare"', *Shakespeare Survey* 57 (2004), 159–68. dlsan, *HyperMacbeth: An Hypertextual Dramatic Piece* http://www.dlsan.org/macbeth/the_mac.htm [accessed 25 August 2012].

Dobson, Michael, 'Improving on the Original: Actresses and Adaptations', in *The Oxford Illustrated History of Shakespeare on Stage*, ed. by Jonathan Bate and Russell Jackson (Oxford: Oxford University Press, 2001), pp. 45–68.

Dollimore, Jonathan, *Sex, Literature and Censorship* (Oxford: Polity Press, 2001).

Donaldson, Peter S., *Shakespearean Films, Shakespearean Directors* (London: Routledge, 1990).

—'Surface and Depth: *Throne of Blood* as Cinematic Allegory', in *Shakespearean Films/Shakespearean Directors* (Boston: Unwin Hyman, 1990), pp. 69–91.

Donohue, Joseph, *Dramatic Character in the English Romantic Age* (Princeton: Princeton University Press, 1970).

Dowden, Edward, *Shakspere. A Critical Study of his Mind and Art* (London: Routledge and Kegan Paul, 1857; repr. 1953).

Drakakis, John, ed., *Alternative Shakespeares* (London: Methuen and co. 1985).

Dusinberre, Juliet, 'Wilfred Owen and *Macbeth*', *Borrowers and Lenders: The Journal of Shakespeare and Appropriation* 6.2 (Fall/Winter 2011) < http://www.borrowers.uga.edu/cocoon/borrowers/pdf?id=782958 [accessed 1 September 2012].

Eagleton, Terry, *On Evil* (New Haven and London: Yale University Press, 2010).

—*William Shakespeare* (Oxford: Basil Blackwell, 1986).

Edelman, Lee, *No Future: Queer Theory and the Death Drive* (Durham and London: Duke University Press, 2004).

Editorial, 'In Praise of … sonnet 18', *Guardian*, 22 April 2012 http://www.guardian.co.uk/commentisfree/2012/apr/22/in-praise-of-shakespeares-sonnet-18 [accessed 5 May 2012]

Elliott, G. R., *Dramatic Providence in 'Macbeth': A Study of Shakespeare's Tragic Theme of Humanity and Grace* (Princeton: Princeton University Press, 1958).

Empson, William, *Essays on Shakespeare*, ed. by David B. Pirie (Cambridge: Cambridge University Press, 1986).

—*Selected Letters of William Empson*, ed. by John Haffenden (Oxford: Oxford University Press, 2006).

—*Seven Types of Ambiguity* (London: Chatto and Windus, 1930; Harmondsworth: Penguin Books, 1965).

Erasmus, Desiderius, *Collected Works of Erasmus, Paraphrase on Matthew*, trans. by Dean Simpson (Toronto and London: University of Toronto Press, 2008).

'Exams to Include Scottish Texts', in *The Scottish Government News* http://www.scotland.gov.uk/News/Releases/2012/01/exams25012012 [accessed 15 May 2012].

Fedderson, Kim and J. Michael Richardson, '*Macbeth*: Recent migrations of the cinematic brand', in *'Macbeth': New Critical Essays*, ed. by Nick Moschovakis (London and New York: Routledge, 2008), pp. 300–17.

Feerick, Jean E. and Vin Nardizzi, (eds), *The Indistinct Human in Renaissance Literature* (Basingstoke: Palgrave Macmillan, 2012).

Felperin, Howard, 'A Painted Devil: *Macbeth*', *in Shakespearean Representation: Mimesis and Modernity in Elizabethan Tragedy* (Princeton: Princeton University Press 1977), pp. 118–44.

Flatter, Richard, *Shakespeare's Producing Hand* (New York: W. W. Norton and Co., 1948).

Fletcher, George, *Studies of Shakespeare* (London: Longman, 1847).

Florio, John, *Queen Anna's New World of Wordes* [...] (London: Melchior Bradwood, 1611).

Floyd-Wilson, Mary, 'English Epicures and Scottish Witches', *Shakespeare Quarterly*, 57, 2 (2006), 131–61.

Focus on 'Macbeth', ed. by John Russell Brown (London: Routledge & Kegan Paul, 1982).

Foucault, Michel, 'Nietzsche, Genealogy, History', in *The Foucault Reader*, ed. by Paul Rabinow (London: Penguin Books, 1984), pp. 76–100.

Fowler, Elizabeth, '*Macbeth* and the rhetoric of political forms', in *Shakespeare and Scotland*, ed. by Willy Maley and Andrew Murphy (Manchester and New York: Manchester University Press, 2004), pp. 67–86.

Fox, Alice, 'Obstetrics and Gynecology in *Macbeth*', *Shakespeare Studies*, 12 (1979), 127–141.

Freud, Sigmund, 'Some Character-Types met with in Psychoanalytic Work', in *The Pelican Freud Library*, vol. 14, ed. by Albert Dickson (Harmondsworth: Penguin Books, 1985), pp. 301–8.

Fulke Greville, Lord Brooke, *The Remains Being Poems of Monarchy and Religion*, ed. by G. A. Wilkes, (Oxford: Oxford University Press, 1965).

Furness, Horace Howard, ed., *Macbeth: A New Variorum Edition* (Philadelphia: Lippincott, 1873).

Gainey-O'Toole, Charita, and Elizabeth Alexander, '"Three Weyward Sisters": African-American Female Poets Conjure with *Macbeth*', in *Weyward 'Macbeth': Intersections of Race and Performance*, ed. by Scott L. Newstok and Ayanna Thompson (New York: Palgrave, 2010), pp. 205–10.

Gardner, Helen, *The Business of Criticism* (Oxford: Clarendon Press, 1956).

Gifford, George, *A Sermon on the Parable of the Sower* [...] (London: Roger Warde, 1583).

Gil, Dan Juan, 'Avant-Garde Technique and the Visual Grammar of Sexuality in Orson Welles's Shakespeare Films', *Borrowers and Lenders: The Journal of Shakespeare and Appropriation*, 1, 2 (2005) http://www.borrowers.uga.edu [accessed 24 September 2012].

Goldman, Michael, *Acting and Action in Shakespearean Tragedy* (Princeton: Princeton University Press, 1985).

Green, Ian, *The Christian's ABC: Catechisms and Catechising in England c. 1530–1740* (Oxford: Clarendon Press, 1996).

Greenblatt, Stephen, 'Shakespeare Bewitched', in *New Historical Literary Study: Essays on Reproducing Texts, Representing History*, ed. by Jeffrey N. Cox and Larry J. Reynolds (Princeton: Princeton University Press, 1993), pp. 108–35.

Griffith, Elizabeth, *Essays Addressed to Young Married Women* (London, 1782).

Groves, Beatrice, *Texts and Traditions: Religion in Shakespeare 1592–1604* (Oxford: Oxford University Press, 2007).

Gurr, Andrew. 'Why was the Globe Round?', in *Who Hears in Shakespeare? Auditory Worlds on Stage and Screen*, ed. by Laury Magnus and Walter Cannon (Madison, New Jersey: Fairleigh Dickinson University Press/ Lanham, Maryland: The Roman & Littlefield Publishing Group, 2012), pp. 3–16.

Hallock, Thomas, Ivo Kamps and Karen Raber, (eds), *Early Modern Ecostudies: From the Florentine Codex to Shakespeare* (Basingstoke: Palgrave Macmillan, 2008).

Harris, Jonathan Gil, *Untimely Matter in the Time of Shakespeare* (Philhadelphia: University of Pennsylvania Press, 2009).

Harrison, Peter, *The Bible, Protestantism and the Rise of Natural Science* (Cambridge: Cambridge University Press, 2001).

Harvey, Paul A. S. and Bernice W. Kliman, 'Ninagawa *Macbeth*: Fusion of Japanese and Western Theatrical Styles', in Bernice W. Kliman., *Shakespeare in Performance: 'Macbeth'* (Manchester: Manchester University Press, 2004), pp. 159–82.

Hatchuel, Sarah, ' "Prithee, See There! Behold! Look!" (3.4.69): The Gift or Denial of Sight in Screen Adaptations of Shakespeare's *Macbeth*', *Borrowers and Lenders: The Journal of Shakespeare and Appropriation*, 1.2 (2005) http:// www.borrowers.uga.edu [accessed 24 September 2012].

Hateley, Erica, 'Lady Macbeth in Detective Fiction: Criminalizing the Female Reader', *Clues: A Journal of Detection*, 24, 2 (Summer 2006), 31–46.

Harding, D. W., 'Woman's Fantasy of Manhood: A Shakespearian Theme', *Shakespeare Quarterly* 20.3 (1969), 245–53.

Harvey, William, *Two Anatomical Exercitations Concerning The Circulation of the Blood* (London, 1653).

Hatchuel, Sarah, '"Prithee, see there! Behold! Look!" (3.4.69): The Gift or the Denial of Sight in Screen Adaptations of Shakespeare's *Macbeth*', *Borrowers and Lenders: The Journal of Shakespeare and Appropriation*,1.2 (Fall/ Winter 2005), p. 3. http://www.borrowers.uga.edu/cocoon/borrowers/ request?id=781443 [accessed 1 September 2012].

Haverkamp, Anselm, *Shakespearean Genealogies of Power: A Whispering of Nothing in 'Hamlet', 'Richard II', 'Julius Caesar', 'Macbeth', 'The Merchant of Venice', and 'The Winter's Tale'* (London: Routledge, 2011).

Hawkes, Terence, 'Dr. Blair, the Leavis of the North' in *London Review of Books*, vol. 21, no. 4 (1999), pp. 23–24.

—'Introduction', in *Twentieth Century Interpretations of 'Macbeth'*, ed. by Terence Hawkes (New Jersey: Englewood Cliffs, 1977), pp. 1–2.

—*Shakespeare in the Present* (London and New York: Routledge, 2002).

—*Shakespeare and the Reason: A Study of the Tragedies and the Problem Plays* (London: Routledge and Kegan Paul, 1964).

—*Shakespeare's Talking Animals*, (London,: Edward Arnold, 1973).

—ed., *Twentieth Century Interpretations of 'Macbeth'* (New Jersey: Englewood Cliffs, 1977).

Hawkins, Michael, 'History, Politics and *Macbeth*', in *Focus on 'Macbeth'*, ed. John Russell Brown (London: Routledge and Kegan Paul, 1982), pp. 155–88.

Hays, Mary, *Appeal to the Men of Great Britain in Behalf of Women* (London, 1798).

Hazlitt, William, *Characters of Shakespeare's Plays*, (London: Dent, 1906).

—*Characters of Shakespeare's Plays* (Oxford: Oxford University Press, 1917).

Herman, Peter C., '*Macbeth*: Absolutism, the Ancient Constitution, and the Aporia of Politics', in *The Law in Shakespeare*, ed. by Constance Jordan and Karen Cunningham (New York and Basingstoke: Palgrave, 2007), pp. 208–32.

Holderness, Graham, '"To be observed": Cue One *Macbeth*', in *Re-Visions of Shakespeare: Essays in Honor of Robert Ornstein*, ed. by Evelyn Gajowski (Newark, DE.: University of Delaware Press, 2004), pp. 165–86.

Holland, Peter D., 'The Age of Garrick' in *Shakespeare: An Illustrated Stage History*, ed. by Jonathan Bate and Russell Jackson (Oxford: Oxford University Press, 1996), pp. 69–91.

—'"Stands Scotland Where It Did?": The Location of *Macbeth* on Film', in William Shakespeare, *'Macbeth': Authoritative Text, Sources, and Contexts*, ed. by Robert S. Miola (New York: W. W. Norton, 2004), pp. 357–80.

Holloway, John, *The Story of the Night: Studies in Shakespeare's Major Tragedies* (London: Routledge and Kegan Paul, 1961).

Honan, Park, *Shakespeare: A Life* (Oxford: Oxford University Press, 1999).

Hopkins, John, *A Sermon preached before the Kinges Maiestie* [...] (London: W. W., 1604).

Huang, Alexander C. Y., 'Introduction', *Borrowers and Lenders: The Journal of Shakespeare and Appropriation*, 4.2, special issue on 'Asian Shakespeares on Screen: Two Films in Perspective', ed. Huang (Spring/Summer 2009) http://www.borrowers.uga.edu/cocoon/borrowers/request?id=782328 [accessed 1 September 2012].

Hulme, Hilda, *Explorations in Shakespeare's Language: Some Problems of Word Meaning in the Dramatic Text* (London: Longman, 1962, 1977).

Hunter, G. K., '*Macbeth* in the Twentieth Century', *Shakespeare Survey* 19 (1966), 1–11.

—ed., *Macbeth* (London: Penguin Books, 1967; repr. 2005)

Huntley, Frank L., '*Macbeth* and the Background of Jesuitical Equivocation', *PMLA*, 79, 4 (1964), 390–400.

Innes, Paul, 'Harming *Macbeth*: A British Translation', in *Shakespeare and the Translation of Identity in Early Modern England*, ed. by Liz Oakley-Brown (London and New York: Continuum, 2011), pp. 103–30.

Jack, Jane H., 'Macbeth, King James and the Bible', *ELH*, 22.3 (1955), 173–93.

Jameson, Anna, *Shakespeare's Heroines: Characteristics of Women, Moral, Poetical and Historical* (London: G. Bell and Sons, 1913).

Johnson, Samuel, *A Dictionary of the English Language [...]*, 2 vols (London: 1755–56).

—, ed., *Plays of Willliam Shakespeare. Volume the Sixth* (London, 1765).

Jonson, Ben, and others, *Eastward Ho*, ed. R. W. Van Fossen (Manchester: Manchester University Press, 1979).

Jorgens, Jack, 'Kurosawa's *Throne of Blood*: Washizu and Miki Meet the Forest Spirit', *Literature/Film Quarterly*, 11 (1983), 167–73.

Jorgensen, Paul A., *Our Naked Frailties: Sensational Art and Meaning in 'Macbeth'* (Berkeley, CA.: University of California Press, 1971).

Kahn, Coppélia, *Man's Estate: Masculinity on Shakespeare* (Berkeley and London: University of California Press, 1981).

Kendall, R. T., *Calvin and English Calvinism to 1649* (Carlisle: Paternoster Press, 1997).

Kerridge, Richard, 'An Ecocritic's *Macbeth*', in *Ecocritical Shakespeare*, ed. by Lynne Bruckner and Dan Brayton (Farnham, Surrey and Burlington, Vermont: Ashgate, 2011), pp. 193–210.

Kernan, Alvin, *Shakespeare, the King's Playwright: Theater in the Stuart Court, 1603-1613* (New Haven: Yale University Press, 1995).

—'The Politics of Madness and Demonism: *Macbeth*, Hampton Court, August 7, 1606', in *Shakespeare, The King's Playwright: Theatre in the Stuart Court, 1603-1613* (New Haven: Yale University Press, 1995), pp. 71–88.

Kinney, Arthur F., *Lies Like Truth: Shakespeare, 'Macbeth', and the Cultural Moment* (Detroit: Wayne State University Press, 2001)

—'Macbeth's Knowledge', *Shakespeare Studies* 57 (2004), 11–26.

—'Scottish History, the Union of the Crowns and the Issue of Right Rule: The Case of Shakespeare's *Macbeth*', in *Renaissance Culture in Context: Theory and Practice*, ed. by Jean R. Brink and William F. Gentrup (Aldershot: Scolar Press,1993), pp. 18–53.

—'Shakespeare's *Macbeth* and the Question of Nationalism', in *Literature and Nationalism*, ed. by Vincent Newey and Ann Thompson (Liverpool: Liverpool University Press, 1991), pp. 56–75.

Klein, Joan Larsen, 'Lady Macbeth: "Infirm of Purpose" ', in *The Woman's Part: Feminist Criticism of Shakespeare*, ed. by Ruth Swift Lenz, Gayle Greene and Carol Thomas Neely (Urbana: University of Illinois Press, 1980), pp. 240–55.

Kliman, Bernice, 'Another Ninagawa *Macbeth*', *The Shakespeare Newsletter* 52.4 (2002/3), 93–106.

—*Shakespeare in Performance: 'Macbeth'*, second edition (Manchester and New York: Manchester University Press, 2004).

Knights, L. C., 'How Many Children Had Lady Macbeth?' in *Explorations: An Essay in the Theory and Practice of Shakespeare Criticism* (New York: G. W. Stewart, 1947), pp. 15–54.

—*Some Shakespearean Themes and An Approach to 'Hamlet'* (London: Chatto and Windus, 1959).

Kolb, Laura, 'Playing with Demons: Interrogating the Supernatural in Jacobean Drama', *Forum for Modern Language Studies*, 43, 1 (2007), 337–50.

Kott, Jan, *Shakespeare our Contemporary* (London: Methuen and Co., 1964).

Kranz, David L., 'The Sounds of Supernatural Soliciting in *Macbeth*', *Studies in Philology* 100, 3 (2003), 346–83.

La Belle, Jenijoy, '"A strange infirmity": Lady Macbeth's Amenorrhea', *Shakespeare Quarterly*, 31 (1980), 381–86.

Lamb, Charles, 'On the Tragedies of Shakespeare, considered with Reference to their Fitness for Stage Representation', in *English Critical Essays: Nineteenth Century*, ed. by Edmund D. Jones (Oxford: Oxford University Press, 1919), pp. 95–119.

—*Tales from Shakespeare. Designed for the Use of Young Persons*, 2 vols (London, 1807)

Landrigan, Stephen, and Qais Akbar Omar, *Shakespeare in Kabul* (London, Haus Publishing, 2012).

Laqueur, Thomas, *Making Sex: Body and Gender from the Greeks to Freud* (Cambridge, MA. and London: Harvard University Press, 1992).

Lehmann, Courtney, 'Out Damned Scot: Dislocating *Macbeth* in transnational film and media culture', in *Shakespeare, the Movie, II: Popularizing the Plays on Film, TV, Video, and DVD*, ed. by Richard Burt and Lynda E. Boose (London and New York: Routledge, 2003), pp. 231–51.

Lei, Beatrice Bi-qi, '*Macbeth* in Chinese Opera', in *'Macbeth': New Critical Essays*, ed. by Nick Moschovakis (London and New York: Routledge, 2008), pp. 276–99.

Lemnius, Levinus, *An Herbal for the Bible* [...], trans. by Thomas Newton (London: Edmund Bollifant, 1587).

Lemon, Rebecca, 'Sovereignty and Treason in *Macbeth*', in *'Macbeth': New Critical Essays*, ed. by Nick Moschovakis (London and New York: Routledge, 2008), pp. 73–87.

—*Treason by Words: Literature, Law, and Rebellion in Shakespeare's England* (Ithaca: Cornell University Press, 2006).

Lessard, Bruno, 'Hypermedia *Macbeth*: Cognition and Performance', in *'Macbeth': New Critical Essays*, ed. by Nick Moschovakis (London and New York: Routledge, 2008), pp. 318–34.

Levin, Joanna, 'Lady Macbeth and the Daemonologie of Hysteria', *ELH*, 69 (2002), 21–55.

Levin, Richard, 'The New Refutation of Shakespeare', *MP* 83.2 (1985), 123–41.

Lewin, Jennifer, 'Murdering Sleep in *Macbeth*: The Mental World of the Protagonist', *Shakespeare International Yearbook* 5 (2005), 181–88.

Li, Ruru, '"A Drum, A Drum – Macbeth doth come": When Birnam Wood Moved to China', *Shakespeare Survey* 57 (2004), 169–85.

Liebler, Naomi Conn, *Shakespeare's Festive Tragedy: The Ritual Foundations of Genre* (London and New York: Routledge, 1995).

Lindfors, Bernth, 'Ira Aldridge as Macbeth', in *Weyward 'Macbeth': Intersections of Race and Performance*, ed. by Scott L. Newstok and Ayanna Thompson (New York: Palgrave, 2010), pp. 45–54.

Lopez, Jeremy, 'A partial theory of original practice', *Shakespeare Survey* 61 (2008), 302–17.

Lopez Roman, Blanca, 'Sir William D'Avenant's So-Called Improvements of *Macbeth* (1674)', *Actas del I congreso nacional* (1990), 211–22.

Love, Heather, 'Milk', in *Shakesqueer: A Queer Companion to the Complete Works of Shakespeare*, ed. by Madhavi Menon (Durham and London: Duke University Press, 2011), pp. 201–8.

Macbeth, dir. by Geoffrey Wright, perf. by Sam Worthington, Victoria Hill and Lachy Hulme (Revolver Entertainment, 2007). DVD.

Macbeth, dir. by Jack Gold (BBC/Time-Life films, 1983).

Macbeth, dir. by Rupert Goold (Chichester Festival Theatre, 2007; DVD PBS, 2010).

Macbeth, dir. by Rupert Goold, perf. by Patrick Stewart and Kate Fleetwood (PBS, 2009) http://www.pbs.org/wnet/gperf/episodes/macbeth/watch-the-full-program/1030/ [accessed 1 September 2012].

Macbeth, dir. by Trevor Nunn (UK, Royal Shakespeare Company); television film dir. by John Casson (UK, Thames Television, 1979).

Macbeth, dir. by Roman Polanski (Caliban Films, Playboy Production, 1971).

Macbeth, dir. by Aaron Posner (Folger Theatre/Two Rivers Company, 2008).

Macbeth, dir. by Orson Welles (Mercury Productions, 1948).

Macbeth, dir. by Geoffrey Wright (Palace Films, 2006).

Macbeth, dir. by Geoffrey Wright, perf. by Sam Worthington, Victoria Hill and Lachy Hulme (Revolver Entertainment, 2007). DVD.

'Macbeth': New Critical Essays, ed. by Nick Moschovakis (London and New York: Routledge, 2008).

MacDonald, Joyce Green, 'Minstrel Show *Macbeth*', in *Weyward 'Macbeth': Intersections of Race and Performance*, ed. by Scott L. Newstok and Ayanna Thompson (New York: Palgrave, 2010), pp. 55–64.

Macdonnell, Hamish, 'Alex Salmond's Holyrood Address on Being Re-Elected First Minister', *Caledonian Mercury*, 18 May 2011 http://caledonianmercury.com/2011/05/18/alex-salmonds-holyrood-address-on-being-re-elected-first-minister/0020027 [accessed 12 May 2012].

Magnus, Laury., 'An Interview with Arin Arbus of the Theatre for a New Audience', *The Shakespeare Newsletter* (Spring/Summer 2011), 10–14.

—'"Bearing the Weight of this Sad Time": *Macbeth* at the Delacorte, *Lear* at LaMama', *The Shakespeare Newsletter,* 56:1 (Spring/Summer 2006), 11–35.

—'Playing the Moments: *Macbeth* at the Theatre for a New Audience', *The Shakespeare Newsletter*, 61.1. Spring/Summer 2011), 3–14.

—and Walter W. Cannon, (eds), *Who Hears in Shakespeare? Auditory Worlds on Stage and Screen* (Madison, New Jersey: Fairleigh Dickinson University Press/Lanham, Maryland: The Roman & Littlefield Publishing Group, 2012).

Mahood, M. M., *Shakespeare's Wordplay* (Methuen and Co.: London, 1968).

Maley, Willy and Andrew Murphy, (eds), *Shakespeare and Scotland* (Manchester: Manchester University Press, 2004).

Malone, Edmond, ed., *The plays and Poems of William Shakspeare. Volume the Fourth* (London, 1790).

Mapstone, Sally, 'Shakespeare and Scottish Kingship: A Case History', in *The Rose and the Thistle: Essays on the Culture of Late Medieval and Renaissance Scotland*, ed. by Sally Mapstone and Juliette Wood (East Linton: Tuckwell Press, 1998), pp. 158–93.

Maqbool, dir. Vishal Bhardwaj (Kaleidoscope Entertainment, 2004).

Marx, Stephen, *Shakespeare and the Bible* (Oxford: Oxford University Press, 2000).

Maslin, Janet. '*Men of Respect*: Car Bomb and Chianti in "Macbeth" Variation', *The New York Times*, 18 January 1991 http://movies.nytimes.com/movie/review?res=9D0CE7D81230F93BA25752C0A967958260 [accessed 1 September 2012].

Mason, David, 'Dharma and Violence in Mumbai', in *Borrowers and Lenders: The Journal of Shakespeare and Appropriation*, 4.2 (Spring/Summer 2009) http://www.borrowers.uga.edu/cocoon/borrowers/pdf?id=782302 [accessed 1 September 2012].

Mason, Pamela, 'Sunshine in *Macbeth*', in *'Macbeth': New Critical Essays*, ed. by Nick Moschovakis (London and New York: Routledge, 2008), pp. 335–49.

Mathias, T. J., *The Pursuits of Literature, A Satirical Poem in Four Dialogues* (Dublin, 1799).

—*The Pursuits of Literature: A Satirical Dialogue. With Notes: Part the Fourth and Last* (London, 1797).

McCoy, Richard, '"The grace of grace" and Double-Talk in *Macbeth*', *Shakespeare Survey*, 57 (2004), 27–37.

McDonald, Russ, *Look to the Lady: Sarah Siddons, Ellen Terry, and Judi Dench on the Shakespearean Stage* (Athens: University of Georgia Press, 2005).

McDowell, Sean H., 'Macbeth and the Perils of Conjecture', in *Knowing Shakespeare: Senses, Embodiment, and Cognition*, ed. by Lowell Gallagher and Shankar Raman (Basingstoke and London: Palgrave Macmillan, 2010), pp. 30–49.

McLuhan, Marshall, *The Gutenberg Galaxy* (London: Routledge 1962).

—and Quentin Fiore, *War and Death in the Global Village* (California, Ginko Press, 1977).

McLuskie, Kate, '*Macbeth/uMabatha*: Global Shakespeare in a Post-Colonial Market', *Shakespeare Survey*, 52 (1999), 154–65.

McLuskie, Kathleen E., 'Humane Statute and the Gentle Weal: Historical Reading and Historical Allegory', *Shakespeare Survey* 57 (2004), 1–10.

—*William Shakespeare, 'Macbeth'*, Writers and their Work (Horndon: Northcote House Publishing, 2009).

Menzer, Paul, *Inside Shakespeare: Studies on the Blackfriars Stage* (Selinsgrove, Pennsylvania: Susquehanna University Press, 2006).

Montaigne, Michaell [Michel] de, *The Essayes: Or Morall, Politike and Millitary Discourses of Lo: Michaell de Montaigne […]*, trans. by John Florio (London, 1603).

Morse, Ruth, 'Monsieur Macbeth: From Jarry to Ionesco', *Shakespeare Survey* 57 (2004), 112–25.

Moschovakis, Nick, 'Introduction: Dualistic Macbeth? Problematic Macbeth?', in *'Macbeth': New Critical Essays*, ed. by Nick Moschovakis (London and New York: Routledge, 2008), pp. 1–73.

—ed., *'Macbeth': New Critical Essays* (London and New York: Routledge, 2008).

Msomi, Welcome, *uMabatha*, in *Adaptations of Shakespeare: A Critical Anthology*, ed. by Daniel Fischlin and Mark Fortier (London: Routledge, 2000), pp. 164–87.

Muir, Kenneth, ed., *Macbeth*, Arden 2 (London: Methuen and Co., 1951; London and New York: Routledge, 1984).

Mullaney, Steven, 'Lying Like Truth: Riddle, Representation, and Treason in Renaissance England', *ELH*, 47, 1 (1980), 32–47.

Nathans, Heather S., ' "Blood will have blood": Violence, Slavery and *Macbeth* in the Antebellum American Imagination', in *Weyward 'Macbeth': Intersections of Race and Performance*, ed. by Scott L. Newstok and Ayanna Thompson (New York: Palgrave, 2010), pp. 23–34.

Needham, Alex, 'Taking South Sudan to the Globe: Shakespeare from the Newest Nation', *The Guardian*, 21 March 2012 http://www.guardian.co.uk/stage/2012/mar/20/south-sudan-globe-shakespeare-cymbelin [accessed 27 May 2012].

Neely, Carol Thomas, *Distracted Subjects: Madness and Gender in Shakespeare and Early Modern Culture* (Ithaca: Cornell University Press, 2004).

Nemerov, Alexander, *Acting in the Night: 'Macbeth' and the Places of the Civil War* (Berkeley, CA.: University of California Press, 2010).

Newstok, Scott L., '"Why *Macbeth*?": Looking Back on *uMabatha* after Forty Years: An Interview with Welcome Msomi', *Shakespeare in South Africa*, 21 (2009), 74–80.

Norbrook, David, '*Macbeth* and the Politics of Historiography', in *The Politics of Discourse*: *The Literature and History of Seventeenth-Century England*, ed. by Kevin Sharpe and Steven N. Zwicker (Berkeley, CA.: University of California Press, 1987), pp. 78–116.

The Norton Facsimile: The First Folio of Shakespeare, Based on Folios in the Folger Shakespeare Library Collection, prepared by Charlton Hinman. 2nd edition. Intro. by Peter W. M. Blayney (New York and London: W. W. Norton, 1996).

Nosworthy, J. M., *Shakespeare's Occasional Plays* (London: Edward Arnold, 1965).

Orgel, Stephen, '*Macbeth* and the Antic Round', *Shakespeare Survey* 52 (1999), 143–53.

Orkin, Martin, '"It will have blood they say; blood will have blood" – Proverb Usage and the Vague and Undetermined Places of *Macbeth*', in *Shakespeare Without Boundaries: Essays in Honor of Dieter Mehl*, ed. by Christa Jansohn, Lena Cowen Orlin and Stanley Wells (Newark, DE.: University of Delaware Press, 2011), pp. 189–202.

—'Shifting Shakespeare', *PMLA*, 118 (2003), 134–6.

Oxford English Dictionary, http://www.oed.com/ [accessed 20 September 2012].

Paul, Henry N., *The Royal Play of Macbeth: When, Why, and How it was Written by Shakespeare* (New York: Macmillan Company, 1950).

Pedicord, Harry William, and Frederick Louis Bergmann, ed. by *The Plays of David Garrick*, 4 vols, (Carbondale: Southern Illinois University Press, 1981).

Perkins, William, *A treatise tending vnto a declaration whether a man be in the estate of damnation or in the estate of grace: and if he be in the first, how he may in time come out of it: if in the second, how he maie discerne it, and perseuere in the same to the end* (London: R. Robinson, 1590).

Polka, Brayton, *Shakespeare and Interpretation, Or, What You Will* (Newark, DE: University of Delaware Press, 2011).

Polwhele, Richard, *The Unsex'd Females; A Poem, Addressed to the Author of The Pursuits of Literature* (London, 1798).

Poole, Kristen, *Supernatural Environments in Shakespeare's England: Spaces of Demonism, Divinity and Drama* (Cambridge: Cambridge University Press, 2011).

Pope, Alexander, ed., *The Works of Shakespear, from Mr Pope's Edition [. . .]*, 6 vols (London, 1768).

—and William Warburton, (eds), *The Works of Shakespear In Eight Volumes [. . .]* (London, 1747).

Pound, Ezra, 'Hugh Selwyn Mauberley', in *Selected Poems, 1908–1959* (London and Boston: Faber and Faber, 1975), pp. 98–112.

Prescott, Paul, 'Doing all that becomes a man: the Reception and Afterlife of the Macbeth Actor, 1744-1889', *Shakespeare Survey* 57 (2004), 81–95.

Proser, Matthew N., *The Heroic Image in Five Shakespearean Tragedies* (Princeton: Princeton University Press, 1965).

Purcell, Stephen, *Popular Shakespeare: Simulation and Subversion on the Modern Stage* (Basingstoke and New York: Palgrave, 2009).

Purkiss, Diane, *The Witch in History* (London and New York: Routledge, 1996).

Ramsay, Jerold, 'The Perversion of Manliness in *Macbeth*', *Studies in English Literature*, 13, 2 (1973), 285–300.

Reynolds, Bryan, '"Untimely Ripped": Mediating Witchcraft in Polanski and Shakespeare', in *Performing Transversally: Reimagining Shakespeare and the Critical Future* (New York: Palgrave Macmillan, 2003), pp. 111–35.

Roberts, David, *Thomas Betterton: The Greatest Actor of the Restoration Stage* (Cambridge: Cambridge University Press, 2010).

Rogers, Rebecca, 'How Scottish was "the Scottish play"? *Macbeth*'s national identity in the eighteenth century', in *Shakespeare and Scotland*, ed. by Willy Maley and Andrew Murphy (Manchester and New York: Manchester University Press, 2004), pp. 104–23.

Rose, Jacqueline, 'The Iron Rule' in *London Review of Books*, vol. 30, no. 15 (31 July 2008), pp. 21–4.

Rose, Mark, *Shakespearean Design* (Cambridge, Mass.: Belknap Press of Harvard University Press, 1972).

Rosenberg, Marvin, 'Macbeth and Lady Macbeth in the Eighteenth and Nineteenth Centuries', in *Focus on* Macbeth, ed. by John Russell Brown (London: Routledge & Kegan Paul, 1982), pp. 73–86.

—*The Masks of Macbeth* (Delaware: University of Delaware Press, 1993).

Ross, Alexander, *Arcana Microcosmi: Or, The hid Secrets of MAN'S Body discovered; In an Anatomical Duel Between Aristotle and Galen concerning the Parts thereof* [...] (London, 1652).

Rothwell, Kenneth, *A History of Shakespeare on Screen* (Cambridge: Cambridge University Press, 2001).

Rowe, Katherine A., 'Humoral Knowledge and Liberal Cognition in Davenant's *Macbeth*', in *Reading the Early Modern Passions: Essays in the Cultural History of Emotion*, ed. by Gail Kern Paster, Katherine Rowe and Mary Floyd-Wilson (Philadelphia: University of Pennsylvania Press, 2004), pp. 169–91.

—'The Politics of Sleepwalking: American Lady Macbeths', *Shakespeare Survey* 57 (2004), 126–36.

Rowe, Nicholas, ed., *The Works of Mr. William Shakespear, Volume the Fifth* (London, 1709).

Royal Shakespeare Company http://www.rsc.org.uk/ [accessed 22 September 2012].

Royster, Francesca, 'Riddling Whiteness, Riddling Certainty: Roman Polanski's *Macbeth*', in *Weyward 'Macbeth': Intersections of Race and Performance*, ed. by Scott L. Newstok and Ayanna Thompson (New York: Palgrave, 2010), pp. 173–82.

Salgādo, Gāmini, ed., *Eyewitnesses of Shakespeare: First Hand Accounts of Performances of Shakespeare, 1590–1890* (London: Chatto and Windus, 1975).

Sanders, Wilbur, *The Dramatist and the Received Idea: Studies in the Plays of Marlowe and Shakespeare* (Cambridge: Cambridge University Press, 1968).

Schlosser, Eric, *Fast Food Nation: The Dark Side of the All-American Meal* (New York: Houghton Mifflin, 2001).

Schmitt, Carl, *The Concept of The Political*, trans. by George Schwab (Chicago and London: University of Chicago Press, 2007).

—*Political Theology: Four Chapters on the Concept of Sovereignty*, trans. by George Schwab (Chicago: University of Chicago Press, 1985).

—*Political Theology II: The Myth of the Closure of Any Political Theology*, trans. and intro. by Michael Hoelzl and Graham Ward (Cambridge: Polity Press, 2008).

Schoenbaum, S., ed., *'Macbeth': Critical Essays* (New York and London: Garland Publishing, 1991).

Scotland, PA, dir. by Billy Morrissette, perf. by James LeGros (Joe 'Mac' Mcbeth), Maura Tierney ('Pat' Mcbeth), Christopher Whalken (Lieutenant Macduff) (Abandon Pictures, 2001). DVD. 104 min.

Scott, William O., 'Macbeth's – and Our – Self-Equivocations', *Shakespeare Quarterly*, 37, 2 (1986), 160–74.

Shakespeare, William, *Hamlet*, ed. by Harold Jenkins, Arden 2 series (Methuen: London and New York, 1982).

—*Macbeth*, ed. by A. R. Braunmuller, New Cambridge Shakespeare (Cambridge: Cambridge University Press, 1997; updated edition 2008).

—*Macbeth*, ed. by Nicholas Brooke (Oxford: Clarendon, 1990).

—*Macbeth*, ed. by John Russell Brown, The Shakespeare Handbooks (Houndsmill, Basingstoke, Hampshire: Palgrave Macmillan, 2005).

—*Macbeth*, ed. by Anthony Dawson, Internet Shakespeare Editions http://internetshakespeare.uvic.ca/Library/plays/Mac.html [accessed 25 August 2012].

—*Macbeth* (F1), Project Gutenberg http://www.gutenberg.org/ebooks/2264 [accessed 23 August 2012].

—*Macbeth*, ed. by Rex Gibson, Cambridge School Shakespeare (Cambridge: Cambridge University Press, 2005).

—*Macbeth*, ed. by Jeremy Hylton, The MIT Shakespeare http://shakespeare.mit.edu/ [accessed 17 June 2012].

—*Macbeth* (for iPad and iPhone), Shakespeare in Bits http://www.MindConnex.com [accessed 23 August 2012].

—*Macbeth*, ed. by Robert S. Miola, Norton Critical Editions (New York: W. W. Norton, 2004).

—*Macbeth*, in *The Oxford Shakespeare: The Complete Works*, second edition (Oxford: Oxford University Press, 2005; The Complete Works Collection, distributed by Kindle Books, 2011).

—*Macbeth Online* (Personal Playscript and Website Registration Code) (Oxford: Oxford University Press, 2010).

—*The Tragedy of Macbeth*, ed. by Barbara Mowat and Paul Werstine, New Folger Library Shakespeare (New York and London: Washington Square Books, 1992).

—*The Two Gentlemen of Verona*, in *The Norton Shakespeare*, ed. Stephen Greenblatt et. al. (New York and London: Wm. Norton and Co., 1997).

Shakespeare's Globe http://www.shakespearesglobe.com/ [accessed 22 September 2012].

Shakespeare Illustrated, <http://shakespeare.emory.edu/illustrated_index.cfm> [accessed 22 September 2012].

Shakespeare Set Free: Teaching 'Romeo & Juliet', 'Macbeth' & 'A Midsummer Night's Dream', ed. by Peggy O'Brien (New York: Washington Square Press, 1993).

Shohet, Lauren, 'The Banquet of *Scotland (PA)*', *Shakespeare Survey*, 57 (2004), 186–95.

Shuger, Debora, *The Renaissance Bible: Scholarship, Sacrifice and Subjectivity* (Berkeley: University of California Press, 1994).

Siddons, Sarah. 'Remarks on the Character of Lady Macbeth', in Campbell's *Life of Mrs. Siddons*, reprinted in *William Shakespeare, A New Variorum Edition of Shakespeare: Macbeth*, ed. by Horace Howard Furness, Jr. (New York: Dover Publications, 1963), pp. 472–77.

Sinfield, Alan, '*Macbeth*: History, Ideology, and Intellectuals', *Critical Quarterly*, 28 (1986), 3–77.

—'*Macbeth*: History, Ideology and Intellectuals' in *Faultlines: Cultural Materialism and the Politics of Dissident Reading* (Oxford: Clarendon Press, 1992), pp. 95–108.

—ed., '*Macbeth*': *New Casebooks* (New York: St Martin's Press, 1992).

Smith, Alexander McCall, 'Baboons with bassoons: Why Alexander McCall Smith monkeyed with *Macbeth*', *The Daily Mail*, 14 July 2012. http://www.dailymail.co.uk/tvshowbiz/article-2173484/The-Okavango-Macbeth-Alexander-McCall-Smith-unusual-opera.html [accessed 10 September 2012].

—and Tom Cunningham, *The Okavango Macbeth*, conducted by Michael Bawtree (Delphian, 2011).

Smith, Gay, *Lady Macbeth in America: From the Stage to the White House* (New York: Palgrave, 2010).

Smith, Thomas Sir, *De Republica Anglorum: The Maner of Government or Policie of the Realme of England* (London: Printed by Henrie Midleton for Gregorie Seton, 1583).

Smuts, Malcolm, 'Banquo's Progeny: Hereditary Monarchy, the Stuart Lineage, and *Macbeth*', in *Renaissance Historicisms: Essays in Honor of Arthur F. Kinney*, ed. by James M. Dutcher and Anne Lake Prescott (Newark, DE: University of Delaware Press, 2008), pp. 225–46.

Spencer, Christopher, *Davenant's 'Macbeth' from the Yale Manuscript: An Edition, With a Discussion of the Relation of Davenant's Text to Shakespeare's* (New Haven: Yale University Press, 1961).

—ed., *Five Restoration Adaptations of 'Macbeth'* (Urbana: University of Illinois Press, 1965).

Sprat, Thomas, *History of the Royal Society, For the Improving of Natural Knowledge* (London: Printed by T. R. for J. Martyn, 1667).

Spurgeon, Caroline, *Shakespeare's Imagery and What it Tells Us* (Cambridge: Cambridge University Press, 1935; repr. 1968).

Stachniewski, John, 'Calvinist Psychology in *Macbeth*', *Shakespeare Studies*, 20, 1988, 169–89.

Stallybrass, Peter, '*Macbeth* and witchcraft', in *Focus on 'Macbeth'*, ed. by John Russell Brown (London: Routledge & Kegan Paul, 1982), pp. 189–209.

Stewart, John, *Travels Over the most Interesting Parts of the Globe, to Discover the Source of Moral Motion* [...] (London, 1792).

Stoll, Abraham, '*Macbeth*'s equivocal conscience', in '*Macbeth*': *New Critical Essays*, ed. by Nick Moschovakis (London and New York: Routledge, 2008), pp. 132–50.

Stone, Lawrence, *The Crisis of the Aristocracy, 1558–1641* (Oxford: Oxford University Press, 1967).

Streete, Adrian, *Protestantism and Drama in Early Modern England* (Cambridge: Cambridge University Press, 2009).

—' "What bloody man is that?": Questioning Biblical Typology in *Macbeth*', *Shakespeare*, 5, 1, 2009, 18–35.

—ed., *Early Modern Drama and the Bible: Contexts and Readings, 1570-1625* (Basingstoke: Palgrave Macmillan, 2012).

Taylor, Gary, ed., *Macbeth*, in *Thomas Middleton: The Collected Works*, ed. by Gary Taylor and John Lavagnino (Oxford: The Clarendon Press, 2007), pp. 1165–201.

—and John Lavagnino, (eds), *Thomas Middleton: The Collected Works* (Oxford: Clarendon Press, 2007).

Teague, Frances, *Shakespeare and the American Popular Stage* (Cambridge: Cambridge University Press, 2006).

Thompson, Ayanna, 'What is a "weyward" *Macbeth*?', in *Weyward 'Macbeth': Intersections of Race and Performance*, ed. by Scott L. Newstok and Ayanna Thompson (New York: Palgrave, 2010), pp. 3–10.

Throne of Blood, dir. Akira Kurosawa (Kurosawa Production Company, 1957).

Tillyard, E. M. W., *Shakespeare's History Plays* (Harmondsworth: Penguin Books, 1944; repr. 1989).

Tredell, Nicholas, ed., *Shakespeare: 'Macbeth'* (Houndmills, Basingstoke: Palgrave Macmillan, 2006).

Trivedi, Poonam, '"Mak[ing] . . . Strange/Even to the disposition that I owe": Vishal Bhardwaj's *Maqbool*', *Borrowers and Lenders: The Journal of Shakespeare and Appropriation*, 4.2 (Spring/Summer 2009), p. 2 http://www.borrowers.uga.edu/cocoon/borrowers/pdf?id=782301 [accessed 1 September 2012].

Tromly, Fred B., *Fathers and Sons in Shakespeare: The Debt Never Promised* (Toronto: University of Toronto Press, 2010).

Valbuena, Olga, *Subjects to the King's Divorce: Equivocation, Infidelity, and Resistance in Early Modern England* (Bloomington, IN.: Indiana University Press, 2003)

Vicary, Thomas, *A Profitable Treatise of the Anatomie of Mans body* (London, 1577).

Vickers, Brian, *Shakespeare, Co-Author: A Historical Study of Five Collaborative Plays*, (Oxford: Oxford University Press, 2002).

—ed., *Shakespeare: The Critical Heritage*, 6 vols (London and Boston: Routledge and Kegan Paul, 1974–81).

Wain, John, ed., *Shakespeare: 'Macbeth': A Casebook*, (London and Basingstoke: Macmillan, 1984).

Waith, Eugene M., 'Manhood and Valour in Two Shakespearean Tragedies', *ELH* 17.4 (1950), 262–73.

Walker, Roy, *The Time is Free: A Study of Macbeth* (London: Andrew Dakers, 1949).

Walsham, Alexandra, *Providence in Early Modern England* (Oxford: Oxford University Press, 2001).

Weil, Judith, *Service and Dependency in Shakespeare's Plays* (Cambridge: Cambridge University Press, 2005).

Weimann, Robert, 'Theatrical Space in Shakespeare's Playhouse: Revisiting *locus* and *platea* in *Timon* and *Macbeth*', *Shakespeare International Yearbook* 2 (2002), 203–17.

Wells, Stanley and Gary Taylor, eds, *William Shakespeare: The Complete Works* (Oxford: Clarendon Press, 1986).

Wendel, François, *Calvin: The Origin and Development of his Religious Thought*, trans. Philip Mairet (London and New York: Collins/Fontana, 1973).

Weyward 'Macbeth': Intersections of Race and Performance, ed. by Scott L. Newstok and Ayanna Thompson (New York: Palgrave Macmillan, 2010).

Wickham, Glynne, 'Hell-Castle and Its Door-Keeper', *Shakespeare Survey*, 19 (1966), 68–74.

Wilder, Lina Perkins, *Shakespeare's Memory Theatre: Recollection, Properties, and Character* (Cambridge: Cambridge University Press, 2010).

Wilders, John, ed., *Macbeth*. Shakespeare in Production (Cambridge: Cambridge University Press, 2004).

William Shakespeare's 'Macbeth': Texts and Contexts, ed. by William C. Carroll (Boston and New York: Bedford/St. Martin's, 1999).

Williams, Gordon, *'Macbeth': Text and Performance* (London: Macmillan, 1985).

Williams, Simon, 'Taking Macbeth out of himself: Davenant, Garrick, Schiller, and Verdi', *Shakespeare Survey* 57 (2004), 54–68.

Willis, Deborah, 'Strange Brew', in *Malevolent Nurture: Witch-Hunting and Maternal Power in Early Modern England* (Ithaca: Cornell University Press, 1995), pp. 209–37.

Wills, Gary, *Witches and Jesuits: Shakespeare's 'Macbeth'* (Oxford and New York: Oxford University Press, 1995).

Wilson, John Dover, ed., *Macbeth*, The New Shakespeare (Cambridge: Cambridge University Press, 1947).

Wilson, Richard, 'The Pilot's Thumb: *Macbeth* and the Martyrs', in *Secret Shakespeare: Studies in Theatre, Religion, and Resistance* (Manchester: Manchester University Press, 2004), pp. 186–205.

Wilson Knight, George, *The Imperial Theme* (London: Methuen and Co. Ltd., 1931; repr. 1968).

—*The Wheel of Fire: Interpretations of Shakespearian Tragedy With Three New Essays* (London: Methuen, 1954).

Wimsatt, W. K., ed., *Dr Johnson on Shakespeare* (Harmondsworth: Penguin, 1969).

The Windsor Shakespeare, ed. Henry H. Hudson, 20 vols (London: Blackwood, Le Bas and Co, nd.).

Woudhuysen, H. R., ed., *Samuel Johnson on Shakespeare* (Harmondsworth: Penguin Books, 1989).

Wright, George, *The Lady's Miscellany; Or, Pleasing Essays, Poems, Stories, and Examples, for the Instruction and Entertainment of the Female Sex in General, in Every Station of Life* (London, 1793).

Wright, Lawrence, '*uMabatha*: Global and Local', *English Studies in Africa*, 47, 2 (2004), 97–116.

Xenophon, *The Polity of The Athenians and The Lacedaemonians*, trans. by H. G. Dakyns, http://www.gutenberg.org/files/1178/1178-h/1178-htm [accessed 3 April, 2012].

Ziegler, Georgianna, 'Accommodating the Virago: Nineteenth-Century Representations of Lady Macbeth', in *Shakespeare and Appropriation*, ed. by Christy Desmet and Robert Sawyer (London: Routledge, 1999), pp. 119–41.

INDEX

Literary works are listed under author
Films/theatrical performances are listed by director and title
Stage productions are listed by director